Writings of
Fermín Francisco de Lasuén

Translated and edited by

Finbar Kenneally, O.F.M.

Volume I

ACADEMY OF AMERICAN FRANCISCAN HISTORY

WASHINGTON, D. C.

MCMLXV

NIHIL OBSTAT:

Reverend Antonine Tibesar, O.F.M.
Censor Deputatus

IMPRIMATUR:

✝ Patrick A. O'Boyle
Archbishop of Washington

December 4, 1964

Foreword

HISTORIANS MAY AT TIMES CAST ENVIOUS glances at their professional colleagues in the physical sciences who in their laboratories are able to control the circumstances of their experiments. Historians are seldom that fortunate, but in a way the history of colonial Upper California does offer the scholar analogous advantages. Spaniards first settled in the area in July, 1769, and the colonial era ended with the arrival of the Americans in the 1840's. The closest Spanish settlement in Upper California was separated from Mexico proper by a distance of about 1500 kilometers of uncertain sea routes and dangerous land trails. In addition to this physical isolation and limitation in time, California history offers a large amount of extant documentary material. The present study demonstrates this in presenting an almost complete file of the letters and reports of Lasuén, Serra's successor as president of the missions. Thus the advantages to the historian of Upper California history are evident since he can control his material more than in any other area of history.

To encourage studies in California history the Academy of American Franciscan history some years ago began to collect the letters and reports of the presidents of the California missions. Most of the correspondence of Serra has been published. Now Father Finbar Kenneally has compiled and translated the collection of material writen by Lasuén. It is a pleasure to welcome this magnificent edition which has cost the editor years of study and discipline.

It is hoped that these volumes will be followed soon by the publication of the official papers of the other mission presidents. At the same time perhaps this collection may stimulate some group in California to undertake the publication of a companion series of the documents of the colonial governors. Each series would complement and enrich the other and lead to a fuller understanding of the policies, aims, and activities of both State and Church in colonial California. Father Finbar Kenneally's work certainly does contribute to such an understanding. All students of Upper California history are in his debt.

ANTONINE TIBESAR, O.F.M.
January 15, 1965

Preface

UTHORS COULD ASSIGN MANY REASONS why they became writers, and the reasons would be almost as numerous as the authors. In the case of Lasuén, the motives are easy to discover. He wrote, and these volumes make it clear that he wrote extensively, because circumstances made it necessary for him to do so.

Many of his letters are addressed to higher officials in Church and State, and these are written in the formal style so dear to Spanish writers in the eighteenth century. The remainder, for the most part, even when they deal with matters of business, are friendly, informal letters to confreres in the missions of California or in San Fernando College, Mexico. They were never intended for publication, and for that reason they have a charm, a freshness, and a value not usually found in formal, official letters.

A brief study will reveal that the thought expressed in these letters is usually elevated, and the presentation pleasing, often subtly so. At times the words seem to obscure the meaning, and this may be more than an accident. This often appears in letters to the local governor when a reply had to be made before there was an opportunity to consult the higher superior in Mexico. There is another reason, too. Lasuén was a Basque, and on his own admission his mastery of the Spanish language was never complete. In a letter dated August 21, 1787, he speaks of his "knowledge, such as it is, of the Spanish language" ["mi tal cual inteligencia del castellano"]. No letter of his is written in Basque, but there can be little doubt that he used his native language often, for many of the missionaries, and some of the governors, were Basques.

In this collection a total of approximately four hundred and eighty papers are classified as Letters. It is an impressive number, but it is by no means complete. The vast majority were written during the period when he exercised the office of President, and they have survived either because he retained a copy of them, or the recipient of them held an official position and retained them along with other official documents. Those he wrote as a private individual, with a few exceptions, seem to have vanished, as do millions of private letters at the present day.

The list of the letters he wrote as President is far from complete. As early as September 18, 1787, he wrote that "my pen, which is not idle for a moment, is all you see or know of me." Yet, only a few letters for the entire year have survived. Towards the end of 1797, in a letter dated November 2, he adds that he is "ceaselessly busy with the painful task of writing," and in the same letter he looks forward to spending the entire winter "with a pen in my hand." Few of these letters have come to light. Yet, despite the numbers that are lost, there is no evidence that important ones are missing.

Lasuén preferred to transact important business, not by letter but by conference; and when such conferences took place, the reasonable attitude he assumed, the charm of his personality, and his willingness to accommodate whenever possible, all contributed towards the smooth and successful operation of the mission system. The historian, in his perverse way, may regret this, for such conferences are never described in detail; but when conferences were not held, and Lasuén, much against his will, was obliged to pen lengthy reports, we are given clear and dramatic pictures of mission life, with all its incidental problems. For this reason the three lengthy letters dated respectively July 3, 1786, October 20, 1787, and June 19, 1801, will, without doubt, be regarded as the most valuable. He wrote them with much reluctance, and sometimes in the midst of many distractions. At times he had to depend on unaided memory to supply the details, for the archives which contained the authentic information were too far distant for easy consultation. On at least one occasion, shortly after the founding of San Luis Rey Mission, he wrote one of his characteristic letters, although at the time he lacked the facilities afforded by both a table and a chair.

Circumstances such as these did not unduly disturb him, for he did not have a high regard for what he wrote. In a letter to the guardian of San Fernando College, written on August 29, 1802, less than a year before his death, he voiced the opinion that no one could read his letters without being annoyed by them, so numerous and so somber were they—an opinion with which readers will not agree.

In an effort to present in modern English the contents of these letters the translator has allowed himself a certain degree of liberty. In his more formal letters, Lasuén tended to express himself in long, involved sentences, with many dependent clauses and qualifying conditions. In view of the declining classical tradition at the present day, and the more accelerated tempo of living, it was deemed better to reduce such sentences to their components, in the hope that clarity of thought may compensate for fastidiousness of expression.

In the early mission days writing paper was often in short supply;

but in the case of a Father President it was a necessity of life. Inspired, no doubt, by motives of economy, Lasuén at times paid scant attention to paragraphing. When his divisions seemed unduly long and the parts too varied, the present writer has not hesitated to break up the larger paragraphs into smaller ones.

Notes, Doctor Johnson informs us, are a necessary evil—he was speaking about literature. In a work of this kind, no doubt, their use does not call for a lengthy defense. They have been employed mainly for purposes of identification and clarification, with a leaning towards the side of mercy as regards their number.

As should be expected in writings of that period, accents are used infrequently—Lasuén did not add an accent even to his own name. Furthermore, the writer has been informed that Basque proper names, in instances where they carry an accent in their Castilian form, are not necessarily pronounced in that manner in the land of the Basques. In all such cases, a conscious effort has been made to follow common sense and common usage as the norm.

Acknowledgments

No work of this magnitude could be carried forward without the co-operation and good will of many. Initially the project owes its origin to the vision and foresight of the early directors and members of the Academy. The late Father Benjamino Gento, O.F.M., pioneer member of the Academy, was the first to make a systematic attempt to assemble the writings of Lasuén. At a later date the work was continued with equal zeal and energy, and with unflagging perseverence, by his confrere, Father Lázaro Lamadrid, O.F.M. The present writer gladly and gratefully acknowledges his indebtedness to these pioneer researches in the field of Lasuén writings. To Father Antonine Tibesar, O.F.M., a special word of thanks is due. It was during his administration as Director of the Academy that these letters were assembled and translated. The writer is grateful for the opportunities for research which Father Tibesar so generously accorded, for his professional advice which was often availed of, and for his encouragement and moral support which made the issuing of these volumes not a task, but a pleasure.

A deep debt of gratitude is due, also, to Father Maynard J. Geiger, O.F.M., custodian of the archives of Santa Barbara Mission and distinguished authority on the Mission Period; to the different superiors of Santa Barbara Mission for gracious hospitality; to the Most Reverend John J. Mitty, late Archbishop of San Francisco, for permission to obtain a microfilm of the entire Taylor Collection; to Fray Ignacio Omaechevarria, O.F.M., of the Franciscan Province of Cantabria, for invaluable information and for illustrations from the home land of Lasuén; to Dr. George P. Hammond and the staff of Bancroft Library, especially to Mrs. Helen Harding Bretnor; to Mr. Paul O'Brien and the staff of the California Historical Archives, Sacramento; to Miss Ellen C. Barrett, Los Angeles Public Library; to the directors of the Archivo General de la Nación, of the Biblioteca Nacional, and of the Museo Nacional, Mexico City; to Professor Manuel Servin of the University of Southern California for many helpful suggestions and for professional assistance; to Professor Lionel U. Ridout of San Diego State College for numerous courtesies; to my confreres at the Academy of American Franciscan History for constant co-operation and generous forbearance, and especially to Father Fintan Warren, O.F.M., for unselfish assistance in the tedious task of proofreading; to Fray Rafael de la Torre, O.F.M., for the line drawings; to Mrs. Myra J. Boland of Washington, D. C., for illustrations of the mission brands; and to Mr. Willis Shell, Jr., and the staff at the William Byrd Press, Richmond, for courtesy, co-operation, and professional competence.

The writer is deeply grateful to Mrs. Walter H. Hoffman, Jr., of Ventura, California, whose generous financial assistance facilitated the publication of these volumes.

Introduction

IN COMMUNITIES LARGE AS WELL AS SMALL, some individuals leave an impress on their contemporaries by reason of their character or personality. Others achieve a more lasting fame because of their achievements. A few win a temporary pre-eminence because, although their talents and achievements may be mediocre, they are seen against a background of personalities more mediocre still.

Occasionally, a self-effacing Boswell will appear, to record the words and deeds of someone who soars above his contemporaries; but more often it will be the lot of a later writer to rescue from unmerited oblivion the name and achievements of some "mute inglorious Milton."

Hispanic California has had its popular heroes. Rivera and Neve, Fages, Borica, and Argüello—each has had its coterie of admirers; and even Figueroa and Pico, begrimed and tarnished although they sometimes appear, have their defenders, their apologists, and their devotees.

In the long roster of California's celebrities, one name and one alone has withstood the searching test of time and the scrutiny of friend and foe: the enduring name of Fray Junípero Serra. With clear vision he drew the ground plan for California's mission system, and in his heroic determination to make it a reality, hand and brain never ceased until both were stilled in death.

Serra had an advantage not shared by others. He was the first bearer of good tidings, the herald of a new day. And the beginning of a new day is often colorful and glamorous. It brings challenge, and hope, and promise; and nothing is more soul-stirring than a bold leader as he presses onward into the dawn.

Serra was fortunate, too, in having among his missionaries a devoted friend, a keen observer, and a faithful scribe who committed to writing what he had heard and observed. Father Francisco Balou's *Life of the Venerable Father Fray Junípero Serra*[1] is invaluable because it preserves for posterity a picture, as contemporaries saw it, of a great leader, missionary, administrator, friend of the Indians, and man of God.

[1] See Maynard J. Geiger, O.F.M. (ed.) *Palou's Life of Fray Junípero Serra* (Washington, D. C., 1955).

xi

But Spain, in the days of its power and glory, rarely suffered from a shortage of leaders, and the canvas of California's mission history is too wide to be restricted to one man, no matter how heroic his achievements.

Fray Fermín Francisco Lasuén was a missionary with only a few years of experience when he attracted the attention of superiors who were looking for someone to succeed the aged and venerable Junípero Serra. Once appointed to the position of President of the Missions, he was confirmed in office again and again. World visitors who were his guests at Carmel were unanimous in their tributes to their host, and the story of the progress of the missions in spiritual and temporal matters, as revealed in his writings, is further proof that in Lasuén the missions of California had a President worthy to be compared with his better-known predecessor, Junípero Serra.

Serra first saw light in the sun-kissed Island of Mallorca. By reason of his race and language his kinship was with Catalonia. Lasuén was a Basque. His kinsfolk were the hardy mountaineers of the Basque province of Álava. There he was born in the city of Vitoria on July 7, 1736, "between five and half past five in the morning," as the meticulous *cura* of the parish church of San Vicente recorded in the Baptismal Register, with the added information that on the following day he was given the sacrament of Baptism, and the name of Fermín Francisco. Like a true Basque, fastidious for family honor, on each occasion the *cura* entered the name "de Lasuén," for the added "de" carried a hint of nobility. Nevertheless, so numerous were those who laid claim to such titles, and so remote were their connections with the original holders of the distinction, that for the sake of brevity and simplicity writers who are not Basques often omit the added prefix. But not Lasuén himself. He invariably signed himself "de Lasuén," and offered the same courtesy to other Basques with similar claims to noble origin.

His father's name was Lorenzo, and his mother's maiden name María Francisca de Arizqueta.[2] On the paternal side, his grandmother was Magdalena de Aspiunza, and on the maternal side, Agueda de Murua.

Despite the multiplied hints of nobility in the family tree, it seems clear that the family of Lasuén was not unduly encumbered with worldly wealth. Early in his career in California he felt it necessary to enlist the aid of his superiors in obtaining financial help for his parents in their declining years; and almost three decades later, when his own last years were approaching, he felt obliged to do a like service for his sister Clara.

[2] In the certificate of Baptism, the *cura* wrote the name as *Arasqueta*. This is possibly an older form of the name, or a local corruption in spelling. The name is still a common one in that region, but the spelling is invariably *Arizqueta*. This, too, is the spelling employed in the certificate of Lasuén's reception into the Order and his Profession in it.

Official record of Lasuén's Baptism

CROSSING THE THRESHOLD

Lasuén becomes a candidate for membership in
the Franciscan Order

In the circumstances, it should not be a matter of wonder that no further details of the early life of Lasuén have survived. As in countless similar cases, the few particulars in the Baptism Register sum up the "short and simple annals of the poor"—at least for their early years. When fame and pre-eminence come moderately late, as they did in the case of Lasuén, companions of early years are scattered or departed, memories of distant days are obliterated, and in the brilliance of the noontide it is too late to pursue the chase that could bring promise only when the "dews of morning" are fresh.

No record survives of the schools he may have attended in his early years. Perhaps he received some instruction in the church and school of his parish; but it is more likely that he was an attendant at the church of St. Francis, the ruins of which are still pointed out. Even in the days of Lasuén it was an ancient church. As early as the middle of the thirteenth century the church and friary were already in existence; and if local tradition can be trusted, St. Francis himself, when on a pilgrimage to the shrine of St. James at Compostela, was present at their founding. They were administered by the Franciscans through all the centuries of their existence, and were frequently the recipients of favors from the lords and lesser nobility of the neighborhood.

The friary attached to the church of St. Francis was more than a residence for Franciscans. It was, in addition, a novitiate and a house of studies where young men received their initiation into the Franciscan Order and their early training in the spirit of it.

The thoughts of the youthful Lasuén turned to the religious life at an early age, and he applied for admission to the Franciscan Order at the above-named Friary of St. Francis. His application was viewed favorably by the superiors, and on March 19, 1751, a few months before his sixteenth birthday, he was clothed with the habit of the Franciscan Order.

Ordination to the priesthood was still in the distant future, and the intervening years would be busy, exacting, and challenging. By far the greater portion of the time would be devoted to study. Any gaps in the literary and scientific training of the young man would have to be filled. A minimum of two years was normally devoted to Philosophy, with emphasis on the subtle and thought-provoking system of Duns Scotus, with a minimum of three years devoted to Theology. But first would have to come the year of the novitiate, the year of testing when the youth for the first time is brought face to face with the ideals of the Franciscan Order, seeks to regulate his own life in accordance with them, in the light of his own personal experience, decides whether or not it is a way of life which he would freely choose. If he decides to live according to these ideals, and if the superiors are satisfied about his aptitude to do so, at the end of the year of novitiate he is admitted to full membership in the Order, provided he has reached, as a minimum, his seventeenth birthday. Lasuén, however, had not reached the minimum age, and his Profession, or formal reception into the Order, had to be deferred until July 7, 1752.

No records have survived regarding the studies he pursued or his progress in them. It is evident that they were not completed in his native Vitoria, for in February, 1759, we find him at the Franciscan house of studies at Aránzazu, already raised to the rank of deacon, but not yet a priest.

What the shrine of Guadalupe is to the devout Mexican, and what Beaupré is to the Catholics of Quebec, Aránzazu is to the Basques of Spain. It is their sacred city, the home of a religious shrine that, century after century, has symbolized their faith, their culture, and their uniqueness among the people of Spain.

It was in such surroundings that Lasuén pursued at least some of his higher studies, and it was there that word reached him that a Franciscan delegate from Mexico had come to Spain with the purpose of visiting the Franciscan provinces in the hope of inducing priests and seminarians to volunteer for missionary work in Mexico. Similar appeals had been made in the past, and the Basque people had responded most generously. A glance at California's long list of early missionaries will reveal an astonishingly high percentage of Friars of Basque origin: Fathers Landaeta, de Miguel, Zalvidea, Sarria, Martiarena, de la Peña, Murgia, Mugartegui, and Quintana. These are but a few, taken almost at random; but they serve to indicate that the missionary spirit was strong in the land of the Basques.

The delegate from Mexico was authorized to accept twenty recruits. He succeeded in obtaining eighteen, six of whom were Basques. Of these six, two were priests: Fathers Arenaza and Pangua; two were deacons: Lasuén and Prestamero; and two were theological students: Fermín Juanena and Juan de Medinaveitia. The first four subsequently exercised much influence on the mission history of California.

No record is extant regarding the date on which Lasuén volunteered for missionary work, but his application was accepted on February 19, 1759, and the delegate, Fray Gaspar Gómez, in sending him the formal acceptance, sent him this further information:

It has been made clear to us . . . by trustworthy reports that you possess the virtue, aptitude, and other gifts which are requisite for so high a ministry. We here and now admit you as one of the above missionaries by virtue of our letter patent, signed by our hand and under our seal. These you will present to the

Very Reverend Father Guardian of the Friary in order that he may countersign them; and having received his blessing you will proceed to the port of Cádiz where you are to stay at the Friary of St. Francis, under obedience to the Very Reverend Father Vice-Commissary of the Indies, and will await the occasion to embark with the others.

This is not a personal letter. It is a printed form, with blanks where the delegate filled in names, dates, and similar details. It is countersigned by the guardian, who testified that on March 6, 1759, Lasuén set out on his journey to Cádiz. From his passport and other official documents regarding him, we gather the following information regarding his physical appearance at this time. He was twenty-three years of age, white, of medium stature, rosy complexion, but face pitted with marks of smallpox. His eyes were dark, his beard ample, and his hair black and curly.

No doubt he visited his native Vitoria to take leave of his family, to which he was devoted, as his later letters reveal. To reach the port of Cádiz he had to make an overland journey of one hundred and seventy or more leagues. He went by way of Zafra, which he reached on April 18, and Llerena (Badajoz) where he arrived on May 2, and thence by way of Seville to Cádiz, which he reached on May 14.

The voyage to the New World was not yet to begin. First there was a delay of thirty days, for a new superior had failed to comply with all the formalities insisted on by the government. Other delays followed, and it was late in August before the last of the requirements was met, and formal approval for sailing obtained. Finally, on September 5, 1759, Lasuén and his companions bade farewell to their homeland, and, with Don José de Sierra as captain, a ship named *El Jasón* engaged in the quicksilver trade weighed anchor, set its prow to the west, and the voyage to the New World had at last begun.

With winds and tide favorable, the journey could be made in a little more than two months. Much would depend on the unpredictable nature of the elements, on the number of ports which the ship would visit in the Caribbean, and the length of time in each port. Ten years previously, Junípero Serra had made a similar journey. He left the port of Cádiz at the end of September, 1749, but did not reach Veracruz until December 7. No record has come to light regarding the length of time Lasuén needed to reach the same port.

VERACRUZ TO MEXICO CITY

At Veracruz, Lasuén set foot on the new continent which he was destined never to leave. His immediate destination, however, was Mexico City, many days' journey distant. We may assume that the Spanish government made transportation available, as it normally did for incoming missionaries; yet, in his day Serra and a companion chose to make the journey on foot.

Few journeys can be more trying, few more rewarding. Sandy beaches give way to tropical vegetation. Then the sultry and humid atmosphere of the lowlands is refreshed by gentle breezes from the foothills. Canyons and gorges appear, such as the rugged mountains of the Basque country had never known, and occasional torrents strike terror into Europeans accustomed to the tamed and placid rivers of the old continent. Mountain ranges give way to ever higher mountains, and snow-capped volcanoes, with their towering peaks wrapped in clouds as a rule, keep watch and ward on every side.

After scaling range after range, the weary traveler at length descends to the picturesque valley where the City of Mexico nestles, seven thousand feet above sea level. And Mexico City, for the present, was journey's end. The home of his childhood was more than five thousand miles away, separated from him by land and ocean. The toils and hazards of travel, for the moment, were over. Another Franciscan house opened its portals to receive him. Its cloisters were soon to become familiar, and its way of life more dear to him than anything he had left behind. He was now incorporated into San Fernando College, and to his dying day it would always be to him the "holy" college. Tomorrow would bring its own cycle of problems, and many a tomorrow would follow in its wake; but today began a period of respite—peace after anxious days, a reunion, perhaps, with confreres of earlier years, and a fraternal welcome from future comrades in arms. Here at last was restful repose. "Home is the sailor home from sea, And the hunter home from the hill."

San Fernando College

The College of San Fernando was a comparatively new institution when Lasuén first entered it. It had been established in 1733, a little more than a quarter of a century before. It was one of a group of such institutions, subject to the jurisdiction of the Franciscan Order. Each college enjoyed a certain measure of autonomy, independent of the jurisdiction of the local bishop or Franciscan superior, subject immediately to a resident superior called a guardian, and, through him, to a commissary general who was the representative in the New World of the highest official in the Order.

The purpose of each college was to facilitate missionary work in the New World. Academic courses were conducted for those who had not yet completed their formal studies; there was a novitiate for those not yet received into the Order; and for all there were courses in the languages and customs of the Indians to whom they were to minister. Many of those who entered San Fernando were already priests who now wished to devote their lives to more specialized missionary work. These would normally spend a year at the college to deepen and strengthen their spiritual life by following the rigorous discipline that characterized such colleges.

At the conclusion of their respective courses, some might be retained at the college to assist in the different kinds of work it had assumed, others, in response to requests, might be sent from church to church to preach sermons and conduct religious exercises in order to quicken the faith of those who were already Christians, and the others were available for misisonary work among aboriginal tribes.

The college, moreover, served as an intermediary between the missionaries and the civil authorities in Mexico City, and as a rule it undertook to supervise the forwarding of requisites intended for the various missions. Finally, each college was a home to which missionaries could return when fatigued by labors, or incapacitated for any reason.

Early Days in the New World

San Fernando College was Lasuén's first home in the New World. We do not at present know the exact date on which he entered it, or when he left to become a missionary. On March 17, 1760, the superiors of San Fernando issued a formal request for the ordination to the priesthood of Lasuén and his companion, Prestamero, and on February 25, of the following year they requested that Father Lasuén be granted faculties for preaching and hearing confessions, because, as they testified, he had shown that he possessed the knowledge, virtue, and prudence requisite for such an office. The ordination to the priesthood, therefore, took place some time between these two dates.

No record has come to light regarding the years immediately following his ordination. In the letters that comprise these volumes he makes but a few references to these early days. He tells us that for five years he was a missionary among the primitive Indians of the Pame tribe whose home was in the rugged Sierra Gorda country in the northeast corner of what is now the state of Querétaro, and the adjoining regions in San Luis Potosí and Guanajuato.[3] At that time the College of San Fernando conducted five mission centers there, but for the most part the records have disappeared, and up to the present it has been impos-

---

[3] For a description of the Sierra Gorda missions, see Maynard J. Geiger, O.F.M., *The Life and Times of Junípero Serra* (Washington, D. C., 1959), I, 102-134.

sible to determine to which of the missions Lasuén was assigned, and what was accomplished during his administration.

In the year 1768, the College of San Fernando assumed control of the missions of Lower California, and Palou informs us that Lasuén was among the five missionaries who journeyed from the Sierra Gorda in order to labor there. From this point on it becomes easier to trace the life and labors of Lasuén.

In Lower California

The Jesuits began their first permanent settlement in Lower California in October, 1697. The story of their apostolic labors, of the missions they founded, and of their eventual departure from the land they evangelized has been told by many writers.[4] It is not deemed necessary to recount it here.

On the departure of the Jesuits, sixteen missionaries of San Fernando College assumed control, at the request of the Mexican administration. They reached Lower California at the beginning of April, 1768, and Lasuén was assigned to the Mission of San Borja.

This mission had been founded less than six years before. It was rather isolated and remote; but it had strategic importance for, although it was but one among thirteen missions then functioning, it comprised about twenty per cent of all the Christian Indians of Lower California.

A few years later, when writing to the guardian of San Fernando College on February 12, 1772, Father Palou reported in regard to San Borja that it was located more than thirty-five leagues from Santa Gertrudis, the nearest mission in the south, and about forty leagues from Santa María, the nearest to the north; that it was about twelve leagues from the Pacific Ocean and ten from the Gulf of Mexico; that it had a church and cloister of adobe, both roofed with tule, and recently built by Lasuén; that all the pagans in the region had now become Christians; and that in addition to San Borja there were five dependent settlements, each with an Indian population, making a total of some fifteen hundred Indians, and thus constituting it the most populous of all the missions of Lower California.[5]

Lasuén was not destined to spend the remainder of his life in this peninsula. Members of the Dominican Order for some time had been eager to engage in missionary work in that region, and the Franciscans gladly ceded Lower California to them. The agreement between the two

[4] See, for instance, Peter Masten Dunne, S.J., *Black Robes in Lower California* (Berkeley and Los Angeles, 1952). The book contains an extensive bibliography.
[5] Cf. Herbert Eugene Bolton (ed.) *Historical Memoirs of New California by Fray Francisco Palóu, O.F.M.* (Berkeley, 1926), I, 205-207.

Orders was signed on April 7, 1772, and the approval of the Viceroy was obtained before the month was ended.

Although some Dominicans arived in October of that year it was not possible for them to take formal possession of the missions at that time, for their Father President, who had been authorized to make the transfer, died on the way. A few months later, on April 8, 1773, a new letter of authorization reached them, and the formal handing-over of the mission began.

Now that his work in Lower California was coming to an end, Lasuén would have preferred to return to San Fernando College. He had devoted ten years of his life to some of the most difficult missions in Mexico; but a new mission field had been opened in Upper California, and in response to a plea for missionaries sent from Carmel by Father Serra, Lasuén "resigned himself to obedience with total indifference,"[6] as Palou expresses it.

On June 21, he bade farewell to San Borja, the mission over which he had presided for five years, and in company with Palou set out for Upper California. On the twenty-fourth they reached Santa María Mission, where they stayed for three weeks. By that time other missionaries had joined them. On July 13, they arrived at the frontier outpost, Mission San Fernando de Vellicatá, the only mission founded by the Franciscans in Lower California. On July 21, accompanied by five other missionaries, Lasuén set out from Vellicatá. The balance of the journey was made by slow stages, for in addition to the six missionaries there were also fourteen soldiers and six families of Indians, as well as a mule team laden with corn for the missions of Upper California. It was a toilsome journey, as the burning rays of the summer sun beat down mercilessly, and the hot breath of the desert was on every side, with little to break the monotony of sand and rock and sage and chaparral. They reached San Diego on the morning of August 30, 1773.

In California

The California they entered had little in common with the California of later years. There were in all but five missions, and these were little better than palisades coated with mud and roofed with tule. There were no towns, no settlements of white people, and nothing beyond the barest trappings of civilization. Each mission had a few soldiers to protect it, and the military defense of the entire territory was entrusted to two presidios located at each extremity of the newly acquired prov-

[6] Bolton, *op. cit.*, I, 263.

ince, and separated from one another by an expanse of some five hundred miles. There were no roads; but connecting the presidios and missions there was one principal trail from north to south which was euphoniously called the *Camino Real*, the King's Highway.

The Indians far outnumbered those of Lower California; but in the five years which had elapsed since the first coming of the missionaries the number of converts had been lamentably small. A whole year had passed in San Diego before the first Indian was baptized; and at San Gabriel, one of the more flourishing of the missions, in the course of three years there had been less than eighty baptisms.

Food supplies had been running low, and the specter of famine was beginning to cast ominous shadows across the new foundations. There was a new Viceroy in Mexico: Bucarelli; a new guardian at San Fernando College: Verger; and a young and energetic governor in California: Fages. The latter was capable, ambitious, loyal to military traditions, and devoted to the Crown. But he was new to frontier life, inexperienced in civil administration, and inclined to chafe at the restrictions imposed on his freedom of action by the rights and prerogatives conceded to the missionaries.

It was evident to the experienced eye of Serra that a crisis was fast approaching unless there was to be a drastic change in the policy then pursued. Despite the hazards of the long journey, in the preceding October Serra had set out for Mexico City to lay before the Viceroy and the guardian of San Fernando College the multiple problems of Spain's newest acquisitions. As a result of these conferences, officials in Mexico obtained a clearer and more sympathetic understanding of California's problems, and these conferences resulted in a series of salutary regulations which had a profound influence on the development of the new territory. Serra returned to California in March, 1774, after an absence of eighteen months.

Serra was still absent in Mexico when Palou and his companions arrived in San Diego, and Palou found himself in the role of Interim President of the Missions. In that capacity he assigned Lasuén to San Gabriel Mission. It was intended as a temporary appointment, but it lasted two years. They were unhappy years for Lasuén. He had come to California under the impression that there was a scarcity of missionaries, and if circumstances had been normal he would have been given a permanent assignment immediately. Instead, for two years he was a supernumerary, and at the end of that time became chaplain to the military governor, with rights and status vaguely defined.

In the late summer of 1775, hope was rekindled, and it seemed as if Lasuén's years of waiting were to win their reward. He was authorized to found and preside over a new establishment, a mission that would bear the name of San Juan Capistrano.

On October 29, he reached the site selected for the new mission, and on the following day conducted the religious services prescribed for such a founding. For seven or eight days he and his companions worked with enthusiasm. Then came the blow that shattered his hopes once more. On the morning of November 5, Indians attacked and sacked the neighboring Mission of San Diego, killing Father Jayme, a missionary, and some others. Work at San Juan Capistrano had to be suspended, and all withdrew to the protection of the presidio at San Diego. There for a time he was a guest, neither a full-time missionary nor even a supernumerary; and for a time, too, he was chaplain once more to the unpredictable Rivera, the military governor.

It seemed as if disappointments and frustrations in his case were destined to be compounded, for day followed day, and weeks lapsed slowly into months, and the weary missionary, so eager for work and so sensitive by nature, was still without an assignment. Then, in the early summer of 1777, eighteen months after he had been forced to suspend work on the Mission of San Juan Capistrano, the sorely-tried Friar received an appointment in which he could exercise his zeal to the full. He was made superior of San Diego Mission.

It was not the most flattering of assignments, but, as Serra pointed out, it was the only one then available.[7] As others before him had found out, the Indians of San Diego were not very responsive, and the soil, in great part arid, was more suitable for pasture than for cultivation. Here he labored for eight years, and during that time the number of baptisms increased from 431 to 1,075, and the livestock increased tenfold, from 245 to 2,462, which is the figure for the year 1784, the last full year of his administration. It can scarcely have been a matter of surprise to anyone when, shortly after the death of Father Junípero Serra, Lasuén was appointed President of the Missions.

Fresh Fields and Pastures New

The patent appointing him President of the Missions was signed by the guardian of San Fernando College on February 6, 1785. Months were to pass before it reached San Diego, and in September of that year Lasuén bade good-bye to the mission that had cost him so much effort, took the road to Carmel, and squared his shoulders to bear the burden that only the hand of death would remove when eighteen toilsome years had run their course.

[7] Cf. Antonine Tibesar, O.F.M. (ed.), *Writings of Junípero Serra* (Washington, 1956), III, 155.

Under his benevolent administration the story of San Diego was duplicated wherever missionaries labored throughout California. The Letters and Reports that fill these volumes are the clearest proof. Serra in his day had seen as many as nine missions spring up in the wilderness that was California. Lasuén enabled the wilderness to blossom and bear fruit, and lived to witness the founding of nine additional missions. Some of these latter are familiar wherever the lure of California has penetrated, and three of them have won worldwide fame: Santa Barbara, "betwixt the mountains and the sea"; San Miguel, whose cool, sequestered cloisters offer shade to sun-drenched travelers along Highway 101; and San Luis Rey, where gentle breezes from the ocean and a backdrop of distant mountains more than compensate for the drabness of the valley in which it is located. They add a borrowed loveliness to the graceful proportions of the mission, and to the simple charm of its architecture.

His life at San Diego had been hidden, and his influence restricted to the mission and presidio, for San Diego was but the gateway to California. Carmel was different. It was the central headquarters for the entire mission system and but a few miles from Monterey, the executive center for civil and military administration. From now on, he was to be in frequent, almost daily, contact with viceroys and governors; with distinguished visitors and ordinary sea captains; with local commanders and lesser officials; with missionaries and their manifold problems of sowing and harvesting, of building and rebuilding, in the world of matter as well as in the realm of spirit; and with the perennial problem of every mission, the neophytes as they came and went.

Problems seemed to grow in number and complexity as if keeping pace with his advancing years, and all who saw him judged him to be much older than he really was. But he who in early years had chafed at his own enforced inactivity, in maturer years never shirked a duty no matter how repellent it might be. The wearied frame might clamor for rest, but an active brain and a burning zeal kept steady the hand at the rudder.

Frequent allusions in his letters make it clear that throughout his busy life he had set his course steadily towards the eternal shores, and on June 26, 1803, it was a weary voyager in a frail bark who crept into port "on a flowing tide." He died at San Carlos Mission after an illness which kept him confined to his room for twelve days. He was buried the following day, and in the sanctuary of that mission he rests beside the body of Junípero Serra. No eulogy is carved into the stone that guards his dust—just the simple name Fermín Francisco de Lasuén. It is enough.

Shepherd of a larger Flock

When Lasuén assumed the office of President of the Missions he was not venturing into the unknown. He was to preside over a system with which he was quite familiar. He had been instructed in its techniques when at San Fernando College, and he grew more familiar with it in the years that followed, for he had lived in accordance with it. It was not the only system employed by the Franciscans in the New World, but it was the one adopted by San Fernando. In many respects it was a rigid system, allowing but little freedom of action to the individual missionary, or even to the President of the Missions.

Under the Spanish system there was a close alliance between Church and State, and in missionary regions such as California, sword and cross, for good or ill, were intertwined. No matter how diverse their individual aims and methods might have been, soldier and missionary marched forward in step, and many undertakings were joint enterprises. The founding of a new mission is a clear instance. Those who were familiar with the locale could recommend the establishment there of a mission, but many preliminaries had to take place before the first step in actual construction could be undertaken. Before the site could be approved certain requirements had to be met. There had to be an adequate supply of water, of good soil, of available timber; there should be a reasonably large number of Indians within reach; and the site chosen should be not only suitable for the purpose, but accessible to the main highway. Missionaries should be available, as well as a military guard of five or six or more soldiers. Food supplies would have to be provided for the sustenance of the missionaries, the soldiers, the workers, and the neophytes whom, it was hoped, the mission would attract. There should be livestock, tools and implements for farming purposes, and a supply of grain for sowing so that the future of the enterprise might be safeguarded. It was the Viceroy who authorized the establishment, and it was he who selected the title for the new mission. Thus, both in its founding and in its functioning, Church and State co-operated.

Lasuén succeeded to the position of President at a critical time. A year before, as the administration of Serra was drawing to a close, there was a distinct possibility that even in Upper California the Franciscans might be replaced by Dominican missionaries. Paradoxical as it may seem, it was a Franciscan bishop, Don Fray Antonio de los Reyes of Sonora, who advocated such a change, and it was the governor of California, Don Filipe de Neve, who strenuously opposed it and eloquently defended the Franciscans, despite the fact that he had often been at odds with them. The problem arose in this wise.

California was a missionary country, far from the residence or jurisdiction of any bishop. In 1779, the new diocese of Sonora was formed, with California as an integral part of it. In 1782, Reyes became its first bishop. The area subject to his jurisdiction was immense. A few places, the more populous settlements, had the status of parishes, but the rest was mission territory. There was a relatively small group of Dominicans in Lower California, but the rest of the missionaries were Franciscans, members mainly of the College of San Fernando, or of Querétaro, or of the Province of the Holy Gospel, Mexico City.

Reyes devised a plan for the organization of his diocese which was idealistic, if not fantastic. He wished to divide his diocese into four administrative units, called *custodies*. Each would be independent of the province or college to which it had been assigned. California and Lower California would make up one of these custodies, and for greater uniformity it was thought that the entire region should be entrusted to just one religious group, preferably the Dominicans, in the opinion of Reyes. The bishop was not very explicit when explaining how, under the new system, future missionaries were to be recruited, educated, and maintained, and how residences and churches were to be provided.

Opposition to such a scheme came, not from Neve alone, but from the missionaries who objected to being ejected in this fashion from the province or college to which they had belonged. Wiser and more disinterested administrators were quick to see the problems and pitfalls inherent in the system, but the bishop had friends at the Spanish court. Such was the situation as Serra lay dying.

The risk of being replaced by Dominicans was passing when Lasuén assumed office, but the threat that a custody might be set up was still very real. Not until August, 1791, was the project finally ended by royal decree.

With the death of Serra the early pioneer stage in California drew to a close. The missions founded by him were but temporary structures erected in the midst of a wilderness. Yet, when the conquest of Upper California was planned, it was hoped that from the beginning the mission churches would be adorned "as if they were cathedrals" so as to impress the natives with the superiority of the new religion,[8] and some of the church furnishings for the early missions would not be incongruous in many an American cathedral today. But hopes and ideals had to be tempered to fit the hard realities of life in the new mission territory.

Serra and many of his companions had ministered for years in the ornate stone churches of Sierra Gorda. They now had to be content with the most primitive of buildings, for the first mission structures, of

[8] Cf. Bolton, *op. cit.*, I, 56-57.

necessity, had to be of a temporary nature—upright poles arranged as palisades, with beams for a roof, and reeds or earth for further covering. This was inevitable, for time was pressing, skilled workers were few, and even willing workers were not always in proportion to the need. The first buildings to rise were usually the chapel, a few rooms for the missionaries and their assistants, together with the military guard, and storerooms to house the supplies.

When Indians expressed a desire to become Christians they were required to reside at the mission during the period of instruction, and this made additional building imperative. After the instructions were completed, and the Indians had become Christian converts, they were encouraged to live in the neighborhood of the mission, "within sound of the mission bell." As a further safeguard, unmarried Christian Indian girls were required to live within the mission compound in a place set apart for them—a policy that necessitated additional building. Use had to be made of whatever building material was available, and it often happened that what was constructed one year had to be reconstructed the next.

Towards the end of Serra's administration, structures of a more permanent nature were beginning to appear. Roofing tile, so prominent a feature of typical mission buildings, did not come into use until 1780, when it was employed at San Antonio Mission, and shortly afterwards at San Luis Obispo. Of all the mission churches to be seen now in California, not one was in existence in the days of Serra. In San Juan Capistrano Mission what is known as the "Serra Chapel" is still in use. It is quite probable that it is one of the few links with the first President of the Missions, but, like so many other mission structures, it has undergone many alterations, reconstructions, and "restorations" in the meantime.

From the beginning some instruction in domestic arts was given to the Indians in the missions, for Indians from Lower California had come for that purpose, and members of the armed guard and their wives cooperated in many instances; but the results were evidently mediocre. Beginning in 1790, a systematic attempt was made to teach the Indians a variety of arts which were basic in the mission system—masonry, carpentry, pottery making, spinning, weaving, leather work, and such like. Skilled technicians were sent from Mexico at royal expense to teach these arts. From this period, occurring in the middle of Lasuén's administration, can be traced the rise of architecture that is characteristically Californian—the graceful arches, stately corridors, and sheltered patios, the bell towers and belfry walls, the cupolas, the Moorish windows, and the ornate church façades.

More important than the imposing architecture was the teaching of less spectacular arts, such as the building of dams, the constructing of canals for the wider distribution of water, and the manufacture of baked clay pipes to convey it, for these and similar innovations contributed to the notable increase not only in farm products but in livestock, too.

From time immemorial the Indians had ground corn by hand, making use either of the mortar and pestle or the metate and handstone, or *mano*. It was a slow, laborious method which, no doubt, was moderately satisfactory for supplying the needs of a small group of families. It was still the method in use for many years when large numbers of Indians were concentrated in the individual missions. When La Pérouse visited California in 1786, he and his party were astonished to observe the antiquated method of grinding; so a member of his party donated a grinding mill so simple to operate that it needed but the attention of four women to do the work of a hundred. There is no evidence, however, that extensive use was made of it, for habits change very slowly among primitive people. But change was pending, and among the technicians sent to California in the 1790's was at least one whose duty it was to teach the Indians how to construct and operate grinding mills. It was the beginning of a trend, and soon mills operated by waterpower became a feature of individual missions. One of the best examples may be seen at San Antonio Mission, although it was not completed until two years after the death of Lasuén. It was operated by water power, and the water was brought from a source three miles distant, and across open and rugged country, by means of a masonry conduit, to an artificial lake, whence it was released as needed.

Grapes were cultivated and wine produced in Lower California when the Friars were missionaries there, even at a mission as poor and remote as Lasuén's San Borja. In what precise year vines were planted in California it is difficult to say, for the Reports of the missionaries are mainly answers to questions, and many years passed before any questionnaire was sent to them in regard to vines. However, in the spring of 1779, Fray Mugartegui, superior of San Juan Capistrano Mission, in a letter to Serra reported that the vine cuttings, which had been sent from Lower California at Serra's request, had been planted. That similar cuttings had been sent to San Diego Mission around the same time can be deduced from a letter sent by Serra to Lasuén on December 8, 1781. In it he expressed the hope that the "vines would survive and bear fruit, for the lack of wine for Mass is becoming unbearable." By the year 1784, San Juan Capistrano was producing wine for table use, and in the Biennial Report for the years 1787-1788, Lasuén mentions that in San Diego, San Juan Capistrano, San Gabriel, San Buenaventura, and

Santa Barbara they now had grapes at table, and they were making some wine, too. From such small beginnings grew one of California's great industries, wine making.

Good harvests in such basic necessities as wheat, barley, corn, peas, and beans were much more important in the early pioneer days than they became at a later date. The success or failure of the Spanish conquest depended in great measure on them, and for that reason the returns for them occupy much space in the mission reports. But farming in California was a highly speculative enterprise. The missionaries were not farmers either by profession or by training; but many of them had acquired a measure of proficiency in it by reason of their experience in the missions of Sierra Gorda and Lower California. Books on agriculture, too, formed part of the library of certain missions. However, more than skill was needed for success in farming. A knowledge of both soil and climate was essential; and in regard to these the missionaries had much to learn. Too often their fate was similar to the Scriptural sower who "went forth to sow his seed." Some brought no return, for it was swept away by unforeseen floods; others failed to reach maturity because of prolonged drought; and still others fell a prey to locusts. Prior to the conquest, the soil of California had been virtually uncultivated. Now it needed to be broken so that it might bring forth a variety of products, and the chief implement by which this was to be achieved, the Spanish plow, was one of the most primitive of farming devices. It was simply a crooked branch from a tree, with one handle, no mould-board, and containing no iron except at the point where contact was made with the ground. It was attached by means of a long beam to the horns of two oxen, and as they trudged slowly across the rough terrain the iron socket opened a tiny furrow. It was necessary to cross and recross the field several times before the soil could be regarded as sufficiently broken. The plowman, however, had auxiliaries, for other Indians with machetes, axes, crowbars, and pickaxes in their all too clumsy hands sought to clear the ground of shrub and bush and rock, and to render smooth the rugged contour of a region exposed without protection to the seasons' fitful forces of erosion. It was a task that was slow and tedious, and often unrewarding. Throughout the period of colonial administration there was but little change in the system of cultivating; but with the skill acquired by practice, and with better methods of irrigating, and a better understanding of the vagaries of a climate that even then could prove to be "unusual" at critical times, more abundant harvests rewarded the missionaries' efforts.

Livestock arrived with the first settlers. To make certain that the stock would not be depleted, in the early years there were stringent regulations regarding the slaughtering of cattle. Within a few years the tiny herds had increased and multiplied, progenitors of the herds that, many decades later, won for the southern part of the State the title of Cow Country, and for the State as a whole gave substance to the boast of "Cattle on a Thousand Hills."

The horse was ordinarily used only for riding. It was the ox, not the horse, that was yoked to the plow; and for the transport of goods by means of packsaddle or the *carreta*—the crude vehicle used for travel and transport—it was the mule, not the horse, that was employed.

The cow contributed greatly to the economy of early California. It was a source of milk and meat; and its hide was always valuable not only for the leather into which it could be converted, but also for many other incidental reasons, for strips of cowhide often substituted for nails in building operations, served to fasten the beam of the plow to the horns of the oxen, and to attach the bells to the crossbeams from which they hung. The domestic uses of hides were almost unlimited. They could be fashioned into seats for chairs, and normally did duty for bedsprings and mattress, and in case of necessity for blankets or coverlet, or both. Where lumber was scarce a cowhide could serve for a door; and since glass was virtually unknown in early mission days, a carefully processed hide served the purpose quite well.

Among the artisans who arrived in the 1790's there were two who were experts in the tanning of leather, and two whose specialty was the making of saddles. A more diversified range of uses thus opened at a time when, as can be seen from the statistical tables, mission livestock had grown to vast dimensions. The export of tallow was already a source of income in the days of Lasuén, and a decade or more after his death the export of hides would loom large in the foreign trade of California, and the New England ships that traded in such products would be familiar sights.

In the year 1786, the first full year of Lasuén's administration, the gross returns for all the missions indicated that they owned 8,266 cows, and 9,713 sheep. By the year 1802, these had increased to 67,782 cows, and 107,172 sheep. These figures, however, are necessarily incomplete, for they do not include the numbers slaughtered each year to maintain the ever-increasing number of Christian Indians. There were times when in individual missions the number so slaughtered amounted to as many as sixty a week. Towards the end of Lasuén's administration some of the missions indicated that they were slaughtering as many as two thousand head of cattle each year.

The vast increase in the number of sheep is noteworthy. It implied not only diversity in the menu of the Indians, but it made available, too, a vast quantity of wool. This, in turn, afforded opportunities for the instruction of the Indians in shearing, in washing and carding the wool, and in spinning and weaving it into fabrics. Since the missionaries were not required to furnish detailed information on such matters, we are dependent in great measure on the information they volunteered, and on what visitors observed. A considerable amount of textile work was carried on in certain of the missions towards the close of Lasuén's administration, and blankets, wearing apparel for the Indians, riding mantles for the vaqueros, and even carpets for the sanctuary came from the looms of the missions. Vancouver, when he visited San Francisco Mission in the year 1792, mentions that he saw some of the cloth manufactured there, and it was "by no means despicable." He had words of praise, too, for the work done on the looms of Santa Clara.

The compiling of Reports was one of Lasuén's severest trials, as he indicates more than once in his letters. Still, as he added up the totals, and compared them with previous totals, and observed the steady upward trend, the rising barometer of progress, he must often have felt a tinge of legitimate satisfaction and a pride which he did not manifest. However, his personal sentiments would have differed profoundly from those of government officials who read the same Reports in the offices of the Viceroy in Mexico, or of the King in Spain.

As early as the year 1787, when writing to the commandant general, Ugarte, Lasuén did not hesitate to assert, in his own name and in that of the missionaries: "We are not administrators of haciendas. We have not the responsibility to make them a success, and we are not accountable if they fall short of expectations."[9]

All such items were of secondary importance; they were but means to something incomparably more important, the evangelization of the Indian population. This was the ultimate goal towards which his efforts were directed, the objective towards which he had dedicated his life. But spiritual values, of their nature, are basically intangible; they cannot be determined in terms of weights and measures. Only a few aspects of the spiritual life of neophytes yielded themselves to statistical study: the numbers who received the sacraments of Baptism and Confirmation. With this limitation the following data are given; they are not offered for purposes of comparison, or as proofs of efficiency. When Serra ended his career after sixteen years of missionary work in California there was a total of 7,700 baptisms and 5,308 confirmations. Some eighteen years later, when Lasuén's career as a misionary came to a close, the number of baptisms had risen to 33,717, and the number of confirmations to 15,440.

[9] Cf. Letter 65, p. 164, *infra.*

Father to the Indians

The role of father to the Indians was not one which Lasuén felt he was at liberty to assume or to lay aside. He regarded it as inseparably connected with the office of missionary, and especially with that of President. Writing to Governor Fages on July 26, 1790, he reminded him that "all, from the King down to Your Lordship desire that I should safeguard [the Indians] as would a father. . . ." Long before he assumed the office of President he took a paternal interest in them. It is a trait that appears in his earliest letters. On October 22, 1768, in a letter to Gálvez, the Visitor General, he pleads for his "children," for San Borja Mission is poor, and these are "numerous and hungry and naked," and he is moved to do so because of his "affection as father to these miserable creatures." It is a theme that becomes familiar as letter succeeds letter.

His is not an impulsive, instinctive love that is blind to the limitations of the loved ones. Lasuén knew but too well the faults and weaknesses of his Indians. In a lengthy Report which he penned on June 19, 1801, when he had been a missionary in the New World for almost forty years, without a tinge of bitterness or cynicism, he described the Indians of his acquaintance as men who in their native state had to be taught to act as men, for they recognized "no law but force, no superior but their own free will, and no reason but their own caprice. . . . They are a people without education, without government, religion, or respect for authority, and they shamelessly pursue without restraint whatever their brutal appetites suggest to them."

As father to his Indian flock he had to provide for their support, and the preceding pages, with their story of notable increases in livestock and farm produce, reveal how abundantly he provided for their needs. There was no tradition of labor among California's Indians. Before the coming of the missionary they had maintained themselves by fishing, hunting, and collecting such seeds, nuts, and fruits as nature supplied. They had to be taught that work was a necessity; that it was something befitting human nature; and that it was a venture noble and rewarding, not a drudgery to be avoided.

The Indians were not only untutored; they were warlike, and their wars were almost ceaseless. As Lasuén explains in a letter to Viceroy Branciforte on April 25, 1797, "to speak a different dialect and to be an enemy" are one and the same. They had to be taught to live in peace, and to observe at least the rudiments of civilized living. To people who had rejoiced in the freedom of the mountains, such restraints did not come easily. For this reason the missionary learned from the beginning that the enforcing of discipline was one of his unpleasant duties. He had to learn, almost instinctively, when to be severe, when to be mild, and when to scan with eyelids closed.

In dealing with delinquents, even recalcitrant ones, Lasuén counseled patience, endless patience, with corporal punishment only as a last resort. And the punishment should never be more severe than a loving father would mete out to an erring son in similar circumstances. But Lasuén was prudent enough to recognize that this principle was subject to interpretation, as he pointed out in his Report to Branciforte mentioned above. One type of punishment is appropriate in the case of children of those who are "cultured and enlightened, and where the ways of doing things are restrained and mild." However, a different kind is expedient in the case of those who are "barbarous, fierce, and ignorant." But kindness and patience are never wasted.

Vancouver and others who visited California when Lasuén was President imply that discipline in the missions was very rigid, and punishments very severe. It must be kept in mind that none of these visitors stayed long enough in the missions to garner the information for themselves. They obviously obtained it from others, and none would have been more willing to supply it than those who, for personal motives, were critical of the mission system. The identity of such possible sources can readily be discovered when one reads Lasuén's Report of June 19, 1801.

Loyalty

Lasuén was a man of many loyalties. He was a Basque, with all the high intelligence, social graces, and steady self-respect of that ancient race. He even possessed a Pauline pride in the country of his origin. But there is nothing parochial or provincial in his outlook. A number of his countrymen had attained to high office in Church or State. He acknowledges the kinship, is cordial in responding to their friendship, but he seeks no favor from a superior and extends no concession to a subject by reason of their Basque origin. His is a broader loyalty. Spain was his motherland, and to the King of Spain he gave a loyalty second only to that which he gave to God. His devotion to both he summed up more than once in the phrase "their two majesties." Even the growing regalism of the monarchy and the restrictions it placed on the free exercise of religion did not dampen his ardor for the King, for, in the simple world of Lasuén, Church and State were partners, and the King of Spain was the Pope's most faithful vassal, his delegate, and, within limitations, his *alter ego*.

Lasuén was occasionally the witness, and sometimes the victim, of the efforts of civil officials to restrict the freedom of ecclesiastics and to extend the range of civil authority on the plea that it was part of the prerogatives accorded to the King by the Holy See, an aspect of the royal *patronato*. Lasuén never questioned the propriety of the patronato, even when it imposed hardships on him because of the delays to which it gave rise. But he resented the attempts of lower officials to extend the scope of the patronato, and was ready to invoke the aid of San Fernando College to defend what he regarded as the rights of the missionaries and to restrict what he regarded as the pretentions of local officials.

He resided at San Fernando College for a relatively short time, for a year, or for a few years at most. It was his Alma Mater in the New World, and for the rest of his life the guardian at San Fernando was his major superior. Despite his short residence in it, he was, in modern parlance, one of its most devoted alumni. To him it was always the "holy" college, its ideals the lodestone to be followed unswervingly, and the wishes of its guardian his chosen rule of life. The language in which he expresses this attitude at times may seem exaggerated; but he expresses it so often and in such varied forms that it obviously reveals his true mentality. In fact, he became a missionary in California not because of choice on his part but because of the wishes of his superiors, and in these early years he would gladly have retired to Mexico if his superiors had given their consent.

He was devoted to the Indians. In the *Laws of the Indies,* the King of Spain had given his approval to many enactments drawn up for the purpose of protecting the native races. These regulations were not always carried out in practice. The labor of the Indians was exploited; their lands were seized without due authorization; their loved ones were treated with dishonor; and their few possessions were in constant danger of passing too easily into the hands of white men. The missionary had to be their defender, and the voice and pen of Lasuén were often active in their defense. Even when the Indian was at fault (and in the early years of the conquest he was often at fault), Lasuén used his influence both in California and often even in far-off Mexico City to insure that punishment would not be unduly severe, that justice would be tempered by charity.

Lasuén was but twenty-three years of age when he left the land of his birth and the home of his childhood. He never revisited either again. No doubt he wrote to the members of his family, and possibly to some of his boyhood friends, for he was affectionate and kindhearted, but no letters of that period have come to light. They are not needed in order to prove that he was devoted to his family, for there is other evidence.

He was in California but a short time when he had to beg his superiors, as an act of charity, to find some way to help his aged and impoverished parents who were no longer able to help themselves. Towards the end of his career he had to make another appeal, this time in behalf of an aged and impoverished sister. The letters are brief, but they are touching, for they are the cry of a heart that was crushed because loved ones needed help, and he was unable to come to their aid.

Tact and Prudence

The position of Lasuén, and of every President of the Missions, was a delicate one. Under the Spanish system the civil and military forces had rights and spheres of influence guaranteed by law. So did the Church. Inevitably the two spheres often touched and sometimes overcrossed. Even with good will on both sides, misunderstandings and disagreements were almost inevitable. In a frontier settlement such as California then was, far from centers of authority, with a social order still in a fluid state, and where laws and regulations that might be admirable elsewhere had but a limited application, it needed more than ordinary tact and prudence to hold an even balance. But Lasuén was gifted with these qualities to an eminent degree. They were not something acquired as a result of long experience; there is evidence of them even in his earliest letters. The powerful Gálvez, for instance, when engaged in his official investigation of conditions in Lower California, soon discovered that in certain arid regions of the peninsula many Indian settlements were attempting, with little success, to eke out a bare subsistence, while elsewhere in the peninsula, but at a considerable distance, there was an abundance of fertile land with far too few to cultivate it. He decided on a solution that seemed simple, logical, and practical. Let the Indians from the arid regions be transferred to the more fertile regions.

When Lasuén received an order to put this into effect, in his reply to Gálvez he did not refuse to obey, and neither did he show his disapproval. He refers to the order as a "very just and necessary one"; but he points out how attached the Indians are to their place of origin, and to the environment and customs with which they are familiar, and adverts to other practical difficulties which an experienced missionary could foresee. The Indians were permitted to remain undisturbed, and help from Gálvez, combined with self-help, took care of their more pressing needs.

It is in his later letters, when his status as President added weight to his words, that the delicacy of his tact becomes apparent. A good example of his letter of September 26, 1787, to the commanding general.

He apologizes for seeking a favor for another, but, he adds, "as long as there are some who find comfort in the fact that I try to do them a favor, they place me under an obligation to give them comfort. . . . I confess that in this petition I have completely forgotten who I am, and I have kept in mind solely who Your Lordship is . . . and if the favor is granted it will be due exclusively to you, and I shall add eternal gratitude to the homage and obedience which, in justice, I owe Your Lordship."

The courtly Englishman, Vancouver, was so impressed by Lasuén that he sent valuable gifts as a token of his esteem. The gifts Lasuén sent in return were in keeping with the poverty of the mission, but he reminded his English guest, in his letter of December 15, 1792, that "it is no less a mark of honor to receive insignificant gifts than to confer valuable ones."

His letters to his superiors, whether religious, civil, or military, are models of courtesy. To the new Bishop of Sonora he wrote on July 15, 1790: "It is my desire and my delight to hold second place to no one in homage and submission, in deference and obedience to Your Illustrious Person and to your superior orders." When Ugarte was promoted to a higher office, Lasuén wrote to him on September 7, 1796: "You have merited the confidence of our temporal sovereign; may you also merit that of the Eternal Sovereign."

Lasuén did not write as a sycophant, a flatterer at the courts of the great. He was always a simple and humble misisonary who used every talent he had in the interests of his Indians; and among his many talents was the fine art of diplomacy. His language was always courteous, but by no means obsequious. He never surrendered a principle, and rarely lost a cause.

Less noble characters might have debased the office—used it to promote their personal whims, to reward their friends, or to frustrate their rivals. Lasuén was cast in a different mold. He made it his aim to carry out scrupulously the legitimate commands of all superiors, clerical and lay alike. But he was very conscious, too, of the sensitivity of those under him. He sought to fit, not the back to the burden, but the burden to the back. When he wrote to the guardian of San Fernando College on January 2, 1800: "I'll do the best I can in everything," he was not formulating a resolution for the New Year—or even for the new century. He was expressing in simple language his whole philosophy of life.

Kindheartedness

There were general and particular regulations pertaining to the missionary work in progress in California. Some emanated from the

College of San Fernando, others from higher superiors in Spain and Rome. It was the duty of the President to adapt them to the particular needs of the missions' neophytes. Hence, in local affairs he exercised a deep influence. He was in a position to inspire, direct, and regulate the activities of those subject to him. But first he had to win their good will and co-operation. He succeeded. He won the hearts of others because he himself was kindhearted to a notable degree.

He was kind to the Indians. In his first letter to Gálvez, October 22, 1768, he makes clear that it was with a heavy heart he had been compelled by circumstances to reduce the rations of the natives. He refers to them as "poor, penniless neophytes who look to me as a father." When some of those dependent on him became a source of concern because of their evil ways, no sooner were they apprehended than Lasuén's chief concern invariably was charity and mercy towards the guilty.

He was kind to the missionaries who served under him. He tried to assign them to places where the climate would be suitable for their health, and where the temperament of the companion missionary would be harmonious. Towards the sick Friars he was sympathetic and accommodating. At times this would have tested the patience and endurance of many a superior, for occasionally the percentage of those who were mentally or physically incapacitated threatened the efficiency of the entire work of evangelization. In such circumstances he had recourse to the guardian of San Fernando College, and in the meantime took whatever steps he could to assist the sick missionaries, even to the extent of taking their places.

Philosophical Calm

When Lasuén arrived in California he was less than forty years of age. Compared with other missionaries he was still a young man—and he was a "young man in a hurry." He chafed under the disappointments and frustrations which he met with on every side. He would gladly have returned to San Fernando, if only his superiors would give the word. But superiors understood him better than he understood himself. They withheld the permisison, and Lasuén submitted to their will and reconciled himself to the life that lay ahead.

He soon grew familiar through personal experience with every phase of the life of a missionary. He knew the agony and the fascination of founding a mission, and in a few days the frustration of being forced to abandon it. Then, at San Diego Mission, as year succeeded year he became more and more familiar with the difficulty involved in keeping in existence an impoverished mission that seemed to be ill-starred from the day of its founding.

Difficulties such as these might have embittered many another, and must have been very trying for the sensitive soul of Lasuén. However, the self-pity which appears in the early letters soon disappears. He had begun to acquire a philosophy of life by means of which he later sought to sustain others, as he mentions in his letter of December 20, 1797. It is a simple philosophy, but a heroic one. Man's largest schemes and best intentioned plans often end in frustration. But all is not in vain, for by means of such trials the virtue of patience is enabled to flourish.

For the kind of life which he had to live, and the work in which he was engaged, Lasuén needed the perspective which philosophy gives. He had devoted his life to the betterment of the Indians. It was a discouraging task, for the rank and file of the Indians showed not the least concern for their own betterment. Vancouver, who had opportunities to observe, asserts that they "seem to have treated with the most perfect indifference the precepts and laborious example of their truly worthy and benevolent pastors, whose object has been to allure them from their life of indolence and raise in them a spirit of emulous industry. . . . Deaf to the important lessons, and insensible to the promised advantages, they still remained in the most abject state of uncivilization."

Despite all that had been done for them over a period of almost three decades, it was Vancouver's conviction that the Indians had benefited but little as a result of the labors and instructions of missionaries "who seem entirely devoted to the benevolent office of rendering them a better and a happier people."

Another world traveler who visited California at that time, the Frenchman La Pérouse, reached substantially the same conclusion. He found the Indian "too much of a child, too much of a slave, and too little of a man."

Lasuén's problems were not confined to the Indians. Different governors contributed their share. The letters that follow supply ample evidence. One example will suffice, for it is fairly typical.

There were many reasons why missionaries had to travel. They had a legal right to retire from missionary work after they had served for ten years. Sickness compelled others to retire at an earlier date. Occasionally a missionary discovered only after he had arrived that he was not fitted for such work. Travel of this nature involved expense; but not government expense. A fund known as the Pious Fund of the Californias had been established by private individuals for the support of the California missions, their founding, their upkeep, and the expense involved in the daily sustenance and incidental traveling of the missionaries who labored in them. The Jesuits had established the Fund, and when they were suppressed the government assumed control of it, but without interfering with its objectives. Lasuén occasionally discovered, however, that, even when the reasons were legitimate, governors at times were very slow to grant missionaries permission to travel, assigning as the reason the need for economy. Writing to his superior in Mexico on February 29, 1796, Lasuén adverts to the fact that the very same officials who had invoked economy when the missionaries were concerned, seemed to feel no scruple about increasing their own salaries. Then he added, without bitterness, "Perhaps if we were lay people we would look on things in the same way."

Occasionally missionaries asked him to assign them to other missions, or to give them different companions. Circumstances which could not be overcome often placed restrictions on his freedom of action. Either he lacked supernumeraries who might serve as replacements, or his sense of justice would not allow him to change personnel in other missions that were functioning satisfactorily. As a consequence, he could do little beyond recommending more patience and forbearance, or making such minor adjustments as circumstances permitted, and then calmly admitting, as he does in his letter of October 2, 1800, that he had merely succeeded in demonstrating that it is impossible to please everyone.

"The glory dies not and the grief is past"

Lasuén made no effort to create a favorable "image" of himself. He gave no thought to the judgment which later generations might pass on his efforts and accomplishments. He was too humble to claim credit for success achieved, and he did not need to be reminded that without the co-operation of both college and missionaries the best laid plans of every president would come to nought.

He had been assigned a task; he tried to accomplish it to the best of his ability. He was the representative of an organization; he sought to be loyal to its traditions, to uphold its prerogatives, and to keep its reputation unsullied. His duties brought him into daily contact with missionaries and Indians. He made a determined effort to be a brother to the one, and a devoted father to the other. But California in his day was not peopled exclusively by Indians and missionaries. There were civil and military forces, too. Lasuén, we may deduce from his letters, at times must have experienced some regret that their presence was indispensible, for he was painfully aware that his best efforts to live in harmony with them were not always successful.

He began his career in California with a deep conviction of his own worthlessness, and to the end he retained a lowly estimate of himself. It was an assessment that was not shared by others. The College of San Fernando reappointed him again and again to the position of President.

The Holy Office of Mexico made him its local representative. And the Bishop of Sonora chose him as his personal vicar for California, and judge in matters of ecclesiastical import.

Although geographically remote and still in great part inaccessible, California in the closing decades of the eighteenth century was visited by some distinguished world travelers. Deserving of special note were the visits of two scientific expeditions, the one commanded by the learned Frenchman, La Pérouse,[10] and the other by the less known but equally versatile Malaspina,[11] Italian by birth and Spanish by adoption. Each group partook of the hospitality of the missions, and all paid high tribute to Lasuén. Both parties seemed to be equally at a loss to decide whether to praise him as man or clergyman, as friend of the Indians, or cultured gentleman, or genial host. Perhaps the strangest tribute of all is to be found in the writings of another guest of the missions, the distinguished navigator George Vancouver.[12] More than once in the course of his writings this typical English nobleman forgot his native reserve and the national prejudice against Spain, and referred to Lasuén as his "highly esteemed and venerable friend" whose many good qualities "fitted him in an eminent degree for presiding over so benevolent an institution."[13]

In due time the English ship weighed anchor, resumed the voyage along the poorly mapped coast line of California, and soon approached two unnamed promontories. On the one, Vancouver conferred the title "Point Fermín," and on the other "Point Lasuén," and as such they appear to this day on the maps of California,[14] the tribute of a Protestant Englishman to a Spanish Franciscan.

Historians, although laboring under the handicap of very limited documentation, have been generous in their expressions of esteem for Lasuén. In his standard work, *A History of California: The Spanish Period*, Charles E. Chapman devotes an entire chapter to him,[15] in the hope that his words would in some measure rescue this "worthy rival" of Junípero Serra from the "obscurity" and "almost complete oblivion" into which he had passed.

Ridout, in an unpublished thesis devoted to the economic develop-

[10] See Charles N. Rudkin *First French Expedition to California. Lapérouse in 1786.* (Los Angeles, 1959).

[11] See Donald C. Cutter *Malaspina in California* (San Francisco, 1960), especially pp. 31-38.

[12] The observations of Vancouver relative to California have been edited by Marguerite Eyer Wilbur, under the title *Vancouver in California*, as part of the "Early California Series" (Nos. 9, 10, and 22) published by Glen Dawson, Los Angeles.

[13] Wilbur, *op. cit.*, I, 63-64.

[14] They are at the entrance to the port of San Pedro, the harbor of Los Angeles.

[15] See Charles E. Chapman *A History of California: The Spanish Period* (New York, 1921), pp. 364-382.

ment of California during the administration of Lasuén, concludes his study by extolling the Father President as a "teacher, builder, architect, agriculturalist, rancher, director of local industries, administrator of labor, practical economist and ecclesiastic who directed the growth of an untried, unproved province"[16] during its formative period.

Engeldhardt, the Franciscan historian of the missions, recounts at considerable length the achievements of his confrere, then tersely sums up the record by saying that Lasuén "must be numbered among the territory's best men and greatest benefactors."[17]

The most generous words of praise come from the least likely of sources, the writings of Bancroft, one of the most consistent and uncompromising critics of the missionaries. "In [Lasuén]," he writes, "were united the qualities that make up the model or ideal padre. . . . He was a frank and kind-hearted old man, who made friends of all he met. . . . Visitors were impressed . . . with his sweetness of disposition and quiet force of character. His relations with others were always harmonious, often in somewhat trying circumstances, though no one of the Franciscans had more clearly defined opinions than he. None of them had a firmer will, or were readier on occasion to express their views. His management of mission interests for eighteen years affords abundant evidence of his untiring zeal and of his ability as a man of business. . . . Of his fervent piety there are abundant proofs. . . . He based his hopes of future reward on purity of life, and a zealous performance of duty as a man, a Christian and a Franciscan."[18]

These comments, admittedly, are eulogistic. If the writers had had an opportunity to study the wide range of letters presented in these volumes they might have tempered their judgments to some extent. It is not likely that they would have altered them substantially. They might have been slower to proclaim Lasuén "the noblest Roman of them all"; but few would have hesitated to assert that

> His life was gentle, and the elements
> So mix't in him that Nature might stand up
> And say to all the world "This was a man!"

FINBAR KENNEALLY, O.F.M.

Academy of American Franciscan History
Washington, D. C.

---

[16] Lionel Utley Ridout, "Fermín Francisco de Lausén and the Economic Development of the California Missions" (Master's thesis, University of California, 1940), p. 145.

[17] Zephryn Engelhardt, *Missions and Missionaries of California* (Santa Barbara, 1930), II, 613.

[18] Hubert Howe Bancroft, *History of California* (San Francisco, 1885), II, 8-9.

Table of Contents

Illustrations

Writings of Fermín Francisco de Lasuén

I

The Baja California Prelude

These are the earliest extant writings of Lasuén. They were composed in Baja California between October 12, 1767 and June 15, 1773. Prior to this period Lasuén had been missionary for five years in the Sierra Gorda missions near Querétaro, Mexico, but no writings from that period have been discovered.

I

The Baja California Prelude

These are the earliest extant writings of Lasuén. They were composed in Baja California between October 12, 1767 and June 15, 1773. Prior to this period Lasuén had been missionary for five years in the Sierra Gorda missions near Querétaro, Mexico, but no writings from that period have been discovered.

1. To the Guardian and Council of San Fernando College[1]

WORD HAS REACHED US OF A LETTER FROM His Excellency the Viceroy to the commandant of the expedition who resides in this pueblo of Tepic. It is to the effect that he is to proceed to the provinces of California and Sonora and there, according to the instructions and commands of His Excellency,[2] assign the Reverend Fathers of the Province of Jalisco to the missions of California and all of us, those from the College of San Fernando of Mexico as well as the Reverend Fathers of Santa Cruz of Querétaro,[3] to the missions of Sonora,[4] in accordance with the representations and request of our Most Reverend Father Commissary General.[5]

Your Paternities[6] will bear in mind that it was for this very objective all of us gladly offered our services with no thought in mind but the good of those poor souls and the glory of our apostolic college. And now we see our hopes frustrated.

We beg Your Paternities to see if it would not be possible to stand by the former resolution, for otherwise our college will emerge without missions in these parts, and we ourselves will be obliged to withdraw to the college. In that eventuality we take this opportunity to ask for that permission, in case the California project is abandoned. We were all so happy and contented at the prospect of going there that we did not cease to offer up praises to God; and now we are so disheartened that not one of us has it in mind to go to Sonora, in case there should be some missions available for the college. It is our hope that the Venerable Fathers will do what they can to insure that there is no change of plans, for the glory of the apostolic college is involved. If we accept California, we have active missions for as long as the college is a college, and with many opportunities to spread the Catholic faith. This is not the case in Sonora according to the information we have gathered from close contact with it, and from the letter of the Bishop of Durango in which he states that he is coming with forty of his clergy to take possession of the missions there.

It is our hope that the Venerable Fathers will pay particular attention to this matter which is so conducive to the glory of God and of the holy college.

Thus we petition God Our Lord and Our Most Beloved Lady.

Hospice of Santa Cruz de Tepic,
October 12, 1767.

Fray Juan Morán	*Fray José Antonio Murguía*
Fray Antonio Martínez	*Fray Juan Crespí*
Fray Juan Ramos de Lora	*Fray Juan Ignacio Gastón*
Fray Miguel Campa	*Fray Fernando Parrón*
Fray Juan Sancho	*Fray Francisco Gómez*
Fray Juan Villumbrales	*Fray Fermín Francisco de Lasuén*

[1] San Fernando College, Mexico City, was established in 1733 for the specialized training of Franciscan missionaries. The highest official in it was known as the Father Guardian, and he was assisted by a council of four members elected from among the missionaries of the college. The guardian at that time was José García, and the members of the council: Juan Escudero, Antonio de Vega, José Vélez, and Francisco Palou.

[2] The Marqués de Croix. His term as viceroy ended in September, 1771.

[3] A college for the training of Franciscan missionaries was founded at Querétaro, Mexico, in 1683. Fifty years later San Fernando College was founded from it. Each sent many missionaries to California. See Michael McCloskey, *The Formative Years of the Missionary College of Santa Cruz of Querétaro, 1683-1733* (Washington, D. C., 1955).

[4] Lasuén and his companions had left their former assignments under the impression that they were to labor in the Californias. At the same time a group of Franciscans from the Province of Jalisco was on its way to assume charge of missions in Sonora. At Tepic, where both groups were assembled, word reached them that these plans had been changed, and there was clear evidence that those from Jalisco were responsible for the change. For details see Maynard Geiger, *The Life and Times of Fray Junípero Serra, O.F.M.* (Washington, D. C., 1859), I, 183-190.

[5] Fray Manuel Nájera. His authority was higher than that of the guardians and local superiors.

[6] A term of respect for major superiors in certain Religious Orders, corresponding to the term "Excellency" as now applied to bishops.

2. Inventory of San Borja Mission

MISSION OF SAN FRANCISCO DE BORJA, May seventh of the year one thousand seven hundred and sixty-eight. On this day, in the name of my captain, Don Fernando de Rivera y Moncada, I, Ignacio de Higuera, corporal of the guard and major-domo of said mission, delivered unto Reverend Father Fray Fermín Francisco de Lasuén, Apostolic Preacher of the College of San Fernando of Mexico, the adornments of this church and the goods and chattels of the house, in the presence of two witnesses, and I beg His Paternity to grant a receipt for the transfer of the following:

First, a set of vestments of cloth of silver with the antependium[1] of other material.

A set of vestments of cloth of gold.

A set of vestments of cloth embroidered with flowers.

A set of vestments of white cloth, with corresponding antependium.

A set of vestments of Persian silk, with antependium to match.

A set of vestments of Persian silk in floral pattern with antependium to match.

A set of violet vestments with ante-pendium to match.

A set of ordinary violet vestments with-out antependium.

A set of ordinary red vestments with antependium quartered in violet.

A set of black vestments with ante-pendium.

An antependium of cloth of silver.

A cope of Persian [silk].

A black cope.

A humeral veil of Persian [silk].

Two lace tabernacle veils.

Two others, red.

Another veil, purple.

Another veil, blue.

A black veil.

Five albs, two in fair condition, and three ordinary.

Two surplices, old.

Six amices, three cambric, and three ordinary.

Six altar cloths.

Eight finger towels.

Two stoles, one for baptisms, the other for funerals.

A silver chalice, gilded, with its silver cruets[2] and paten.

Three other chalices of silver.

A silver ciborium,[3] gilded.

Other silver cruets, with stand to match.

Two silver thuribles with boats[4] of the same.

Two silver vials for chrism.[5]

A silver holy water stoup with sprink-ler.

Fourteen metal candlesticks.

Nine paintings on canvas.

A silver shell [for baptisms].

Twelve purificators.

Two silk canopies.

Twelve corporals[6] of Breton linen and cambric.

Two carpets.

One copper holy water stoup with its sprinkler.

Two small copper urns for baptismal fonts.

An iron for making wafers.

Three cassocks with their rochets.

Two lecterns of tortoise shell.

Two manuals, one Roman, the other by Betancurt.

Four bells, two small ones for the altar.

A set of altar cards.

Thirteen silver two-peso coins,[7] with two rings, for marriages.

Three cloth cinctures.

House Furnishings

The Holy Bible in two volumes.

Montenegro's *Itinerario*.

La Croix in two volumes.

Luz de Verdades Católicas.

Concilio de Trento.

Indice Práctico Moral.

Father Busembaum's *Medula*.

Fuero de la Conciencia.

A *Diurno*.

Vida de S. Francisco de Borja.

Seven volumes by Father Señeri.

Two volumes by Father Natali.

Two small volumes of Ovid.

Four small books on administration.

A small book of devotion.

Kitchen and Table

Four small saucepans.

Three dozen china plates.

Nine vessels for the pozole.[8]

Half a dozen cups.

Four small vessels of glass.

Five candlesticks of copper.

Nine spoons and nine forks, metal.

A table knife.

Two brass metates[9] with their pestles, and another, broken.

Two frying pans.

A bottle case with twenty flasks, eight of them broken.

Two tablecloths and a dozen napkins.

HOUSE FURNISHINGS

One large table and another small.

Nine small glass flasks with a case for them.

Two boxes and one chest of drawers for vestments.

A nonstriking clock, of silver.

Five large maps.

Two saddles.

Two beds, one of cowhide, the other of coarse hemp cloth.[10]

A *pabellón* of home-made unbleached cotton cloth.[11]

A hand claw-hammer.

Four locks for a door, two of them broken.

Some tailor's scissors.

A small scale and its weights.

In testimony of the above, and because the above-mentioned corporal and major-domo does not know how to sign, I signed it on the above day, month, and year.

Guillermo Carrillo.
Mariano Carrillo, witness.

On the above day, month, and year, I, Fray Fermín Francisco de Lasuén, of the Regular Observance of our father St. Francis, Apostolic Preacher of the College of *Propaganda Fide* of San Fernando of Mexico, and assigned by my superior as minister of this Mission of San Francisco de Borja, received all the items contained in the foregoing entries, these being the properties of the church and house of this mission. In testimony thereof I have signed it on the said sixth day of May of the said year one thousand seven hundred and sixty-eight.

Fray Fermín Francisco de Lasuén.

The following is a copy of the Inventory of the goods pertaining to the church and house of this Mission of San Francisco de Borja and of the receipt therefor. It agrees in all respects with the original which was sent to Loreto to Captain Don Fernando de Rivera y Moncada,[12] in accordance with the instructions of said captain, as appears from the instructions which he left in writing with the corporal-major-domo of this mission. In testimony thereof I signed it the twenty-sixth day of May of the same year one thousand seven hundred and sixty-eight in the said Mission of San Francisco de Borja.

Fray Fermín Francisco de Lasuén.

The following is an Inventory of the temporal goods, the grain, moveable goods, and other assets both of the house and lands of this Mission of San Francisco de Borja which the soldier Don Ignacio de la Higuera had in his charge and under his administration during the present interim, and which he on this day and date made known and delivered to me, Fray Fermín Francisco de Lasuén of the Regular Observance of our father St. Francis of the Apostolic College of Propaganda Fide of San Fernando of Mexico, missionary minister of the said Mission to attend to its economic administration, as so ordered by His Most Illustrious Lordship Don José de Gálvez, Visitator General of New Spain in a decree given at the mining camp of Santa Ana in this peninsula of the Californias on August 12 of the current year of 1768.

THE HOUSE

Three large cauldrons for the pozole, somewhat battered, but sound and serviceable.

Three other small ones, very old, have holes, and are not fit for use.

Another, smaller still, which cannot be used because of holes.

One fairly large which is used to make candles, and is almost new.

A dozen large boilers, used but still good. They are used for preparing the pozole and atole.

Two others, not in use for they are old and bent.

Two false bottoms for casks, new.

A dozen crowbars, six ironshod and sharpened, the other six blunt.

Two other crowbars, small, and also blunt.

Two adzes.

Seven axes, two carpenter's, five woodman's, all blunted.

Four ladles of copper for serving the atole and pozole; two are good and serviceable, the other two are not for use.

An iron anvil, new, tongs, and a hammer for use when there is a forge.

Five chisels, two files, and compass.

Two carpenter's squares, iron, good quality, and one plumb.

Four syringes, good.

Twenty-seven sets of harness, very old and ill-treated, with the accessories in the same condition.

One new set, defective, and without accessories.

Eighty-four leather sacks, most of them old and repaired, but all still serviceable.

One new hand saw and one carpenter's saw, good.

A Roman balance with its weights.

Two balances with their weights, one new and the other broken.

Eleven goads, five new, six blunted.

A hoof parer, hammer, and pincers for shoeing [horses], all good.

A still, good.

A vat (?) of stone, new.

Eighteen barrel hoops.

Three arrobas[13] and nineteen pounds of shot; one arroba and sixteen pounds of powder.

One saddler's set, with four awls, three needles for leather work, and some scissors for the same.

Fourteen hides, five of rams and the rest of he-goats.

One bronze astrolabe.[14]

The remaining furnishings of the house where I live are not entered in this Inventory, for the Royal Commissioner delivered them at the time I arrived, and I received them by an inventory which was sent to Captain Don Fernando de Rivera y Moncada, and for that reason they would not be a matter of concern to the commissary in question. These are neither greater nor less than those that appear in the inventory mentioned, with the exception that there are in reality eleven additional arrobas of cotton, and these do not concern him, either.

THE BARN

Forty fanegas[15] of bearded wheat, and four almuds[16] of corn.

Eight fanegas of summer wheat.

Two hundred and fifty tallow candles.

Eight pounds of lard.

Two large earthenware wine jars

THE FIELD

Two dozen hoes, all much the worse for wear and still used because there are no others.

Another dozen and a half of the same. These are broken in pieces and are not fit for use.

Thirteen warren hoes, seven new, two half worn out, and four very old and worn.

Two plowshares, new.

Five cowboy saddles very much worn, and their accessories in the same condition.

Three pieces of ground in which are sown a little less than one fanega of corn, and it is now almost in season to be harvested. It is neither very good nor very bad, and we do not know how much it will bring in.

THE RANCH

One hundred and twenty-three head of cattle, tame, the parent group.

Fifty-eight head, the offspring of this parent group.

Nine ranchos.

Four hundred and twelve head of said cattle rounded up.

Eleven hundred and eight head of sheep, large and small.

Seven hundred and seventy-two goats, large and small.

Ninety-six brood mares in six droves, two of them with he-donkeys.

Twenty-three two year old bulls.

Thirteen two year old fillies.

Twenty-five colts, yearlings.

Twenty-five yearling fillies.

Fifty-two tame horses.

Twenty-one young horses, broken in.[17]

Twelve saddle mules for the vaqueros, and twenty-five pack mules.

One two year old female mule; three two year old males, one of them broken in.

Three female and two male yearling mules.

Three small copper cauldrons.

Two saddler's knives for hamstringing.

Three goads for the vaqueros.

Two crowbars, blunted.

One axe, blunted.

A set of gear with all accessories for the vaqueros to take their supplies.

There are in this mission nineteen saddle and pack mules belonging to the Mission of Santa María. Also, three tame horses, and three colts. Also, a herd of twenty mares with the stallion. Also, ten offspring born of this herd. Also, three female and two male donkeys.

DEBTS

The Commissary, Don Ignacio de la Higuera, informs me that he has already sent the governor a record of what the soldiers of the guard owe this mission, and what this mission owed those serving it up to the twelfth of July of the present year, and what Don Hernando Rubio owes from that date up to the date of the Inventory, namely, nine almuds of wheat, fifty-one pounds of meat, and five and a half pounds of lard; that there is due to those employed on the launch and the ranch, the salary to which they are entitled from the above-mentioned twelfth of July to the present date; that the captain of the launch receives fifty pesos a month, and the other two receive twelve pesos each, with rations; that those who work on the ranch had received for it half an arroba of jerked meat in addition to the ration they received. At the same time the said commissioner informs me that there had been sent to the Mission of Santa María for its use and that of its escort thirty-six fanegas of wheat, and one arroba and four pounds of lard; that of the hundred beasts that had been on this mission ranch but belonging to Santa María Mission, twelve were killed by order of Captain Don Fernando de Rivera y Moncada, and were written off as an impost on it. He reports that afterwards eighteen animals on the hoof had been sent to it and one hundred and ten arrobas of meat.

In order to send back this number of arrobas, he reports that the medium sized beasts had been slaughtered, irrespective of whether they belonged to this mission or to that, and that he does not know what number of arrobas is equivalent to each beast that had been slaughtered, because in providing the two missions with meat by means of the slaughterings that had been held, he informs me that the meat which was weighed was sent to Santa María Mission, and that that which was used here was not weighed; that all he was able to say was that all the beasts that were slaughtered had been two- or three-year olds, for they did not have at this ranch cattle of a greater age, with the exception of fifteen or twenty milking cows; and that therefore in the number of cattle which were entered in this Inventory there are included some that could be due to Santa María Mission.

In addition to this, he reports that thirty he-goats had been sent to the above mission, twelve of them gelded, as well as twenty-five hides of animals.

The items contained and expressed in this Inventory are those which, neither more nor less, are actually to be found in this mission; and I, the above-named minister thereof, have been entrusted with the care and economic administration thereof, for the welfare of the poor Indians of this mission under my charge, and for the royal service. And the soldier-commissary who was charged with the administration of it is freed from this obligation.

In proof of these particulars and of their transfer we hereby certify

in duplicate so that proof may now be at hand for His Lordship the
Most Illustrious Visitor General individually, and for the purposes of
each in person, and we hereby sign it in this said Mission of San Francisco de Borja this nineteenth of September of the present year of 1768.

Fray Fermín Francisco de Lasuén.

And because the Royal Commissioner does not know how to sign, I
sign it

Bernardo Rubio.

The original Inventory, to be found at this mission, enumerates all
the above, and this is a copy of it, word for word. And in proof thereof
I so affirm in this same Mission on the third of April of 1772.

Fray Fermín Francisco de Lasuén.

[1] An ornamental veil or hanging placed in front of an altar below the level of the altar table. Its color usually varies according to the color of the vestments worn at Mass that day.

[2] For the wine and water used at the Mass.

[3] A sacred vessel resembling a chalice. In it the Blessed Sacrament is permanently reserved, and from it Holy Communion is normally given.

[4] The vessels that contain the incense to be placed in the thurible, or censer. They usually have the shape of a boat.

[5] An oil blessed for use in Baptism and Confirmation.

[6] A corporal is a small piece of linen on which the sacred vessels are placed.

[7] These are given by the bridegroom to the bride according to the marriage rite as often observed in Spanish speaking countries. The giving is symbolic; the coins are normally the property of the church.

[8] A thick soup made of wheat, corn, beans, and sometimes meat.

[9] Derived from the Aztec word *metatl*, it is a mortar, usually of stone and resting on three legs of the same material and continuous with it, so hollowed out that, with the aid of a pestle, substances such as corn can be pounded or pulverized in it.

[10] Beds consisted of a simple wooden frame, collapsible and portable, covered with a tanned cowhide or strong cloth, and without mattress.

[11] This is a type of net shaped somewhat like a bell, and lowered around a bed to exclude mosquitoes. It is used extensively in tropical countries. In this instance coarse cotton, a local product, took the place of the more commonly used and more expensive net.

[12] A controversial figure in the history of early California. For a time Lasuén regarded him as a devoted friend, but subsequently found him to be somewhat erratic and unpredictable. Rivera lost his life in the Yuma massacre in 1781.

[13] A Spanish weight equivalent to 25.36 pounds avoirdupois.

[14] A type of sextant used for determining the altitude of heavenly bodies as an aid to determining latitude.

[15] A Spanish bushel, equivalent to 100 pounds avoirdupois.

[16] A Spanish measure, equivalent to 6.88 dry quarts.

[17] For a description of the process of breaking-in horses in mission days, see the picturesque account by one who understood the traditional ways, Jo Mora in *Californios: the Saga of the Hard-riding Cowboys* (New York, 1949), p. 114 and *passim*.

CHURCH OF ST. VINCENT, VITORIA
where Lasuén was baptized

3. To Don José de Gálvez[1]

WITH THE RESPECT AND ESTEEM which I always show them, I received Your Most Illustrious Lordship's two letters and the two accompanying proclamations. I wish to pay tribute to the zeal with which Your Most Illustrious Lordship has undertaken the task of uprooting pernicious tendencies, and to express gratitude for it. I hereby assert and testify that the orders of Your Most Illustrious Lordship and the instructions of the Reverend Father President were carried out punctually and in detail. The proclamations were read to the soldiers, and were explained through an interpreter to the residents of this mission, and were affixed in the most public place. I shall exercise great diligence in seeing that they are observed to the letter.

Insofar as these apply to the Indians, Most Illustrious Lord, there is no reason for concern; and my motive for explaining these salutary regulations to them was, I assure Your Most Illustrious Lordship, solely the desire to carry out to the letter the commands I had received. And since it will afford satisfaction to Your Most Illustrious Lordship I cannot refrain from pointing out that, by the great mercy of God, neither of the vices which according to your most salutary and Christian edict you are eager to eradicate, as yet exists among the Indians of the mission entrusted to my care.

Not that of cards; for there is not even one individual among them who knows how to play, and there are not more than six who by chance may have seen the soldiers play. Nor that of tobacco, either; for although it is certain that they have some inclination towards its use, it is hardly any discomfort or hardship for them to do without it. And I am sure, from what I have observed, that in order to obtain it, not one of them would deprive himself of the slightest thing that he values.

It is already five and is now approaching six months, Most Illustrious Lord, since I came to this mission. In that time I have not given even a particle of leaf-tobacco to any Indian. Yet, I have neither heard nor known any complaint that they feel the need of it; but I have heard and known that they miss other things previously given them with a less sparing hand. Furthermore, I can assure you that in all this time only one pagan and one Christian have come to me to ask for leaf-tobacco, and I did not give it to either of them, for I first gave them something to eat (and I can recall that even that was very little) with the intention of giving them the tobacco later; but there was no need, for they went away very happy and content without waiting for, or giving further thought to, the tobacco.

This happens frequently in the case of those who ask for snuff, to which, I have observed, they are more inclined, or they became more inclined under the Jesuit Fathers. It is true that there are many who ask me for it; but if I treat them in the manner I have mentioned above, there are very few who will wait to receive what they asked for. Furthermore, several make a pretext of asking for snuff in order to obtain either food or clothing; and if they fail to receive the latter, they scatter the snuff along the way.

And finally, Most Illustrious Lord, if there are a few (and there are) who would wait for the tobacco they asked for, even after they had been given something to eat, there would not, I think, be even one person who would wait if, in addition, he were given a rag with which to clothe himself.

Most Illustrious Lord, what in this region is called wild tobacco[2] is a kind of herb or shrub; and it is rare to find a place where it does not exist in abundance. Consequently, they neither sow, nor buy, nor sell, nor exchange it.

It is used without any restraint among the pagans, I am informed, especially when they are planning a raid or an attack on some enemy or hostile ranchería.[3] And because of this reason and because they know that it harms them even when used in moderation, they hold it in horror and detestation as soon as they are converted to Christianity. This is my opinion. It is based on what they themselves have told me and on the experiences gained during the time that I have been among them. For during this time I have both frequently talked with those living in the mission and, at various times, visited those of the rancherías at the place where they stay when they come to the mission for their weekly visit; and when it has been necessary for me to go out from these, I have met great numbers of Indians living together in places adjacent to the roads; and I can swear that I have not met a single Indian smoking or chewing.

I have observed also that no one carries with him the herb or shrub called wild tobacco nor any instrument for its conveyance, whereas many carry a piece of cane or reed to keep snuff; and I have been in the habit of giving small quantities of it occasionally to those who ask me for it.

Assuming then, Most Illustrious Lord, that what I say is true, and keeping in mind what Your Most Illustrious Lordship tells me in your esteemed letter that, in your opinion, I shall agree with Your Most Illustrious Lordship in this, that from the general stock of each mission there should be drawn on account from the royal warehouse such quantities of tobacco as are needed by the male population of the mission, and that these should be distributed daily or weekly under the prudent direction of the Father missionary; I would give it as my opinion, Sir, (but with humble submission and compliant subjection to what Your Most Illustrious Lordship may determine) that it might be advantageous if from the common fund or from that which the mission might have, there were drawn from the royal warehouse, and not from anywhere else (for as a most loyal, humble, and cheerful vassal of our Catholic King and Lord, whom God preserve, I will guard his royal interest by seeing to it that no one is guilty of fraud in the payment of the tobacco revenue), a small quantity of snuff and of leaf-tobacco so as to make it possible to treat the Indians occasionally and to give them their allowance when they ask for it. But what is needed should not be drawn from that fund in order to make daily or weekly distributions, for my dependents are many, Most Illustrious Lord, and they are hungry and naked; and therefore I consider that it would be more pleasing to both their Royal Majesties[4] and to Your Most Illustrious Lordship, if priority would be given to this need, which is greater, rather than to the other, which is less, or, more properly, non-existent.

After this, Most Illustrious Lord, my affection as a father to these poor creatures obliges me to bring my troubles to the notice of Your Most Illustrious Lordship in whom, after God, I have placed my hopes of relief. And so I shall speak as frankly as in prayer.

The illustrious person of Your Lordship has been the object with which I have consoled the poor dependents maintained at this mission entrusted to me. Before Your Illustrious Lordship arrived in this peninsula, I told them that on your arrival their most pressing needs would obtain some alleviation, And when you arrived, I revealed in public my great joy, for I saw the approaching fulfilment of the hopes I had held out.

When I received the two most prudent and righteous decrees of Your Most Illustrious Lordship, I published them, letting them see very clearly that they were the most expressive confirmation of all I had told and promised them.

And now, Most Illustrious Lord, it is my misfortune to be very short of food and clothing. The wheat is being sown at present; and when it is completed there will be very little left over. The corn crop has been very small, for they have harvested only fifty fanegas, and some of these have been lost; and therefore I hope, because of Your Illustrious Lordship's charity, that you will provide at least some measure of help as quickly as possible in this emergency.

This mission, Most Illustrious Lord, even with larger harvests and even if it did not have the obligation which it has had and still has of helping the Mission of Santa María de los Angeles[5] and its military guard, has always been in need of frequent and copious assistance, which it has received in times past from the other missions; but ever since I first came here, it has not received even a mite from any source.

Once when this assistance failed, Most Illustrious Lord, I am informed that the residents were maintained on meat alone. I am keeping this alternative for the greatest emergency and for a more opportune time, since the cattle at present are in very poor condition. Candidly, I look on them as the most essential and fundamental treasure of this mission, and so I shall aim at keeping them at least in the condition in which they are today. If we have recourse to them only in situations like the above, or in other critical moments, we can be assured of the continuance in the mission of the residents, who are so necessary for the labor in the fields, and also be certain of the good will of the rancherías which we have today; and as a result we shall be able, with the help of God and of our own efforts, to make some progress in regards to the cattle and to an increase of the crops for the relief of these my children, and for a somewhat larger number of them.

It is with great sorrow of heart, Most Illustrious Lord, that for the present I have taken the precaution of reducing their ration, serving it to them with a ladle that is much smaller than usual.

Other measures, too, I have taken; and because I plead necessity in the past and the present as the reason, I should be able to avoid hostile criticism. By these means I shall continue to save some of the corn until the middle or the end of next month, for it is at that time, they say, the cattle will be in reasonably fit condition. Then, if God wills it, I am resolved to have a slaughtering[6] that will be somewhat larger than is usually made in this mission each year at that time, as I am told, to provide for our own needs and to supply meat and fats for the Mission of Santa María de los Angeles and its military guard.

I trust Your Most Illustrious Lordship, for the love of God, will pardon the importunity of this lengthy letter. I would certainly refrain from writing it if my aim were the petitioning of some favor for myself. But I cannot plead that excuse, for it is written for the benefit of these poor penniless neophytes who look to me as a father.

With the affectionate devotion and esteem of times past, I am Your Most Illustrious Lordship's humble servant. May God Our Lord preserve Your Illustrious Lordship for many years in health and in His holy grace.

San Borja Mission,
October 22, 1768.

[1] Gálvez was sent to Mexico by Carlos III in the capacity of Visitor, or Inspector General. He was "invested with well-nigh absolute powers to investigate and reform

the administration of the government in its different branches, particularly in matters pertaining to the royal finances. Independent of the viceroy in many respects by virtue of his position . . . he was to all intents the highest authority in New Spain." Hubert H. Bancroft, *History of California* (San Francisco, 1884-1886), I, 114. This accounts for the general tone of the letter, and for the frequent use of the term "Your Illustrious Lordship."

Gálvez held office from 1765 to 1771, and during that time replaced the Jesuits in Lower California by Franciscans, organized the expedition to Upper California, and helped to establish the first missions there. On his return to Spain he became Minister to the Indies. He died in Spain in 1787.

[2] Marijuana

[3] A group of Indian huts.

[4] God and the King.

[5] San Borja Mission, where Lasuén was then stationed, was founded by the Jesuits in 1762. It is located in the north central portion of the peninsula of Lower California, a little to the south of the twenty-ninth parallel, approximately midway between the protected harbor of Los Angeles on the Gulf of Mexico, and the more open roadstead of Santa Rosalia on the side of the Pacific Ocean. Santa María Mission is located further north, among the mountains, a little to the south of the thirtieth parallel.

[6] For a description of a *matanza*, or slaughtering of cattle in mission days, see Jo Mora, *op. cit.*, pp. 154-157; see also Edith Buckland Webb *Indian Life at the Old Missions* (Los Angeles, 1952), pp. 176-177.

4. To Don José de Gálvez

I HAVE RECEIVED Your Most Illustrious Lordship's esteemed letter dated October 29 and written from the mining town of Santa Ana. Accompanying it was an edict with which I have duly complied. I subsequently received, on the 17th of last month, a letter written from Puerto de la Paz in which Your Most Illustrious Lordship ordered that the launches *San Borja* and *San Ignacio* be used to convey some Indians of this mission or some Indian women from their rancherías to the territory of Mission San José del Cabo.[1] Two days later I received two additional letters with an accompanying decree and an order for Captain Don Fernando de Rivera. These were written on November 23 from Puerto de la Paz. And there was another decree from the same place, dated the 21st of the same month.

In compliance with your command I have carried out, as far as possible up to the present day, all that Your Most Illustrious Lordship disposed, decreed, and ordained; and I am making provision for what remains to be done, with the exception of that portion dealing with the transfer of the Indians to the Cape, as mentioned in your letter. My reason for this attitude is as follows: Although I recognize that the order is very just and necessary, I consider it inexpedient at the present time, and I would regard it as almost impossible to bring it to a successful conclusion.

Apart from the fact that the mission cannot acquit itself of the responsibility for the Indians who would embark in the two launches, there is the further difficulty that, even though they are few, I do not have the provisions with which to supply them for their journey. I am short of clothing to give them so that they may have some protection against the inclemency of the weather. And the weather at the present time is extremely cold.

These Indians, Most Illustrious Lord, are quite inexperienced and are but recent converts,[2] and it is difficult to lead them to understand the benefits that would accrue to them from the generous compact which Your Most Illustrious Lordship offers them.

Let them first see others enjoying these advantages. Let them find out by experience the effects of the generous way in which Your Most Illustrious Lordship makes provision so that, supplied with foodstuffs and clothing, they may live in community, even if it be but for a short time. Then it will be easy to persuade them that they cannot be supported in this manner here where the soil is so barren and unproductive and that they should migrate, instead, to a place where they can enjoy comforts and conveniences for the rest of their lives.

It is in this manner, I think, that Your Most Illustrious Lordship's most worthy project, which is as masterful as it is wise and prudent, will have the desired effect.

On the other hand, I am sure that merely to propose it and, still more, to attempt it, will greatly disturb the converts and frighten away the infidels altogether. And another result of it may be that the project will be rendered impossible; or at least the execution of it will be made more difficult.

I have proof of this, and I could place it before Your Most Illustrious Lordship; but I am refraining from doing so, for I do not wish to be boring and tedious. But I am prepared to give it, if and when requested.

This is my opinion, and it is based on these reasons. I submit it as always to Your Lordship's better judgment after you have considered this suggestion.

It seems to me that Your Most Illustrious Lordship implies that you are to some extent in agreement with my views. It is expressed in one of the letters attached to the decrees just mentioned. It followed the letter which ordered that the decree was to be carried out without attracting attention in this particular Mission of San Borja.

Your Most Illustrious Lordship wisely forsees (but not as something to be hoped for) that the agents of your salutary decrees may not be as ready in carrying them out as is required—and truly it is only in this way that your magnanimous intentions could be frustrated. But if they were duly and promptly carried out, I am convinced that, with God's help, they would attain their end quickly and to the satisfaction of all.

The Indians who can come together and live as a group at the head-

quarters of the mission and in the two places it possesses for that purpose will, in my judgment, amount to approximately one hundred and
fifty families. This being so, after the people have settled down and
everything is running smoothly, we can give a fairly accurate estimate
of the number of otter skins these Indians can gather in the course of
a year.

In the meantime I am sure the number could be quite considerable
if a little encouragement were given the Indians. This, however, should
be done only when we have on hand the means of giving them a just
reward for their labors and for their goods. The present time, they assure
me, is not seasonable for trapping these creatures, Most Illustrious Lord;
in fact, it is most unseasonable. For this reason I am sending Your Most
Illustrious Lordship merely a few samples which the Indians have given
me. I had been keeping them for the Indians, or for myself, in case I
decided to discard the ragged blankets with which I cover myself at
night.

I am well aware, Most Illustrious Lord, that Your Most Illustrious
Lordship accepts gifts from no one (May the Lord fill you with blessings and give you the gift of perseverance); but I also know that if you
were to accept these pelts in the spirit in which they are sent, you would
certainly not be receiving any gift, but a well-deserved proof of Christian gratitude, or a mere token payment of a heavy debt. If my poor
Indians and I consider carefully the benefits and favors we have recently
received and those which Your Most Illustrious Lordship provided and
allocated in the past, no matter how much we may strive, we shall always
remain debtors and fall far short in rendering the thanks that are due.

Nevertheless, Most Illustrious Lord, I shall do my utmost to discharge my obligation of gratitude without prejudice to my religious
state, and I shall pray that God may bestow upon Your Most Illustrious
Lordship success, preferment, His holy grace, and in the end the life of
glory.

But if, despite all I have said, Your Most Illustrious Lordship should
insist on paying a price for this trifle, let it be what your natural generosity dictates in behalf of these poor hapless natives.

In regard to Your Most Illustrious Lordship's request that I should
notify you regarding what I actually lack at the present time for the
upkeep of the mission rancherías and for clothing the men and women,
I beg to report, Most Illustrious Lord, that what I need is not less but
greater than what I had told Your Most Illustrious Lordship four months
ago, for in that time I have not received anything at all. Instead, they
have removed two hundred head of cattle and many yearling calves
from this rancho—I could not even prevail on them to keep a record

of the number. Other things, too, were taken, and other cattle which the worthy Captain Rivera, on his own authority, had slaughtered here for the use of his soldiers. Not that I regret it, for it is in the interest of His Majesty's Service and is in behalf of the renowned Monterey expedition for which I have even volunteered. I cannot do less than admit that I need help, or, to speak more correctly, that it is needed by these poor wards of mine. I have already informed Your Most Illustrious Lordship that I regard the cattle of this mission as its most prized possession; and may I now add that they could be regarded, too, as the most prized possession of both this and Santa María Mission. Only a few days before the cattle mentioned were taken away, I sent sixty arrobas of meat and smaller amounts of other things so that those at Santa María would not perish from want, even though it entailed sacrifice and aggravated our own pressing needs.

I am completely at your service, Most Illustrious Lord, for anything it may please you to command me, and I pray that God may keep you in His holy grace through the many long years of life which I wish you.

San Borja Mission,
December 20, 1768.

[1] "Gálvez saw that many of the missions could never support the Indians whom they had on their books, and that it would be necessary in the future for them to live as they formerly did, in the hills like deer, supporting themselves with wild fruit, while there were other missions with an abundance of land and water and with few Indians, though able to support many more. . . . He therefore decided to remedy the evils which would follow from this situation by moving the surplus Indians from some missions to others which had few Indians but plenty of land." Herbert Eugene Bolton (trans.), *Historical Memoirs of New California by Fray Francisco Palou, O.F.M.* (Berkeley, 1926), I, 38. The transfer of Indians, to which Lasuén refers, was part of this plan. The Mission of San José del Cabo was founded by the Jesuits in 1730. It had many advantages: a good harbor, water, good land in abundance, and many groves of trees. It was located near Cape San Lucas at the lower end of the peninsula. For a description of the older missions of Lower California from another point of view, see the comments of the Dominican missionary, a contemporary of Lasuén, Fray Luis Sales in his *Observations on California 1772-1790*, trans. Charles N. Rudkin (Los Angeles, 1956), p. 91 *et seq.*.

[2] When Lasuén wrote this letter, San Borja Mission was but six years old, and the neighboring mission, Santa María de los Angeles, the last of the Jesuit missions, was but eighteen months.

5. Memorandum

ON THE DATE MENTIONED there arrived at this mission the master of the launch *San Borja* to carry out the instructions he had received.

I have duly explained to the Most Illustrious Inspector General, Don José de Gálvez, the very serious difficulties which may arise if his plan is put into execution, and the inconveniences which may result and which may be feared if it is even proposed. And I repeat here that I have neither clothes to give to the people who would have to embark, nor food with which to supply them. For these reasons, and for the further reason that I have received from His Most Illustrious Lordship a letter, one written subsequent to the decree of which they hold copies, in which he gives me to understand that the necessary preliminaries must be attended to before this transfer of people takes place. For all of these reasons I am suspending the execution of the order until further instructions are received.

It might be thought that this mission was provided with supplies at the present time by virtue of a decree the Most Illustrious Lord deigned to enclose in a letter to me so that I might make it known, or forward it, to Captain Don Fernando de Rivera, so that the most urgent needs of this mission and of Mission Santa María de los Angeles might be met from the supplies intended for the Monterey expedition, which would be brought to the Bay of San Luis by the launches *San Borja* and *San Ignacio*. Although the captain replied several days later in a letter which I have kept—he retained the decree for himself—stating that he would carry out in full all that had been stipulated by His Most Illustrious Lordship, nevertheless, he placed many obstacles in the way of bringing our supplies by land. He gave as his reason that the pack mules were in rather poor condition and that in number they were about two hundred, or perhaps more.

On account of this I then expected the decree to be fulfilled by means of sea transportation. Instead, I witnessed the return of the launch *San Borja* from the Bay of San Luis with not an ounce of relief on board for this mission, and with no prospect whatever that it will be sent by another launch.

San Borja Mission,
January 15, 1769.

6. To Fray[1] Francisco Palou[2]

IN A LETTER from Your Reverence, written at the former Mission of San Luis,[3] I received a copy you enclosed of an official letter sent to Your Reverence by Governor Don Matías de Armona.[4] In this letter he begs Your Reverence, on the instructions of His Excellency the Viceroy, the Marqués de Croix, to instruct and direct us, the missionaries of the peninsula, to supply the information sought in that letter: namely, whether among the archives of these missions there is a record of their establishment, their endowments, their pious foundations; the number of pueblos and their population; how to establish in them an administration that will be most just and adaptable so as to promote the spiritual happiness of the Californians, and reconcile all this with the interests of the royal treasury, so that the latter will not be overburdened but can attend to the important objectives mentioned, and not render them difficult or impossible of attainment.

Gladly complying with the instructions of Your Reverence in regard to what is entrusted to my care, I beg to report that in this mission there is no book or document which contains a memorandum or an account of its establishment, endowment, or pious foundations.

This mission has no other pueblo than itself or its immediate surroundings. Forty-two families live here, and together with their children they total one hundred and fifteen persons.

Besides these, there are four widowers, one of whom has a son. And there are three widows, and two of these have one daughter each. Here, too, but living as a distinct group, are twenty-two orphan boys, eleven orphan girls, six disabled old women, and eleven old men in the same condition. There are varying numbers of sick persons who may later recover; and of these there is always a goodly number who return to their rancherías when they regain their health.

At present there are six rancherías where the rest of the dependents of this mission live.

The rancherías are named, respectively, San Juan, San Regis, Los Angeles, Guadalupe, El Rosario, and San Ignacio.

What these rancherías are like, and how they are conducted; who are attached to them, and who have no fixed abode; the minor differences between the status of these Indians now and when they were pagans; the homes or dwelling places: they are not to be found; they have none in these regions, for one sees in [these regions] scarcely more evidence of life than would mark the place where a chance wanderer rested or slept, etc.—all of this I have reported at length to the Most Illustrious Inspector General, Don José de Gálvez, indicating specifically to His Most Illustrious Lordship whether the Indians live in groups in towns or are scattered through the hills, for His Most Illustrious Lordship requested such information in his decree of July 12, 1768, issued from the mining town of Santa Ana. I refer to this report because I do not wish to be tedious and because I can neither add anything to it, nor can I who know the situation say less.

In reply to the decree above-mentioned, I sent the said Most Illustrious Lord a lengthy and detailed census register of each and every one who resided at this mission. The number, I think, was one thousand six hundred and sixteen or eighteen persons.

In the little less than two years that have elapsed since that report, one hundred and twenty children, and one hundred and six adults have received baptism, a total of two hundred and twenty-six.

Two hundred and twenty adults, and one hundred and four children —three hundred and twenty-four in all—have died. And since there is an excess of deaths over births and baptisms, the mission has actually fewer in residence now than it had then.

Although it should be pointed out that, owing to the fact that the Mission of Santa María de los Angeles had been abandoned or that there was no Father there, the Ranchería of San Pedro y San Pablo (which had belonged to that mission and is near the Arroyo de Calangujuet) and the people of that arroyo (where the mission was first established), together with the Ranchería of Guadalupe, were obliged to attend to their religious duties at the Mission of San Borja. This was decided on because the Mission of San Fernando de Velicatá was situated at a great distance in one direction, while in the other the Arroyo was but approximately twenty-five leagues[5] from this mission.

With these people added, there will still be in this mission as many individuals as I enumerated individually in the register mentioned above.

I have already told the Most Illustrious Lord, the Inspector General, the various reasons why I could not give in more exact figures the number of souls under the jurisdiction of this mission, and for the same reasons I cannot in this instance give a report that is more definite and absolute, despite the fact that I have carried out searching inquiries in an effort to do so. Keeping these investigations in mind, I can affirm that the true figures will not be much greater or much less than what can be read in this report.

As regards the last question, I freely admit that it is not within my capacity to make a reply; and I cannot fail to perceive that for a complete solution it would be right and fitting to employ someone gifted with more talent. But I am persuaded that the ability of Your Reverence, coupled with the long and valuable experience you have had in the management of missions and with what you have personally observed in this peninsula, as well as with what you have not observed but of which you have received reliable and detailed information from others— all of this will enable you to bring this important and grave matter to a successful end.

Finally, I should like to suggest that, in my opinion, it is very important that there should be two Fathers at each mission. But, Reverend Father, whatever decision you may reach in regard to this, you may be assured that it will receive my approval or, to speak more correctly, my co-operation for the attainment of the Christian objectives we have in mind.

May God Our Savior grant Your Reverence the guidance you need; and to those who are appointed or destined to carry out what in your opinion and judgment seems best, may He grant the strength to fulfil their obligation so that neither the inquiry, nor our efforts, nor the end sought shall have been in vain.

This I ask of His Most Holy Majesty—that He keep Your Reverence for many years in His holy grace.

San Borja Mission,
August 31, 1770.

¹ Equivalent to "Brother," and in Spanish lands applied without distinction to all members of the Franciscan Order and to certain other religious groups similarly organized.

² Palou was born on the Island of Mallorca on January 22, 1723, joined the Franciscan Order, and in 1747 became a priest. He later volunteered for mission work and reached San Fernando College on January 1, 1750. He served as missionary in different regions in Mexico, including Lower California, and for a time (in the absence of Junípero Serra) was President of the Missions. He is the author of two very important works: the *Historical Memoirs* already mentioned, and a *Vida* of Father Serra, translated by Maynard J. Geiger under the title of *Palou's Life of Fray Junípero Serra* (Washington, D. C., 1955). Palou returned to Mexico in February, 1786, and on July 1, of the same year was elected Guardian of San Fernando College. He died in office on April 6, 1789.

³ In the interests of economy, and in order to promote a better distribution of the Indians, Gálvez suppressed two of the missions, Dolores and San Luis Gonzaga.

⁴ He accepted the office of governor with reluctance, for he was not in complete agreement with the policies of Gálvez. His administration extended from 1769 to 1771.

⁵ In Spanish possessions the length of a league varied. In Mexico it was 2.6 miles.

7. Conveyance of San Borja Mission

IN COMPLIANCE WITH the order of the Very Reverend Father Preacher Fray Rafael Verger,¹ Guardian of my apostolic College of Propaganda of San Fernando of Mexico, communicated by the Reverend Father President Fray Francisco Palou, to the effect that there be handed over to the Reverend Fathers of the sacred Order of Preachers² of our Father St. Dominic³ all these old missions of California; and this having been agreed to by the Reverend Fathers, the Reverend Father Fray Juan Pedro de Iriarte⁴ on the part of his venerable Order and the said Reverend Father Guardian on the part of the aforementioned college, the latter freely and voluntarily relinquishing all the aforesaid, and the guardian in question agreeing to deliver them, and the above-mentioned vicar general agreeing to receive them in the name of his religious Order; and the Reverend Fathers Fray Manuel García and Fray José Aibar, representatives of their Reverend Father President and Vicar General, Fray Vicente Mora, having arrived at this mission, the delivery of this mission was proceeded with, and there was delivered to them, in accordance with the census, the Indians who comprise it, the church and sacristy, house and land, an inventory being made of all the ornaments and fixtures of the church and sacristy, and of everything else that belongs to this mission, this being carried out on this, the twelfth day of June in the year one thousand seven hundred and seventy-three.

Fray Fermín Francisco de Lasuén.

This mission, according to the census register which has been drawn up and in accordance with which it has been handed over, has two hundred and fifty-four married families, one hundred and eighty-nine widowers, one hundred and twenty widows, and these with their sons and daughters make up one thousand souls.

INVENTORY OF ALL THINGS BELONGING TO THE MISSION

First, a new adobe church, an entire thirty-three varas[5] in length, eight in width, and five and a half in height. The walls are two varas wide, with five windows, their arched upper portions being of carved wood.

The arch of the door is of carved stone, and the same is true of the lintels of the sacristy and baptistery doors. The entire roof is flat, with palms for beams, jamb-posts of willow, and covered with tule.[6] The door of the church is also new, a double door, three varas and about three-quarters high, and two varas and three-quarters wide, with wickets.

In the sacristy are two new doors, one with a key and the other with a lock for the inside.

Three altars. In the principal, a tabernacle completely gilt; a set of altar cards with gilt frames; a statue of Christ a little less than half a vara high with corresponding baldachin;[7] another baldachin of silk with gold braid and fringe; eight painted canvases, some one and a half varas, the others two varas, seven of them saints of the Society of Jesus and the other of St. John Nepomucene,[8] all with gilt frames.

On the altar at the Gospel side, a canvas of Our Lady of Guadalupe, one and two-thirds varas, a small cross, and a remnant of blue silk fabric with red ribbon shaped in the form of a canopy for the said canvas.

On the Epistle side, a crucifix of more than a vara, with its baldachin of silk, with braid and fringe of gold; a tabernacle painted in vermilion, with gilt moldings and carving.

THE SACRISTY

A table with three cases for sacred vestments, and a large case with key for the same.

A vestment of silver cloth with the antependium of other material.

A vestment of cloth of gold.

Another of cloth embroidered with flowers.

Another of white cloth with its antependium.

Another of silk with its antependium.

Another of silk, with a floral pattern, and antependium.

Another of violet with its antependium.

Another, of the same, ordinary, without antependium.

Another, green, without antependium.

Another, ordinary red, with antependium quartered in violet.

Another, black, with antependium.

An antependium of silver cloth.

A silk cope.

A black cope.

A silk sash.

Two lace tabernacle veils.

Two others, red.

Another, violet.

Another, blue.

Another, black.

Seven albs, three good classical ones and the other four ordinary.

Two old surplices.

Three cassocks with their rochets.

Seven amices, four of cambric and very good, and three ordinary.

Fifteen purificators.

Nine finger towels.

Thirteen plain corporals, some of cambric, the others of fine linen.

Six altar cloths of fine linen.

Three altar covers, cotton.

Two stoles, one for baptisms, the other for funerals.

A silver chalice, gilded, with its silver cruets and paten.

A silver ciborium, gilded.

Two silver thuribles with their incense boats.

Two silver vials for chrism.

A holy water stoup.

A silver shell for use at baptisms.

Fourteen large candlesticks and two small ones, of metal.

Three carpets.

Two missal stands of tortoise-shell and another lined with sheepskin.

A copper holy water aspersorium with its aspergillum.

Two urns for baptismal fonts.

An iron for making wafers.

Three cloth cinctures and four cotton ones.

Two ordinary missals and one small one.

Two manuals, one Roman, the other Venegas'.

Two altar stones, in addition to the three of the altars.

Four bells.

Two small ones for the altar.

Thirteen silver two-peso coins, with two rings, for marriages.

Three small purses and a large one of silk.

Two hand towels.

One ribbon of gold cloth for the tabernacle key.

Five linen cloths for the chalices and baptistery.

A baptismal font of well-carved stone.

House Furnishings

Two large cases, one a good one with a key, the other old and lacking one.

A trunk of tanned cowhide.

Some pine boxes.

Three tables, one large and two small.

A bookstand.

A dresser with its stand for jars, etc.

Two chairs.

Four rattan chairs with seats of reed.

Two small beds, one of cowhide, the other of coarse hemp cloth.

Two small *pabellóns* of homemade unbleached cotton cloth.

Five large maps.

A bottle case with twenty flasks, eight of them broken.

Another bottle case, small, with five glass bottles.

The Holy Bible in two volumes.
Montenegro's *Itinerario*.
Lux de Verdades Católicas.
Concilio de Trento.
Indice Práctico Moral.
Fuero de la Conciencia.
A diurnal.[9]
Vida de San Francisco de Borja.
Six volumes of Father Señeri.
Two volumes of Father Natali.
Three, of Father Sautel.
Two small volumes of Ovid.
A small devotional book.
Manojito de Flores.
Florilegio Medicinal.
Four books on administration.
A nonstriking clock of silver.
A small case with three bottles for holy oils.
Another, for the wax
Four small saucepans.
Four new frying pans.
A basin and two chamber pots, copper.
An inkwell and sandbox, metal.
Two and a half dozen china plates.
A milk bowl.
Two small ones.
Four oil cruets and a very good salt-cellar.
Three metal plates.
Nine spoons and nine forks, metal.
A table knife.
Two brass *metates* with their pestles, and another, broken.
Five metal candlesticks.
Three good syringes and one broken.
Four tablecloths and twelve napkins.
One small hand hammer and another for blacksmith's use.
A pair of tailor's scissors.
One dozen animal clippers.
Another of the same kind for shearing, large, new.

Two medium metal locks for a door, new; and one for a box.
Two large metal locks, used.
Three cowboy spurs.
Two small kettles, two chocolate pots, and two jars, copper.
A small scale and its weights.
Three bottles and a number of troughs, native.
Two wire strainers.
Four of the same, white; and four black, for flour.
Some pliers and about half a pound of wire.
Three large machetes, new.
Three others, used.
A dozen large knives.
Two candle extinguishers.
A large quantity of century plant fiber.
A wooden astrolabe.
A bottle of oil of roses, another of almond oil.
A flask of catholic balsam.
Two gallipots of white ointment, another two of yellow.
A pound of diapalma[10] in its container, and half a pound of senna leaves.[11]
Another half pound of manus-dei.[12]
One straw basket of cassia fistula and a large supply of aniseed, camomile, rose of Castile, and cumin seed.
Three or four ounces of silk of different colors and two or three of *salón y muñequilla*[13] thread.
A pound of blue agave thread, a half a pound of white, a pound of soft thread, and four papers of pins.
Four primers and three children's reading books.
A yardstick for measuring, a cuartillo, a half cuartillo, and two funnels.
A number of water casks.

All the above are in a new house joined to the church with which it forms a perfect square. In the first side is a hall suitable for living quarters. It has two doors with locks, three windows; all the doors are wooden, double, each with its grating executed in wood. Two pantries.

On the second side, two workrooms and a porch, each with its doors and keys, all very spacious.

On the third side, a hall and a living room with three windows, one with a lattice and folding doors, the other two with lattices of wood, one new door with its lock.

The whole house has thick walls, high and whitewashed, and a good flat roof.[14]

Also, a cemetery, new and very spacious, enclosed with walls of adobe, with a door and a wooden cross above it, and in the center a cross of carved stone.

Also, a chicken run with two roosters and eighteen hens.

A house for the use of the guard. The mission built it without the intervention of the presidio or the soldiers.

A place for cooking, and two infirmaries.

GRANARY

There are left in the granary eight hundred and two sacks of wheat in the ear, well preserved.

Seven fanegas and eleven almuds of barley.

Eight sacks of corn on the cob.

Two arrobas and twenty-two pounds of tallow.

Five hundred and thirty-six tallow candles.

Three arrobas and fifteen pounds of lard.

Five arrobas and three pounds of jerked beef.

Three large pozole pots, copper.

Another, medium sized.

Four others, small; two are good, two with holes.

Three of the same, to be repaired at Loreto.

Fourteen crowbars.

Five chisels, a small crowbar, and two gouges.

Five engraving chisels.

A large auger for beams.

Two of the above, medium.

One of the same, small.

A carpenter's square, a joiner's gauge, and an iron compass.

Two levels, and a small adze, and another large adze.

A carpenter's plane, a jack-plane, and a small plane.

An iron square, another of wood, and a plummet.

A frame-saw and two small ones.

Three carpenter's axes, good.

Sixteen woodman's axes, in good condition and new.

Five of the same, a little used; and six old ones.

An anvil, tongs, and a hammer for the forge.

Eleven *picaderas*.

A Roman scale.

Two balances with their weights.

A shoemaker's heel-knife, three lasts, and five awls.

Four mason's trowels.

A ruler and a yardstick.

Four copper ladles for pozole.

Three of the same, new.

A small copper jug.

An almud; two half measures; a cuartilla[15] measure; nineteen barrel hoops.

A quantity of shot.

A good supply of chile and salt.

MAIN ALTAR
Church of St. Vincent, Vitoria

THE WINECELLAR

A quite large, new adobe winecellar, with a good flat roof, with a door and padlock.

Two new vats and one old one, made of stone, with a capacity for seventy or eighty earthenware jars, well tarred, and with wooden covers in good condition.

Two large earthenware wine jars, good.

Two others, repaired, serviceable.

Two small ones, local products.

Four small jars.

Four large waterjugs, tarred for wine.

Six others of the same, four from Mission San Fernando and two from San Ignacio Mission.

A large still, good.

Fifty-one arrobas and fifty pounds of cotton, uncarded.

Three arrobas and fourteen pounds of the same, spun.

Sixteen arrobas and twenty-one pounds of wool, uncarded.

Also one arroba of the same, spun.

A small loom, equipped.

Three combs, six used cards, and four pairs of the same, new.

THE SADDLE SHED

Fifteen packsaddles, new, with harness.

Six of the same, old.

Three blankets for the herd.

A good supply of sheepskins, tanned and to be tanned.

A supply of goatskins.

A supply of burlap sacks.

Eighty-five sacks of tanned cowhide.

A sheath with various needles and awls.

Seven tanned cowhides.

Twelve of the same ready to be delivered from the tannery.

Two cowhides.

THE FIELD

Eighteen large hoes, good.

Twenty warren hoes, new.

Twenty of the same, used, good.

Six of the same, medium.

Two pruning hooks.

Two plowshares and two sockets for the plow beam.

The arable land at the mission produces three and a half fanegas of wheat for seed; and under our administration the land was prepared for one and a half of these fanegas, while there was likewise a considerable increase in the planting of fig trees, pomegranates, cotton, and some olive trees.

A large and well cultivated garden, with all kinds of garden produce, with fruit trees, mostly of our time; and in the same period, by using the irrigation ditches, etc., a vineyard of one hundred and twenty vines has been planted in that garden, and almost all bear fruit.

Item, a vineyard of nine hundred and twenty-eight vine stocks, four hundred and sixteen old, and the remainder of our time.

Four and a half almuds of corn were actually sown in that place, and most of it has germinated.

THE SAN REGIS SETTLEMENT

In this place and during our administration the following have been built or brought into use:

A large house which serves as a chapel, fully sixteen varas in length, five wide, and four high, all of adobe and with a good roof.

A good granary, adobe, with door and key.

Two pools for [treating] hemp, of stone and clay, large and in good condition.

A tract has been opened up, nine hundred varas in length and more than twenty-eight varas in width at the narrowest part.

Enough water has been obtained to irrigate it, and it is all completely suitable for corn and wheat; and for the past three years good results have been obtained.

One hundred and three fig trees have been planted in the trenches, and they are doing well.

Two hundred and three pomegranates, likewise doing well.

Eight hundred and twenty cotton plants which have already produced.

Three hundred varas of wet land have been drained and put in condition to be planted with corn and it will be about twenty varas wide.

In the parts that are less humid and almost useless for sowing, two hundred and forty vine cuttings have been successfully planted; most of them have yielded some grapes, and at the present time they have a good crop.

GRANARY OF THE ABOVE PLACE

In the above-mentioned barn of San Regis there are at the present time two hundred and fifty sacks of bearded wheat in the ear, and eight of barley in the ear, and about eight almuds of corn in grain.

Six almuds of corn and other grain for house use have been sown in this place.

PARAISO

Under our administration a small granary of stone and mud, well roofed, with a door and key [was built]. In it are stored six hundred and fifty-eight sacks of wheat in the ear and twelve sacks of barley in the ear.

In this place there is land where about two and a half fanegas of wheat, more or less, have been planted; and in this land, too, an almud and a half of corn and other grain have been sown.

Some pomegranates, fig trees, and a good number of cotton plants have been planted.

The sacks of wheat in the ear and of wheat stored in these barns total one thousand seven hundred and eleven.

The Rancho

An adobe house well roofed, and having corrals enclosed with palm, belongs to the ranch.

Five cowboy saddles, in poor condition, with their trapping in the same condition.

Two goad-points.

Two saddle knives for hamstringing.

A packsaddle for cowboys to carry their supplies.

Two small copper pots.

Three and a half pairs of cowboy's stirrups, iron, new.

Five used bridles.

Three branding irons.

Cattle

Six hundred and forty-eight head of cattle, branded, as well as many yearlings.

Horses

Thirty-eight tame horses	38
Thirty-seven colts, broken in and unbroken included	37
Twenty yearling colts	20
One hundred and twenty breeding mares, with many young ones, this year	120
Fillies of two or three years, forty-six	46
The same, yearlings, twenty-two	22

Mules

Twenty-four mules, broken for riding and for pack animals	24
Fifteen broken in	15
Ten unbroken, some yearlings and some from two to three years included	10
From the last branding, twelve	12
Seven stallions	7
Three brood burros	3
One male burro, two females, and a young one	4

SHEEP AND GOATS

Two thousand three hundred and forty-three head of sheep 2,343	One thousand and three head of goats 1,003	

In this ranch there are eight head of cattle belonging to Mission Santa María. Also, fifteen brood mares, with four yearling colts, and three of this year. Also, three male burros and four female burros.

LAUNCH

The mission has a large well-equipped launch.

DEBITS

This mission owes one hundred and ninety pesos and seven reales according to the statement of account arrived at in agreement with the Loreto warehouse.

CREDITS

In payment of the above debt the sub-syndics[16] of this mission delivered to the Reverend Fathers eighty pesos and four reales in cash, and they received it .... 80 pesos, 4 reales

Also, in favor of this mission, sixty pesos and seven and a half reales were delivered in drafts.

Furthermore, at the present time the cattle, mares, mules, and horses which were taken from it for the expedition are to be credited and regarded as due to it, and they are as stated below:

First, for seventeen mules: three hundred and forty pesos	340.	of cattle: one thousand and twenty pesos	1,020.
Eight horses: eighty pesos	80.		
Six mares and a breeding burro: fifty-six pesos	56.	Grand Total: one thousand four hundred and ninety-	
Two hundred and four head		six pesos	1,496.

In addition, there is a large number of calves that followed their mother which no one took the trouble to count, as Captain Don Fernando Rivera clearly stated in the receipt which he gave for all the things mentioned.

Also, a hammer, a paring knife, and some pincers for shoeing.

All these items are shown to be legitimately due to this Mission of San Borja by the receipt which Captain Don Fernando Rivera y Moncada gave for them on the fourteenth of December of seventeen hundred and sixty-eight; and I gave a copy of this receipt to the Reverend Fathers who remained as ministers, and the original is to be found in the archives of Loreto.

All the families and individuals who are named in the beginning and all that is contained in this inventory, we have received in the name of our institute of the sacred Order of Preachers from Fray Fermín Francisco de Lasuén, Apostolic Preacher of the College of Propaganda Fide of San Fernando of Mexico, Minister of the above Mission of San Francisco de Borja, with the exception of seven families whose names are:

Jorge with his wife María Antonia	daughter named Brígida
Everado with his wife Petra	Nicolás with his wife Gertrudis
José with his wife Sinforosa	Antonio with his wife María Salomé
Esteban with his wife Clara, and one	José Borgino with his wife Gertrudis.

Also four orphan boys, single, named: Fabián, Gaspar, José, and Saturnino, all healthy and strong and able to work. This makes in all nineteen souls who are being taken by the Fathers for the missions of Monterey. We affix our signatures in this Mission of San Francisco de Borja on the fifteenth day of June in the year one thousand seven hundred and seventy-three.

Fray José Aibar
Fray Manuel García
Fray Fermín Francisco de Lasuén.

We hereby declare that this Mission of San Francisco de Borja was handed over, and received, as well as everything expressed in the above census and inventories, as also the state of the accounts above cited; and for testimony to the said delivery we the respective presidents sign in this Mission of Our Lady of Loreto on the twenty-fifth day of June in the year one thousand seven hundred and seventy-three.

Fray Vicente de Mora
Fray Francisco Palou.

[1] Rafael José Verger (1722-1783) was a distinguished member of the Franciscan Order. A native of Mallorca, he held the position of professor in the local university, and later at San Fernando College. He was guardian at San Fernando for six years, and died as bishop of Nuevo Leon.

[2] The more correct title for the Order instituted by St. Dominic, and popularly known as Dominicans.

[3] By reason of the close friendship between St. Dominic and St. Francis, the members of the distinct Orders they founded refer alike to each saint as their "Father."

[4] Iriarte was the Dominican procurator for Mexico. He petitioned the King for permission to enter the field of missionary activity in Lower California. Gálvez and the Viceroy were opposed, but were overruled by the King. Iriarte was appointed superior of the group of missionaries. In 1771, on his way to take over the new mission field, he and some of his companions lost their lives. See Sales, *op. cit.*, pp. 157-158. For Iriarte's motives in undertaking such a mission, see *ibid.* pp. 143-153. He was succeeded in office by Fray Vicente Mora.

[5] Although the vara was the standard of distance, even in Spain it varied according to location, from 30.3 inches in Huesca to 35.6 inches in Valencia. In the New World, too, it varied, but not so widely. It was reckoned at 32.99 inches in Mexico, and in California, at a later date, it was 33 inches.

[6] A Spanish word derived from the Indian (Nahuatl) word *tollin*, meaning a rush, and applied to different species of bulrushes which grow abundantly in certain swampy regions of the Southwest.

[7] A form of canopy above an altar or shrine.

[8] Father Link, the Jesuit founder of San Borja, was a native of Bohemia, whose patron saint is St. John Nepomucene. Furthermore, throughout Spain and in many regions of the New World there was a widespread cult of this saint who sacrificed his life rather than divulge confessional information.

[9] A Book of Hours containing the principal parts of the Divine Office, with the exception of Matins.

[10] In the form of a plaster it was used extensively for the relief of aching joints.

[11] Senna, of the family of casia, was used as a purgative.

[12] A medicine for the treatment of tumors, concussions, and the like. One of its constituents was lead monoxide.

[13] Maguey or cotton yarn. The name is derived from the role which the wrist (muneca) plays in the manufacture of it. See Lesley Byrd Simpson (ed.) *The Letters of José Señán, O.F.M.* (San Francisco, 1962), p. 28, n. 17.

[14] In the *jacalon* style of construction the roof was flat. It was supported on the forked ends of upright posts, and over the rafters a layer of tule or branches was spread, and this in turn was covered with earth. The walls were usually upright posts placed close together, interwoven with tule or branches, and often covered with mud or adobe.

[15] A *cuartilla* is equivalent to three almuds, or 20.64 dry quarts. It is not to be confused with a *cuartillo*, which is 1.72 dry quarts. See Manuel Carrera Stampa, "The Evolution of Weights and Measures in New Spain," *The Hispanic American Historical Review,* XXIX (February, 1949), 2-24, especially p. 15.

[16] "St. Francis forbade the commercial use of money to his friars. In time, however, money became the sole medium of exchange to the civilized world. To enable the friars to continue loyal to their rule without abandoning their chosen work, the Pope sanctioned the appointment of laymen to accept and expend money given for the use of the friars. Such laymen were called syndics." See Antonine Tibesar (ed.), *Writings of Junípero Serra* (Washington, D. C., 1956), II, 468, n. 11. Syndics could have local representatives called sub-syndics.

The Oven

II

First Years in California

These are the first letters of Lasuén written in California. The period, April 23, 1774 to October 21, 1776, was one of many frustrations and disappointments for him, for either he lacked a permanent assignment, or met with unexpected difficulties in filling those given to him.

8. To Reverend Father Guardian [Fray Francisco Pangua]

AY YOUR REVERENCE ENJOY THE BEST OF health. I offer my congratulations and best wishes on your appointment as prelate.[1] I pray that He who conferred this favor on you may grant you the grace to carry out its duties in accordance with His most holy pleasure.

In me Your Reverence beholds your most willing, devoted, and least subject; and this is what I profess to be. For this reason, then, I take the liberty of bringing to your notice the fact that I have devoted myself to the work of the missions, in accordance with the will of my superiors, the predecessors of Your Reverence, for ten full years, five of them in the Sierra Gorda, and the other five in California.

At the very time that the missions of the peninsula were being given up they were going to gratify an earnest wish I had had for a long time, and one that has persisted, and I was to put it into effect, namely, that of returning to the college. To bring this about I did not have recourse to any form of pressure, great or little. By the same token, when I could have departed from there and gone to the destination mentioned, it was the suggestion, the request, and the pleading of my Reverend Father President, Fray Francisco Palou, that I ought to come north to these new establishments, that robbed me of this pleasure—for to me [the wish of a superior] is equivalent to a command.

Ever since I left the college, as I mentioned, I have been and am resolved to be submissive in all things, neither opposing nor failing to carry out any order of the presidents who are my superiors; and seeing that there was nothing in this case to hinder me, as soon as the articles of conveyance for my Mission of San Borja were sealed and delivered, I set out with the other Fathers for this new Department, with the impression, and on the understanding, that there would be a scarcity of missionaries here.

Well, when I arrived and saw there were Fathers to spare, I made known my wishes to my Reverend Father President, above-mentioned. I begged him in view of the superabundance of Fathers, to put my name at the head of the list, and to permit me to embark at the first opportunity, so that I might return to the college. In this I was not successful; and so, for the past eight months I have been retained as a member of the community of this Mission of San Gabriel.

A few days ago the Reverend Father President, Fray Junípero Serra, arrived, and he left yesterday for Monterey. I brought to his attention once more the fact that I am the person most expendible. I mentioned what I would like to do, and gave my reasons. In this connection, it seemed to me, he was determined that for the present there would be no new foundations, and he merely gave me the same negative answer which Father Lector[2] Palou had already given, and which is in accord with what Your Reverence's predecessor, the Reverend Father Lector, the venerable Father Fray Rafael Verger had in mind, that I should stay in these new missions. I submitted without question.

But, my dear Father, now that I seem to be just a supernumerary with nothing in particular to do, while such a condition may be agreeable to human nature, it is by no means in accord with our institution. It may be, too, that it is not in accord with your wishes; and this is what I would like to find out. So, in all humility, I am asking you to inform me. I am by no means suggesting that you should bring your way of thinking into harmony with mine. My aim instead is, that my will may be subject in all things and in all respects to that of Your Reverence.

No matter what conclusion Your Reverence reaches, and no matter what decision you make in regard to me, whether it be that I should return to the college, something that would please me greatly, or whether it be that I should continue here, something to which I would humbly submit, I beg, for the love of God, if there is time for it and an occasion offers, I beg that I be sent a complete outfit, for I have been and am appallingly short of clothing. Without exaggeration, I have reached the stage of indecency. Just keep in mind that an under-habit which I brought from Sierra Gorda serves me as a tunic, and that the habit which I brought from there I have now had in continuous use for five years. I have done what I could to keep the clothes in repair; but they no longer can be repaired, partly because there is nothing to repair, and partly because there is nothing with which to repair them. Possibly some one from the Colorado expedition who was here will testify, alas, to the truth of this. In the only request for supplies sent to the college in five years of residence and administration at San Borja Mission, among different things which I asked for and which they failed to send me, was a habit of coarse wool. And the supplies they did send were not equivalent to the stipend for one year. This, I suspect could be due to forgetfulness, some mistake, or carelessness. So, for this reason I repeat my request, for the love of God, and I beg Him to preserve Your Reverence through many years in His holy grace.

San Gabriel Mission,
April 23, 1774.

¹ Lasuén was aware that a Chapter was soon to be held in San Fernando College for the election of officials for the forthcoming three-year term. At the time of writing Father Verger was still guardian. Three weeks later the chapter was held, and Verger was succeeded by Fray Francisco Pangua.

² In the Franciscan Order professors in such faculties as Philosophy and Theology were known as *lectors*. Since the recipient of the title at that time enjoyed more rights and prerogatives than a modern professor, the term *lector* is retained throughout.

9. To Fray Francisco Pangua

Being now free from the anxieties, cares, and worries of the Californias and enjoying a life of ease in this new department, I wish to convey to Your Reverence an expression of my deep and unvarying affection; and I am assured that this does not consist in an exchange of letters, for even without them (and I have scarcely had a chance to write) my affection for you has continued undiminished.

I wish an abundance of health and happiness for Your Reverence, and that you may have been successful in meeting the heavy tasks of your vicariate; but perhaps you have already assumed the more onerous duties of guardian, and in that case accept my congratulations—not just those of a close friend and fellow countryman,¹ but those, too, of a devoted subject who, in another letter by this mail, sends his felicitations.

I had already left my few belongings in Loreto, and only awaited the handing over of my Mission of San Borja before going down to the presidio so as to embark and return to the college. With that in mind I wrote a number of letters to my Reverend Father President Palou. He answered each one of them and gave his approval to what I had in mind.

However, when he arrived at San Borja to arrange for the transfer of the mission, he implored and pleaded with me to go to these new missions; and as I have held the firm conviction ever since I was ordained that I can never succeed if I oppose the wish of any president, I accompanied the aforesaid Father, thinking to myself that there must be a scarcity of missionaries. But this is so far from the case that half of us are not needed.

I have already written to the Reverend Father Guardian on this point (although with entire submission to his decision), because I find it hard to be idle for such a long time; and in view of the circumstances which I explain in the letter, it may not be in accordance with his will that I should remain here. It is my conviction that no new foundations will be established for some time, despite the fact that the Reverend Father President Junípero² says that when the commandant Don Fernando arrives—all we know about him is that he has reached Loreto with thirty soldiers and their families—it will be easier to proceed with one or more foundations.

I am now awaiting the reply from my superior, and I shall carry out his will in all humility.

The aforementioned Father President Junípero left this mission yesterday for his Mission of Carmel.

Father Mugartegui[3] remains in San Diego. He has already recovered but not entirely from the chills which forced him to interrupt his voyage aboard the frigate to Monterey. Father Amurrió[4] took the former's place up to that port, and he will return overland to this mission with the emoluments and salary of one promised the assignment.

Prestamero[5] and Peña,[6] I believe, are in the San Luis Mission and are dissatisfied with their status as supernumeraries; and although they are entitled to double maintenance, they cannot be received to full membership at the mission. And I believe that they will renounce the assignment they were awaiting, for they accepted it with much reluctance in the first instance.

Regarding the land expedition from the Colorado River under the command of Captain Don Juan Bautista de Anza,[7] Your Reverence already knows how great the expectations are. I have heard it said by some well-informed persons that it will be a long time before it leads to any improvement of these new settlements, nor will it free them from the hazards they have good reason to fear.

I have vague hopes to the contrary. The land is very beautiful. The pagans are numerous and very docile; and if we had the wherewithal for sowing, we could assert with absolute certainty that, by the grace of God, most abundant harvests could be obtained, both temporal and eternal.

It has been more than a year since I wrote to Father Lector Verger, my former guardian, enclosing two letters in regard to a very particular business with which, perhaps, Your Reverence may be acquainted; and as I have not received a reply, I am kept in a state of constant and serious agitation. Therefore, I beg Your Reverence, for the love of God, to make inquiries and to notify me concerning their receipt and the action taken or the lack of action, for in that event the Reverend Father President will assist me to obtain an answer to this request that is so important and means so much to me.

In a letter of this date I am also asking the Reverend Father Guardian to do me the kindness of furnishing me a complete outfit of clothes, because in the five years during which I was in charge of the Mission of San Borja I did not receive as much as a single stipend. I left that unfortunate province entirely devoid even of under-clothing and sandals. I know, of course, that this was due to the fact that the college found it impossible to send them. Perhaps it was because of my very necessities that the Indians became so devoted to me, for if "like attracts like" I resemble them closely in scantiness of attire.

Your most affectionate friend, servant, and (in case something happens)[8] your subject.

San Gabriel Mission,
April 23, 1774.

[In the first and last pages there are the following marginal notes:]

I will be much indebted if Your Reverence will do me the favor, for the love of God, of forwarding the letters with all possible care to their destination; and if the addresses are inadequate, will Your Reverence kindly add what is needed. [Here follow two lines too garbled to be deciphered.]

To avoid multiplying letters, I beg that this may serve as a personal greeting to the Reverend Fathers, my masters and friends, Fray Esteban Antonio de Arenaza and Fray José de Jesús María Vélez;[9] and to this I would add that I have offered a Mass each month according to the intention we agreed on, and I console myself with the assurance that you do me a like favor.

[1] Like Lasuén, Pangua was a native of the Basque country, and was Lasuén's senior by some ten years. He served as a member of the college council of San Fernando for two terms of three years each, and was a guardian of the college from 1774 to 1777, and from 1780 to 1783.

[2] The renowned and saintly Fray Junípero Serra, founder of the mission system in California.

[3] "Pablo de Mugártegui was born in 1738 in Marquina, Spain. He joined the Franciscan Order in 1759, becoming a member of the Franciscan Province of Cantabria. He entered the College of San Fernando, Mexico, in 1770. He accompanied Serra to California in 1774, arriving at San Diego on March 13, of that year. He served mainly at San Luis Obispo and San Carlos Missions, and on the death of Serra became the vice-president of the missions. For three years, 1789-1792, he was guardian of San Fernando College." Tibesar, *op. cit.*, II, 467, n. 6. See also Ignacio Omaechevarria, O.F.M. *Fr. Pablo José de Mugártegui* (Bilbao, Spain, 1959).

[4] Fray Gregorio Amurrió was a Basque, born in Bastida, Spain, in 1774. He joined the Franciscan Order in 1760, became a member of the Province of Cantabria, and transferred to San Fernando College in 1770. He served in Lower California from 1771 to 1773, when he was sent to Upper California. For a time he was associated with Lasuén at San Juan Capistrano. In 1779 he returned to Mexico, joined the Province of Jalisco, but later returned to San Fernando College.

[5] Lasuén's familiar tone when writing to, or concerning, Fray José de Prestamero makes it clear that there was a close bond of friendship between them. They were approximately the same age. Both were residents of the same Basque city, Vitoria. Both were novices in St. Francis Friary in that city in the years 1751 and 1752. Prior to ordination both volunteered for missionary work in Mexico, and, while still deacons, were companions on the same boat to Mexico. Later they worked in the same mission fields: Sierra Gorda, Lower California, and Upper California.

[6] Fray Tomás de la Peña y Saravia, also a Basque, was born at Brizuela, Spain, in 1743, and entered the Franciscan Order in the Province of Cantabria on November 13, 1762. Shortly after his arrival at San Fernando in 1770 he was sent to Lower California.

On August 4, 1772, he arrived at San Diego, where he remained for a few months. In 1774, he was one of the chaplains who accompanied Juan Pérez on the *Santiago* during the exploration of the northern waters. In 1777, he assisted in the founding of Mission Santa Clara. He served this mission until 1794, when he returned to Mexico. He was made a member of the college council in 1795, and died in 1806. Cf. Tibesar, *op. cit.* I, 420, n. 123.

[7] The object of the first Anza expedition was to test the feasibility of an inland route from northern Mexico across the Colorado River to California.

[8] Lasuén knew that a Chapter would soon be held at San Fernando College, and he is here indicating that it would please him greatly if Pangua, the recipient of the letter, were to become guardian, so that the writer, Lasuén, might become his subject. The Chapter was held three weeks later, on May 14, 1774, and Pangua did become guardian.

[9] Little information is presently available on either Arenaza or Vélez. The former was born about the year 1720, became a member of the Basque province, and, like Lasuén, later transferred to San Fernando. He was a member of the college council for two terms, from 1774 to 1777, and from 1783 to 1786. Vélez was born about the year 1714, became a Franciscan at San Fernando College in 1737, was a member of the council from 1764 to 1767, and from 1780 to 1783.

10. To the Council of San Fernando College

I was under the impression that my letters to Your Reverences would be carried by one of the Fathers of Querétaro who arrived at this mission by way of the Colorado River; but this did not happen because the gallant Captain, Don Juan Bautista de Anza (commandant of the land expedition who came to these missions of San Diego and Monterey by way of the Colorado River) did me the favor, and thus anticipated them. I have deemed it fitting to make this known to Your Reverence so that he, as the bearer of these letters, may receive the courtesy that is his due.

He is a devoted friend of the College of Santa Cruz, a distinguished benefactor, and a source of great encouragement to the missionaries of the Pimería.[1] It should be our hope that he will take the same interest in the Fernandino missionaries of this Northern California.

He has acquitted himself in these parts with great Christian integrity, and he has carried out his duties to the satisfaction of all interested in the objectives of this enterprise. And everyone is already convinced that in a short time the enterprise will lead to much progress in this new territory.

Will Your Reverences kindly bring all of this to the attention of the Reverend Father Guardian, who is also receiving my letter from the same bearer. And remind him that the Fathers of the College of Santa Cruz, the Reverend Fathers Fray Francisco Garcés and Fray Juan Díaz,[2] furnished me with much needed clothing some months ago, and they deserve to be thanked. One gave me a light habit and cowl, and the other a tunic and sandals. To another Father, Fray Francisco gave a cloak.

May God keep Your Reverences many years in His holy grace.

San Gabriel Mission,

May 2, 1774.

[1] The international boundry line intersects the lands of the Indians of the Pimería country beginning in the neighborhood of Tucson, Arizona, and extending westwards towards, and perhaps beyond, Ajo. The missionaries at that time were from the College of Santa Cruz, Querétaro.

[2] Garcés and Díaz were missionaries from the College of Querétaro. Garcés, an intrepid explorer, is the better known. Both lost their lives at the Colorado River near Yuma when the Indians attacked in the month of July, 1781. See Maynard J. Geiger (ed.), *Palou's Life of Fray Junípero Serra* (Washington, D. C., 1955), pp. 223-225.

11. To the Guardian of San Francisco College [Fray Francisco Pangua]

I wish Your Reverence all happiness and respectfully beg you to consider the request that I made in a preceding letter.

The purpose of this letter is to inform Your Reverence that I am much perturbed these days, for I find myself obliged to solicit help for my poor, aged, beloved, and venerated parents. They are in need of help, and they have asked me for help. My efforts failed, for no one would answer the pleas which I made for that purpose and addressed to Your Reverence's predecessor,[1] the Reverend Father Fray Rafael Verger. I brought these requests to the attention of the Reverend Father Lector Fray Francisco Palou, the former Reverend Father President; and he regarded what I had done as sufficient to discharge what is for me a very grave obligation, and therefore enough to overcome my opposition and to induce me to agree with his request that I come up here to these newly established missions. And when I made the same request to the Reverend Father President Fray Junípero Serra, they sought to persuade me that I had satisfied in full my strict natural obligation, and as a consequence, being free of all anxiety, I could continue in the department, biding my time until a new foundation would be established which would afford me ample field for labor and a permanent appointment. Both presidents[2] thought, and were even certain, I believe, that in a matter of such importance there could be no danger of an oversight—which naturally is presumed when there is no reply, unless, perchance, the letters had been lost.

I am disillusioned to discover that nothing has resulted from those plans of both Father Presidents, one of whom required me to come to these missions and the other to continue in them as supernumerary, despite the fact that I was inclined, and in fact eager, to return to the college. I could not do otherwise than repeat these earnest requests; but for the present the Reverend Father President Junípero has deferred action, devising with this end in view other measures which are communicated to the Reverend Father Fray Martín Crucélegui[3] through the Reverend Father Fray Pablo Mugartegui at the request of the above-mentioned Reverend Father President.

In view of all this, I beg Your Reverence for the love of God that you be so kind as to assist me by the aid of any influence you can exercise. However, if it should not be found expedient to fulfill this request, or if no good would follow from the carrying out of it, I ask that Your Reverence may permit me to withdraw to the holy college at the first opportunity.

In the meantime, in order to expedite a matter that is so urgent and so important, and on my part to leave nothing untried that might lead to a favorable outcome, I might add that it occurs to me that it might be found possible to assign to this purpose either in whole or part the stipends still undisbursed, accruing from the administration of San Borja Mission in Lower California.

I leave in the hands of Your Reverence the solution of this difficulty; and should the outcome be favorable, I beg and pray, for the love of God, that you take every step necessary so that the needed help may reach the hands of my parents. And for this purpose, any further information or explanation required may be obtained from the Reverend Father Fray Juan Prestamero or the Reverend Father Lector Fray Francisco Pangua.

May God Our Lord keep Your Reverence for many years in His holy grace.

San Diego,
July 29, 1774.

---

[1] At San Fernando it was not the custom to reelect a guardian to succeed himself in the same office, and prior to 1832 there is not a single instance of it. Hence Lasuén assumed that there was a new guardian, for the date of the Chapter was past. Between the years 1770 and 1783 Verger and Pangua alternated in office. Pangua was elected to the office of guardian no fewer than four times.

[2] Serra held the position of President from the beginning of the California project until his death in 1784. However, when Serra departed from Lower for Upper California in 1769, Palou became interim president of the missionaries who still continued for some time in Lower California, and one of these was Lasuén. Later, for part of the years 1773 and 1774, during a prolonged absence of Serra in Mexico City, Palou once more became interim president, and by this time all the missionaries from Lower California had reached Upper California. Serra had returned from his Mexican journey some two months before the date of this letter. See Geiger, *Life and Times,* I, 348-417.

[3] Also a Basque, and Lasuén's junior by about six years.

12. To Fray Francisco Pangua

I have received Your Reverence's two letters, dated November 8 and November 24, of last year. I was unable to reply to them by return mail because we in San Gabriel learned of the arrival of the packet boat in San Diego (through word received from the Fathers of that mission) on the same day on which it began its return trip to San Blas.

It seems that the lieutenant of that presidio found himself without a courier through whom to send this information, which had been requested and is customary, because various duties concurred to keep the troops occupied and dispersed.

I thank Your Reverence with all my heart for the charity that has been shown to my aged father. May God reward you for it and grant you a place in the Kingdom of Heaven.

I have already pledged myself to keep in mind so keen a recollection of your kindness that I shall never be wanting in the gratitude that is due. I had tried a thousand ways and taken every possible step in regard to the matter; and the only result was that I had to presume that all was in vain, for of those to whom I wrote, not one replied. I felt that it would be easier for them to do what I had in mind, rather than for Your Reverence; and so my first requests were to them. As it turns out, it was on Your Reverence that the burden and the reward for such a holy work (may God grant it to you) fell; and it was I that received the joy that a matter of such urgency was taken care of, and the added privilege that it was taken care of by a superior for whom the love of a friend is sufficient incentive. I repeat: May God reward you for it.

I obtained permission from the Reverend Father President to go to Monterey where I arrived on the 21st of last month. On the journey I saw great numbers of Indians who live largely in the vast expanse of territory that lies between San Gabriel and San Luis [Obispo]. The Channel of Santa Barbara is in that region, and it is a place that is deserving of the greatest attention. It is a matter of deep regret that by deferring the founding of a mission in that region, which manifestly offers many sites that are suitable for that purpose and conveniently located for the natives, many of them will suffer in the continual wars which they wage among themselves, as the signs of their attacks and manifest evidences of their destruction indicate.

Furthermore, due to this delay in establishing a mission, the Indians are becoming more conceited; and with their more frequent opportunities of observing our men in their frequent and necessary trips—trips during which unfortunately they are often attacked—there is danger that in time the conversion of these Indians will be rendered more difficult and more costly.

When we were on our journey and reached the place popularly known as Dos Pueblos[1] (for two rancherías adjoin one another there), but now known by the name of San Pedro y San Pablo, six of these unfortunate Indians met death at the hands of our soldiers; and the greatest wonder is that the losses were not on our side instead, and that I was not one of them.

It happened in the ranchería that a soldier struck a pagan a sharp blow with the flat side of his sword, for the latter had cut off the tail of the soldier's mule and had tried to disarm him. In a rage the Indian ran to fetch his arms, raised the alarm, and excited his neighbors to follow his example. They all rushed out armed and caught us in their midst, the soldier and myself. I was on foot, for I had just dismounted from the mule in order to give glass beads to the children whom the Indian mothers were bringing to me in their arms. They began to shoot arrows. I tried to mount my mule, but found I could not do so, for the animal had become very restive because of the vociferous yelling. But because the first volleys had not been directed against me, and because three soldiers promptly rushed to the rescue, I was able to make my escape on foot, and although it was difficult because of my weight, with God's help I found myself very shortly beyond the range of their shafts. The Indians were now shooting their arrows without distinction of persons for they saw that there were others who replied to their attack and came to the defense of the first target of their arrows.

There were no casualties on our side, thanks be to God, although the other side had all the strategic advantages, entrenched as they were behind their houses, well armed, and superior in numbers, while our forces were caught off guard, poorly equipped, and quite outnumbered—there were only four when the skirmish started and was at its worst.

When our men were able to draw their guns, the guns failed to go off; and when at length they began to fire, the first three rounds were ineffectual. In addition to this, the four soldiers were steadily retreating, either to protect me (although my armed guard only made matters worse for me, for he was so upset at the thought that he was the cause of the commotion that he used neither shield nor leather jacket), or to find a more favorable ground, for the place where the engagement began was very soft and full of holes and small depressions which did not allow the use of horses, which the engagement called for. This situation caused the Indians to become haughty and made them so daring that they followed us for a long distance yelling and discharging arrows until at last we reached level ground. There we were joined by four of our soldiers, who had followed behind with the horses, and another four, who had gone ahead with the pack train. The twelve charged the Indians and killed three in the encounter. This did not suffice to stop them, and they pursued the Indians right up to their ranchería, where they killed three more of them. They might have killed more of them if they had not sued for peace, raising their hands and giving up their arms.

The most surprising thing is that so many arrows could have been shot, and shot at close range, without wounding the soldier who was responsible for the brawl, for he was either so stupified or so taken by surprise, that he used neither his leather jacket nor his shield, for these are the safeguards that these soldiers employ in their campaigns. And although many arrows were shot without aiming, it is astonishing that one did not reach its objective, for the soldier is of unusual stature and of gigantic frame. It was God who brought us through the ordeal in safety, and may He be blessed for ever.

I am of the opinion that these Channel Indians know that they are strong, and that they act on the principle that whoever harms them will have to pay the price. May His Divine Majesty grant that the innocent may not have to pay for what they have not done.

Already a report has reached us from the Mission of San Luis [Obispo] that there is a widespread rumor among their natives that the Channel Indians have killed two soldiers who were on their way from San Diego, and that they have invited the pagans of the Sierras to prevent the passage of our people.

The rumor does not yet deserve much credence, considering the vague rumors these people are in the habit of spreading, and the orders which have been issued well in advance by the commandant to ensure that such a thing should not happen. Nevertheless, such an incident may be feared. In view of the investigations which have been set on foot, we should not have long to wait to ascertain the truth.

Word reaches us from San Antonio that there is an epidemic of dysentery in that mission and that the death rate is particularly high among the children. Steps are being taken to send the surgeon there in the hope that he may be able to find a remedy.

We have no further news from the different missions. The wheat crop is very good in all of them, except at San Gabriel. In the hope of availing themselves of a new water supply they report that they had decided to sow in soil that had been arid, and as a consequence the crop is somewhat retarded. But they are taking whatever steps are needed, and any losses will in all probability be compensated for by an increased yield of corn, for this was sown in the more fertile soil.

The work of evangelization is progressing all along the line, and I think it is true that each of the missions will have as many converts as it can feed and clothe becomingly. This is all I have to say in response to the obligation Your Reverence has imposed on me; and if I had failed in regard to it, it would have been unpardonable.

I am grateful for the faculties and for the clothing. The latter I had already pledged as security because of the extreme need I was in. With it I repaid the Father who helped me last year with what had been brought in the packet boat *San Antonio* or *El Principe* for his use. I was left with only the cloak; and therefore, in preparation for the coming year I beg, for the love of God, for the rest. And I pray that His Most Holy Majesty may keep Your Reverence for many years in His holy grace.

Presidio of Monterey,
July 19, 1775.

[*On the margin:*] The commandant[2] tells me that he is thinking of writing to Your Reverence; and if he fails to do so, it will be on account of his many duties. He wishes to be remembered to you and sends his kindest regards. May God Our Lord and His Majesty the King keep this good man many years in this assignment. I cannot persuade myself that another could be found more fitted for the post or more helpful in the great and glorious undertaking we have assumed, and it will be a big achievement if someone is found who can match his accomplishments.

[1] These places are located along the Santa Barbara coastline between the modern settlements of Goleta and Gaviota.
[2] Don Fernando Rivera.

13. To Fray Francisco Pangua

On the nineteenth of last month I sent Your Reverence the Reports; and now I am going to write in this letter about some problems of my own.

I have already set forth and explained to Your Reverence how, on the occasion of the transfer of the Mission of San Borja, it was within my power, and it was also my desire, to retire to the college. Instead, at the instance of Father Lector Fray Francisco Palou, who was then the president, and of Fray Junípero Serra, who holds the office now, I proceeded to the missions of Upper California which had just been established. Father President Fray Junípero Serra further assured me that such a step would be pleasing to my former Reverend Father Guardian Fray Rafael Verger; so I continued in them.

I found out later that there was actually no scarcity of missionaries, although this was the reason given by the one why I should come, and by the other why I should stay in California. In view of this, I begged both of them to give me priority among the supernumeraries so that I could qualify for an early return to the college. I have just learned that they have given me the priority I sought, but this will not lead to the objective I had in mind. It has now been decided to proceed with two new missions; but they have informed me that I am neither destined for them nor needed at them, but that I am being held in reserve for missions not yet decided on.

In these circumstances there remains to me no other consolation—it is a big one—than knowing that I am carrying out to the letter the mandate of Your Reverence, expressed in your letter of November 24, of last year. It was expressed in these words: "It seems to me that even though it be in the capacity of supernumerary, Your Reverence should continue as missionary." But if Your Reverence recalls your motive for disposing things in this fashion, subsequent events should disabuse you of the notion that your information was correct. It is clear that the only talent I have (it's the plain truth) is to act as supernumerary, and that the other ministers do not want me, for the Reverend Father President informs me that since the Reverend Fathers Palou and Murgía, the superiors of the new missions, may each select a companion according to his own choice, he is not assigning me as companion to either.

Relying on the repeated promises of the Reverend Father Presidents, some of these promises being verbal and others written, I have cherished the hope that I would be engaged in one or other of the new missions. And when I was not, it caused me anguish, for during nearly two years at San Gabriel it was my unpleasant duty to maintain a number of Indians from Lower California who were disconsolate, with good reason. By virtue of an agreement entered into with the Dominican Fathers and by reason of their love for me, they became exiles from their own land so that they might work for the improvement and enrichment of this.

I was very happy to undertake the task, and, as may be imagined, devoted my best efforts to it, although I could not place them in charge of activities in the field, not being in complete charge myself. It is they, and the Indians who came ahead of them from the same place, who put the mission on its way to prosperity; and to their toil is due if not all, at least the greater part, of what the mission produces and what it needs for its sustenance. Despite all this, they are treated like stepchildren. Not only do they fail to receive the big returns they were promised when they were recruited, but they work much harder and receive less in return than in their own country. It becomes difficult, and some deem it impossible, to induce them to settle down, or to get the single to marry.

And there are many of these, and many families, too, that have no place they can call home. They are awaiting the establishment of a mission to which they can belong. And consequently, far from improving their own lot as a result of their labors, they continue to bear the heaviest of burdens, that of giving a start to a new settlement.

In the missions and in this presidio I have seen servants who, in addition to wages, were given good rations; yet these Indians, although they were paid no wages and were given poor fare, could equal if not surpass them in work. All of these considerations, and the fact that I was urged to bring these poor creatures to settle here, oblige me to bring to Your Reverence's attention the condition in which they are; and although the Reverend Father President in some of the matters mentioned has made some provision in their favor, I am aware that it is not always carried out, or is carried out with great reluctance. It is but too true that the others who have come up from Lower California are just as eager as those from San Borja Mission to accompany me wherever I might be sent, even though during all this time I have lacked the means of rewarding them adequately, by which it might have been possible to ensure their continuing loyal affection.

Perhaps they reckoned that if they were with me they would receive the preferential treatment they were promised, to which they know they are entitled, but which seems to be forthcoming from hardly anyone else. Their discontent, I think, will not be so great if they can be spared the discovery that there are some missionaries who find it difficult to extend to them the same treatment and to show them the same affection that they give to the natives of their own missions.

I trust Your Reverence will pardon and overlook this lengthy digression, devoted as it is to problems that are extraneous. But I have dwelt on them so often that I have made them my own, and they are closely connected with the obligation I undertook when I removed these Indians from their own country, and which still binds me to maintain them contented here. If some remedy is not found, I fear that some day they may begin to complain about me and attribute their misfortunes to me.

My hopes have been frustrated. The things I foresaw as reasons for not coming to these missions and later for not staying here, have come to pass. This I have reported more than once to the two Reverend Fathers, Serra and Palou. If at that time they had disabused me in regard to the course they are now following, or if they had not assured me that they favored the opposite of what is actually happening, without a doubt I would have returned to the college. All that remains to me is the happiness of obeying the above-mentioned order of Your Reverence, and the consolation of being a companion in this presidio to my great, intimate, and cordial friend, Don Fernando. By serving in this capacity I shall keep this worthy gentleman from giving up hope, and from carrying out his intention of relinquishing this office. He was already on his way to Mexico and would have abandoned this great project which he, in my opinion, is the most competent to carry out.

I am aware that my present position is not completely in accord with our way of living; and it is very different from, and (I think) at variance with, what I had in mind when I agreed to come to this department and to continue in it. I am certain that by holding this position, which the Reverend Father President has approved, I am working for the good, the great good, of all the Fathers, and of the Indians, and of the entire country—for the influence of a commandant like Don Fernando reaches out to all. And nowhere do more regrettable and deplorable setbacks occur more often than in places like this, and in enterprises like these, when there is lacking a leader comparable to ours in Christian life and conduct. Therefore, I think he was sent to us by God Our Lord to be an instrument for some great and distinctive favor which the almighty Majesty wished to bestow on this country.[1]

For this reason I think I am employing my talent to good advantage, and am very happy in doing so, for, although I do not cease to be a supernumerary, there is no dearth of duties for me at the presidio, and, as I have already said, in a sense I serve the entire department. Nevertheless, as this is a matter of serious consequence, it seems to me appropriate to explain in detail to Your Reverence the manner and circumstances of my appointment to it.

When Don Fernando passed through San Gabriel Mission, he indicated to me that it was his earnest desire that I would accompany him to the presidio he commanded, and that I would remain with him until I was assigned to a mission of my own, and that when that time came, it was his hope that my mission would be the one least distant from his residence. In the meantime he undertook to pay for my maintenance. As an obedient subject, I had to decline him such a just and well-merited favor until I referred the matter to the Reverend Father President. In my letter I informed him of what the new commanding officer had proposed and offered, so that with this information in mind he might decide as he thought best.

The reply I received was written in a tone of reproof tempered with kindness; it indicated clearly that there was no intention of assigning any Father to the presidio. This took me by surprise because there had not been the least doubt in my mind, and it was also the thought of the other Fathers, that since there were so many supernumeraries he would assign one of them to the presidio. Disabused of my error or my mistaken notion, I offered an appropriate apology and returned to San Gabriel.

There I received a letter from Don Fernando every time the mail arrived from San Carlos, and in all of them he begged me earnestly, even asking me for charity' sake, at least to come closer to San Luis [Obispo] Mission so that we could meet from time to time, because it would be impossible for him to come to where I was.

I humbly excused myself and tried to comfort him; but as the requests were repeated, I begged permission of the Reverend Father President to come here in response to them. This was the main objective, although I did not disclose it when I asked for the permission. I felt it would but displease the aforesaid Reverend Father, for there were rumors that there was an absence of harmony between him and the captain; and there were instances known to me which could give ground for such suspicions.

In my request for permission I, therefore, alleged another reason which was, indeed, both true and adequate for my petition; but before I could obtain a reply I received a letter from the commandant written from San Luis Mission, where he then was, in which he renewed his requests and entreaties that I join him. Accompanying the letter was another unsealed letter. It was addressed to Señor Echeveste[2] and was written with the sole objective of entreating him, in all humility and earnestness, to do all that lay in his power and to use all his influence in order to obtain for him as soon as possible a release from his command and a transfer.

He gave me the option of withholding the letter, but on the express condition that I would then have to live at the presidio, or at least at some mission less remote. If this could not be done, I was to permit the letter to proceed to its destination, for in that case the writer did not wish to retain the command he then held.

Soon after this it happened that Reverend Fathers Dumetz and Cambón, who were bringing the cargoes that had been seized and detained at San Fernando de Velicatá,[3] passed by the mission; and I resolved to accompany them. A few days later the permission to do so arrived, although I was unaware of it. It was contained in a letter addressed to Father Paterna, and he was instructed to communicate it to me. This is what the Reverend Father President told me when we met.

I finally arrived safely at Carmel, and there I recognized as a fact what up to then I could but suspect, namely, that the coldness and aversion for the commanding officer extended also to his friend, even though the latter was far away at San Gabriel and was simply an unbiassed supernumerary who held aloof from all parties. And my good friend Don Fernando was not the one who supplied the information that led to that conclusion.

More than eight days passed before I was able to get even a moment's conversation with the Reverend Father President, despite all the efforts I made to secure it. Then I received the letter which I enclose. I showed it to the said Reverend Father, and he at the same time had received another on the same subject. He invited me to a conference and opened it with a remark that implied that his wish was that I should return to San Gabriel; and he ended by asking me what I had in mind as regards the request of Don Fernando.

When I replied that my wish was to carry out what he enjoined, he was inflexible in his insistence that I return to where I had been so long —a point he had begun by merely suggesting.

"Very well," I said, "I shall return to San Gabriel, although it is a place for which I have the greatest aversion; and I cannot help regretting (I added), that my destination is not elsewhere, especially since there are plans to found two missions in San Francisco."

It was then that I learned that to them had been assigned the Reverend Fathers Palou and Murguía,[4] each to his own mission and with a companion of his own choosing. Until then it had always been rumored and presumed that the two Fathers were going to the same mission. When I mentioned this to the Reverend Father President he replied, after giving some further reasons, that even if both had been assigned to one of the two missions to be founded, it would be far from his mind to send me as the sole companion of Father Amurrió for the administration of the other.

The compatibility between Father Amurrió and myself has been noted ever since my arrival in these missions, and on several occasions has won the commendation of the former and present presidents.

Well then, my dear and revered Father Guardian, it does not pain me that the matter should have been disposed of in this manner. Nor am I any less of the opinion that a different procedure should have been followed. What grieves me is that they did not recognize my uselessness at a time when I was doing my utmost to return to the college. I then drew attention to my own limitations as compared with so many other Fathers, all of whom were available; and each and all of those who volunteered for this kind of work were more fitted for it than I. Of course they may try to put me off by saying up to now they had not known it, or had not been disabused. It is nonetheless regrettable that their protestation should be so tardy and their misunderstanding so prolonged.

The conference came to an end with the above-mentioned statement, and the two days that followed were passed in silence. On the third day he sent for me; and handing me a letter, he told me that I was to give it to Don Fernando, and that at the same time I could take my bed to the presidio.

I expressed resentment, not with the order, but with the antipathy with which I realized it was being conceded, and I gave this as the reason for my dissatisfaction. He replied that it was not possible to follow any other course in the matter since the decision in regard to it would eventually become known at the court and at the college; and that furthermore, it probably would not be well received if he were to deny a request of this nature, made by the commanding officer and urged with such earnestness.

And now, dear and very esteemed Father Guardian, (permit me, for the love of God, to speak from my heart, for as a father and a superior you will not refuse me this solace), if good Father President repays one to whom he owes so much by an arrangement like this, one which I obeyed,—when I carry it out, why should it involve such displeasure on his part, such coldness and aloofness, such a marked departure from the treatment to which I am accustomed, whether I meet him on the few occasions on which he visits the presidio, or on the more numerous ones when I go to Carmel to make my confession?

It has reached such a stage that no matter what art I employ to conceal it, it can be perceived by the people; and this is what concerns me most. No hint has been given me, nor, God be thanked, do I know of any other reason for so notable a change unless it be, impossible as it may seem, my close friendship with the commandant. But this has no connection with the exercise of his military duties. It is a friendship that is disinterested, upright, and proper. It springs from a knowledge of the attractive qualities of the person in question, qualities which have inclined me to be greatly attached to him; yet in this there is nothing inordinate, nothing that did or could savor in the least of suspicion, for everything is pointed to, and directed to, a holy purpose; and for that reason I neither can nor shall be the worse for so close a friendship.

Nor can it be supposed that the cause can be found in the manner in which our good friend, the commanding officer, discharges his professional duties; for in all that pertains to his office he has undergone no change. He is so Christian and so prudent, so discreet and so wise that through the many years of his administration he has never received a reprimand. He has earned, instead, the highest commendation of superiors who were notable for their high character and their disinterested and calm judgment.

In his attitude towards us he is as friendly and kindly as one could desire. He does us the favor of professing that he feels indebted for our friendship, and his conduct is in accordance with this virtuous sentiment. He relinquishes his rights as far as he may, and even avoids [submitting complaints in] writing when one might expect it in regard to certain matters. And what is more, he deliberately avoids communicating certain information which, far from jeopardizing his status, would be strong evidence in favor of his good administration, and would even protect him against the recriminations which, with good reason, could be feared when appeals are made against decisions he has rendered. Certainly an attitude of mind that is heroic.

He is accommodating whenever possible, and only refuses when what is sought is at variance with the instructions of the central government, or with what his prudence, maturity, and long experience dictate. And above all, whether he assents or declines, it is always because of Christian, upright, pure, and religious motives; and I have ample grounds for making this statement.

But, dear and deeply esteemed Father Guardian, there are some who look on this with doubt, suspicion, and mistrust. Many of his actions are held to be in opposition to us. If he fails to give his assent, it is interpreted as a slight, as evidence of animosity, and as a lack of good will. From this springs a kind of antipathy—or perhaps antipathy, instead, has been the source of all the trouble. If this antipathy is not moderated by allowing this noted commandant to have a Father at his side, or not too far away —a Father who would somehow appreciate the straightforwardness he seems to have possessed all his life, and who would be convinced, as he should be, of his good intentions—I foresee that it will be almost impossible for this officer to continue in his command; and from what has been said, it will be impossible for us to escape a feeling of guilt.

Finally, whatever be the cause, it is certain that I am the one who is paying the price. Furthermore, in order to counteract the harm which, as I say, has already begun to threaten, I will not relinquish the task imposed on me, unless I receive orders to the contrary.

When speaking to other persons I shall limit myself merely to expressing the firm conviction I have formed, which is, that Father Junípero is a saintly religious and a most worthy president, and that Don Fernando is a saintly man and a praiseworthy and indispensable commandant.

Without qualifying this sentiment in any way, I am sending the above information in order to carry out the injunction you imposed, and deemed it proper to impose, on me. And if it is my lot to continue in the role of chaplain, I humbly beg that it be to none other than Don Fernando, and under no other circumstances than with Father Amurrió as companion. Even this temporary appointment I would find it impossible to endure without a priestly companion, if it had not been demanded by so urgent a necessity.

It has just happened that as a result of certain correspondence, Father Palou was successful in his efforts to have the two superiors hold a lengthy conference so that in future they will treat one another with more trust and harmony.

On the twenty-seventh of last month the packet boat *San Carlos* set sail with a good wind to reconnoiter the port of San Francisco. There, for two or three days ten soldiers will be detailed to guard the ship in the operations that may be necessary for the exact carrying out of the objective in mind. The Reverend Fathers Palou and Peña have decided to accompany the convoy. What their purpose is, I do not know.

If you can let me have a small sundial, and if you can spare a copy of the *Doctrina* by Cantero, I shall appreciate it very much. And if, in view of what I have already said in my previous letters and what I have added in this, it should appear desirable to Your Reverence to recall me to the college, it will be a decision that will be most pleasing to me.

May God Our Lord keep Your Reverence many years in His holy grace.

Presidio of San Carlos of Monterey,
August 3, 1775.

[1] Lasuén cannot have forgotten that seven years before, in order to procure supplies for the expedition to Upper California, Rivera had to some extent despoiled his impoverished Mission of San Borja in Lower California. (Lasuén to Gálvez, December 20, 1768, *supra*). Possibly Lasuén's personal interest in the success of the expedition, and his respect for Gálvez, account for the absence of any recrimination.

[2] Juan José de Echeveste was a capable and trusted official of the viceregal court in Mexico. He was often consulted in regard to California problems, and was largely instrumental in drawing up the first *reglamento*, or body of ordinances, for California.

[3] The story of the impounding of the supplies at Velicatá is long and involved. See Zephyrin Engelhardt, *The Missions and Missionaries of California* (Santa Barbara, 1929), I, chaps. xiv-xvi.

[4] Fray José Antonio Murgía was born in the Basque country on December 10, 1715, became a member of the College of San Fernando, was ordained in 1744, labored in the Sierra Gorda missions for many years, served in Lower California, was founder of Santa Clara Mission, and died there in 1784.

14. To Fray Francisco Pangua

His Excellency the Viceroy has written to the Reverend Father President and to my friend the Señor Commandant, informing both of them that it was his earnest desire that steps should be taken without delay for the establishing of four missions in the places designated by the President, and that for this purpose these two superiors should come to an agreement on a common policy and should take steps to carry it out as far as possible, without, however, unduly weakening the garrison needed at the presidios and the military guards at the old missions.

With this in mind, Don Fernando went down to Carmel; but as nothing was achieved at that meeting, the Reverend Father President and Fray Murgía came up to this fort on the twelfth of this month.

The Fathers proposed the establishment of a mission in honor of St. Bonaventure at the entrance to the Channel as the most important beginning. The captain opposed this, on the ground that such a mission would require more than six men as a military guard, for, as he went on to say, he had received instructions not to exceed that number either in the missions already built, or in those to be built at the port of San Francisco. To this the Father President took exception, stating that he had received a letter from the Viceroy, written in his own hand, in which, as the Fathers interpreted it, he set the limits at thirteen. (In this he was mistaken, for the handwriting was very poor, and when studied closely did not yield the figure thirteen as the limit for the garrison or for the armed guard.)

"My orders are for six," said the captain commandant. And he continued to insist on this throughout a great part of the session, repeating the same words whenever occasion called for it.

The President became so indignant at this that he raised his voice and banged the table saying, "There is no such order!"

"There is," said Don Fernando in a quiet tone.

"There is not!", the Father shouted back.

And so they continued for some time with "There is!" and "There is not!" until the Father President put an end to it by remarking that such an exchange could keep up all night.[1]

The señor commandant relaxed for a while, and then rising, produced two letters from the Viceroy. In them there was a clear statement of the order limiting the number of men to six—the order [the officer] had quoted so often. Then he expressed himself deeply hurt that there should be so little confidence in his judgment and experience, and that anyone should think that he was concocting orders just to have an excuse for opposing, and a chance to avoid co-operating.

Because of the serious clash of opinion that had arisen, there was no further progress in the discussion that day. The Fathers stayed at the presidio overnight, and on the following morning it was decided to found the Mission of San Juan Capistrano between San Diego and San Gabriel; and at the same meeting, and there and then, the Reverend Father President assigned me to it. It is in every respect the place for which I have felt the least attraction; and, thanks be to God, for that very reason I find the greatest satisfaction in going there.

With God's help, I shall be on my way there in three days. I shall be joined by Fray Ammurió who is the other Father assigned to the establishing of it. We shall undertake the journey and the task assigned us. May God be with us to be our helper. Amen.

Having come to this settlement of Monterey for the purpose which I explained in my letter to Your Reverence of the third of this month, I am saddened by the thought that the captain will be keenly disappointed because of the news I have imparted, and also because in the assignment given me there was no reference, and no consideration accorded, to his repeated request that I should be given as a companion to assist him in this presidio. He is now submitting his resignation in forceable terms.

I must add that in the light of certain events of the past few days, and of many others that the Fathers have told me, one cannot now attribute to the reverend superiors any lack of harmony or mutual understanding with the captain commandant; and I would not now write on this subject what I wrote in my letter of the third of this month. I would not now mail such a letter, or at least I would erase whatever referred to this particular point, if the mail had not already been dispatched. But it will arrive with this letter, and so can be interpreted in the light of it.

I now see clearly that the sour looks, the coldness, and the indifference on the part of others, which I spoke of as my lot when I last wrote, are due to this, that the Fathers observed that I was deeply devoted to one who had been causing them much displeasure. I was unaware of this; for my warm friendship for the officer has nothing, and will have nothing, to do with either the office he holds or the emoluments within his power.

And this does not, of course, mean that I alter in any way my conviction that my friend is a very necessary and indispensable officer, and that in deference to him some compromise should be sought and arranged.

I wish Your Reverence all happiness, and humbly beg your pious blessing for the happy outcome of the task so recently entrusted to me. I have already made a beginning, for I have taken steps to obtain the implements we shall need.

May Our Lord God keep Your Reverence for many years in His holy grace.

Presidio of Monterey,
August 17, 1775.

[1] For an account of the incident by the president, Fray Junípero Serra, see Tibesar, *op. cit.,* II, 385-395.

15. To José Francisco de Ortega[1]

I have been thinking about the new attitude that has arisen among the soldiers of your presidio with regard to the foundation we have been contemplating. I have had in mind the repugnance which they have shown towards building the house for the Fathers, or towards working on it, and their assertion that they have their own reasons for this— reasons which they will explain whenever and wherever they are asked. Ignoring whether such actions were just or unjust, the thought came to me and to my companion Fray Gregorio [Amurrió] that those who learn about this later development may suspect that the two of us have given some reason for it. We are the ones assigned as ministers to that mission whose construction stirred up the trouble mentioned, and we, as a consequence, are the ones for whom that house would be built on which they, for reasons of their own, do not wish to work.

In this department we have had no connection with the soldiers until after we received our assignment when some of them were appointed to be our escort from Monterey to San Diego, and from that time on our status was that of supernumeraries. It seems to me that we gave no grounds for offense on the way; and on the other hand we are satisfied that we did them what favors we could, as you yourself can testify for you accompanied us. I wish to know if they have some grievance against the two of us, and if so, if they will speak to us about it.

Therefore I beg you, in confidence and in all earnestness, to do what you conveniently can to relieve us of this doubt, or more properly this anxiety, for this is what it amounts to, this surmise that we could be suspected of being the cause of such an attitude, or that we could be connected with it.

I am awaiting this favor from Your Honor, and I shall always recall it, and everything else with it, as an additional motive for being grateful.

October 6, 1775.

[1] José Francisco de Ortega accompanied Portolá to California in 1769. He had a distinguished record as officer in charge of different presidios; he was for a long period associated with the Presidio of Santa Barbara, and was the founder of a distinguished family.

This letter of Lasuén is in the handwriting of Ortega, and is quoted by him in a letter he sent to Lasuén on October 7, 1775. He assigns October 6, 1775 as the date of Lasuén's letter.

16. To Fray Juan Prestamero

I received your letter dated January 30 of last year and the enclosure that accompanied it; and I offer my sincere thanks for your interest and deep affection.

We have experienced all the labor that goes with the selection of a site for a mission and all the happiness that can come when a foundation is made in a good location. And ours was a good location near the stream *La Quema* and three-quarters of a league from the Camino Real [1] in the direction of the coast. And then we found ourselves obliged to give up the enterprise, abandon the site, and withdraw to this presidio because of the dreadful and tragic event that took place in San Diego Mission on the fifth of last December, around three in the morning.[2]

We had just completed seven or eight days of work in that beautiful place. We had erected the mission cross, enclosed a spacious corral, mapped out the building, dug the holes in which to insert the poles, transported the lumber, and gathered a large quantity of tule.[3]

Since we lacked sufficient mules to withdraw with all our equipment, we buried the bells and two metates there.

I am sending minute and detailed accounts of everything to the Reverend Father Guardian, and he will acquaint you with the contents.

Here we were full of anxieties and forebodings until the arrival of Don Fernando who unexpectedly joined forces with Señor Anza at San Gabriel[4] and reached the presidio on the eleventh of this month.

Both have weighed the matter very carefully and have come to the conclusion that there should be no thought of re-establishing this mission at its original site where it was destroyed, that there should be no further construction of the mission just begun at San Juan Capistrano, and that perhaps at this time we should not even proceed with the foundations for San Francisco, pending new instructions from His Excellency the Viceroy.

Everything will have to suffer considerable delay. Consequently, I am applying to the Reverend Father Guardian for permission to return to the college, in case it should prove true that I am not to accompany Don Fernando (and this may quite possibly happen, if one takes into account my present experiences with the Reverend Father President). And even if the outcome should be in accordance with my wishes, I would still ask for permission to return to the college so that I could make use of it in case certain possible contingencies should arise.

This being so, it may be prudent for you to reflect on the decision you have to make;[5] for I assure you that from the day I arrived at Monterey up to the present, I have suffered more than in all the other years which I have devoted to the missions.

I sent the Reverend Father President my journal in which I had recorded all that I had observed and all that had taken place when we were seeking a site for the new mission, its foundation, etc.; but I have not had an acknowledgment of it. He did write, however, to Fray

Fuster,[6] and in that letter he implied that Fray Gregorio and I are to be here merely as guests, until such time as we can resume work on the mission we have begun. For this reason we have the status neither of ministers nor of supernumeraries, and both the Reverend Father Minister and we are in complete agreement with this arrangement.

You should already have received the books and the leather-bound chest which were sent aboard *El Principe* in charge of Reverend Father Usón. An inventory was made of the remaining small items, and they were assigned to San Juan Capistrano Mission; and by order of the Reverend Father President the animals also were included. The cot and bed-screen are being used by the Reverend Father Peña.

As a preparation for whatever may happen (and may it be what is most pleasing to God), I shall be grateful if you will look for a perpetual calendar, one that is recent and detailed, and either bring it or send it to me.

Señor Anza has it in mind to go to Monterey in the early part of next month. And since he has the sealed letters (which you know about) for the Reverend Father President we have no way of knowing the contents until he returns. I shall then send you full information so that you may guide yourself accordingly. At that time, too, if God wills, I shall send a letter with the Lieutenant Colonel for forwarding to our homeland.

Please give my regards to Father Arenaza and my other countrymen; and my best wishes, too, to the Reverend Father Mathe—I have already sent him two letters without getting any reply—and to all my other friends.

And last of all, will you kindly procure a little sundial[7] for me, any kind you like; and either bring or send it to me.

May Our Lord keep you many years in His holy grace.

San Diego,
January 28, 1776.

---

[1] The King's Highway. It corresponds, in the main, with the modern U. S. Highway 101 in California. For a description of its exact location in the days of Lasuén, see Geiger, *Life and Times*, I, 309-320.

[2] The destruction of the mission at the hands of the Indians. For the story, see Tibesar, *op. cit.*, II, 401-407; 449-458.

[3] For a description of the manner in which the first temporary buildings at a mission site were constructed, see the very informative book by the late Mrs. Edith Buckland Webb, *op. cit.*, pp. 100-121.

[4] Anza had just arrived by the inland, or Colorado, route which had just been opened. He was at the head of troops and colonists bound for San Francisco.

[5] Prestamero, who had been in ill health, had returned to San Fernando in 1774. Lasuén implies that Prestamero was contemplating a return to the missions of California.

[6] Fray Vicente Fuster was a native of Aragon, Spain, where he was born in 1742. He arrived at San Fernando College in 1770. For a few years he was attached to the

Santa María and San Fernando missions in Lower California, not far from Lasuén's Mission of San Borja. He was assistant to Lasuén at San Diego from 1775 to 1777. He spent the last ten years of his life at Mission San Juan Capistrano, where he died on October 21, 1800, and is buried.

7 Clocks, even alarm clocks, are frequently mentioned among the *memorias*, or requisitions for the missions. Occasionally, as here, there is a request for a sundial. This, no doubt, was a concession to the ways of the Indians, children of the sun and accustomed to regulating their day by the position of the sun. At San Antonio Mission may be seen a reproduction of a mission sundial made according to sketches supplied by the distinguished student of early California, the late Mrs. Webb. Not only are the hours of the day indicated, but also the various duties of the Indians for each particular hour. According to the sundial, at 8:00 A.M. the Indians departed for the fields; at 11:00 lunch was served; and at 1:00 P.M. they enjoyed a siesta, relaxing in the shade of a tree. At 5:00 P.M. there was prayer, and the day's work ended. A reproduction of such a sundial may be found in Webb, *op. cit.*, p. 31.

17. To Fray Francisco Pangua

I have carried out as required the instructions of the Father President without giving way to the feeling of dejection about which I wrote to Your Reverence in my preceding letter. And although I have done so, I still repeat my former request that you do me the favor of sending me permission to return to the college.

I would not withdraw from this undertaking did I not foresee, from the failure of my superiors to appoint me, that I am unsuitable for this kind of work.

When I left Monterey for my mission, the majority of the missionaries told me that they would not undertake such a project with such inadequate supplies and equipment. But I resolved to do what Your Reverence can read in the enclosed portion of the diary that I am sending, because I did not wish it to be said (as it has been said with less cause) that I preferred to stay with Don Fernando rather than take up my appointed duties, and because I assumed that the letters of recommendation addressed to the missions, especially those of San Diego, San Gabriel, and the one to be named San Buenaventura, would be broad enough to cover the project, I decided on a plan which you will read about in the portion of the diary I am sending you.

My dear confrere, Fray Gregorio, will inform Your Reverence about the high hopes these letters of recommendation produced. And if I am not mistaken, I think you can deduce from this that a mission incurs a liability under the present administration if it becomes known that I am the founder or administrator of it.

I am not implying in the least that I consider myself treated unjustly. On the contrary, such evidence makes me recognize my uselessness. And for that reason I should like to renew my request for permission [to retire].

Furthermore, if there is no thought of rebuilding this mission, and it is taken for granted that the two at San Francisco may be suspended, what is there I can look forward to but more time wasted, over and above the two years that I have already spent without employment?

Here in San Diego there is but one minister, and the Father President in a letter to Father Fray Vicente assumed that Father Fray Gregorio and I are merely guests waiting for a chance to resume the building of the mission we had started. Your Reverence can see how long we may have to wait before that hope is realized.

My staunch friend Don Fernando has forwarded me a letter he received from Father Lector Verger, in which he informs him that Your Reverence has already decided that I am to go with His Worship. If this is so, provided the Reverend Father President gives his approval, it will afford me great pleasure to do so. But in that case, I shall be grateful if Your Reverence will order that all necessary steps be taken to achieve the objective in mind [the chaplaincy] for it is the reward of friendship. But even in this case I still would appreciate it if the permission [to return] were sent. But I assure you that I will not use it without good reason, and subject, too, to any restrictions which Your Reverence may see fit to add.

Because of the uncertainty in my mind as to whether the Reverend Father President may modify what Your Reverence may have decided, for motives that seem adequate to him, I have decided to send a letter with Don Juan Bautista de Anza, for he plans to leave for Monterey around the beginning of next month.[1] In that letter I shall ask for permission to return to the college, provided Your Reverence does not dispose otherwise in letters which the above-named gentleman is bringing.

Should Your Reverence wish to see the remainder of the diary,[2] I shall be happy to send it at the first opportunity, if requested.

San Diego,
January 30, 1776.

[Marginal note:] In regard to the little bottle of wine which they gave us at San Gabriel for use at San Juan Capistrano, all that we have left is wine enough for just one Mass on feast days.

[1] Anza was still in San Diego assisting Rivera to pacify the turbulent Indians who had sacked the mission the preceding November. He left for Monterey on February 9, reaching San Gabriel Mission on February 12. By reason of some desertions from the camp there he was unable to resume the march to Monterey until February 25. See Herbert Eugene Bolton (ed.), *Anza's California Expeditions* (Berkeley, 1930), II, 99-107.
[2] The entire diary is missing.

18. To Fray Francisco Pangua

I received Your Reverence's letter of February 6 of last year, enclosing a document in which I am instructed to accompany Captain Commandant Don Fernando de Rivera y Moncada wherever that gentleman may reside within the limits of his command.

With all my heart I shall obey, and I shall strive so to acquit myself that the college may derive satisfaction from what I do, and from the way in which I do it.

The circumstances in which I received this particular order were in keeping with what has been my lot in this respect; that is, the assignments given me since (against my will) I left the college have not, as a rule, brought me any pleasure, satisfaction, or peace of soul, save what obedience affords. It so happens that your last letter reached me just a few days after the Indian, Carlos,[1] under cover of law and forcibly had been removed from the church. Because of this there followed a period of deep resentment which I believe Your Reverence will have shared already. When Don Fernando returned from Monterey, there were some moments of embarrassment, for it was necessary to discuss the return of the Indian who had sought sanctuary, as a prerequisite for absolution from the censure. I said to him what I judged was appropriate, and, thanks be to God, the matter has been brought to a happy and satisfactory conclusion.

Now I have finally come to understand why the attitude of my distinguished friend seems to many people so inflexible. It is due to the way in which he understands the duties of his office. This gives him no latitude, hems him in, and allows him no leeway for conventional courtesies, amenities, and compliments such as others know how to engage in without detriment to their office.

Despite all this, he has praiseworthy principles which render him an officer particularly well-fitted for work among new reductions. He is a man deeply endowed with singleness of heart and good intentions; but he is rather slow to believe that those who deal with him officially, and must work with him, are endowed with these same estimable qualities. This gives rise to an overweening distrust which does not make it easy for him to accept the kind of advice which would enable him to follow a middle course, which would be the prudent and discreet way.

With this in mind, and in compliance with the instructions of your Reverence, I shall be very happy to accompany him and to assist wherever he takes up residence, trusting in God that all may redound to the Glory of His Divine Majesty, to the good of my soul, and of all others who stand in need of help.

I have not had an opportunity to write as fully as Your Reverence has requested, and I have been unable to do so because I have been constantly preoccupied with the very serious incidents with which, I have no doubt, Your Reverence is in part familiar. To these I have had to devote an incredible amount of attention and anxious care, sometimes writing, sometimes dictating, sometimes moderating hot tempers, and sometimes even openly opposing certain decisions of the commandant, but always keeping mind the honor of Holy Church, and of the Order, the good name of the college, and the cause of peace.

I hope that the uprightness of these motives, and the urgency and need of intervening in such difficult affairs, despite my shortcomings, will win pardon and sanction for whatever mistake or indiscretion may be found in the manner in which I made use of these means.

I know that Father Fray Vicente will give Your Reverence a detailed report of what has happened. This, together with what Lieutenant Colonel Don Juan de Anza has reported, or will report, will make Your Reverence acquainted with what is transpiring. Still, I can imagine it is not easy to get a complete and adequate understanding of the true state of affairs that one can give to each item the weight and consideration it deserves, without first hearing in person from some Father who is well acquainted with the events. What a pleasure it would be if Your Reverence would appoint me the companion to the Father who might be selected for that purpose, if I had also the permission, which I have so often sought, to retire to the college. Your Reverence will decide what is deemed best, and I will carry it out with the same deference which I always show.

May Our Lord God keep Your Reverence for many years in His holy grace.

San Diego,
May 22, 1776.

[1] Carlos, an Indian, had claimed the "right of sanctuary," a right recognized by Spanish law. Rivera, for reasons that seemed adequate to him, forcibly removed him from the church, and for so doing was formally excommunicated. For an account of the event, see Tibesar, *op. cit.*, III, 3-7, and 443, n. 1. For a critical estimate of the incident, see Geiger, *Life and Times*, II, 88-99.

19. To Fray Francisco Pangua

With the coming of the packet boat *San Antonio* which anchored in this port on the eleventh of last July, I received your letter dated the thirteenth of last December. Under the impression that I was still in charge of the new Mission of San Juan Capistrano, Your Reverence and the venerable council leave it to my choice either to continue in the appointment I was then presumed to have, or to return to the one given me previously. Now, in regard to the mission I had already begun, I have already written to Your Reverence regarding what happened. I am under obligation to observe the patent you sent me, for I regard it as most in accord with your will and that of the venerable council. And I wish to carry it out even at the cost of personal sacrifice in order to serve the holy college as best I can.

No sooner had I begun to feel the need of Don Fernando's help, than there arose in me the suspicion that he had changed very much from the time when he needed me. I gave intimations of this in letters which I sent Your Reverence from Monterey; but by this time I am entirely disillusioned, because what I had vaguely suspected is now stark reality; and the entire community of the holy college should be made aware of it, for it is so obvious to everyone of its members here that nobody has the least doubt about it.

In view of his words and his attitude in times past, I formed so high an opinion of that gentleman that I felt extraordinarily devoted and attracted to him; but when I see his actions and behavior at the present time, I must say that I have been deceived. For neither I, nor any Father as an individual, nor all of us as a whole, have received more consideration from this individual than we would reasonably expect from one who had never known us; and we have to be as much on our guard against him as against our worst enemy.

I should add that I did not change my mind easily, and that I was slower in doing so than I should have been, for I was hoping to come upon new grounds for my original opinion. Instead, I received more shocks than were necessary in order to disillusion me.

I have referred to some of these when writing to Your Reverence. The Reverend Father President has given many instances, and in due time will cite plenty additional items of a similar nature. From all of these, in addition to inferring the truth in the matter, Your Reverence will be most distressed by the conclusion that under such a military leader there is no hope whatever for even the slightest progress in our conflict with paganism.

For this reason, and because it is fourteen or fifteen years since at the request of my superior I left the college; and furthermore, since it is three years since I have had a permanent appointment, and in the present circumstances I have no hope of one after this present one runs out, as it probably will when there is a change of command (a change which the captain commandant is awaiting, and which he has sought as well as deserved), I humbly beg Your Reverence and the Reverend Fathers of the council that you grant me permission to retire to the college. Meanwhile, I shall continue to carry out the orders of Your Reverence and of the venerable council.

The provisions intended for Father Fray Gregorio and for me which were to have arrived on the packet boat *San Carlos,* as Your Reverence informs me, have been detained at San Blas on the instructions of the overseer of supplies. The same has happened to most of what belonged to the northern missions and to everything intended for the missionaries there. For this reason the Reverend Father President graciously determined that I may appropriate what I need from what was sent to the supernumerary of this mission, and that Father Fray Gregorio may use what pertained to the late Father Fray Luis.[1]

The warehouse-keeper of the Royal Presidio of San Diego, Don Rafael de Pedro y Gil, a native of the city of Daroca in Aragon, has earnestly begged me to ask Your Reverence for a favor in behalf of himself and his wife, Doña Josefa de Chavira y Lerma, a native of Tepic. The favor they ask is a Letter of Affiliation with the holy college. I was very favorably impressed by the attitude of the gentleman when we were face to face with great reverses and difficulties, and I have seen him give proof of the nobility of his character and of his deep and warm affection for the Franciscan Order.[2] He often attributes the same sentiments to his parents and grandparents, and certainly his own actions and conduct are the clearest proof of it.

He helps the missions and the Fathers to the best of his ability, and, in short, I consider him worthy to share in this privilege to the fullest extent.

So I humbly ask Your Reverence to confer this upon him and to send me, at the earliest opportunity, the Letter in question so that I may have the happiness of granting him this favor. We shall all be the gainers from this proof of our religious gratitude.

I am enclosing unsealed letters that are destined for Spain. Will Your Reverence kindly enclose them in the same envelope as the previous ones, or forward them under whatever cover you deem best to ensure their delivery.

We who reside at San Diego have an excuse for being so troublesome and so insistent, and may Your Reverence pardon us, for the love of God, whom I beseech and entreat to grant Your Reverence patience, and to keep you for many years in His holy grace.

San Diego,
September 13, 1776.

---

[1] Fray Luis Jayme, the missionary who was killed by the Indians when they attacked the San Diego Mission the preceding November.
[2] Literally, the "apostolic habit" (*la apostolica ropa*).

20. To Fray Francisco Pangua

Under date of September 13, of this year I disclosed to Your Reverence my sentiments regarding what was going on at that time. At the present moment, however, although my feelings have not definitely changed, many circumstances have forced me to suspend judgment.

On many occasions when Don Fernando thought (as he told me) of proceeding to Monterey, he spoke of his journey without any connection or reference to the fact that I was assigned there as a favor to him. On one occasion I asked him to advise me in good time, for he had asked me if I had mules, and when I replied that I had only those intended for San Juan Capistrano, he answered in his usual style: "Well, won't they be heard from when they have to take to the road."

He has shown the same lack of fellowship and unity with us in regard to the living allowance which the Reverend Father President, through force of necessity, had to request for us, the Fathers who are to be at the presidio. This was after I had remonstrated with him on the point, and he had raised a thousand objections to granting it, thereby causing no little extra strain on our relations.

Because of these and other incidents I am led to the conclusion that peace and harmony and friendly relations are unattainable in regard to him, whether on the part of good Father President or any other missionary, despite the fact that this is what Your Reverence and the venerable council could expect by reason of my assignment to this gentleman. However, in view of the latest happenings, and the instructions that have arrived from His Excellency the Viceroy, in which (it would seem) some reprimands reached him, it seems to me that the above objectives are attainable, even though it be with difficulty.

I have already spoken to him with the freedom of a spiritual guide. I have explained to him what true gratitude consists in, and how fitting it is that he should give evidence of it to the College of San Fernando and the members of it. I pointed out that Your Reverence and the venerable council had yielded to his request that I be assigned to his residence in order to keep him company, and that in that case I would be in a position to contribute to the good of all the missions, and to the attainment of the objectives mentioned. In the meantime he has no intention of carrying out these projects in accordance with this agreement, or at least he does not give the matter the consideration it deserves in view of the purposes stated above. Nor can I bring about what I am ordered, since by this time this latter [relationship] is not what the college had in mind.

I mentioned in detail some incidents which caused grave concern to the Reverend Father President and the other missionaries; and finally he told me that he had always had very cordial relations with Fathers and religious, and that he appreciated being on terms of harmony and friendship with them. To this I replied, sincerely and calmly, that our greatest regret was that this was true of his relations with the Jesuit Fathers, while the opposite was true regarding ourselves. And I assured him that he himself would realize this if he would recall what his conduct and attitude towards the friars had been, for this had begun to shock those who had observed how different had been his bearing towards the members of the Society [of Jesus]. I urged him to make his standard of conduct in the future the same ancient and very Christian maxim, for it is so important for the success of the missions here. I urged him to keep clearly in mind that the Reverend Father President and all the Fathers, and the entire college, far from having placed the slightest obstacle in the way, were striving, every one of us, by every means possible and imaginable, to co-operate.

Here the matter rests; and I am unable at present to reach a definite judgment in regard to what has taken place, and what may happen.

To do what is most fitting and most in accord with the views of Your Reverence and the venerable council is all that I wish; and with the concurrence of the Reverend Father President I shall try to carry it out. And for this reason I humbly ask the blessing of Your Reverence on what shall be decided on; and I also ask it for myself, and with it the permission I have so often sought to return to the college. Yet, although I have urged this plea at different times, sincerely and earnestly, I accept any other decision that appears more fitting to Your Reverence before God.

I have already notified Your Reverence regarding the restlessness and almost mutiny of the soldiers of this presidio, for they objected to working on the buildings and other things pertaining to the mission now under construction at San Juan Capistrano. This assignment was given them by Lieutenant Ortega, for he inferred from the instruction sent him by his commandant regarding this enterprise that such was the will of that officer.

Various steps were taken in order to appease them, including the formidable one (but an effective and necessary one, as it transpired) of training guns on them and bringing them to bear on the barracks; and by this means it was possible to seize the ringleaders.

The action on the part of the soldiers received something more than a negative approval from their captain, for he took no steps to press any charges against them; he took part in a celebration over what they had done. But as for the conduct of the lieutenant, in the judgment of the commandant this deserved a private censure. Judging by what we have heard, the matter was regarded quite differently at the Court [in Mexico]. In case Your Reverence should wish to know the reason why the soldiers began to declare themselves in favor of this resistance, I am sending you a copy of a letter of mine addressed to the lieutenant on that occasion, and of his reply.

From it Your Reverence will learn that the disaffection of these forces, degrading and foolhardy as it was, had its origin in a reproach that was just, made opportunely, and delivered as delicately as is possible for me. In fact, it could not have been more kind or restrained if the mule[1] in question had been his own. The way in which they insist on maintaining their unreasonable attitude is most ridiculous, for, recalling after a long interval some cause for displeasure, they gave as an excuse for this grave offense a reprimand given by the Fathers, one that was just, merited, and very moderate. And although this reprimand was given, the great favors which they had been enjoying until then continued as before. In short, they are like leopards: The more you do for them, the worse they get.[2]

In the letter mentioned it can be clearly seen that the soldier, Ignacio Vallejo, is the principal cause of the trouble, and we are informed that the Viceroy, without naming him, has ordered him to be removed or dismissed.

We now know that they are putting on board another who was arrested at that time for a forced statement he made but later withdrew. It is suspected that this is in accordance with the orders of His Excellency, for he is accused of being the leader of the mutiny.

This man Vallejo[3] is held in high regard by the commandant and is the recipient of favors from him to the same degree that he is detrimental to the country, for he is a braggart, and is completely lacking in obedience.

Good Father President has ordered me to submit this information to Your Reverence for consideration, so that you might make determined efforts to remedy this grave situation.

May God Our Lord keep Your Reverence many years in His holy grace.

San Diego,
October 7, 1776.

---

[1] On October 6, 1775, Lasuén wrote to José Ortega to ascertain the cause of the unfriendliness on the part of the soldiers (Letters 15, *supra*). Ortega could find no cause for grievance at first; then he found one soldier, Rafael Márquez, who professed to have a grievance in regard to a mule that had been requisitioned—but, as further questioning revealed, the mule was the property of San Juan Capistrano Mission.

[2] Lasuén gives the quotation in Latin: *quibus cum benefeceris peiores fiunt.*

[3] Ignacio Vallejo (1774-1831) was born in Jalisco, Mexico, of Spanish descent. He is described by Bancroft as a "coarse-grained man . . . haughty in manner, insubordinate and unmanageable as a soldier, and often in trouble with his superiors." Bancroft, *op. cit.*, V, 756.

2 1. To Fray Junípero Serra

I wish Your Reverence and all the good Fathers with you, health and every happiness, and to all of you I send regards.

Nothing of special interest occurred during my trip with the caballero, beyond the fact that I shared with him a meal of rice and jerked meat which I had obtained from the mission for my own use.

Once I told him, half in jest and half in earnest, that I had almost made up my mind to stay in San Diego, because the manner in which he had planned the trip without consulting me made me suspect that perhaps he had not accepted the favor the college had conferred on him, for in that case I would not feel bound by such an obligation. He answered me in the same vein, saying that this was so far from being the case that if that stage were ever reached he would prefer to be a mail-carrier in the Californias.[1] Having said this, he changed the conversation.

There and then I spoke to him in all seriousness about the obligation under which he was placed by the concession extended to him by the college to make all needed provision for my transportation and accommodation. Of course, I knew quite well that Your Reverence and all the Fathers, at the slightest hint, would give me any support that I might need. But in reality it would and did cause me a certain amount of uneasiness to have to trouble them about such a matter, when it was really a matter that should concern him.

His reply was that he would ask the Fathers here to supply all the mules that were needed for my baggage, because they had offered him as many mules as he might need.

The answer was quite unexpected; and keeping in mind what we had just discussed, I feared that new misunderstandings would arise when we tried to put it into effect. So I told him that, since he was on his way to San Francisco and some kind of residence was under construction for me at Monterey, I would have to find accommodation elsewhere, and that I might as well stay here. He proposed Mission Carmel as a more suitable place in the circumstances; but the sudden illness of Father Sánchez served me as a pretext and excuse for not proceeding further, for the Father was eager to begin taking treatments as soon as possible, beginning with a laxative.

I beg Your Reverence, for the love of God, to remember me in your Masses and prayers so that His Most Holy Majesty may grant me what is most fitting for His honor and glory, and the good of my soul. And I pray that He may keep Your Reverence for many years in His holy grace.

San Gabriel Mission,
October 21, 1776.

As regards the suspicion arising because of the departure by boat of Juan de Ortega, there is no ground for it. It is sufficiently clear to me, from casual conversation, that the reasons are very different from those that were rumored, although there was some foundation for them.

[1] The translation is admittedly obscure. The following is the text as given by Lasuén: me respondio en el mismo tono, que estaba tan lejos de esto, que luego al punto en este caso hubiera hecho correo por Californias, y dicho esto mudo de conversacion.

The Crown & the Cross

III
Missionary at San Diego

These letters were written from California's old-est mission, San Diego, where Lasuén was in charge from midsummer 1777 until late in the year 1785. They reveal how impoverished was the mission and how seemingly insurmountable the obstacles to its progress. Yet, in a subsequent volume of this series the Annual Reports from San Diego will demonstrate how eminently successful Lasuén really was.

22. To Felipe de Neve

N JANUARY 21 OF THIS YEAR 1779 WE RE-ceived an official letter from Your Lordship dated December 22 of last year. In it it is deemed proper that the provisions of the laws of the kingdom be observed and executed in the old missions established in these parts; and you request and charge us, beginning with the current year of 1779, to make due arrangements so that the natives of this Mission of San Diego may proceed to the election of two alcaldes and two regidores[1] from among those residing in it. It is further ordered that all this is to be carried out in accordance with the system under which elections are held in Spanish and Indian pueblos, in the presence of the parish priests, as provided by these laws. After the holding of the elections—and from now on they must be held each year—those who are elected must present certificates of their election at the Presidio of San Diego. There they will be installed in their office in the name of the King by Don Francisco de Ortega, whom Your Lordship has appointed as lieutenant governor so that he may exercise royal jurisdiction in this area. He will likewise give them the necessary certificates for exercising the authority which they shall enjoy, and which will be explained in the same certificates.

We respect Your Lordship's decision; but we cannot proceed to carry it out without first receiving instructions from the Father President without whose sanction, as we have been advised by the College of San Fernando, we are not to introduce in the management of the mission any modification whatever in the system and method in which its missionaries have been trained.

This is the reason why the above-mentioned college maintains a President of the Missions near the residence of the commanding officer of them, so that through him as intermediary, and with the benefit of his experience, new provisions of the secular officer in charge may be passed on to the ministers of the missions. And it is evident to us that when Your Lordship despatched from Monterey the above instructions the Father President was still in Carmel. And since we have had no letter from him, the lack of such a letter constrains us from putting this into execution, leaving out of consideration any doubt we might have regarding the aptness of this new instruction for those under our charge in San Diego Mission.

The very terms in which Your Lordship issues the decree force us to conclude that here we are dealing with a notable innovation. What the laws envisage are elections which take place in the presence of the parish priests, and where there are no parish priests, by inference, there are no elections.

We, Sir, are not parish priests; we are apostolic missionaries bound by papal bulls to depart from the missions as soon as we recognize that the neophytes, whom we have brought together by our missionary efforts, are sufficiently instructed in the divine law, and sufficiently competent to care for the economic welfare of their families and for the political government of their pueblos. When that stage is reached, they may then come under the jurisdiction of the parish priests sent by the bishops to whose care they are to be entrusted. As for us, we then return to our college; or we look for other Indians to take under instruction, beginning at their level of intelligence and continuing the training until they can exercise average discretion. And we know that if we were to appropriate the name of parish priests, even inadvertently, we would draw down on ourselves a severe rebuke from our college. And we would fear lest, by interfering in matters that pertain to the rights of parish priests but which do not extend to missionaries, we would be excluding ourselves from cherished membership in the college.

We know that Your Lordship would not have us incur so sad a privation. And it must of necessity be assumed that we would not wish anyone to be more zealous than our Indian converts in rendering to His Catholic Majesty the gratitude they owe him, and to the judges and officials appointed by His Majesty the corresponding deference. Hence, we humbly beg Your Lordship to be so kind as to suspend your ruling until such time as we are notified by our Father President. Only thus shall we be free from the misgivings we have noted above, based as they are on our own constant and minute observation of the status of these Indians; for it is only by sacrificing and accommodating ourselves as far as we could that we have brought about the present reign of peace, which is as novel as it is welcome. And we shall not mention their manifest incapacity for carrying out the duties which it is sought to entrust to them, nor the inability of the mission, year by year, to support those whom they would elect, for we have to apportion the grain sent to us by San Gabriel Mission among those whom we employ in the more specific types of work, as long as they engage in that work. And on a permanent basis we support the following natives of California: an interpreter, a cook, shepherds and cowboys, the sick, the aged, and

WHERE STUDENT DAYS WERE SPENT
The shrine and college of Aránzazu
as they now appear

the orphans. And if the supply proves inadequate, there will be nothing for them, nor will we be able to maintain (for such is our experience up to the present) this poor apology of a leader whom one half of our scattered Christians are to recognize in turn every eight days,[2] and all this because just now we are denied the ration which the King had been giving us, for by means of it in great measure we took care of all these items just mentioned. And even though other obstacles may be encountered, nevertheless, when the decision is made, we will carry out the instructions with the certainty and satisfaction that, should something transpire that merits reproof, Your Lordship will answer for us that, being well acquainted with all circumstances, you so ordered the matter, and our Reverend Father President, being well acquainted with his duty in the matter, so executed it.

May God Our Lord keep Your Lordship for many years in His holy grace.

San Diego Mission,
January 25, 1779.

[1] The office of alcalde combined many of the functions of magistrate and mayor. A *regidor* had the status of an alderman or councilman.

For a discussion of the institution of such offices among the recent converts, and of the attitude of the pioneer missionaries, see Geiger, *Life and Times*, II, 244-254.

[2] Unlike the other missions, San Diego was so poor that it could accommodate only one half of the Indians during the time they were receiving instructions. The groups rotated periodically, one half at the mission, the other half in their native rancherías.

23. To Fray Francisco Pangua

I am deeply grateful for Your Reverence's letter of January 10, and with all my heart and mind I accept your saintly advice to accept whatever obedience enjoins, so that my coming and my going may please God and conduce to the attainment of His purposes.

If it was not in Your Reverence's power, nor in that of your successor, to issue orders according to your good pleasure, it is but just that a subject should submit himself to the dictates of his superiors when what they order runs counter to his own wishes. I humbly submit, dear Father, and (thanks be to God) I am determined to silence for ever any urge to seek a different assignment. I merely plead, in extenuation of my previous request, that you might recall the high hopes of a favorable answer which my superiors held out.

I am much perturbed that I am having difficulty with the inflections of this dialect, for I cannot grasp its syllables, although I have been here a long time. This is an experience I did not have at the other missions. It may be that there are circumstances peculiar to this mission[1] which are responsible for this difference which is so notable and so obvious. I am not pleased with the interpreters, and I have but little time to devote to study, for I have to devote a great deal of attention to the Christian converts. These latter are quite numerous and are widely scattered. Then, on the part of the Indians, there is no love whatever for anything resembling civilization or rational culture. And worst of all, the duties at the presidio are burdensome and almost insupportable, overcrowded as it is with so many families.

In addition to the Mass on all days of obligation, its requirements distract me greatly from fulfilling my principal obligations. I am convinced that if a chaplain were stationed there my greatest burden would be removed.

Fierce-looking scarecrows (you will say) to frighten a timid soul like Father Lasuén; anyone else when face to face with difficulties that arise at the mission would solve them with dispatch, and then would have both time and courage to overcome difficulties of greater moment. And this, dear Father, is exactly what I tell myself. And it was thoughts like these that inspired my previous petition.

Your Reverence sent me news of the province and other places, and I am grateful for it. But the part that pleased me most was the plan agreed on to have recourse to Señor Gálvez regarding mission affairs. This is very necessary, things being as they are; and it gives a foundation for the hope that results will be favorable.

In these places of seclusion and exile from the civilized world the only news is, that troops are expected by land and sea for the foundation of a mission at the Channel at Santa Barbara.

San Diego Mission,
December 6, 1780.

---

[1] The Indians of San Diego belonged to a family with which the missionaries were not well acquainted. They were related to, and had close ties with, the Indians of Yuma. Despite the fact that San Diego was the site of the first mission, few if any Indians resisted the spread and influence of Christianity more stubbornly than did those of San Diego. There were no converts the first year, and only a hundred in the course of the first five years. Kroeber comments thus: "[The Indians of San Diego are described as] proud, rancorous, boastful, covetous, given to jests and quarrels, passionately devoted to the customs of their fathers, and hard to handle." A. L. Kroeber, *Handbook of the Indians of California* (Washington, D. C., 1925), p. 711.

24. To Father Guardian [Fray Francisco Pangua]

First let me gladly express my obedience, and beg Your Reverence's holy blessing. Then I wish to inform you that the Reverend Father

President has forwarded me the enclosed letter giving me permission to open it, and to add to it a copy of the letter which His Reverence wrote to the Commandant General, all of which I have done.

Because there is so short a time between the mails I cannot write at length; but I must not fail to bring to Your Reverence's notice the great trial through which we are passing.[1] The troops under command of Don Fernando de Rivera, which are on their way to the founding of the mission at the Santa Barbara Channel, are expected at any moment,[2] and the governor has reached San Gabriel Mission already. He arrived there on the eleventh of this month in order to receive them.

Twenty-seven or thirty-seven families, one hundred and thirty-three persons in all, have arrived by sea and are already in Lower California. They are on the point of starting out for these parts with the same objective in mind. And from a letter that I received from Mission San Luis I learn that not one word has been communicated to our good Father President regarding this undertaking.

His Reverence has good reason to doubt if the new foundation may not be a purely secular one, and he is almost persuaded that if a spiritual one is intended, it will be given to some other missionaries. Your Reverence will give this unexpected development the value it deserves and the corresponding attention when the opportune moment arrives.

The mails are already leaving, and there are other points worthy of consideration, but I cannot touch on them. I invoke the aid of our Heavenly Queen and commend our cares and anxieties to her.

May God Our Lord keep Your Reverence for many years in His holy grace.

San Diego Mission,
April 16, 1781.

[1] Among the trials of the missionaries were problems such as these: the desire of the governor to reduce to one the number of missionaries at each mission, his determination to require them to serve as chaplains at the presidios, even without remuneration, and his reluctance to supply them with a military escort even on essential trips through lands largely pagan. The missionaries, however, had grown somewhat accustomed to these problems; but a new one was now emerging. The governor had in mind a new type of mission organization in which control of temporalities and in great measure the training of the Indians would pass from the missionaries to the secular authorities.

[2] Rivera had received orders to go to Sonora and Sinoloa in Mexico to recruit soldiers and settlers as well as to collect supplies. Part of the group so collected was taken to Lower California and made the journey thence by land. The balance, under Rivera, were to come by an exclusively land route, following the trail opened by Anza. This part of the expedition was attacked by Indians at Yuma on July 17 and 18, and many of the party, including Rivera, lost their lives. One result of the disaster was the postponement of the projected mission at the Santa Barbara Channel, San Buenaventura. It was not founded until Easter Sunday, March 31, of the following year, 1782.

25. To Fray Junípero Serra

I have complied with the instructions regarding the contribution which is asked from these Indians of San Diego;[1] and now, in the very form in which Your Reverence asked for it, I am sending the information on the subject you requested, for I am forwarding on this occasion a report on the actual state of this mission, showing all that is good and all that is bad in it. When Your Reverence sees it you can decide what is the best course, and your decision will be our rule of action.

So that it may be possible to proceed in this case and to carry out as well as possible what you order, I should like to state that this mission, like the others, has a group of converts receiving instruction in the midst of countless pagans, and that it tries to bring the natives together so that they may form a pueblo in which, of a certainty, after they have found out by experience what it is to be treated as children of our Catholic King, he can rule them as vassals and should not exempt them from the just contribution demanded; nevertheless, in our opinion, these should be exempted from it owing to the particular circumstances of the case.

The commandant general has expressly indicated three considerations which might constitute a basis for such exemption, namely, barrenness, epidemics, and enemy raids.

Epidemics, God be thanked, we are free from at the moment; but we have had some. And persons from Lower California tell us that we have reason to fear an outbreak of smallpox.[2]

Enemy raids are a threat that is always present, and we still suffer from the setbacks and shortages caused by the one that took place six years ago.

The barrenness of the ground is something that is evident and obvious to everyone. This was made clear to the commandant general in the investigation made in the year 1777 under the direction of Lieutenant Don José Francisco de Ortega.

In it this land is described as very barren, unproductive, lacking in all fruit, without humidity or irrigation; and planting is but a speculation made in the hope that the year will be one of abundant rainfall.

Hence it was proposed that because of the needs of this mission an allowance of one or two hundred fanegas of corn should be made to it in the name of His Majesty the King, and that this should be brought on board the vessels of His Majesty which are employed in the transport of supplies for these presidios.

Your Reverence will clearly recall that this was your own thought and that you urged its execution very forcibly. And when I, who had recently been put in charge of this place, expressed a doubt that it would be carried out, you replied, firmly and resolutely, "If they do not grant me this we shall give up the place."[3]

This shows how barren the region had proved to be from the time it was first settled until then.

The help received from the missions here, especially from that of San Gabriel, and the abundant rains in two out of the last four years, have complicated this action which was as sensible as it was necessary.

We feel, esteemed Father, that there is not to be found in the world an institution with greater needs, and with fewer resources and revenues than our pueblo, and that in this country no greater service is performed for the King than maintaining in the full status of a mission that assignment of San Diego which is so manifestly unsuitable and useless for such an establishment, which receives not even the least help from the government, and which is hampered by having to serve the presidio, thereby saving the royal treasury the salary of a chaplain.

The pagans are very numerous, and the Christians few. Of the latter, the majority are scattered among the hills and beaches, after the pagan fashion. The minority live in settlements like other Christians. The majority are a burden to the community, and the least useful to its welfare. Most of them are content with a loincloth which barely covers their nakedness, and the others wear a blanket of baize or cloth. For neither group is the ration we serve sufficient to satisfy the voracious way of eating in which they were brought up; and none would submit to the slightest discipline if he were denied access to his hunting and fishing; to his mice, snakes, vipers, and insects; to his acorns and other loathsome and unpalatable seeds which are rendered edible only by being soaked in water and cooked over a fire.[4] And there is none among them who knows or uses any other medium of exchange than these coarse and contemptible foodstuffs and other items of a similar nature.

My dear and venerated Father, I conclude by saying with devout sincerity that there is much more to be said, and like a true son of Spain I would like to say it with emphasis. But in circumstances like these it is best to conform to the mind of the sovereign and his representatives. And so we hope that when this essential condition is made clear, whatever is decreed in our behalf, in the light of this true information, may be promptly put into effect.

May God Our Lord keep Your Reverence many years in His holy grace.

San Diego Mission,
January 9, 1782.

[1] This was a war tax. Spain had declared war on England on June 23, 1779. It was

ended by a peace treaty in 1783 under the terms of which Spain was awarded Florida and England the Bahamas. Despite its poverty, San Diego Mission contributed 229 pesos.

[2] During the previous year, 1781, a ship entered the port of Loreto, in Lower California. On board were families from Sonora, some of whom were suffering from small pox. Since no precautions were taken to quarantine them, an epidemic spread quickly through all the towns and missions of the peninsula with very disastrous results. See Sales, *op. cit.*, p. 60.

[3] A possible reading is *puerto*, "port," and Zephyrin Engelhardt in his *San Diego Mission* (San Francisco, 1920), p. 115, so interprets it.

[4] Among the descendents of these Indians at the present day, acorns "soaked in water and cooked over a fire" are still a favorite dish, and the writer can testify that as the Indians serve it, it is by no means "loathsome and unpalatable."

26. To Fray Francisco Pangua

I beg Your Reverence's blessing and should like to acknowledge the receipt of your last letter of April 23 of last year, and to thank you sincerely for the sentiments of paternal affection with which you refer to me.

As soon as I learned, by way of the Philippines, that you had been re-elected guardian,[1] I wrote by the next mail to send my compliments and congratulations, together with my homage and joyful submission to your bidding. This letter did not arrive according to schedule, as I learned from the message you included for me in Your Reverence's letter to Father Fray Vicente which I forwarded at the first opportunity. I regret this deeply, and hope that by this time Your Reverence has become cognizant of the matters of considerable importance which I included in it. In any case, I wish to repeat how happy I am to be your subject and to express my humble and filial obedience to your commands.

When rumor regarding the Custodies[2] reached this land, I gave my approval to the scheme solely as a steppingstone for my departure from this administration and assignment. But now, on the one hand, I see that they have been decided upon with much solemnity, and that the two religious who (according to rumor) promoted them have been elevated;[3] and on the other hand, I am finding out by experience that regulations by the head of this province are being multiplied and enforced and that these do not in the least make it easier for me to achieve those objectives which, up to the present, modified the intense reluctance with which, out of religious obedience to Your Reverence and to your predecessors I entered upon, and persevered so long in, this service.

It seems better for me, then, to renew my confidence in the kind of compliance I mentioned, and to be so pleasantly preoccupied with it that there will be no time left to give thought to other projects, and not to permit such projects to have any other effect on me than an urge to pray that God Our Lord may ordain and regulate everything for the greater honor and glory of His name and the greater good of souls.

I take a different attitude regarding the new idea that there is to be but one missionary in each mission; for if I were to receive a notification like that, and could not have recourse to the council through the Most Excellent Lord, Don José Gálvez (to whom, under God, I entrust the solution), I would not hesitate to take what steps my conscience would dictate to withdraw to the college, with no other permission than that given by the Seraphic Patriarch,[4] and the presumed permission (for it could, without rashness, be presumed) of Your Reverence.

This plan (in my own opinion, and I do not wish to place myself in opposition to others, no matter how they applaud it) is not religiously oriented and cannot be legitimately defended as one inspired by zeal for reducing the expenses of the royal treasury.

A missionary priest has to engage in many duties many of which only concern him as means to something else. He is responsible for the spiritual and temporal welfare of people who are many and varied. He has individuals who are more dependent on him than small children on parents, for there are many needs that arise, many affairs to be managed, and many things to be done for the different groups that make up the community. He is surrounded by pagans, and placed in charge of neophytes who can be trusted but little. He is constantly employed in the administration of the sacraments, and day by day offers up the awesome sacrifice of the Mass. He has to be dependent for his spiritual consolation on another Father, engaged in the same kind of labors, at a distance of twenty or more leagues. And neither Father can travel more than a short distance without an escort of soldiers. On some occasions such an escort is hard to obtain; and on others, travel by road is impossible because of severe storms; or the departure is hindered by the needs of catechumens, or by the large number who are sick.

In short, this is to condemn a religious to a life that is more than a burden, to sickness without attendance, and to death without the sacraments. My thought, therefore, is, in such a situation *Nolui venire, nec volo stare seu esse inter infideles.*[5] And this, as I understand it, is a liberty accorded me by the twelfth chapter of our Rule.[6]

The same author of the *Reglamento* has not hesitated recently to appoint an adjutant for himself and his successors, at a salary of two thousand pesos; nor has he refrained from increasing the number of the officials with their corresponding emoluments. I must assume that these offices are essential and their remuneration very justifiable; but I cannot understand how anyone who considers our Lord the King as very prodigal and liberal in regard to the temporal welfare of his possessions should imagine him to be very sparing and parsimonious in spiritual matters, for in the royal mind it is the latter which is the principal consideration while the former is but accessory. Yet, the disbursements for the former are greater, and the returns they bring are only increased luxury for the military personnel; and the disbursements for the missionaries are much less, and more than half of these must be devoted to objectives that are common to both the military and the missionaries.

No one should think that His Catholic Majesty would regard with approval, would desire or permit that a poor friar should endure a loneliness that is so sad and so painful and that in his hour of greatest need he should lack the spiritual help of another priest—he who, in the service of his King, has sacrificed the companionship of many loved ones and now lies dying unattended by anyone, although he has spent himself in the service of all.

Loneliness in this work is for me a savage and cruel enemy which has afflicted me greatly. I fled from it, thanks be to God, in face of evident risk of dying at its hands; and now as I see it raise its ugly head, even from afar, I tremble at the inconceivable danger in returning to the battle. May this latter serve as an excuse for so lengthy a discourse on the matter. I see the matter clearly because it means much to me.

I am not unaware that the missions close to the presidios, like the one in my charge, are cared for in a very different manner. But the supply of missionaries in proportion to the missions is so restricted, and the replacement of those who die or fall sick is so tardy, impeded, and difficult that the misfortune which I fear worse than death could easily become my lot.

Hence, if a regulation of this kind is not revoked, I again declare my absolute and total aversion to serving under such conditions and beg with all earnestness for my removal, relying on the chapter of the Franciscan Rule quoted above.

My confidence in the affection of Your Reverence and in the faculties that you possess make it unnecessary for me to send a personal request to the venerable college council. It may well be that by remaining a member of the college such a request cannot be granted; if so, I would ask and do ask permission to return to my own province, or to join any other one in the world, for with the exception of sin, any misfortune that could befall me would be less than being alone in this service.

We do not know here what has happened elsewhere in regard to the religious we were certainly expecting for the mission at the Santa Barbara Channel.[7] Many of us were of the opinion that the Reverend Father President would not agree to the request of the governor in respect to these establishments.

Your Reverence will know by this time what has been done in

regard to the matter. Without a doubt the immense distance, and what is more important the failure of correspondence which causes us here to be uninformed about the mind and attitude of the missionary center at San Fernando—all these bring it about that whoever holds the office of our esteemed Father Junípero will make mistakes or be in a quandary.

You say very truly that it is not justice that the labors and reputation of the missionaries should be lost and that the college should be outraged by the caprice of one who wants to seek applause and advancement at the cost of this dishonor. And here we may add that the baseless invectives, which cause us so much trouble, lead us to suspect that this is their precise aim and object; and this is not justice. I do not guarantee this. I may be mistaken.

The letter mentioned above, which I sent to Your Reverence by the Philippine packet boat, contained many passages which are a basis for the above suspicion; and in case it has not arrived, I would repeat them here, if I did not reflect that the Reverend Father President will leave nothing unexplained, now that by a fortunate coincidence the frigates have arrived. Nevertheless, in another letter which I may yet write I will relate in substance an occurrence which placed us, and still keeps us, Fathers of this mission, in a condition of grave mental anguish.

After the occurrence His Lordship wrote me in such terms that I felt obliged in reply to inform him that it would be difficult to find someone who would acquaint him with the evil results that had followed from what he had done, and that neither my companion nor I would do so because, even if the indignation which could be aroused among the Indians of San Diego would not make us its victims, at least it made clear to us that not only would he ignore any requests we would make for the benefit of the mission, but that he would order the contrary.

I am grateful for your effort in obtaining the vestments and sacred vessels. I am returning the itemized list of those you sent me, and also a receipt for them. I also include a certificate of our presence here, although I was always under the impression that they were always forwarded by the Reverend Father President. And I close with expressions of kindest regards and deep gratitude from my beloved companion Fray Juan. And I would add that if the missions are to remain subject to the college, a religious from them should be required to appear before you in order to inform you clearly and distinctly regarding what you should know so that you may deal with the matter fittingly.

May God Our Lord keep Your Reverence for many years in His holy grace.

San Diego Mission,
July 8, 1782.

[Marginal note:]

I am enclosing two letters for the two Bishops recently appointed,[8] to be delivered or not, according to your judgment and disposition. It seemed to me that such a procedure is in accord with proper protocol; but I may be mistaken, for there is a vast expanse between my lowliness and littleness and the dignity that is their's.

[1] At the Chapter held on June 17, 1780, Pangua was elected guardian to serve a second term. His first term was from 1774-1777.

[2] From the beginning, the missionaries in California were subject immediately to the President of the Missions who resided at Carmel, and remotely to the Guardian of San Fernando College, Mexico. It was now proposed to place a vast expanse of frontier country, comprising not only the Californias, but also Arizona, New Mexico, Texas, and parts of northern Mexico under a bishop, with the new diocese subdivided into four "custodies," or incipient provinces, thereby drastically changing the status of the individual missionaries and the entire mission system. See Geiger, *op. cit.*, II, 343-374.

[3] One of the two was certainly Fray Antonio de los Reyes, Franciscan missionary attached to the College of Santa Cruz, Querétaro, who seems to have initiated the scheme, and later became the first bishop of the territory so designated. The other was probably Fray Sebastián Flores, who had been guardian at Querétaro for two terms. He accompanied Reyes to the new diocese and was given the next highest office there.

[4] Lasuén is referring to an article in the Rule of St. Francis which permits a friar to petition his superior for a transfer, if local circumstances present an obstacle to his spiritual welfare. The article reads: "And wheresoever there are friars who know and feel they are not able to observe the Rule spiritually, they ought to and can have recourse to their ministers."

[5] I am unwilling, and I have no wish to live or to be among heathens.

[6] This portion of the Rule of St. Francis admonishes friars who wish to become missionaries among infidels to seek the permission of their major superiors. These superiors are warned that they "must give permission to go to none but those who they see are fit to be sent." Lasuén, in his humility, had convinced himself that he lacked all the qualifications.

[7] The college cancelled the appointments it had made and deferred sending the missionaries until it was clear that the projected missions would be established in accordance with the older regulations.

[8] Two missionaries attached to the College of San Fernando had recently been appointed bishops: Fray Rafael Verger in Nuevo Leon, and Fray Juan Ramos de Lora in Merida, Venezuela.

27. To Fray José de Jesús María Vélez

The present letter is but a further proof that there is no change in the sentiments I entertain for Your Reverence; they have always remained constant. I have had it in mind to write, but failed to do so for there was nothing in particular to write about. Now there is a good reason, the kind I have been waiting for, so that I can bring myself to carry out a wish that is dear to me by renewing a correspondence that brings me much happiness.

I have just learned that you have been re-elected a member of the college council;[1] and although I realize that it is not the highest post, especially when I recall the promotions to very high places made from within that cloister,[2] nevertheless it is a post on which I should offer, as I now do, a thousand congratulations and cordial good wishes.

I am already an old man[3] and completely grey; and although it is the toll of years, the pace has been accelerated by the heavy burden of this office which I hold, and especially by the five years which I am completing as superior at San Diego.

This land is for apostles only, and its people should be cared for by those more mission-minded than I; but, thanks be to God, I enjoy good health, and I shall try to use it for some good purpose, even though my strength be waning.[4]

I have been much perturbed by various items of news which have reached me since the boats last arrived; but the one which seems intolerable to me is the idea that there should be but one missionary in each mission.

I have already explained at some length to Father Guardian the repugnance which this regulation inspires in me. But as his numerous activities may divert his attention from the matter, I beg Your Reverence most earnestly, and I shall appreciate it beyond measure if, as a Father and friend, and a member of the council you will interest yourself in this, for it is a matter of the gravest importance. If this plan is put into action, I am now asking for permission to return to the college, or to be relieved of my duties as missionary and to be permitted to return to my own province or to be incorporated into any other province of the Order. For me there is no punishment so cruel as a law like this in circumstances such as these.

Despite the scarcity of wine this year, and the Masses we had to say for the many missionaries who passed away, I have not failed to offer a Mass each month for you, as we agreed; and I hope you have kept, and continue to keep, your part of the agreement.

San Diego Mission,
October 3, 1782.

P.S.

Will Your Reverence kindly inform me if the faculties granted us in these parts *pro utroque foro* [5] in regard to impediments *quoad futura matrimonia*[6] apply also to the *gente de razón*[7] of all races. And if California becomes a diocese (we hear it would be attached to the diocese of Arispe), would it involve a change in the obligation and observance of these points?

---

[1] He had previously held the office from 1764 to 1767. He was thus a member of the council that had accepted the task of continuing the work begun by the Jesuits in Lower California, and of establishing the mission system in the California of today. A friend of Lasuén, he was the latter's senior by some twenty years.

[2] The former guardian, Verger, had recently become a bishop.

[3] Visitors to California, such as Vancouver, assumed that Lasuén was considerably older than he really was; and writers such as Bancroft, Engelhardt, and others kept alive the tradition. Actually, at this particular time Lasuén was only forty-six years of age. He was born on July 7, 1736.

[4] The word employed by Lasuén, *flojeando*, could also mean "in a disheartened fashion," a rendition that could be defended.

[5] A legal term. Literally it means "for both forms (or tribunals)," viz., for the internal tribunal of conscience, and for the external one where law, civil or ecclesiastical, is enforced.

[6] That is, pertaining to marriages yet to be performed.

[7] Literally, "people possessed of reason." This phrase is not to be understood as restricted to whites. It applied, too, to any member of the native races who had made some progress in civilization.

28. Inventory of San Diego Mission Church and Sacristy[1]

10 Albs, two of fine linen, new; two of Breton linen, same; one kept at the presidio, old; three of Brabant linen, new; two of the same, half worn, all with lace to match

2 holy water stoops of copper, with sprinklers, one of brass, the other of wood

3 consecrated altar stones, one in use at the presidio

16 amices, six of cambric, seven of Breton, and three of Brabant linen

1 dalmaisal of damask with gold trimmings, lined with Chinese silk

2 carpets of coarse material, colored, and one small one of cotton

— *arras*, thirteen reales

2 wooden missal stands, one in use at the presidio

2 coffins for the dead, large and small

1 fine large trunk covered on the outside with cowhide and on the inside with muslin, to store white clean church linen

1 baldachin of muslin with Chinese ribbon, where the statue of the Most Holy Mary, Our Lady of the Pillar, may be placed

1 large candlestick of cedar, well ornamented, for the paschal candle, and one of the same for the sanctuary lamp, and two small ones to hold tapers

12 chasubles,[2] one of Persian silk, very faded, with gold braid, and lining of Zandalete; one of ancient fine silk, very old. It was made from the dalmatic which escaped the fire [at the San Diego Mission], lined with Zandalete; one of old Persian, and patched. It is in San Blas, having been sent there last year to be repaired. One in violet damask, old and worn, with silver braid, and this, too, was sent there for the same reason. Three black chasubles, two of them new, one with silver braid, the other of silk, and the other to which there is reference is kept at the presidio. Two white chasubles, one of them new, with silver braid and lined with Chinese silk, another very old and poorly patched; it has a cross in red and is used at the presidio for the Feast of All Saints and other festivals. Three chasubles, red, purple, and green, of damask, with braid of gold and silver to match the color, and lined with Chinese silk, all new, each with a stole, maniple, chalice veil, and burse for corporal, all to match

3 choir copes, new, damask; one black, two reversible—one red and white, the other green and purple,

all with gold or silver braid to match the color, each with accompanying stole

12 corporals, seven cambric, five of Breton linen, in good condition except for two that are rather old

2 dresses for [the statue of] the Infant Jesus, one of fine cambric, the other of Breton linen

9 cinctures, three of interwoven silk, velvet-like and new, three of woven silk, two of white linen, one of cloth, old

6 altar covers of bleached wool

3 silver chalices, each with its paten, and spoon of the same material, one of them kept at the presidio

1 silver ciborium

1 moderately large cross of silver

2 bronze processional crosses, one new, the other broken

2 crucifixes, one in wood a little more than a vara long, the other small, of brass

12 candlesticks, two of silver, half a vara high, four of bronze, and six copper-plated

2 silver crismeros

1 brass shell for baptisms

4 copper hand bells for the altar

2 medium bells for hanging, one larger, one smaller

12 small cannons for firing salutes

1 confessional, of cedar

3 chests, one of cedar for church furnishings, with shelves, and a door with a key; one small one for laundry; and one regular size made of pine for the dress of the acolytes

1 small case with a key to protect the three flasks of holy oils

2 stoles, one reversible, white and purple, for baptisms, the other black, for funerals

14 Stations of the Cross, with molded frames and little hanging crosses

1 mirror, two-thirds of a vara, in a well gilt frame

2 ladders of cedar, one five varas, the other two and a half

6 antependia, two black, of damask, new; one with trimmings and border of silver, and one with silk border; two reversible, of damask, new, the one red and white, the other green and purple, with trimmings and border in gold and silver to match; one in white damask, very old, with trimmings and border in matching silver and gold, another in Persian silk, very old and patched; it was sent to San Blas for repairs.

3 little flasks for the holy oils in addition to those in the little case

2 lanterns of tin

2 irons for making hosts

3 host boxes, one of tin and two of pasteboard, one of them at the presidio

1 carved statue of Most Holy Mary of the Pillar with a corona of gilt silver

2 thuribles of brass, with boats and spoons to match

2 paintings of St. Didacus,[3] one a vara and a half, and the other, which is at the presidio, is two varas

2 idem, one vara, one of them of the Blessed Virgin, the other of St. Joseph

1 idem, of St. John the Baptist, a vara and a quarter

2 idem, small, one of St. Didacus, the other of Our Lady of Light

2 idem, half a vara, the one of Our Lady of Solitude, the other Our Lady of Dolors

1 idem, very old, of Our Lady of Light

5 new damask *manguillas*[4] for the cross, one black, one red, one purple, one white, one green, with trimmings and border of gold and silver to match the color, with lining of Chinese silk

2 idem, old, of damask, deep red and

violet, with trimmings and border of silk, and lined with Zandalete

2 mozzettas for the administration of the sacraments, one of white damask, new, with trimmings and border of gold, and lined with Chinese silk; the other is of glossy silk, old, with trimmings of new gold, and lined with Chinese silk

10 altar cloths, eight of new Breton linen

12 finger towels, four of cambric, linen, and two of Brabant, worn out; all trimmed with lace

4 missals, two proper to the Franciscan Order, one very old and much used, the other good but not new. The other two are ordinary ones, old, but in good condition. One of them is used at the presidio.

3 manuals of prayer. A Roman one is as good as new; the one by Osorio is new, and the one by Betencour is very old

2 altars. The main one, of cedar, is large, and has two gradines; the other, of pine, is small, and is dedicated to the Most Blessed Virgin Mary of the Pillar

1 idem, for the sacristy, of cedar, three varas long and one wide, with three drawers in the center for vestments

1 idem, small, and well proportioned, to be used for the administration of Holy Viaticum and other functions

1 statue of the Infant Jesus held in the arms of the statue of St. Joseph which was stolen or burned or otherwise lost during the Indian uprising of the year '75. When those who committed the sacrilege withdrew, some Indians from the mission were able to rescue it from their hands and to entrust it to the Father who survived

8 cassocks for the acolytes, four of

bright red, four of blue baize

2 new canopies, one of white damask with trimmings and border of gold, lined with Chinese silk, and another of mottled Chinese linen, with a streamer of the same material, with lining of white linen

2 altar canopies of old turquoise-colored cloth, in good condition

1 set of altar cards neatly framed in cedar

2 broken sets of the same

20 purificators of cambric and Breton linen

1 baptismal font in onyx

1 basin for the same, polished and tin-plated

1 pitcher of Chinese brass for washing the hands

2 Filipino sleeping mats, one big and ordinary, the other small, superior, and in colors

4 rochets of linen for the acolytes

1 octagonal cedar pedestal, painted, as are its four arches. On it is to be placed the statue of the Most Blessed Virgin Mary, Our Lady of the Pillar

2 carved tabernacles, one ordinary, built here; the other is well gilt, painted, from Mexico. Both have locks and keys.

8 surplices, four of Breton linen, new, and four of Brabant, in good condition, in boxes

2 tablecloths, one of colored wool, the other of muslin

3 seats of cypress wood, with backs

6 towels, two of Gallician, two of Filipino, and two of Del Reyno material

1 glass case for the storing of silver, with gilt frame and two glass doors

3 sets of altar cruets, silver, one old and very delicate, but in good condition; two are new, large and plain and well designed, but unfit for use, for they corrupt the wine

or give it an unpleasant or unpalatable copper flavor

2 idem, of glass, with corresponding finger bowls of pewter.

San Diego Mission,
April 30, 1783.

[1] In this inventory the items are listed in alphabetical order according to their names in Spanish; hence the seeming lack of order or sequence.

[2] The outer vestment worn by the priest at Mass. Its color varies according to the liturgical season of the year, the feast which is celebrated, or the occasion, such as a funeral. The permissible colors are those given here.

[3] Diego, in whose honor San Diego was named.

[4] A *manguilla* is an ornamental sheath used to cover the upper portion of the staff of a processional cross, and often ends in ornamental streamers. It bears some resemblance to a sleeve (Spanish *manga*); hence the name. It seems to be unknown in English speaking countries, and has no specific name in English.

29. Inventory of San Diego Mission
The House

1 Dough trough and 3 sieves

1 still

2 scales, large and small, with weights up to eight pounds, and 1 (Roman) balance

12 vessels with fiber finish and an equal number of baskets of the same material, and 6 hundred-weight barrels, empty

8 chests, 6 of pine and 2 of cedar, 6 with locks

3 candlesticks and 2 extinguishers

6 kettles

1 medicine chest with 20 gallipots, 2 flasks, and other medicine bottles

6 pairs of carding instruments

2 tin funnels, 1 large, 1 medium

2 containers with 16 flasks each, in good condition

1 syringe, 2 toilet bowls, and 2 bed pots

2 metal cups for drinking water

4 tables and 2 benches

2 sets of razors and 2 shaving mugs

14 drinking cups, 8 china and 6 common ware

3 seats and 1 leather chair[1]

1 inkwell with metal sand-box

1 dresser with 3 shelves

1 tailor's scissors

8 earthen jars, 6 for water, 2 for wine

3 jars, 1 of china ware, 2 from Guadalajara

8 crystal glasses, and 10 flasks

1 brass mortar and pestle

2 large cauldrons for the pozole, and 4 ladles for the same

10 assorted pots, 5 used, 5 new

4 copper table sets

2 iron skimmers, and 3 spoons of the same material

4 grinding stones [*metates*] with pestles to match

1 spit

4 tablecloths and 8 napkins

1 copper cauldron for the pozole, medium size, 8 of the same in a smaller size, 5 used, 3 new

4 griddle cake cooking pans, and 4 copper colanders

3 frying pans and 4 baking pans

1 dozen cups of common ware, 4 cups of china ware, and 6 for serving milk

2 dozen plates, pewter and brass

2 dozen plates of common ware and 3 of china ware

2 beds for the two friars, with 3 blankets and 2 sheep skins for each, and the same bed furnishings for a guest, in case he should not have brought them

1 small supply of clothes for the Indians

200 (approximately) fanegas of wheat for their use and ours

2 fanegas of beans and 3 almuds of rice; lard and fat for candles for a year; chocolate and snuff to last until the boat is expected.

THE LIBRARY

1 The Holy Bible in one volume

4 volumes of the *Mística Ciudad de Dios*

1 volume with Notes, critical Prologue, and Life of the Venerable Mother, Sister Mary of Jesus, of Agreda

3 volumes of the *Flos Sanctorum* by Rivadeneyra

1 volume *Historia* by Fray Diego

1 volume *Párocho de Indios* by Montenegro, large volume

1 volume *Speculum Parochorum* by Abrreu

2 volumes *Theologia Moral* by La Croix

2 volumes *Theologia Moral* by Tamburino

3 volumes *Doctrinas Prácticas* by Calatayud

1 volume *Afanes Apostólicos*

1 volume *Cartas Edificantes*

1 volume, the same by Garciano

1 volume *Manogito* by Tellado

1 volume *Florelegio Medicinal*

4 books on Administration

1 *Martyrologio Romano*

4 volumes of the *Leyes de Indias*

1 volume *Curia Philipica*.

CARPENTER SHOP

1 iron compass and one bronze plumb

3 jack planes, 3 jointing planes, 3 ordinary planes, and a grooving plane

4 carpenter's axes, 3 ordinary axes, 2 crowbars, 6 chisels, and 4 augers

5 saws, 1 buck-saw, 4 hand saws, 2 small hand saws

4 large gimlets, 3 claw-hammers, 3 iron moulds

1 set-square, 1 square, and 1 wooden spirit-level

1 rabbet-plane, a marking gauge, and some carpenter's squares.

THE FORGE

4 bolts, 4 ferrules with goads attached, 2 bellows handles, and 1 airpipe to go with bellows

1 large anvil, 4 anvil blocks[2]

2 hand pincers, and 1 small one

2 chopping knives, 1 poker, 1 nailer's anvil

2 anvils, 1 large, 1 small

1 vise[3] for hatchets, another for hoes

3 vises, 2 large, 1 small some bench vises, 1 chisel to match, and 1 screw plate

10 files, including large and small, and 6 Spanish round files.

THE HARNESS SHED

22 sets of gear, with all accessories, 12 old, 10 new

14 loads of leather sacks

4 of the above from Esmiquilpan

2 sets of harness with all accessories

1 hoof parer, a hammer and pincers for shoeing purposes

4 cowboy saddles, complete, but in poor condition.

SAN FERNANDO COLLEGE CHURCH

Mexico City

THE FARM

The entire gear for 5 yoke of oxen
  5 yoke and 5 additional plows
28 mattocks, 12 large, 16 small
14 hoes, 8 hatchets for felling, and
  12 sheep shears
12 woodcutter's axes, and 2 gardener's hoes
  6 pack-saddle trees [4]
25 yoke of oxen, already broken in
24 tame horses
  6 as above, 5 accustomed to imitation
  bridle, and 1 to bit and bridle

415 head of cattle, counting big and
  little, and including the above oxen
900 head of sheep
484 goats
  7 swine
178 head of horses in 4 herds, 2 of
  them with male donkeys
29 mules, counting male and the fe-
  males broken in
  2 female mules, partly broken in
30 hens and roosters combined, and 34
  doves.

San Diego Mission,
May 4, 1783.

[1] Lasuén uses the word *equipal*, a word from an Aztec root. Originally it meant a seat made to resemble a wicker chair. In its more modern usage it implies a chair made of pigskin leather, as may be seen in Michoacan and northern states in Mexico.

[2] The word *macho* can either mean the block on which the anvil rests, or a sledge hammer—either would be appropriate.

[3] In contemporary Spanish the word *tornillo* can be applied to many different things, from the simple screw or bolt to the most intricate form of vise. Lasuén employs the word three times to describe the furnishings of the forge, possibly describing a different object each time. Many of these objects are not well known today, and they are difficult to define or differentiate.

[4] A possible meaning. Lasuén uses the word *barras*.

30. To Don Pedro Fages

In view of the long exile which three members of this mission—Carlos,[1] Luis, and Rafael—have endured for three years in the Presidio of Loreto, following another period of somewhat similar length as prisoners in this Presidio of San Diego, I have wondered if, perhaps, justice itself does not demand that an application for mercy should be made in their behalf. And since the poor fellows have no one but me to take such a step, and because there is no one who desires their liberty more than I, their father, I make this application to Your Lordship with the greatest respect, begging you for the love of God to take an interest in them, to pardon them, and to restore them to their country.

I did not interfere to suggest that their guilt may already have been blotted out in full by about six years of punishment which they have been enduring. This pertains to justice. My role is to make a plea in the name of mercy.

During the imprisonment and exile of these men, a number of petitions for amnesty have been circulated in the name of our lord the

King, and I do not know why no one intervened for them. They are but neophytes, and this circumstance ought to be enough to excite sympathy. They have wives, who are not old, and they have children; and because of the hope I have had to keep alive in them that they would one day see their husbands and fathers in their rancherías, they have continued to live the Christian life in the midst of relatives and associates who are pagans; and they have recourse to the mission almost every time there is a Mass of obligation there.

Finally, my Lord, if the prolonged and grave punishment which they have endured should be regarded as sufficient warning to them, the pardon and pity for which I plead will, without doubt, be a means towards making the relatives and countrymen of three unfortunates more content in the tranquility, peace, and subjection which we desire.

I await Your Lordship's disposition of this humble petition according to your good judgment, and I pray that God Our Lord may keep your important life for many years in His holy grace.

San Diego Mission,
April 29, 1785.

[1] Carlos was one of the principal leaders in the Indian revolt that resulted in the destruction of the first San Diego Mission and the death of one of the missionaries.

The Missionary Spirit -

IV

President of the Missions

Lasuén assumed the office of President in October, 1785, and an administration that lasted almost eighteen years begins. He founds his first mission, and has his first official contacts with Governor Fages, as each in his own way tries to mold the future of California.

31. To the Missionaries

THE LORD GIVE YOU PEACE.[1] THE REVEREND Father Guardian of our Apostolic College of San Fernando orders me to make a transcript of the patent which appoints me to the office of President of these Missions and to forward it to all Your Reverences, even though, as he tells me, he has advised each one of you of my appointment. It reads as follows:

Fray Juan Sancho[2] of the Regular Observance of the Order of St. Francis, former Professor of Philosophy, former Lector of Theology, Apostolic Preacher, and Guardian of this Apostolic College *de Propaganda Fide* at San Fernando in Mexico to the Reverend Father Preacher, Fray Fermín Lasuén, Member of this College and Minister of the Mission of San Diego in the territory of our Missions of Monterey: Health and Peace in Our Lord Jesus Christ.

Whereas, in the missions of our college in Upper California of Monterey there is vacant the office and administration of president,[3] which rules and governs them, and promotes the works of our apostolic institute for the glory of God and the honor of our apostolic seminary, at a meeting of the venerable council of the college I nominated Your Paternity for this office; and by common consent the members gave their approval, in view of the qualities of knowledge, piety, and prudence which combine in you.

Wherefore, in virtue of these presents, signed by my hand, bearing the seal of the college, and countersigned by its secretary, I choose and name Your Paternity to be president, and legitimate superior of all the missionaries who dwell in the aforesaid missions. And in order that Your Paternity may receive aid from on high in a work that is great and an employment which is glorious, I order you under holy obedience and by virtue of the Holy Spirit to accept the office and duty of President of these Missions; and under the same formal precept I instruct and order all the religious missionaries, present and future, to obey, to revere, and be guided by Your Paternity, as their legitimate superior, not only in what pertains to their individual duties, but also in respect to the greater stability and better administration of the missions.

And because it may come to pass that through death, or some other accident, recourse cannot be had to the person of Your Paternity, with the consent of the Fathers of the venerable council I hereby appoint Father Lector Fray Pablo Mugartegui as superior next in authority to the president.

Given in the Apostolic College of San Fernando in Mexico, the 6th day of February of the year one thousand seven hundred and eighty-five.

Fray Juan Sancho, Guardian.
By order of His Reverend Paternity
Fray Daniel Ayasso, Pro-secretary of the College.

97

The above is a faithful copy; and for this reason, it contains the phrase "Your Paternity" which, due no doubt to lack of knowledge, was used by the amanuensis.[4] Your Reverences are well aware that in our community such a form of address is not used. The Father Guardian, in the letter which accompanies the patent, addresses me as Your Reverence and that is the title I used when replying.

You realize, Reverend Fathers, and no one realizes it more clearly than I, that the holy college, in its desire to fill the vacancy caused by the death of the esteemed Father Junípero, has made us very sensible of the loss we have sustained; but we know, too, that this realization leaves unchanged the precept and obedience which are imposed on us.

In order that we may all make progress, it is particularly necessary that Your Reverences commend me to God, and that you continue your apostolic ministry with the same zeal as hitherto, and if possible with greater and more unselfish zeal, and also that you should not vary, still less that you should slacken in the least, your very praiseworthy course of conduct.

The Reverend Father Guardian, under date of February 23, of this year, sends me this message; "This Royal Audiencia, which at the present time is governing because of the death of the late Viceroy,[5] announces His Majesty's royal order, a copy of which I enclose. Having acquainted yourself with its content, when occasion arises Your Reverences will carry out with the greatest promptness and with religious reserve all that is therein required of us, and you will take care to make it known to the other Father Ministers so that everything may be done in conformity with the intention of His Majesty."

The following is a copy of the document:

There has come to the attention of the King an official letter which had been forwarded to the superior government in the name of the colleges of Querétaro, Zacatecas, and San Fernando of the Franciscan Order in opposition to the establishment of Custodies and the arrangement of missions, which, after mature deliberation and due investigation, His Majesty had decreed in the provinces of this realm, having first obtained the consent of the Holy See.

It is His Majesty's royal will that Your Excellency should disregard the opposition of the colleges and the provinces of this Order and that you should assist and contribute effectively to the establishment of the projected custodies by carrying into effect this our mandate. And I hereby notify you of the royal order so that you may know it and put it into execution.

May God protect Your Excellency for many years.

El Pardo,
January 14, 1784.
José de Gálvez.

The Viceroy of New Spain
Tacubaya, May 12, 1784

Let a certified copy of this royal order be made, and let it become part of the *expendiente*[6] and be forwarded to the Attorney for Civil Affairs so that, having seen it, he may demand what he thinks fitting for its observance.

Signed by His Excellency with rubric.[7]
The above is a copy.

Francisco Hernández de Cordova
Mexico, February 16, 1785.

When Your Reverences have become well informed regarding the contents, the folder, properly sealed, is to be sent from mission to mission as it is received; and the minister of the last mission is to preserve it carefully so that it may be a permanent record that we have carried out the instructions of the Reverend Father Guardian.

May God Our Lord, etc.

San Diego Mission,
October 10, 1785.

[1] Lasuén began many of his letters with this greeting. He always used the Latin form of the greeting: *Dominus det tibi* (or *vobis*) *Pacem.*

[2] Fray Juan Sancho de la Torre, to give his full title, was one of those sent to Lower California by San Fernando College when that mission field was accepted. There he was in charge of Mission Guadalupe. When the Dominicans assumed control he returned to San Fernando, and in 1774, and again in 1780 was made a member of the college council. In May, 1783, he was elected guardian. He had formerly been a member of the Province of Mallorca where he received the Franciscan habit in January, 1746.

[3] The first President of the Missions, Fray Junípero Serra, died on August 28, 1784. During the succeeding months Fray Francisco Palou was interim superior.

[4] It was customary to use abbreviations for titles of honor. The amanuensis evidently wrote "V. P." (Vuestra Paternidad) for "V. R." (Vuestra Reverencia).

[6] A file, or dossier, of documents pertaining to a particular case.

[7] A distinctive and characteristic flourish, not subject to variation, which writers added to their signature. As in this instance, it was often used as a substitute for the complete signature.

32. To Don José Antonio Rengel[1]

On the sixth of this month I received a patent from the Reverend Father Guardian of the Apostolic College of San Fernando in which he ordered me to become the President of these Missions of Upper California.

This letter will serve to advise Your Lordship that in me you have a person subject to you in everything, and that I desire to make this known to you in no other manner than by being particularly submissive to your superior orders. Should I have the honor to receive them, Your Lordship will not fail to observe how very prompt is my obedience.

I well know, Sir, that all this is very much a matter of right; but, as a poor friar, I have nothing to offer but prayers. And in them, such as they are, I have remembered Your Lordship and shall continue to do so, with the added wish that Your Lordship may discharge the duties of your high office to the greater approval of God and the eminent satisfaction of the King, so that having won for yourself the unshaken confidence of an earthly ruler you may also obtain the imperishable rewards of One who is eternal.

May God Our Lord keep Your Lordship many years in His holy grace.

San Diego Mission,
October 11, 1785.

[1] When the office of Commandant General of the Internal Provinces became vacant, due to the death of Neve, Rengel was appointed to the office *ad interim* by the Audiencia at Guadalajara. He was succeeded by General Jacobo Ugarte y Loyola who was appointed to it by a royal order on October 6, 1785.

33. To Don Pedro Fages[1]

On the sixth of the present month I received Your Lordship's esteemed and cordial letter, dated the thirtieth of September of last year, together with a copy of the *Reglamento*[2] now in force.

I greatly appreciate Your Lordship's sincere expression of satisfaction with the new office that has been conferred on me, that of President of these Missions.

I no sooner received the patent appointing me to this office than I placed it, by means of a letter, at the service of Your Lordship in the same way as I had already offered my own person. I now sincerely renew the acknowledgement I then made, for I am always eager to give Your Lordship the most pleasing proofs of my devoted submission.

Without allowing any time to be lost, I am making a study of what the above *Reglamento* lays down in regard to the missions; and Your Lordship need have no doubt that I will carry out with the most minute accuracy all that the King requires.

I am very pleased with the discovery which Your Lordship and Father Fray Vicente de Santa María[3] made of a site suitable for the establishment of Santa Barbara Mission;[4] and it is a pleasure, too, to know that because of the report which Your Lordship made to the commandant general, His Lordship may decide on founding it at an earlier date. This is a work which I had longed for eagerly, without any thought that I would become president; but we are still lacking the missionaries for whom, as Your Lordship tells me, the Reverend Father, my late predecessor, asked our college. I have already made the same request, and I am looking forward with good reason to a favorable outcome as soon as the matter can be arranged.

It has been brought to my attention that the two Fathers who came this year are to replace the one who, on the King's orders, retired from San Francisco, and the other who died in San Diego;[5] and I have given them these assignments in accordance with the orders given me.

My main thought now is to settle down as soon as possible in the Mission of San Carlos so as to place myself personally at the service of Your Lordship, to consult you in regard to different things, to serve you as you may wish, and to give proof in a practical way that in me Your Lordship has one who is subject to you in everything.

Unavoidable and very important details of my new office detain me, and may delay my arrival at the above Mission of San Carlos longer than I might wish. With God's help, however, I shall see to it that I do not lose an instant in achieving that happy objective.

May God Our Lord keep Your Lordship many years in His holy grace.

San Diego Mission,
November 7, 1785.

[1] When Neve was promoted to an official position in the Internal Provinces in 1782, Fages replaced him as governor of California.

[2] This was a new instrument of government drawn up by Governor Neve. It contained many innovations, some of which were very obnoxious to the missionaries for, had they been carried out literally, they would have given rise to a very different form of evangelization to that favored by the missionaries. For a summary of many of the basic articles of the reglamento, and of the attitude of the missionaries, see Zephyrin Engelhardt, *Missions and Missionaries of California* II, 349-370.

[3] He was a member of the Franciscan Province of Burgos, but joined the College of San Fernando in 1769. He labored for a brief period in Lower California, and for approximately thirty years in different missions in Upper California. He died at San Buenaventura Mission on July 16, 1806, at the age of sixty-four.

[4] The place favored by Fages and Santa María is now known as Montecito, a picturesque residential settlement on the eastern outskirts of Santa Barbara. The place actually chosen, and the site of the present structure, was much closer to the presidio, and was known to the Indians as *Taynayan*, and to the Spaniards as *El Pedregoso*, the "stoney place."

[5] Fray Juan Figuer. He died on December 18, 1784, aged approximately forty-two years. He had been a member of the Franciscan Province of Aragon before joining the College of San Fernando.

34. To Don Pedro Fages

On reading Your Lordship's esteemed letter of the eighth of this month I shared deeply in the displeasure which Father Fray Tomás de la Peña occasioned Your Lordship when he declined to supply corn at the price fixed by law, corn which was requested for the provisioning of your presidio.

The copies attached to the letter just mentioned and concerned with the matter in question, all of which Your Lordship has forwarded, on the one hand make very clear to me the reasons given by Your Lordship for not acceding to the claims of the Father in question; and on the other hand they bring to mind what I already knew, namely, that in this province Your Lordship alone has the power to enforce the prices set by law, or to vary them as time and circumstances demand.

I am well aware of Your Lordship's attachment to our holy institute and of your deep understanding, and I am keeping in mind the fact that Your Lordship discharges the duties of your office with such a sense of justice that no one would presume to interfere in the functions proper to it; yet, despite all this, I am still not quite convinced but that it is possible that one can fail to notice the upright and praiseworthy conduct of a missionary such as this.

I would like to think that Your Lordship does not regard the present program of His Majesty, and others of a like nature which he holds, as matters definitely prescribed, but that you would regard them as, in a sense, ideals which, even if not all of them have the force of law, may at times give rise to an undue zeal, with the result that we, the Fathers engaged in apostolic labors here, make it our aim to reduce as much as possible the all too evident needs and necessities of those entrusted to us. And I know how many and how varied are the problems that Mission Santa Clara has to face at times, knowing, as I do, the large numbers who were not only hungry but naked, too.

Keeping in mind all I have just said, and also the fact that on this date I sent Father Peña appropriate admonitions for his future guidance, and that I am placing on him the obligation of seeking my approval and permission in regard to matters of that nature, should occasion arise, I hope and pray there will be no action on the part of Your Lordship's tribunal as a result of the misunderstanding.

Rest assured that in this particular case, as in all others, this poor President, your subject, is resolved to do what pleases Your Lordship insofar as I can, and to act in harmony with your will.

May God Our Lord keep Your Lordship many years in His holy grace.

San Juan Capistrano Mission,
November 22, 1785.

35. To Don José Antonio Rengel

Through the medium of Your Lordship's esteemed letter of the ninth of last August I am informed that I am to use the term "Lordship" when addressing Don Pedro Galindo Navarro,[1] counselor[2] and legal adviser in military matters[3] to the central government, and also to the commandant general, and I am to advise my subordinates to do likewise, both by spoken word and in writing, for His Majesty has deigned to confer on him the honor of *alcalde del crimen*[4] within the Royal Audiencia[5] of Mexico.

No sooner did I receive my patent as President of these Missions than I wrote to Your Lordship, on the eleventh of last October, placing at your command and at your service both my person and my office. I now acknowledge once more my obligation to you and my determination to be faithful in the discharge thereof at all times.

May God Our Lord keep Your Lordship many years in His holy grace

San Carlos of Monterey Mission,
February 20, 1786.

[1] Navarro, a native of Mallorca, accompanied Croix to the Internal Provinces in 1777, served in the capacity of *asesor* for many years, and died in Chihuahua in 1805.
[2] Sp. *Asesor.* An asesor was a lawyer whose duty it was to give advice to judges in legal matters .
[3] Sp. *Auditor de Guerra,* that is, a judge appointed to advise military officers on matters of law.
[4] One who holds the position of judge in a criminal court attached to certain of the audiencias and enjoying a certain amount of autonomy. There were four such judges in Mexico City.
[5] The Audiencia was the highest legal tribunal in Colonial America. Its jurisdiction extended to civil and criminal cases and it possessed a certain degree of legislative power. See Demetrio Ramos Pérez, *Historia de la Colonización Española en América* (Madrid, 1947), pp. 97-98 *et passim,* also C. H. Haring, *The Spanish Empire in America* (New York, 1947), pp. 130-131, 134-135.

36. To Don Pedro Fages

I respectfully acknowledge Your Lordship's letter of the seventh of last month, and the enclosed letter of the Reverend Father Fray Tomás de la Peña, in which it is stated that the said Father declined to co-operate personally and to present, too, the ecclesiastical records needed to make up the census which Lieutenant Don Diego Gonzáles has to prepare. As a result of this, Your Lordship is not able to complete the General Report which has to be sent each year from the whole province to the central government, and you ask me to "see that the document needed for this purpose be made available to the lieutenant."

In the first place, Sir, I am certain that if that worthy officer had made his request in appropriate terms, he would have saved Your Lordship, himself, and everybody else, unpleasant consequences such as these.

Soon after my arrival at this mission this very incident was reported to me, although casually, in the first letters I received from the missionaries of Santa Clara; and although I had already begun to suspect what had provoked it, I wrote to Their Reverences telling them that I had no doubt that they had on hand the census list used in the supervision of their neophytes, and that it would be easy for them to present it, when requested, to any official so that he could carry out the orders of his superior, and that they should hand it over for that purpose when he sought it, without giving rise to an occasion for friction if it could be avoided. On the 5th of last month the Reverend Father Peña replied to me: "If the lieutenant requests the information in appropriate terms, it will be given to him, in accordance with the orders of Your Reverence."

I would suggest, Sir, that Your Lordship would, as a consequence, at least defer judgment so as to decide who it is that is responsible for the delay.

With this in mind I have written to the above Reverend Fathers, repeating the instructions I had already sent; and when a reply is received, there will be an opportunity for Your Lordship, and for myself, to apply whatever remedy is appropriate so that in the future no one will be so irresponsible as to cause the slightest delay in carrying out an order issued by higher authority.

My sentiments, Sir, are not confined to those expressed here. It is my hope that Your Lordship may be spared the least annoyance and that, with the religious subject to me, I may offer you deep-seated allegiance and all the honors and courtesy due to your rank.

In this spirit I place myself at your service, and I pray that God Our Lord may keep you for many years in His holy grace.

San Carlos Mission,
March 31, 1786.

37. To Don Pedro Fages

This very day with all due respect I received Your Lordship's esteemed letter written from San Gabriel on the twenty-seventh of last month. In it Your Lordship is so kind as to inform me that you had received at one and the same time an official notice from the ensign of this presidio and from the commandant of San Francisco regarding the urgent need they both have of corn for the upkeep of the families, and that when the Reverend Father Fray Tomás Peña refused to give any help whatever the presidio pack train returned empty.

By citing what precisely the Reverend Father Peña did I am in a position to submit proof to Your Lordship that, insofar as His Reverence is concerned, the information given Your Lordship is not in accordance with fact; that when the pack train returned without a cargo he did what he could to provide some; and that later that portion was given to the Presidio of San Francisco as the one that needed it the most and had the least resources.

After I had arrived at this Mission of San Carlos and had begun to see how much these presidios were in need, I advised the Reverend Fathers from Santa Clara to San Luis that they were under obligation to help them, even to the point at which they could help them no further. I even suggested that in order to do so it would be well to have recourse to the expedient, admittedly an extreme one, of permitting those who resided at the mission to betake themselves to the forests, but without forcing or compelling them—for Your Lordship is aware that we are charged by the King to make them docile and civilized, and if we keep them away from the forests and busy at the mission in field work [?] [1] and fishing at the very time when the forests have nuts to support them, and then send them to the forests when there is nothing for them to eat there, not only would we be opposing the pious wishes of the King, but we would be introducing a base form of tyranny.

With all this in mind, doubtlessly, the above-mentioned Father Peña hit upon a subtle way, and he imparted it to me in a paragraph in his last letter, and I am going to transcribe it for Your Lordship, for in my opinion it is totally at variance with what has been so perversely attributed to him. He writes as follows:

A few days ago we called together the principal [Indian] leaders at the mission and we said to them: Children, you know already that the corn, wheat, and whatever else there is in the mission does not belong to the Fathers but to you. The soldiers are suffering much from hunger. They have no corn, no wheat, no beans. They are asking us to sell them some of these things so that they can support themselves. If we do sell, there will not be enough on hand to support you until the time of the wheat harvest. If you wish to go away for some weeks to gather nuts, it will be possible to sell them some corn, and there will be that much extra to spend on clothes. You may consult your own people if you wish.

In less than an hour they returned to say that they would choose life in the open, for the pinole was already getting ripe.

De facto, they sought permission, and to none of them was permission refused for the week. But despite all this, if the Presidio of San Francisco does not obtain help from some other source it will be impossible to maintain it until the wheat harvest arrives.

Your Lordship can judge for yourself if this is not a truly severe punishment, for here is a religious who has deserved well of the community because of what he did for it, and now he sees himself charged with having abandoned and deserted it in its hour of greatest need by deceitfully concealing the fact that the mission had more than a moderate supply of provisions.

This is what they tell Your Lordship and me; and now their story is that the grain which was sold to the China galleon as feed for hogs, the one hundred fanegas of corn which were sent from here to the Presidio of Santa Barbara by order of Your Lordship, and the flour that was permitted to be sold to the San Blas ship are responsible for the present scarcity, and that this was something they feared from the beginning. There is no doubt, Sir, that some people have a wealth of words but a dearth of proof, even when they write; and this is something to keep in mind.

The ensign at San Francisco, once he was convinced that the charges he had made against Father Peña were groundless, made amends by saying that the aim of the latter had been to give all possible aid, that he had done so, and continues to do so; and it has been my conviction that in the present emergency this Father is so resolute in helping that no one could ask more of him. The price was not increased because of the scarcity, despite the fact that in the schedule of fixed prices the very author of it himself adverts to such a possibility. But in regard to this matter I hope to have an interview with Your Lordship, and to come to a reasonable decision with you.

Finally, I shall immediately send a copy of Your Lordship's letter to Father Peña. I shall mention once more the steps I had already brought to his attention, ordering him to continue to do what he has taken such pains to do, and nothing more, for it is not in his power to do more, and never to slacken in his determination to help the presidio to the best of his ability.

A thousand thanks to Your Lordship for your kindness, confidences, and considerateness. Like Your Lordship, I, too, shall make it my highest ambition to insure that there will be nothing to endanger the exalted happiness it will bring you, just to prove beyond question how deep is my gratitude.

With the deepest respect and submissiveness I am at the service of Your Lordship, and I pray that God Our Lord may keep you many years in His holy grace.

San Carlos Mission,
April 7, 1786.

P. S.

I am pleased that Albitre and the Indian woman with her little daughter have returned to their country in safety, and I am happy at the way in which Your Lordship has disposed of the matter.

¹ The word is illegible, but the meaning is obvious.

38. To Don Pedro Fages

I beg to acknowledge receipt of Your Lordship's esteemed communication of the eleventh of this month which informs me that Your Lordship has resolved to authorize an increase of two reales in the fixed price of each fanega of corn, that it applies to what the missions of San Carlos and Santa Clara have sold to the presidios of Monterey and San Francisco during four months of this year, and to the balance which they are under obligation to give until the harvest, and that if what they are to supply is hard to obtain there may be grounds for additional increase. I respect the decision of Your Lordship, and look on it as one most in conformity with the best use of the faculties given you, and with the full and perfect acquaintance with the very unusual and serious conditions of scarcity which arise at the present time.

In connection with this matter, and in view of the fact that Your Lordship makes no reference to the missions of San Antonio and San Luis, which seem to be entitled to the same increase, with all due respect, and with the most complete submission to your superior judgment, I should like to bring Your Lordship's attention to what the Reverend Missionary Fathers of these missions tell me in letters that I received from them yesterday and today. The Reverend Father Fray Miguel Pieras, in a letter dated this month, thus writes me:

I have just received a letter from the paymaster to the effect that I am to let him have fifty fanegas of grain, despite the fact that I have written to him repeatedly in regard to the scarcity from which we are suffering, and to the effect that this can not be done without running the risk of losing everything. Over and above this, two days before the team arrived bringing me this demand, I felt obliged to give twenty fanegas to the corporal of the guard here, for by that time he was without a single grain of corn to serve as rations. The inconveniences which these poor men endure, and the losses to the mission in handing over the grain that is not overabundant, seeing it is for the support of the troops, are matters worthy of considerations and deserving of reward.

This past year, during the month of August, in order to meet the request made for grain by the paymaster of this presidio, the rations for these poor men were cancelled (they used to be given them in grain), much to their regret, and they still deeply deplore it. At the second request they were derived of two almuds for every pot of six that they placed in the pozole. Today they are deprived of almost all the pozole and are given atole three times. Because there is no grain, the grounds are not made ready; not a single irrigation ditch is dug, even though these are very useful and necessary, and many useful activities are suspended. As regards things that are necessary, we are eliminating everything that is possible. All of this is bad for the mission, and these are points that deserve consideration.

Perhaps this missionary so writes for he has seen on the one hand that, with my limited resources, it is no longer possible to support the troops, and on the other hand, without the least hint from me, [he writes] in regard to the problem of a higher price. Certainly I had no further information than that, but it was enough to induce me to say to Your Lordship in my letter that I would assume that San Antonio and San Luis would receive the same consideration as San Carlos and Santa Clara missions.

From this latter mission the Reverend Fray Antonio Paterna writes me, under date of the second of this month:

I assure Your Reverence that it may well be that here we shall find ourselves as much in need, or even more so, than those at the presidio, for after a little more cultivating all the wheat at the mission will be exhausted. Much of it turned out to be worthless, and what was poor in quality is yielding little. The only wheat at the mission is what the team brings; that is, wheat of little consequence. In the last trip there was a little from the preceding year; but the sergeant thought it better not to take it, for it was too musty. The little that is brought was used up and I have to admit that that's all there is.

The fact that the missionaries have not planted more was due to the fact that they regarded the presidios as supplied independently, or they did not anticipate an appeal from them, especially because the pueblos have the prior right to accommodate them, and also because of the poor quality of the wheat they sent, there being no better—all of which goes to show how poor was the last harvest, and how grave is the food situation.

Your Lordship is aware that this is my first year in the office of President; and just as Your Lordship did not fail to receive the Annual Reports of the Missions for the purposes expressed, neither will you fail to receive the present one just as soon as the only two that are missing, those from the most distant missions of San Juan Capistrano and San Diego, arrive—unless Your Lordship should wish me to forward the report without waiting for these others.

Furthermore, in accordance with the regulation, it is my duty, Sir, to keep in mind the intent of these documents, namely, that in years when harvests are bountiful they should carefully store up the surplus and reimburse or recompense their subjects for the inconveniences they had to put up with in the years of scarcity.

I repeat once more my expressions of submission to the higher orders of Your Lordship, and my never-ending desire to comply with them. My prayer is that God Our Lord may keep you through many years in His holy grace.

San Carlos Mission,
May 12, 1786.

39. Judicial Proceedings

In this Mission of Santa Clara on the twenty-sixth of the month of May of the year 1786, I, Fray Fermín Francisco de Lasuén, of the Order of Our Holy Father St. Francis, Apostolic Preacher of the College *de Propaganda Fide* of San Fernando of Mexico, and President of these Missions of Upper California, in my mission headquarters at San Carlos of Monterey did receive a letter from Reverend Father Fray Diego Noboa,[1] the tenor of which is as follows:

To the Reverend Father President Fray Fermín Francisco de Lasuén

In the beginning of January I heard a rumor that Father Fray Tomás de la Peña had been accused or denounced to the lieutenant at San Francisco of having killed an Indian irrigation worker with blows of a stick.

As the knowledge, information, and experience which I have of his way of life are proofs to me that he is innocent, I did not regard the report as worthy of attention; but no matter how irreproachable one's life may be, it is never safe from malice.

This rumor, despite the fact that it was so vague and improbable as to be worthy only of contempt, was made the object of a very solemn investigation. It was considered a matter of the greatest importance, and was treated, and is being treated, with the formality which I shall describe.

Lieutenant Don Diego Gonzáles,[2] when he was about to make up the census list, called Plácido, a California Indian, for an interview, and in the presence of Sergeant Grijalva asked him what information he had concerning the incident about which he spoke.

He replied: There was an Indian irrigating the orchard; Father Fray Tomás went to see if he were irrigating correctly. He became so angry with him for irrigating badly that he seized the hoe, and with it struck him some blows that were mortal. Then, (added the Indian) Father Fray Diego came out, took the irrigation worker into the house, and took care of him; but he died after a few days.

Such was the evidence of this witness, but I have some proofs that give rise to a very strong suspicion that the author of this calumny is none other than himself.

The above-mentioned lieutenant, in the presidio of his command, summoned Corporal Mariano Cordero (who, they say, happened to be in this mission at the time of this death and who was removed from it, as I have heard, for having failed to notify the lieutenant of this crime), and asked him what he knew about the incident. He replied that, as far as he knew, there was neither a rumor nor definite information that Father Fray Tomás had wounded or killed anyone. That was all he said. The person mentioned obtained other testimony, too, but I have not been able to find out what it was.

Ensign Don Hermenegildo Sal[3] at the present time is holding six Indians prisoners in the guardhouse and is taking statements from them. Judging by what I have observed, although I do know it for certain, I think they will all pertain to this matter.

I have been in this mission one year, ten months, and twenty days, and did not leave it for more than twenty days when, on different occasions, I happened to be at the Mission of St. Francis. Now, in all that time—I say this in case Your Reverence should so order—I can testify under sacred oath that I have neither seen nor heard that Father Fray Tomás de la Peña has wounded or struck anyone with a hoe, or with any other instrument, and that when he chastises the Indians he uses only the same moderation with which parents generally chastise their own children. And would to God he had chastised according to his merits the person who denounced him! Had this been done, he would not have dared to make such false charges.

The grounds on which I base my suspicion that Plácido is the author of this calumny are these: The fact that, because he had given proof that he could not be trusted, he was required to give up the keys of the storehouse and granaries which until then he had managed. And also the fact that the five who are held in custody with him for the purpose of testifying in favor of what I regard as caluminous accusations are persons who are indebted to him, friends of his, and receivers for the goods he has stolen.

This is what I can tell Your Reverence about this affair which is so false and so mischievous.

I pray that God &c.

Fray Diego Noboa.
Santa Clara Mission,
May 2, 1786.

Having found out later that they had taken some Indians of this mission as prisoners to the Presidio of Monterey and seeing that beyond holding three of them as suspects they sent me no official communication that could be interpreted as a criticism of Father Fray Peña, I had to presume, and did presume, that the Father mentioned was entirely innocent. I was strengthened in this opinion as there had been forwarded to me, some days previously, in writing and officially, complaints of various and serious disputes with the same missionary; and against these His Reverence was able to justify himself in full, and to my complete satisfaction. This I can prove at any time, wherever necessary.

Nevertheless, as I had heard there was a rumor (spread, it is true, by persons little deserving of credence) that the removal to Monterey of the above-mentioned Indians was for the purpose of having them testify that certain deaths at the mission were due to the said Father, I made the journey to the mission with sorrow and anxiety; and in a few days

I discovered that there was good reason for my conjecture that in such a place a rumor as rash as this one could spread far and do much harm.

Therefore, without modifying my firm belief that the missionary mentioned was entirely innocent, and fearing only that intemperate language of this nature would give rise to some charge, suspicion, or question which my immediate or other superior could direct to me as President of these Missions, I determined to take action. I summoned the aid of the Reverend Father Preacher Fray Pedro Benito Cambón,[4] and he came from San Francisco at my request. Then, in the best form to be used, which I am capable of and understand, and which is permitted by our status as religious, I determined to institute an inquiry searching enough to give full satisfaction, and after that to take the steps which I judged necessary in view of the results. This I duly resolved to do, and with the above-mentioned priest assisting I so signed it.

Fray Fermín Francisco de Lasuén,
Fray Pedro Benito Cambón.

In this Mission of Santa Clara on the twenty-seventh of the month of May, 1786, acting in virtue of the official decision which gave rise to this inquiry, there appeared before me, Fray Fermín Francisco de Lasuén, President of the Missions, Fray Diego Noboa, apostolic preacher and minister of the said mission, who, being duly sworn, and testifying *in verbo sacerdotis, tacto pectore*[5] undertook to tell the truth regarding what he knew and whatever he might be asked. Then, having read *de verbo ad verbum*[6] the copy of his letter, which was the first exhibit in this inquiry, I questioned him in the following form, and he answered each of the questions as follows:

Question: Do you know which Indian irrigation worker is the one of whose death Father Fray Tomás de la Peña has been accused?
Answer: I have heard that he is called Sixto.
Question: Were you here when this Indian named Sixto died?
Answer: I was.
Question: What is it you know about that death? Tell all you know.
Answer: Between the sixteenth and the nineteenth of July (to the best of my belief) of the year 1784, the Indian named fell sick of a malignant fever of which there was then an epidemic in this mission, and many were prostrated with it. This fever affected his head and caused him to be so delirious that he was unable to make his confession. On the twenty-eighth of the same month and in the same year he died of it, as did several others.
Question: Did you on that occasion take this Indian, or any other, to the house for the purpose of attending a wound or blow given him by Father Fray Tomás?

Answer: No.

Question: With regard to the statement that Corporal Cordero, in reply to Lieutenant Don Diego Gonzáles, said that he had not heard or known that Father Fray Tomás had wounded or killed anyone: Did you receive that information directly from Cordero?

Answer: No. It was given me by a person whose word is thoroughly reliable.

Question: Do you know whether or not this reply of Cordero was made before or after the investigation which Lieutenant Don Diego Gonzáles made, accompanied by Sergeant Grijalva[7] and using the Indian Plácido as interpreter?

Answer: I do not know for certain, but I would infer that it was before.

Question: Do you now testify, according to your statement in the letter, that you have neither seen nor heard that Father Fray Tomás de la Peña had wounded or struck anybody with a hoe or other instrument, and that he chastises the Indians only with that moderation which fathers generally use with their own children?

Answer: Yes, I so testify.

Question: What do you know about an incident, reported to me from various sources, of an injured or broken ear which Father Fray Tomás caused to a boy?

Answer: This is a case in which Father Fray Tomás pulled the ear of a boy named Bernabé because he was playing and making a noise in the church; and as the boy had a pimple or scab on his ear, it began to bleed a little. The governor was a witness to it. But the ear was not injured or broken, as I am convinced, if I had a mind to call him and examine it. And I am certain that his own father gave His Reverence stronger and more severe blows in the ear.

Question: With regard to the charge filed, or more properly the information lodged, by Plácido before Lieutenant Gonzáles, there being no previous complaint as far as we know, did this take place before or after he had been deprived of the keys?

Answer: It was after.

Question: Did you observe or note any tete-a-tete or any unusual friendliness on the part of Plácido with the Indians who are under suspicion of having been called to give evidence on the death of Sixto?

Answer: Within the previous two months he had frequently been seen playing with these Indians, although previously he had never been seen with them; he had sought their companionship and friendship; and he gave them whatever gifts he could.

Question: What else do you know about Plácido which could be considered a motive for stirring up what His Reverence calls false charges and a false and mischievous affair?

Answer: After they had deprived this Plácido of the keys, I have seen him look spitefully at Fray Tomás, and such was his attitude that, even when I counseled him, he would not ask Father for the things he had previously asked. On a certain occasion, too, when Father Fray Tomás was remonstrating with a soldier, Arellano, for some blows he had given an Indian named Daniel, Plácido took the side of the soldier in the presence of the Father and falsely blamed the Indian. Then the man named Arellano threatened (so he has been told) that he would draw up one or two charges in writing against Father Fray Tomás, and it would seem that it was from then on that Plácido began to fabricate these falsehoods.

Question: In your opinion, how successful is Father Fray Tomás in carrying out his official duties in this Mission of Santa Clara? What is his manner of dealing with the Indians? Do they have a friendly regard for him?

Answer: I consider him very suitable for the office. He is zealous and is very much concerned about both spiritual and material improvements. He is usually genial and affable towards both Christians and pagans. He puts up with and tolerates their importunites, almost to excess, and both parties are reasonably satisfied with him.

Having read all the testimony he had given, he said it was all true and all given under the oath he had taken. He affirmed under oath and signed it with me and the assisting priest.

The day, month, and year as above.

Fray Fermín Francisco de Lasuén,
Fray Diego de Noboa,
Fray Pedro Benito Cambón.

In this Mission of Santa Clara, on the 23rd day of the month of May, 1786, I, Fray Fermín Francisco de Lasuén, President of the Missions, examined with all care the testimony which precedes—testimony which by itself firmly supports my opinion that there has been neither fault nor excess on the part of Father Fray Tomás de la Peña in the matter under consideration—and bearing in mind that nothing has been officially communicated to me on the matter by anyone, [I am cognizant of the fact] that immediately after the inquiries which presumably were made with reference to the death of Sixto, six Indians of this mission were removed as prisoners to Monterey, and that the three elder ones remain there in punishment.

As regards the three who were released and sent to this mission, we know now that they gave Father Fray Tomás de la Peña a verbal message from the governor, couched in these terms: that His Lordship had not asked for these Indians; that he had not intended to give, nor had he given orders for their arrest; that he was therefore sending them back at the first opportunity, but that the other three were wicked and perverse and he was detaining them in order to give them what they deserved.

I had to infer, and did infer as a very fitting consequence, that if their imprisonment and their declarations taken by the Ensign Don Hermenegildo Sal were ordered for the reason put forward by Father Noboa in his letter, a copy of which forms the beginning of this inquiry, they would have convicted these latter three Indians of false testimony, and would therefore continue to hold them as prisoners and in banishment, and in this way, obviously, the complete innocence of Father Fray Tomás de la Peña would be established.

Nevertheless, some very peculiar circumstances, which I continue to uncover in our case, force me to the conclusion that it is necessary to take every possible precaution in order to attain the objectives laid down at the beginning of the inquiry and to ensure, as far as lies in my power, the quiet and tranquility, the stability and good government of this mission.

I, therefore, considered that I should continue, and I did continue, this inquiry, calling as witnesses those whom I knew to be relatives of the deceased Sixto. This I resolved and duly determined, and co-signed it with the same assisting priest.

Fray Fermín Francisco de Lasuén,
Fray Pedro Benito Cambón.

In this Mission of Santa Clara on the 30th day of May, 1785, before me, Fray Fermín Francisco de Lasuén, President of these Missions, and before the assisting priest, there appeared Silverio, an Indian neophyte of this mission, aged about thirty-eight years. Having been warned of the obligation to tell the truth regarding what he knew and would be asked and having been warned too regarding the punishments which he could incur for the contrary, all of which being clearly explained to him through the interpreter, he was questioned by means of the latter:

Question: Are you a relative of Sixto, the deceased Indian?
Answer: I am a relative.
Question: In what way are you related to the Sixto we have spoken of?
Answer: I am an uncle by blood of Sixto.
Question: Did you see him die?
Answer: I saw him die. I took care of him in his illness.
Question: What caused his death?
Answer: It was due to headache.
Question: Did he suffer from something beside a headache?
Answer: No, nothing more.
Question: Did not the sick man say that some other part of the body caused pain?
Answer: He also said that his stomach pained him. (The question was also repeated in this way:)
Question: Did he not complain that he felt pain in some other part?
Answer: Only in the head and stomach.
Question: What did he say? What did this nephew Sixto say when he became ill with that sickness?
Answer: He used the words: 'I have now caught the disease.'
Question: At that time were there others suffering from that disease?
Answer: There were many.
Question: Did some die?
Answer: Many died.

Having set forth through the interpreter all that he had said in reply, he affirmed that these were what he had said and that they were true. To make them official, I signed them, together with the assisting priest.

Fray Fermín Francisco de Lasuén,
Fray Pedro Benito Cambón.

The assisting priest also certified that, according to his knowledge of the Indian dialect, the interpreter observed all the legal requirements in the questions and the testimony given above by the Indian neophyte named Silverio. And to make this official I signed it with the above-named assisting Father.

Fray Fermín Francisco de Lasuén,
Fray Pedro Benito Cambón.

Following immediately, in the same Mission of Santa Clara, on the same thirtieth day of the same month and year, there appeared before me and before the assisting Father an Indian neophyte of this mission named Diego, aged about fifteen years, a cousin or a blood relative of the deceased Sixto. Having been warned of the obligation to tell the truth regarding what he knew and might be asked, and having been warned too about the punishments he would incur for doing the contrary, and being well informed about it because he knew Spanish, he was asked:

Question: Are you a relative of the deceased Sixto?
Answer: Yes, I am his brother-in-law.
Question: Were you here when Sixto died?
Answer: I was here.
Question: Do you know what caused his death?
Answer: Father Fray Tomás struck him.
Question: With what did he strike him?
Answer: With a hoe and with rocks.
Question: Did you see this?
Answer: Yes, I saw it.
Question: Where were you when you saw it?
Answer: I was on the pile of unthreshed wheat.
Question: Was the pile of unthreshed wheat near where the deceased Sixto was?
Answer: No, the pile of wheat was outside the enclosure, close to where they thresh; and the deceased Sixto was irrigating kidney beans on the other side of the orchard.
Question: How could you see it from that distance? Does not the entire orchard with its enclosure of high trees with thick foliage come in between? To this he gave no reply.

Question: Were you, perhaps, at the top of the pile of wheat?

Answer: No, I was on the ground with the boys, catching the ears which Plácido was throwing from above.

Question: How could you see from the ground that Father Fray Tomás was hitting Sixto with the hoe and with rocks?

Answer: I did not see it, but Plácido said he saw it.

Question: When I asked you if you had seen it, why did you say: Yes, you had seen it?

Answer: Plácido told me that I had seen it.

Question: Tell me: Did you see it, or did you not see it?

Answer: I did not see it. Plácido told me that I did see it. Father Tomás was then inside the orchard, and the deceased Sixto was outside of it, irrigating the kidney beans.

I told him then that it was not good to tell a lie, that he was a Christian and knew that God commanded us not to tell lies; and for that reason he should tell what he knew or what he had seen. And the assisting priest added: Do not be afraid. The Father President is our superior, and he wants to know what we the Fathers, do. And if the Fathers do anything bad, he will punish us; and therefore, answer the questions and tell us what you know, or what you have seen.

He answered:

I did not see it; Plácido told me that I saw it.

I repeated the answers he had made, and he affirmed them and said that they were true, and to make it official I signed it with the assisting Father.

Fray Fermín Francisco de Lasuén,
Fray Pedro Benito Cambón.

In this Mission of Santa Clara on the 31st day of May, 1786, I Fray Fermín Francisco de Lasuén, President of these Missions, realize that the two Indians who have given testimony are regarded in the eyes of the law as untrustworthy and interested witnesses against the one who is thought guilty; that the first, who is the uncle of the deceased Sixto, although he was present during the sickness and death of his nephew, makes no mention whatever of blows; and that the *second confesses that in what he imputed to Father Fray Tomás, he was led on and deceived by Plácido, a mean fellow of disreputable conduct, antagonistic to the Fathers, and acceptable to those who persecute them.* After having conducted a sufficient number of judicial proceedings according to the best form which I knew, and could, and thought necessary to attain the objectives expressed and to arrive at a judgment, I now give as my judgment that I find no cause and no reason for correcting, reprehending, or summoning to judgment the Reverend Father Fray Tomás de la Peña.

Therefore, I determined to call, and did call, the above-mentioned Reverend Father, and in the presence of the assisting Father exhorted him paternally to continue in his apostolic ministry, reminding him how appropriate persecutions are in such an occupation.

I pointed out to him that perhaps sometimes by giving an ear-pulling, a punch, a rap on the head, or a slap with the hand, it would be possible to give, now or in the future, an occasion or an excuse for similar false charges, being, as we are, especially in appointments such as these, the center of observation for all men, and not all of them look on us with kindly eyes. And so, he should refrain from such action, even though such punishment is commonly given by the most indulgent fathers to their own sons.

To this the Reverend Father replied that he would gladly obey, and that that was the manner in which he would act, just as he was ordered.

Then he asked me to bear in mind that the grave and repeated complaints that had been made to me against him were not made by the Indians but by the first families of the land and that there was no truth in them nor any foundation for them.

[He added] that the present form of detraction had been started subsequent to these incidents and to others about which he had kept silent, and that besides finding an excuse for it in much earlier occurrences which hitherto had not been imputed to him they try to prove their point, relying solely on the evidence of Indians, who can easily be influenced and instigated against the missionary, for it is he who curbs their excessive liberty, subjects them to justice, and punishes their excesses.

He added that it was very strange, and a matter of deep regret to him, the extraordinary ease with which, it seemed, recourse could be had in such matters to private and judicial inquiries; and these, because they were carried out by the very persons who should have defended us against the boldness of the Indians, had the effect of producing in the latter isolence and haughtiness, and in the missionary sorrow and dismay.

"I take everything into account, Father Fray Tomás," I said to him, "and with the help of God I shall do all that lies in my power to find the best remedy for such troubles and adversities."

The Reverend Father Tomás then proceeded to say that, as I was aware, I had no sooner arrived at this mission than he made representations that I should officially make a request regarding the investigations which, according to rumor, were instituted against him. I replied that I ought not to do this, first, because there was no clear evidence of such proceedings, since nothing specific had been brought to my notice which would be prejudicial to his good conduct; and secondly, because the subsequent imprisonment and immediate banishment of the witnesses should effectively dispel the scandalous public rumor and give rise to one rooted in well-merited esteem for his blameless reputation.

With this he was appeased; and finally he promises, assures, and guarantees me that should there arise any notice, imputation, accusation, claim, petition, declaration, or anything of that nature which would impute to him culpability in this matter, he will give the most adequate answer and fullest satisfaction with testimony given under oath, not just the testimony of persons taken at random, but that of persons *de razón*, God-fearing men of better and blameless life, and even that of Indians, provided they are not those who are excessively vicious or unalterably corrupt.

And for the record, he signed it with me and with the assisting priest.

Fray Fermín Francisco de Lasuén,
Fray Tomás de la Peña,
Fray Pedro Benito Cambón.

[1] He was a native of Santiago, Spain, and reached California in 1783. He spent one year at San Carlos Mission, and ten years at Santa Clara Mission, after which he returned to San Fernando College.

[2] Bancroft (*op. cit.*, I, 470) tells us that he was born at Ceste del Campo, Spain, served as a private and eventually reached the rank of lieutenant, adding that before he left Monterey he was "under arrest for insubordination, gambling, failing to prevent gambling, and for trading with the galleon." At San Francisco his irregular conduct continued in spite of warnings and re-arrest, and in 1787 the governor was obliged to send him away. He never returned to California.

[3] He reached California in the capacity of a private in the Anza expedition. Possessed of talent and a better education than the average, he rose quickly. He held the rank of lieutenant, and at different times was commandant at San Francisco. Bancroft describes him (*op. cit.*, I, 678-679) as a "hasty, quick-tempered man, prone as a commander to order severe penalties for offenses against his strict discipline, and then to countermand the order when his temper had passed away." He died at Monterey in December, 1800.

[4] He was a native of Galicia, Spain. He arrived at San Fernando College in 1770, and at Monterey the following year. He was a participant in the founding of Missions San Gabriel, San Francisco, and San Buenaventura. He was a zealous missionary but was often incapacitated because of ill health. He returned to Mexico in 1791. Cf. Geiger, *Palou's Life of Serra*, pp. 399-400.

[5] On the word of a priest, with hand over heart.

[6] Word for word.

[7] He had been a member of the Anza expedition. He led a group of settlers from San Gabriel, where circumstances had forced him to stay for a time, to San Francisco. See Bolton's *Anza's California Expedition*, III, 386; IV, 424.

40. To Don José Antonio Rengel

The report which, I presume, has been given Your Lordship in regard to certain rumors in the Mission of Santa Clara which impute, but without justification, various crimes of enormous gravity to Father Fray Tomás de la Peña, its missionary, compels me forcibly to refer the matter to the gracious consideration of Your Lordship.

So annoying a report must naturally have moved Your Lordship to indignation, and must have offended your Christian zeal; but the truth which, on my priestly honor, I impart to you will at least serve to hold such sentiments in suspense.

It was with painful anxiety, Sir, that I proceeded to Santa Clara Mission where, in view of what I saw and the inquiries I made, I affirm that the religious in question, who is upright before God and man, is innocent of the crimes imputed to him. He is a good priest, an experienced missionary, and one who upholds the honor of his apostolic calling. He carries out his duties punctually, takes care of that settlement, and develops in it the spirit of peace and progress which His Majesty the King and Your Lordship would desire.

I have gathered abundant proof of this, and shall present it to Your Lordship whenever so ordered, And proofs of my loyalty and devotedness I shall also give without hesitation as often as Your Lordship deigns so to command me.

May God Our Lord keep Your Lordship many years in His holy grace.

San Carlos of Monterey Mission,
July 3, 1786.

41. Report on Judicial Proceedings

Between the twenty-sixth and thirty-first of May of the year 1786, in the Mission of Santa Clara, I instituted certain investigations of a judicial nature, observing due procedure according to the best of my knowledge, capacity, and training. These not only confirmed in me a conviction which I had strongly held regarding the becoming, the religious, priestly, and apostolic conduct of the Reverend Father Tomás de la Peña, minister of the mission above-mentioned, but (if justice be done) should be enough to remove from the minds of the people a most harmful misconception reflecting on the integrity, honor, and good name of the missionary just mentioned. This was occasioned by the holding of a hurried, irregular, and sacrilegious investigation set up, so the public understood, to examine the charges of homicide attributed to the Father mentioned. The proceedings I instituted shall serve as my vindication should my immediate, or some other, superior bring a charge, an accusation, or a requisition against me as President of these Missions because of the publicity which should have been avoided, and which was unwise and showed lack of prudence.

What influences me are motives that are just, causes that are genuine, and reasons that are well-founded so that, ever watchful (insofar as it pertains to me) for the peace and tranquility, the stability and good government of that mission and of the others, I may take the due and fitting means to bring to an end the very serious difficulties and incalculable drawbacks that are certain to result from listening with an avid and vengeful ear to the charges that Indians make against missionaries (who impose on them merely what is just) and, what is more serious still, from suggesting similar falsehoods to them, inducing them to testify to such falsehoods in court, and from flattering them by giving a sympathetic ear to their complaints as if they were genuine.

Taking for granted that the favorable results I had anticipated would follow from the judicial inquiry I instituted (the originals of which I keep in the archives of my office), I dispensed with legal formalities in many cases when the evidence in vindication of the Father was cumulative and well authenticated. I followed this procedure so as not to add to the publicity, and so as not to give the false and opposite opinion more importance than it merits.

Keeping in mind the scandalous publicity given the affair—the fact that the inquiry was held at Santa Clara Mission at the very time when Indians from almost every part of the province had assembled there, especially those who let their ideas be dictated by their whims; and being aware that by this ill-considered action the inquiry had endangered very gravely, or at least exposed to unbecoming criticism, the untarnished good name of this missionary, with no small discredit of his colleagues, I set myself to the task of bringing this missionary's innocence into clearer focus, and of discovering if possible the source of the calumnies that were accumulating.

For this purpose I acted in as affable and friendly a manner as I could towards both Indians and the *gente de razón* at the mission. I gave both to understand that in regard to any shortcomings of the Fathers I would proceed with justice. The result was that there was but one complaint, and this was proved false and groundless by the very witnesses whom the complainant summoned to give evidence in his behalf.

Besides this, I sought opportunities to obtain information discreetly from trustworthy persons who were fully qualified to testify in this matter. Their statements, inasmuch as they were extrajudicial, were made in the presence of Reverend Father Pedro Benito Cambón, and manifested clearly that, in the mind of any man of judgment, the charges against the Reverend Father Peña should be regarded from beginning to end as nothing but a plot inspired by malice, concocted much earlier behind a façade of investigations and inquiries that were at once irregular, heated, and prejudiced. These inquiries were of a nature to give rise to sedition and to brand the leaders and principal promoters of the movement as men who, at the very least, were malicious. They make clear that the procedure they employed was an invasion of privacy, arrogant, exceedingly frivolous, in no way impartial, and a grave menace to the success of this entire conquest.

To supply fuller clarification and proof of this, I will now go on to explain the news and events which the trustworthy people above-mentioned communicated to me privately, (but in the presence of Father Cambón, as already mentioned,) and the offer which they made to confirm their statements on oath, if necessary. I shall do this in accordance with the truth that befits my character, and in accordance, too, with what seems to have been the sequence of steps in this sententious proceeding, without any thought of injuring anyone, or any other purpose than the vindication and exercise of what the law permits.

The Reverend Father Matías Noriega[1] reported that, shortly after his arrival at this mission of San Carlos from the Mission of Santa Clara about October of last year, 1785, Captain Don Nicolás Soler,[2] the adjutant inspector, whose own words and deeds have provoked trouble and critical comment in this province, asserted with indignation that Father Tomás de la Peña had become demented and turned his rage against the Indians, and that the latter were presently opportuning the corporal of that escort and all the guards; and for that reason the mission was in evident danger of revolt.

It was substantially the same story which he recounted briefly at San Antonio Mission, as the Reverend Father Buenaventura Sitjar[3] assured me, for no sooner had the adjutant mentioned arrived at that mission than he made this statement in his presence, namely, that Father Peña frequently punished the Indians by inflicting on them one hundred or two hundred lashes, and this he did after he had exhausted himself by administering buffetings, and thrashings, and kicks to them. What nonsense! May God forgive him for what he said. The normal procedure in the circumstance would be that an officer of his rank, the second highest in this country, should himself take some appropriate measures, or cause them to be taken. What measures have been taken, I do not yet know, unless it be the authorization, which I presume was given in concurrence with His Lordship the Governor, to Lieutenant Don González, who was on his way to San Francisco but who was at that time at the Presidio of Monterey. It is certain that the highly improper inquiries

carried out by this lieutenant at Santa Clara Mission gave rise to calumnies and false accusations similar to, but graver in import, than the
charges made by the adjutant; and that the value and publicity which
the same lieutenant gave to these dastardly fabrications were calculated
to stir up clamorous and sacrilegious accusations against the missionary
in question.

Before presenting the evidence, it seems to me very appropriate to
make mention of my meeting with this adjutant. I met His Honor about
December of that same year of 1785 at the Presidio of Santa Barbara
when I was on my way to take up residence at this mission after my
recent appointment as President of these Missions. There I paid my
respects as courteously and kindly as usual, and I accepted the expressions of respect which he sought to offer, making clear at the same time
how pleased he was because of my new office. I did what I could for
the treatment of his eyes[4] and stayed much longer than I had intended,
solely for the purpose of bringing him some relief and of accompanying
him to San Luis where he was inclined to stay because it offered a more
suitable climate and more comfortable quarters.

In all that time we spoke of the state of these possessions, and never
once by a single word did he make any allusion, direct or indirect, to
the excesses attributed to Father Peña, which he recounted and to which
he gave voice here at this mission and at San Antonio.

This coincidence by itself is enough to help us to draw a conclusion;
but it will be more in accordance with law, more certain, and more
cogent, if we first keep in mind the statements and reports of those who
were in a position to be witnesses, or ought to have witnessed the atrocities which they impute to the Father in question.

Lieutenant Don Diego González had already been to Santa Clara
when on his way to San Francisco and had returned to Santa Clara two
or three times from San Francisco. His superiors and the officers under
him, his subjects and his equals will report better than I can on the
conduct of this officer on the ethical, military, and political level.

It seems to me that a religious in no way merits censure when he
stands up for his rights, no matter how many charges a person makes
against him.

There was then in Santa Clara an Indian known as Plácido who, in
typical Indian fashion, harbored and manifested a grudge against Father
Peña, partly because he had been deprived of keys which until then had
been entrusted to him and partly because of a light punishment that had
been given him for a fault that was not so slight.

It happened at the same time that the same Father reproached a
soldier named Arellano for having struck a neophyte of the name

Daniel. Plácido, in the presence of the Father, defended the soldier and falsely laid the blame on the neophyte. Then, as is known, Arellano threatened that he might have one or two cards to play against Father Peña, and from that time on Plácido and Arellano formed a closer and closer association.

Lieutenant González used to go with undue frequency to the house of Arellano, and even removed by his own authority a restriction or prohibition which, at the instance of the Father, had been imposed on a certain person in that house. I shall now come closer to our problem.

Mariano Cordero, who at that time was corporal of the guard, and who since his marriage[5] has shown good character and good judgment, testifies that the lieutenant reprimanded him for not having notified him of the death of one of the irrigation workers which Father Peña had brought about while the corporal was still there.

In reply, he informed him that he had neither known nor heard anything about a murder of that kind. But the lieutenant in turn replied: "You know it well, but you do not wish to say it." To this the other replied: "If I knew it I would tell it; and if anything as novel as that had happened, without doubt I would have heard, for the Indians usually tell me things of lesser moment, for no corporal has been closer to the Indians, or as close, for I intentionally seek them out, and chat with them, and ask them a thousand questions, all of them weighted, and with the object of testing their good or bad humor. And I do this so that they may not catch me unawares in any of their suspicious movements. In this way they keep me informed about developments; and for this reason, if this murder had taken place, no one would have been better informed about it than I. But I never heard that either a murder, or a wound, or a blow of that kind took place in my time."

On hearing this reply the lieutenant persisted: "Perhaps you know that this was not the only one?" Then the other replied in astonishment: "What do you mean? Not the only one?" The lieutenant in turn replied: "It is not the only one. Isabel, the wife of Corporal Peralta,[6] has informed me that prior to it the same Father was responsible for another murder."

The Corporal brought the interview to an end by saying: "I know nothing about it, and I have heard nothing about it."

This same Cordero testifies that during his entire term of office he neither saw nor heard that Father Fray Tomás had maltreated Indians by administering blows or by inflicting punishment on them; and that he had never heard complaints from them; and that he was not cognizant of, nor did he ever discover in them, the least evidence of discontent, hostility, or insubordination.

He stated that recently the lieutenant, on his return from Santa Clara Mission to the Presidio of San Francisco to which he is attached, informed him that on the very night on which he reached the mission just named, the Indians had decided to destroy it and to flee from it in a body, and that if he had not arrived and calmed them, they would have done so.

How preposterous! There are as many ways of discrediting this statement as there are Indians as witnesses, and as many as there are soldiers, for by an unusual coincidence, some fifteen or twenty of them were assembled there under command of Don Hermenigildo, their ensign. What can one make of it? What conclusion can one draw when a lie is told in the very presence of those who know it is a lie?

I would not be surprised if one who could talk like that would act in the same manner. What I mean is this: If for his own ends he can openly spin fables of this nature, may he not induce the Indians to mutiny just to support his own fault-finding?

In order to find out how reliable Isabel's statement was, I had recourse to her father-in-law, Gabriel Peralta. He is a man advanced in years, respectable, God-fearing, strictly and religiously conscientious, and as exemplary a man as one can find.

On a former occasion he had already told me, as he held in his hand the holy cross on which he was willing to swear, that, having served in the past for a time at Santa Clara Mission, and as corporal at the neighboring Presidio of San José from the date of its founding, and having had frequent contact with Father Tomás, and having helped him in various tasks, he had never seen or heard that His Reverence had struck anyone, even with a rod, or that he had disciplined anyone except after the manner of a parent; nor did he know of any discontent, or restlessness, or evidence of mutiny among the Indians.

He further stated that until Lieutenant Don Diego called to his house the Indian known as Plácido, and others also, he had never heard any of the things later attributed to Father Peña, and that the Indian Plácido, who had been a frequent visitor at his house, never entered it again after the affair of the soldier Arellano mentioned above.

I then asked this good man to tell me what he knew of his daughter-in-law, Isabel, and how one should judge what Lieutenant González said to Cordero. He answered that when he questioned Isabel on the subject, she became quite emotional, as a woman would, and placing her hand on the cross, she replied that she would testify on oath a thousand times that she had made no such statement to Lieutenant González or to anyone else. She said, however, that on a certain occasion when she was with some other women in a house, or in a kitchen, Lieutenant González entered and began by saying: "This Father Peña is bound to be ousted from Santa Clara sooner or later, because blows and insults are all he knows, as far as Indians are concerned. Look at Isabel over there. She knows well that this Father killed an Indian." Looking at him straight in the face, she answered: "This is not so, Lieutenant. I know nothing about a death, nor about blows or insults. All I know and hear is that this Father disciplines the Indians as the other Fathers do."

Shortly after the reproof given to Corporal Cordero by Lieutenant González, arrangements were made to transfer the former from the guard at Santa Clara Mission to the Presidio of San Francisco.

It may be well to note here that from what two astute Indians of San Francisco Mission have said, it is easy to infer that the Indian, Plácido, knew of his transfer before Corporal Cordero did. In addition to this prediction, Plácido informed the two servants it was planned to remove Cordero to the Presidio of San Francisco so that they might investigate one or more deaths that Father Peña had brought about at Santa Clara.

With much regret Cordero in due course departed from the mission, and Corporal Juan José Peralta came to take his place. He is the son of Gabriel Peralta mentioned above, a young man who is well brought up, who carries out his duties, and who will never be the black sheep of the family. He had already served as corporal at that same mission, and he assured me that Lieutenant González had asked him the same questions he had asked Cordero, and had become angered because he gave a truthful answer as Cordero had done, viz., that he knew nothing and heard nothing about the murder regarding which he was questioned, nor of the injuries or blows allegedly inflicted by Father Peña.

He told me further that he had orders from the lieutenant to question Plácido and two or three other witnesses—kinsfolk or associates or comrades of his—as the lieutenant had questioned him in regard to the death or deaths which presumably had been committed or caused by the Father in question; that the Indians informed him that it was true, but that he had never heard anything about such a thing during his duty here, nor ever heard it mentioned until Lieutenant González questioned him about it, and that the Indians had never complained about this, or of being dissatisfied and angry at Father Peña, nor did he ever see the Reverend Father maltreat them, nor did they ever show signs of revolt or rioting. Each further stated that he did not know what the lieutenant had against Father Peña, for on a certain feastday, after the bells had been rung three times for Mass, and the soldiers were bestirring themselves to go and attend it, he asked what priest would say it. When they told him that it would be Father Peña he replied, to the scandal of all,

"Then I'm not going. I would rather miss Mass than attend one said by that Father."

In compliance with the instructions of the lieutenant, Corporal Peralta forwarded him the evidence of these Indians, taken in accordance with the instructions given above. The former then summoned Corporal Peralta and Sergeant Grijalva as witnesses to the inquiry which he held. This [inquiry] was confined to questioning the Indian Plácido, and one or two other Indians, concerning the death or deaths about which Peralta had questioned them and about which they had replied to him that they had been committed by Father Peña. Both Grijalva and Peralta assert that, before they arrived in order to be present at and to hear the interrogation, Don Diego González, who was to ask the questions, engaged in conversation to his heart's content with the Indians who were to answer the questions. This was an observation which they made to me on their own initiative, and they told me how shocked they were at the procedure.

Sergeant Grijalva, who fills his post with honor and stands in high repute, said that, when he was present, what the lieutenant directed to the Indians were suggestions rather than questions, and that the words "So then" were the customary introduction to each interrogation. "So then Father Peña struck the Indian?" "So then the Indian died from the blows?", etc. To these questions the Indians invariably replied, "Yes, Sir"—like a conversation repeated after it had first been rehearsed.

And even if this were not so, it seems to me very appropriate to recall what Señor Montenegro reports when speaking of the prudence which a judge must exercise when investigating charges brought by Indians against parish priests. This learned and experienced bishop writes in his *Itinerario de Párrocos* (Book V of "Los Privilegios," treatise 2, section 5) that a certain visitor, seeing a petition that had reference to very serious charges which certain Indians made against their pastor, said to one of the witnesses: "So, on one Sunday after prayers your pastor killed King David?" And the witness answered: "Yes, Sir, I myself saw him kill him."

It has been our sad lot to suffer precisely what this most illustrious author tried so hard to forestall in the passage quoted; and we see in our day, at great risk and danger, the nullification of these worthy provisions which he drew up at the Third Council of Lima for similar situations:

Since it is well known, (art. 4, ch. 6 states) that Indians can be led by deep-seated malice, while the missionaries are at the mercy of false charges in proportion as they reprove the vices of the Indians, or oppose the avarice or cruelty of the Spaniards, the Holy Synod, desiring to make provision for the good name and stability of the priests who labor among the Indians and are in charge of them, decrees as follows:

"Where there is an urgent reason for obtaining evidence, and the decision will have to be based on the evidence of Indians, let the judges weigh carefully the amount of credence that should be given to the evidence of people such as these, for, as is well known, they can easily be induced to testify falsely."

And in the year 1212 Pope Innocent III, in chapter 17, *Qualiter et Quando de Accusationibus,*[7] states:

Evidence should not be received against a person when it is of this nature, for the inquiry should be confined to charges presented by those who are upright and honorable, and not by those who are vindictive and depraved . . . [incomplete and blurred].

And Canon 23 of Dist. 83 (the first part of the decree) lays this obligation on ecclesiastical prelates in regard to their subjects, and the same should be understood by secular superiors in regard to theirs:

Should some information in regard to any particular cleric come to your knowledge, and should it be of such a nature as to afford you good reason for taking action, do not readily believe it; and unless it is proved, let it not move you to punishment.

Furthermore, the sergeant himself never heard them speak of excesses, nor did he learn anything about them on the many occasions when he was at Santa Clara Mission until Lieutenant González arrived, as mentioned above, despite the fact that he was in frequent contact with the soldiers because of his position, conversing with them, and overhearing their conversation, sometimes with and sometimes without their knowledge, sometimes taking an active part in their confabs, sometimes taking them by surprise, as the duties of his office required.

There is a soldier named Pedro Bojorques. He was a member of the mission guard at Santa Clara for many years, a reasonably well-behaved man about whom nothing evil is known. He reported that he had never seen or heard that Father Peña had ill-treated any Indians, or punished them cruelly, or that they in turn found fault with, or were displeased or dissatisfied with His Reverence. This is the man who heard Arellano make the threat that he held one or more cards against Father Peña.

Finally, Lieutenant González forwarded a report to Governor Fages in regard to what he had learned from the Indians during the inquiry, with the addition that these matters were subjects of conversation among the soldiers.

The governor, who a short time before was pleased to notify me officially of the complaint of the lieutenant in question against Father Peña, and who was satisfied that the charges were not true, on this occasion not only failed to inform me of the denunciation or accusation, but concealed it from me most carefully and commissioned Ensign Don

Hermenegildo Sal to draw up at Santa Clara Mission a brief of the information given by Lieutenant González.

Ensign Don Hermenegildo Sal, who had himself approached the governor with complaints against the same Father, and who found himself in the same unenviable position as the lieutenant after they had been investigated, carried out the commission and set to work on the reports.

These will appear to those who read them as a case of concealing one's head when opposing Indians, and of exposing one's body when opposing the priest. Some of them lack all validity, for they are not faithful copies of the originals; they do not record the decision, the sentence, or the claim. They were entrusted to me, but only confidentially.

At the same time I received a letter from the Reverend Preacher Fray Diego Noboa, minister of the same Mission of Santa Clara. In it he offered to affirm on oath the opposite (according to the rumors then current) to what it was conjectured the Indians had testified. And even before I received that letter, and still more afterwards, I had to presume, and I did presume, that the inquiries conducted by Ensign Sal were nothing but a collection of falsehoods. Despite this, I was strongly impelled neither to cause offense, nor to show lack of good will to another superior officer by drawing attention to a document as spiteful as that. On the other hand, I was requested to deprive Father Peña of all control over the mission, to transfer him to another, and to give my word that I would send him back to Mexico in the first ships.

Well, how was I to agree to something as absurd as that? In *Qualiter et Quando de Accusationibus* taken from the Sacred Text, we read: "Thus we see that God did not give judgment against Adam until He had first called him and heard his defense." And in the chapter *De Causis Possessionis et Proprietatis*[8] the Supreme Pontiff, Gregory VII, when treating of those absent, declared in the year 1075 after the birth of Christ: "Far be it from Us to give judgment against those who have not been heard in their own defense."

I am very desirous that the charges proffered by Sal and already mentioned should be brought before one or more capable and conscientious judges. It seems to me that by itself, independently of what my investigations showed, we can prove to them that the entire record is a baseless fabrication that has its source in a fiery spirit of revenge; that the wily subtlety with which it was concocted is baneful in the highest degree and makes it easy for them to proceed against us in law for any kind of failing. As a consequence of this, such a precedent could lead to delay in, if not to the actual destruction of, the conquests we have undertaken, for it would disqualify us for our apostolic work.

Well, what if my juridical and extra-juridical investigations make all of this clear to them? What if they reflect that, despite the fact that in the legal proceedings the Indians are cited and declared guilty, they are questioned not as if they were the guilty party but as if they are witnesses? No attempt is made to elicit from them the least evidence that could prove that they are calumniators. They are merely asked to confirm the false testimony they have given. And although they are removed to the presidio as prisoners, once within the barracks there are orders that they are to be set at liberty, and the only time they are not seen on the outside is when the President visits there.

In short, I rest my case on the above-mentioned copy, or a faithful transcript of it, for it is necessary for the case so as to ensure that what has been accomplished may not be entirely undone.

I confess I am deeply grieved that I have to be preoccupied with this affair. I find it a mighty obstacle that hinders me from giving my attention to many matters of grave moment. Yet, I am convinced that this affair which has befallen us is the most powerful stratagem which Hell has been able to devise to promote its evil designs against all these reductions, and for that reason I should labor to uncover and defeat it. May God in His infinite mercy do this; and then it will be seen that the snares laid by the Devil entrap but himself, that his stratagems recoil against him, that what he imagines to be hindrances turn out to be helps, and that the Most High laughs to scorn the malice of the Evil One, just as it is by His inscrutable will that the latter is permitted to exist.

No undertaking can win such timely and profitable results for these conquests, in the state in which they are, as this unmasking, just as nothing could be more prejudicial to them than the burlesque just mentioned. This is my reason for pursuring this objective.

After they had made known to me in confidence the commission of Ensign Don Hermenegildo and its results, there were so many summaries given me verbally by both Indians and *gente de razón* of charges against Father Peña that I thought that once I was placed in that Mission of Santa Clara, and close to the Pueblo of San José, I would hear nothing but complaints against Father Peña. This was not the way things developed, because in a few days I neither saw nor heard anything but what was in his favor. This induced me to issue a series of exhortations to both parties, recommending to them to keep the peace, pointing out to them that this beautiful virtue is not an enemy of, but a brother and friend of, justice, and justice I would always render whenever they sought it because of unreasonable actions of the Fathers.

The alcalde of the pueblo in question, as well as the regidor and other residents, on many occasions heard me reason thus. On one occasion when no one had lodged any complaint, the alcalde said to me: "Father President, if there have been some disagreements and dissensions between the pueblo people and the Fathers, all of them were of little moment, and the occasion for them was supplied by the pueblo when the corporal of the guard denied a small favor which the mission requested. He did so with a certain amount of disrespect, but he did it on his own initiative without consulting anyone. However, for some time past we of the pueblo have enjoyed pleasant relations with the two Fathers, and we are very grateful for the favors we all receive from them."

The alcalde, the regidor, and the fiscal[9] of the mission called one at a time and stated through an interpreter that they were all content and that they had no complaint against Father Tomás. And the fiscal added: "All, all, big and little, men and women, Christians and pagans, all are satisfied."

I told each of them that I was much concerned, for I had heard that their people were saying that they were going to flee to the forests. All replied with one voice that that had happened long ago, and that it arose when they asked permission to go to the forests and the Fathers refused it to some, and that these used to say that they would go without permission.

I conclude now with the following information: Joaquín de Castro is an old man of prudent conduct and good repute. After serving for many years as a soldier in the Mission of Santa Clara, he is today one of the most respected inhabitants of the above-mentioned pueblo of San José de Gálvez. He informed me that he was well acquainted with Father Peña; that he had been his escort on journeys and investigations in regard to the Indians; and that he had noticed nothing but a love for them that was too trustful, an extreme good humor, and a degree of patience and courtesy that was unusual.

He stated that he knows Plácido quite well, and that he knows his evil cunning, his treachery and arrogance, and the excessive tolerance of the Fathers for his duplicity; that his representations and those of his companions, based on happenings long past, began to take shape and to be disseminated by means of the investigations instituted in the guard-house and elsewhere; that previous to that time nothing was known or spoken of these calumnies; that if the stories of such Indians were to be the basis for legal proceedings, the judges would have nothing else to do and would not have time for even that; that the imprudent and thought-less assent given to these stories and lies, all of which is known to the Indians, has given them occasion, and perhaps influenced them to say, as in fact some of them have done in his own house, that the corporal of the guard had read them a letter from the governor in which His Lordship promised that he would come in person to remove Father Peña from the mission. And that finally, by means of this method of procedure, what has been accomplished was neither more nor less than the lifting of the hand of the Indian first against the Fathers, and then against all who hold and garrison these possessions.

This last thought, which was in my mind already, is true beyond all doubt, and has kept me preoccupied with this painful task.

This has been, and (assuming the evident innocence of the Father) remains the first and only incentive for my tedious work in these and the other investigations. My sole object is to see whether I can succeed in bringing about the correction and prohibition of such improper and imprudent procedures, for, without any doubt, they rob us of the professional competence so necessary in order to carry out successfully what God wills and the King desires.

By reason of these proceedings we see transformed into adversaries the very individuals whom the King maintains for our help and defense; and by reason of them, too, it is made clear that those who contribute to the insolence and arrogance of the Indians are the very ones who have been entrusted with greater authority by the King in order to bring them into subjection.

May, then, those in authority have sympathy with misfortune, unhappiness, and misery of this kind, and let them know (for we glory not in ourselves but in God) that we have not deserved such abuse and the stirring up of antagonism. Let them examine, inquire, and scrutinize. Let them, if they will, scrutinize our conduct as carefully as they please; and they will be satisfied beyond question that God wills and sees that we carry out in full the obligations and cares confided to us.

Finally, in order that I may not be denied the due procedure which I request, or that which the case itself demands, let thought be given to the following: to the improper method of procedure adopted in this suit, contrary to the provisions of laws invoked in the names of our kings; to the absence of a plaintiff, or in lieu of such, a commensurate public grievance; to the fact that there being no such public outcry needed for even the least judicial inquiry, no sooner did the inquiry begin than it came to life against all reason, and the slanderous publicity grew as the scandal increased; to the absence of legal grounds for the accusation; and to the fact that other considerations were blended with the accusation, with due regard being paid to the identity of the person responsible.

Let attention be given to the pressure which the latter brought to bear on the corporals and to the effect it would have on the Indians; to the discrepancies and the disagreements among the witnesses, testifying as witnesses yet known to be criminals; to the long interval between the alleged crimes and the judicial inquiry into them; to the ignoring of protocol in the appointing of a judge without consulting me; and to the bias of the same and of his deputy. And finally, in testimony to the truth of what is reported above, I, along with the other religious of this mission, sign it as such on the twenty-eighth day of June in the year 1786.

Fray Fermín Francisco de Lasuén
Fray Pedro Benito Cambón.

Extension of the Reflections which have been Cited

Even if it is conceded that the murders imputed to the Father were real, and were the consequence of excessive severity and of indiscreet and frenzied zeal, even granting that this was one of those cases of public scandal in which the royal will "permits" or "regards with favor" (these are the words of Law #73, Book I, Title 14 of the *Recopilación*) that juridical inquiries be instituted by the governors against religious for the sole purpose of informing His Majesty, let us examine the method of procedure it prescribes for a case of this kind.

It orders or (to use the expression of the law) "permits" that juridical inquiries be made secretly, and that the religious superior be obliged to punish the delinquent; and in case he should neglect to do so, the case is to be referred, etc. This shows the sympathy and understanding of our Catholic Sovereigns for the dignity of ecclesiastics, even when they are unworthy; they do not wish that their excesses and scandals should be dealt with in the noisy legal proceedings of ordinary court trials.

The reason for this is given in the Law, No. 152, Book II, Title 15, in these words: "For it is neither right nor fitting that the shortcomings of ecclesiastics be made public. . . ." Wherefore it orders that when it shall happen that charges or claims are made against religious they may not be read in the *audiencias*, regardless whether consent is given for it, or whether the situation warrants it; but they must be held secretly at the *acuerdos*[10] only, so that the information so gathered may be sent thence to those whom it concerns, according to law.

It would be impossible to frame laws that would be more just or expedient. And if one keeps in mind the circumstances of the land in which we live, it becomes clearer still how just, how fitting, and how necessary it is to abide by them.

The Christian religion is but recently established here. There is extreme need of instruction and of good example from the missionaries in order to offset certain impressions which, in the case of such recent converts, may be brought about by those excesses which happen too frequently, and perhaps go unpunished, and have been the occasion for comment in these reductions.

The best remedy for this is the good name of the missionaries.

Missionaries are not so numerous that if one is removed, or one is missing for any reason, it will be easy to replace him. This is what we have learned from experience. Even after religious assigned to a new foundation have arrived, it happens that it will be necessary to employ them in older ones, either because the application was delayed, or the voyage was slow, etc. In the meantime some one dies, or some accident occurs, and it becomes necessary to reduce to two the missionaries at each mission, as the Apostolic Bulls, the royal laws, and the most recent decrees demand.

Hence, if everywhere it is most fitting that those who govern in the name of the King should treat a matter of this kind with the prudence and caution which the laws prescribe, how much the more here? What reason then will there be for instituting proceedings in a juridical and solemn manner with no more foundation than the simple statement of a man who (in the judgment of the judge himself) has a bad reputation? And if there should be nothing but a vague rumor (as they say) spread by some Indians and soldiers, who does not recognize that its origin could be investigated with more becomingness and truth and with none of this clamor, as the law requires, and without entrusting to persons who possess little sense of responsibility the investigation of matters that are very delicate?

If at that very time the governor did not decline to make known to me officially certain charges against this religious, and if I did not fail to satisfy His Lordship fully by showing that they were false and deceitful, what could be the reason that he did not tell me anything about these particular excesses? Who can say! What is certain is that I have never given any cause for presuming that I would fail in zeal for justice in a matter so vicious and so odious to those who preside over these new missions. And since this is the express intention of our supreme legislator, what excuse can there be for not conforming to it in a matter, the delicacy of which can be deduced from the careful wording of the law he has proclaimed?

The noisy legal processes and the additional considerations to which this and similar situations give rise are things that cannot be ignored. It was necessary, in order to set limits to these inconveniences and to preserve intact the privileges of the priesthood, that there should be enacted by the same supreme lawgiver such rules and limitations that, when they are observed, the ecclesiastic would have no grounds for complaint if he should find himself summoned before a civil tribunal. Moreover, since he cannot go beyond this rule or exceed these terms, why should he be required to give up such an advantage, especially when by more convenient methods and procedures in accordance with the law he would be able to refute the calumny and to establish the truth with greater certainty? And what do these secret proceedings denote if not that, wrapped up in them, is some other enigma?

The controversy between the governor and this minister is well known. It arose because this mission was not able to supply the troops with grain, and because the grain which, in view of the pressing needs of the presidio he made great efforts to obtain, called for a higher price, because of the present scarcity of foodstuffs, than that fixed by the old tariff.

In regard to this latter, numerous reports were passed from the paymasters and others to the governor. All were prejudicial, especially to this missionary, and for the most part they were believed by the governor.

Now, these reports were forwarded to me, and the corresponding charges were preferred against the Father. However, he vindicated himself in the most complete and convincing manner without omitting even the least charge, whether raised by the person who made the complaint or by the individual to whom they were made.

He did this with so much success that it would seem as if the governor felt himself mortified; and then His Lordship thought it over (I find myself obliged to say it), liked the idea, and then made up his mind blandly to impugn the honor of the religious, bringing to light no less than three or more homicides which, although they had reference to individuals who had been dead for a long time, seemed to him to be problems of current interest.

Now, if true zeal for justice had been the motive for action in this instance, the same should have applied to other cases in the past, for they had equally good reason for being credited.

In addition to the very grave and scandalous excesses associated with this most unbecoming process, there have been widespread reports of cruel murders of unfortunate Indians and the governor could not escape hearing them. We do not know whether any action has been taken, nor what reparation has been made to society, especially in this latter point which is of such concern to the sovereign. Everything seems to have been hushed up.

True, there is no lack of officers of character who openly threaten to make up for what is culpably lacking here by notifying higher authorities of those excesses of which they have clear proof. One that can be regarded as certain in this connection took place when the governor passed through San Gabriel. He summoned an Indian, who was acting as interpreter for soldiers who were detailed to search for and apprehend certain criminals, because he wished to inquire personally into rumors that were current. He asked the Indians if it was true that the soldiers had hung up a certain Indian in a swing, and had proceeded to beat him until he started to bleed from the mouth and nose, and finally died as a result. The Indian testified that this was so, and the other, by way of reply, assured him it would not happen again. And the interpreter added that he had heard that on a similar occasion the soldiers had acted in the same fashion at Monterey.

But perhaps such evidence was regarded as suspicious or weak, and the governor felt he could disregard it, for we see no response to it. Well and good; but if an exception is made in favor of these others, why is it not extended to the poor priest? And if, in this way, one is zealous and considerate for the honor of a soldier, and for residents of this land, why cannot at least the same amount be done for the honor of a poor religious?

This is clear evidence of the esteem in which they are held by this government, and of the sinister reports that, no doubt, will be sent to higher authorities in regard to their conduct.

As proof of this it may be opportune to mention what happened in the year 1783 to my predecessor, the Venerable Father Fray Junípero Serra, a man well known for his outstanding virtue wherever he came or went. When, as a concession to his age and chronic ailments, he took ship at Monterey on his way to the port of San Diego with the intention of returning by land, of visiting the missions, and of confirming the neophytes, there was an officer at hand to notify him, in the name of the governor, of an order forbidding any religious to travel by boat because of the drunkenness and other disorders which used to occur.

This was the attitude towards a religious at whose death, which was most exemplary, the troops of land and sea displayed those external manifestations which piety dictates for the death of saints, while at the same time we were witnessing soldiers and civilians at liberty to go on board and travel by boat.

At the present time we are hampered by a very strict rule according to which no missionary without exception can set out with an escort, even for another mission; nor may he join a group of passengers, or pack trains, or those carrying mail, without express permission, except for purposes of administering the sacraments.

For this reason, religious who suffer much from sicknesses are unable to enjoy little outings with which perhaps they might alleviate their ills, for here we are not as well supplied with doctors and medicines as elsewhere, and there are some to whom such recourse is very burdensome or useless owing to the distance.

Such are the straits to which we have been reduced by this government; and at the same time we can see even the wives of soldiers passing from place to place supplied with an escort, and without any need of this permission from higher authorities such as we need.

To vindicate the justice of the steps taken so that they would not seem to be uncalled for, evidently it was deemed necessary to prejudice the minds of higher superiors by means of stories of happenings which, thank God, never took place here.

This is the kind of protection and sanctuary we receive at the hands of those to whom our sovereign most kindly recommends us as persons who are poor and helpless, and this is the response to what is no less than a royal recommendation. And if we are to judge by the course things are taking and the amount of concern that is shown, we have reason to anticipate greater persecution.

And who can doubt that if a governor should make up his mind to charge a religious with any crime he pleases, in the condition in which we live it would be very easy to find evidence to support it? The religious here have assumed charge of temporalities, watching over them in the interest of the Indians and guarding them from those *de razón*. They impose on the former the obligation of attending Mass, of prayer, of work, of living together according to the law. If they run away, they search for them; if they commit theft, or polygamy, or other barbarities no matter how scandalous for such a people, the Father has to correct, restrain, and discipline them with practically no help from the secular authorities. If they look to the soldiers, they find in them nothing but models for their own lust and license, and they feel impelled to regard the missionaries as enemies of their liberty and as men armed with a cane in order to hold them in subjection. And on the other hand, since they are not fully capable of realizing the religious value of an oath, or the evil of calumny, etc., it is easy to understand how difficult it will be to raise them to an acceptable standard.

I have no doubt if the present governor should undertake to prove that the missionary mentioned is guilty, not only of the killing of three or more, but of as many of the residents of Santa Clara as have died, provided that at one time or another he had to impose discipline on [the Indians], or had given them medicine in their sicknesses, he could carry out his desire, seeing the kind of witnesses available. And if he would pay attention to gossip and legend, he would be able to institute not just one formal charge but a bulky volume of them. But he did not go that far, for the exaggeration would be self-evident.

Finally, the higher authorities cannot investigate these matters for themselves. Instead, if they would send here an impartial person who would make a report on what is going on, the result would be that they would be convinced that the picture of us which they have been given is nothing but a caricature and in no way resembles the original.

San Carlos of Monterey Mission,
July 3, 1786.

[1] He was a native of Oviedo, Spain, where he was born in 1736. He arrived in San Fernando College in 1779, served San Carlos Mission from 1781 to 1787 when he returned to the college.

[2] Soler was appointed to the position of *habilitado* in 1781, charged with the reception and distribution of pay and rations, and the keeping of the company accounts. He seems to have been an inveterate fault-finder. In 1788 he was removed from that office, became commandant at Tucson and died there in 1790. Cf. Bancroft, *op. cit.,* I, 234-235, 397-398.

[3] A native of Mallorca where he was born in 1739, he entered San Fernando College in 1770, and reached Monterey the following year. A few months after his arrival he took part in the founding of San Antonio Mission, where he stayed for almost thirty-seven years. See Geiger, *Palou,* p. 400.

[4] Just six months before, Fages reported that Soler was "almost completely blind, with little or very remote hope of recovering his sight." See Pedro Fages to Fray Francisco Palou (January 2, 1787) in Bolton, *Historical Memoirs,* IV, 380.

[5] His was the first recorded marriage of a white person in San Francisco. The date was November 28, 1776.

[6] He was a corporal at San Francisco in 1777, was assigned to Santa Clara at its founding the following year, and in 1790 was entered as an *inválido* at San José.

[7] Problems of "In what circumstances" and "When" in Accusations.

[8] Problems of Possession and Ownership.

[9] In government documents the office of *fiscal* was akin to that of attorney-general. In the California missions the office was a much more lowly one. It combined the functions of sacristan and church usher.

[10] A deliberative council which held its sessions in secret, defined as "la reunión de los magistrados de un tribunal con su presidente y los fiscales, para deliberar y resolver sobre objetos de aplicación general."

42. To Don José Rengel

In your esteemed official letter of March 24, of this year, Your Lordship justly complains that, according to the report made to you by His Lordship Governor Don Pedro Fages, for more than two years I have failed to have Mass said in the Presidio of San Francisco; and you direct me to arrange that one of the two religious of the adjoining mission serve the above presidio in the manner which the *Reglamento* of the peninsula requires, and which was formerly observed.

I was unaware, Sir, that Mass was not said at the presidio outside of the times when there was no church or other suitable place there.

If on the part of the different presidios there is no obstacle of the kind mentioned, Your Lordship need have no fear that on the part of the missionaries there will be any lack of the assistance which is due to them. I gave the same answer to the above-mentioned governor each time we discussed the matter.

Even the Fathers of Mission San Buenaventura, despite the long distance of twelve or more leagues from the Presidio of Santa Barbara, assist there as far as they can in all that pertains to its spiritual administration.

In conclusion, Sir, even the slightest suggestion from Your Lordship is all that is needed for the prompt carrying out of everything you may require from me and my religious; and if Your Lordship will be pleased to hear what we have to say when complaints are made against us, especially under the present administration, it may be that our priestly explanation will serve to overcome the natural resentment they have caused Your Lordship.

Renewing my entire submission and humble subjection to the commands of Your Lordship, I pray that God Our Lord may keep your important life for many years in His holy grace.

San Carlos of Monterey Mission,
August 4, 1786.

43. To Don Pedro Fages

In your esteemed official letter of the ninth of this month Your Lordship informs me that, in accordance with the decision of the commandant general, Your Lordship will assume the office and exercise the functions of Commandant Inspector which, as governor of this province, pertain to you in virtue of the royal *Reglamento* which governs it, and you offer me the prestige which this new honor brings for any contingency connected with it that may arise for me.

On the one hand I offer my congratulations to Your Lordship, and on the other I offer a thousand thanks, and I hope that these proofs of confidence which our sovereign places in Your Lordship may be but a step to others of greater importance.

I renew my submission and subjection to the higher orders of Your Lordship, and I pray that God, etc.

Santa Clara Mission,
August 12, [1786]

44. To Don Pedro Fages

Through the medium of your esteemed official letter of the ninth of this month I am advised of the decision of the commandant general regarding the preliminary examination of the place mistakenly called *La Gaviota*, but in reality *Santa Rosa*, for the purpose of founding Purísima Mission there. I am advised, too, of Your Lordship's kindness in extending me the favor of accompanying you next spring on a further exploration, so that the site selected for the location of the above-mentioned mission may meet with my approval.

I wish to express gratitude in keeping with a courtesy so delicate, and to express my entire readiness, at Your Lordship's first call, to reciprocate with ready obedience in this matter, and in any other which Your Lordship may desire from my humble self.

May God Our Lord keep Your Lordship for many years in His holy grace.

Santa Clara Mission,
August 12, 1786.

45. To Don Pedro Fages

Since it was almost at the end of last year that I received the patent appointing me President of these Missions, I assumed that the prescribed certificate regarding the administration of the Fathers in their respective missions had already been requested and obtained. In a letter which I have just now received from the Reverend Father Guardian of our College of San Fernando he reminds me that this matter has not been attended to, and he instructs me to ask Your Lordship for such a document, one that will apply both to last year and to this. With the greatest respect, therefore, I beg Your Lordship to do me this favor so that I may comply with the orders of my superior.

I place myself in all humility at the service of Your Lordship, and I beg that God Our Lord may keep you many years in His holy grace.

San Carlos of Monterey Mission,
September 7, 1786.

46. To Don Jacobo de Ugarte y Loyola[1]

The least of Your Lordship's servants, the President of these Missions of Upper California, together with all his religious, extends a thousand congratulations to Your Lordship on your promotion to the high office of Commandant General of this and the other Provinces.

I am fully aware, Sir, that whatever I may offer in the way of deference, services, and compliance with your orders, and even with your very wishes, would not be more than I owe; but I do promise, Sir, to fulfil every duty with pleasure.

As regards what remains to be done here for the propagation of our holy faith, and the means to be found for such holy purposes, Your Lordship will be gratified with your new assignment, for it gives you the power to wield much influence in a work that is most noble. As for ourselves, being fully aware of Your Lordship's Christian zeal, we are overjoyed; and we give thanks to God that He has come to our aid with such powerful support.

May His Divine Majesty bless the government of Your Lordship, so that while meriting by means of it the utmost confidence of our temporal sovereign, you may receive the imperishable rewards of the Eternal Sovereign.

May God Our Lord keep Your Lordship many years in His holy grace.

San Carlos of Monterey Mission,
September 7, 1786.

---

[1] He was born in the Basque country in 1728, entered military service at an early age, rose quickly to high rank, and was a colonel by the time he was forty. In the New World he was appointed military governor of Sonora in 1779 by Teodoro de Croix, and in 1783 was assigned to the same office in Puebla. In 1785 he was appointed governor of the Internal Provinces with immediate jurisdiction over California, Sonora, and Sinaloa. He died in Guadalajara in 1798.

47. To Don José de Gálvez

In reply to the esteemed letter of Your Excellency dated March 1, in which you graciously inform me that I, and all the religious subject to me, are to afford protection and assistance to Don Vicente Vasadre[1] as need may arise, so as to bring about the useful and advantageous establishment of reciprocal trade between the Chinese and this part of the coast of California by trading in otter skins and seal skins, taking advantage of the trading ships[2] to Asia in the transaction, I beg to state that the aforementioned Don Vicente will be able to satisfy Your Excellency that when you give a strong recommendation, to me it is equivalent to a direct command, and as such I extend to it the ready obedience it merits. This is the manner in which I take it upon myself to act whenever I have the honor to receive the least suggestion from Your Excellency.

May God Our Lord preserve the important life of Your Excellency for many years in His holy grace.

San Carlos of Monterey Mission,
September 8, 1786.

[1] For further comment on the fur trade in California and Vasadre's connection with it, see Donald C. Cutter, *Malaspina in California* (San Francisco, 1960), pp. 68-69, 76-77. For the otter trade in general along the west coast, see Adele Ogden, *The California Sea Otter Trade, 1784-1848,* ("University of California Publications in History," No. 26.) Berkeley, 1941, and, by the same author, "The Californians in the Spanish Pacific Otter Trade, 1775-1795," *Pacific Historical Review,* I (1932), 444-468.

[2] Lasuén uses the word *azogues*, ships used for the transport of quicksilver to the New World where it was extensively used in mining operations to separate gold from less valuable ore. For a time it was hoped that the sale of otter pelts would help finance the purchase of quicksilver. In 1790 the government ended the monopoly in pelts and paid for the quicksilver from other sources.

48. To Don Pedro Fages

This is in reply to Your Lordship's esteemed official letter of the eighth of this month, which was in response to mine of the seventh of the same month. Seeing that there has been a change in the appointments of several missionaries, and seeing that Your Lordship is unaware of the date or time of such transfers, you ask me to forward you a list of these particulars.

I beg to remind you, Sir, that I did not assume the office of President until almost the end of last year, and for this reason it is extremely difficult, if not impossible, for me to make such an investigation, for it embraces the preceding year when my sole duty was the administration of San Diego Mission.

However, in an effort to obey Your Lordship as far as I can, and to do what seems to me sufficient so that you can issue the certificate sought, I am sending Your Lordship the enclosed list, and I hope I have succeeded thereby in carrying out your superior orders. This, indeed, is what I desire: always to observe in full whatever Your Lordship commands me.

May God Our Lord keep Your Lordship many years in His holy grace.

San Carlos of Monterey Mission,
September 9, 1786.

49. Assignments of Missionaries

Mission of	1785	1786
San Diego	Fermín Francisco de Lasuén** Juan Riobó	Juan Riobó Juan Mariner
San Juan Capistrano	Pablo Mugartegui Vicente Fuster	Pablo Mugartegui Vicente Fuster
San Gabriel	Antonio Cruzado Miguel Sánchez	Antonio Cruzado Miguel Sánchez
San Buenaventura	Francisco Dumethz [Dumets] Vicente Santa María	Francisco Dumethz [Dumets] Vicente Santa María
San Luis Obispo	Antonio Paterna (four months) José Caballero (entire year)	Antonio Paterna José Caballero
San Antonio de Padua	Miguel Pieras Buenaventura Sitjar	Miguel Pieras Buenaventura Sitjar
San Carlos de Monterey	Matías Noriega (entire year) Antonio Paterna	Fermín Francisco de Lasuén, President Matias Noriega
Santa Clara	Tomás de la Peña Diego de Noboa	Tomás de la Peña Diego de Noboa
San Francisco	Francisco Palou Pedro Cambón	Francisco Palou Miguel Giribet

** The prefix "Fr." [Fray], meaning Brother, accompanies each name in the original. It is omitted in this and subsequent lists of missionaries. [Tr.]

50. To the Governor [Don Pedro Fages]

[This letter is identical in content with Letter 44 supra, except for the date which, in this instance, is given as September 12, 1786.]

51. To Count de La Pérouse[1]

I gladly place at Your Lordship's disposal both my person and my resources. And because I have heard that among the things which would bring you happiness would be to take back to your own country samples or specimens of the most curious objects to be found in the countries through which you pass, I shall be happy if Your Lordship will be pleased to accept these three objects which are made of rush, and the one that is made of stone. All were fashioned by the Indians of the Santa Barbara Channel.

In the region between San Diego and San Francisco, which are the limits of Upper California, I have not seen among the natives any artifacts of greater value.

Certainly the smallness of the gift makes me blush; but the ardent desire I have to please Your Lordship is what emboldens me.

Beginning tomorrow, with God's help, we shall forward for the use of the ships under your command the seventy fanegas of grain which have been requested from this mission. The Fathers, the residents of the mission, and myself, we all rejoice at the thought that Your Lordship and all those with you will derive pleasure and happiness from partaking of it.

Sir, If Your Lordship should observe that I can be of some use, be firmly convinced that I sincerely desire to serve you; and in the meantime, when Your Lordship does me the honor and favor of imposing on me commands which I [am happy to] obey, I pray the Almighty Lord to assist, favor, and prosper Your Lordship in every way during this very creditable and useful expedition so that, having attained by such deserving effort the highest rank and the most intimate confidence of your sovereign, you may obtain, in addition to many years of health in the grace of God, the priceless reward of heavenly glory.

San Carlos of Monterey Mission,
September 18, 1786.

[1] Jean-François de Galaup La Pérouse was born in France in 1741. In 1785 he sailed on an expedition the purpose of which was mainly scientific—one of its objectives was the discovery of the "North-West passage." In the course of his Pacific Coast explorations he spent ten days at Monterey and left an interesting, if not always accurate, description of what he saw. Early in September of the following year he sent Baron de Lesseps back to France with the records of his observations to date. A few months later, in the opening months of 1788, the expedition ended in disaster in the region of the New Hebrides with the loss, it would seem, of all hands on board. See Charles E. Chapman, *A History of California, The Spanish Period* (New York, 1921), pp. 401-403; Bancroft, *op. cit.*, I, 428-438. See also Charles N. Rudkin, *First French Expedition to California. Lapérouse in 1786* (Los Angeles, 1959).

52. To Don Jacobo Ugarte y Loyola

At the beginning of this month I had the honor to receive Your Lordship's official letter of April 22, in which you graciously inform me of your well-merited promotion to the rank of Commandant General of these and of the other provinces, with the same powers as those of the late Brigadier Don Felipe de Neve.

Some time ago, by chance and privately, I heard this happy news; and at once, under date of September 7, I wrote to Your Lordship offering fitting congratulations and placing at your disposal and command myself, my office, and all my religious. It affords me great pleasure now to renew the same sentiments and to await the esteemed orders of Your Lordship so that I may give clear proof and evidence how prompt and humble is the obedience of the least of your dependents.

Since the end of October I have been staying at this Royal Presidio of Santa Barbara. I arrived here with two missionaries for the purpose of founding in this vicinity a mission of the same name.

Since our arrival we have been attending to a number of preliminaries and to the sowing of wheat, which we have already commenced. In the meantime, too, we celebrated the feast of the patron saint, and in the evening we raised and set up the holy cross in the place already selected; but the actual laying of the foundation and the building of any habitation and shelter has been forbidden us by the governor, pending His Lordship's arrival.

Because of circumstances peculiar to it, and because of its unique importance, this establishment was precisely what Your Lordship's government needed.[1]

May Heaven favor and expedite in Your Lordship's time whatever remains to be done so that it may become possible to bring into our holy Church the very large number of pagans of our coast.

In all humility I place myself once more at the service of Your Lordship, and I pray that God Our Lord may preserve your valuable life for many years in His holy grace.

Royal Presidio of Santa Barbara,
December 11, 1786.

---

[1] Santa Barbara had strategic importance. The Indians of that region were more numerous and more warlike than those to be found elsewhere. Further, the Camino Real, the lifeline of California, for some miles at this point was little more than a wagon trail between mountains that rose abruptly on one side and the ocean on the other. If the Indians were to become hostile, the consequences could be very grave.

V
The Year 1787

Lasuén discovers that a President of the Missions must be concerned about many things, such as the price of otter pelts, and the sifting of evidence to discover the truth when testimonies are in conflict.

53. To Don Pedro Fages

THIS EVENING I HAVE HAD THE HONOR TO receive Your Lordship's communication under date of yesterday. In it you were gracious enough to apprise me of two instructions forwarded to you by the commandant general: the first, that the Indian woman named Pelagia, a neophyte of Santa Clara Mission now detained in this Mission of San Gabriel, be restored to her home; and the other, that the Indians of San Diego, Carlos, Luis and Rafael, after being exiled to Loreto,[1] are returning free to their mission and ranchería after having been well admonished to amend their ways.

With regard to the first, Your Lordship instructs me to take such steps as I judge best for the transfer of said Pelagia, observing such safeguards as decorum demands. But Your Lordship knows quite well that I have no means of arranging the conveyance of any one, not even of myself, except by having recourse to you or to those under your command.

In view of this, my suggestion would be that it might be found best to effect the transfer by taking advantage of one of the occasions, which sometimes arise, when some woman from among the *gente de razón* is on her way up there. What I can do and will do, is to instruct the mission Fathers to help her with whatever is necessary for the journey.

With regard to the second point, for a long time I have had in mind the same thought as Your Lordship, that when the Indians return home they be required to live permanently in that same Mission of San Diego so that being more closely observed by us, their conduct may be more easily scrutinized, and they may thus be prevented from, or guarded against, a relapse. And with this object in mind I shall transmit appropriate orders to the Reverend Missionary Fathers concerned, in accordance with your recommendations.

As ever, I remain your obedient and devoted servant, and I pray that the Lord Our God may keep Your Lordship for many years in His holy grace.

San Gabriel Mission,
January 6, 1787.

[1] These were Indians who had taken part in the attack on San Diego Mission in 1775. The following April they were banished for six years.

54. Memorandum

Having seen the foregoing statement of defense, and keeping in mind the judicial and extra-judicial measures I adopted in regard to the same affair, copies of which I have remitted to the holy college, as well as other very authentic evidence, as an aid to arriving at a proper judgment in this matter, I must and do infer that this particular religious who has been persecuted for so long and by so many who had to rely on lying and deceit in order to achieve their purpose, is free of all suspicion.

On this assumption, it seems to me that the aggrieved religious is demanding what is just in order that his innocence may be vindicated and his good name restored. And for this purpose I am forwarding the present copy with the same signature as the original to our Apostolic College *de Propaganda Fide* of San Fernando in Mexico. It is the course of action, in this instance, which is within my competence as President of these Missions which are subject to the college mentioned.

In proof thereof, I hereby sign it in the above Mission on the day, month, and year mentioned.

San Juan Capistrano Mission,
February 12, 1787.

55. To Don Pedro Fages

Having given all due attention to the pertinent items in the evidence taken at the inquiry held at Santa Clara Mission and forwarded to me by Your Lordship, I instructed the Reverend Father Tomás de la Peña, its minister, to go to San Carlos Mission as soon as possible and when there to reply, on the word of a priest and in due legal form, to the charges made against him, after he had first seen a copy which I left him of the evidence above-mentioned.

He had already promised me that he would act in this case as he had done when confronted with the false rumors, spread abroad by reason of the judicial proceedings of Ensign Sal at Santa Clara, at the time when I went to that mission myself and conducted the type of investigation within my competence, as Your Lordship is aware.

A few days ago I received the answers and the defense submitted by this missionary. I have studied the entire matter carefully and given it the fullest thought, and I find myself obliged to inform Your Lordship that he has convinced me of his innocence, and that as soon as the case is reviewed from beginning to end both Your Lordship and every judge whose duty it is to investigate it will have to concede to this religious the justice he demands, namely, that those who destroyed his good name, and worked together to sully it, should themselves restore it to what it had been.

This is my judgment; and as Your Lordship knows, it is directly and absolutely subject to that of our College of San Fernando. I am seeing to it that all documents are sent there so that they may clearly understand the facts of the case; and at the same time I am sending them to the tribunal which, having the power and obligation to call me to account in regard to this case, may be pleased to give heed to the decision I have reached and to the memorandum submitted by this religious.

I place myself at the service of Your Lordship, and I pray that God Our Lord may keep you many years in His holy grace.

San Juan Capistrano Mission,
March 21, 1787.

I certify that the above is a faithful copy of the original which I sent to Don Pedro Fages.

San Carlos of Monterey Mission,
July 7, 1793.

56. To Don Pedro Fages

I have the honor to acknowledge receipt of Your Lordship's official letter of the twenty-second of this month in which you reproduce and bring to my attention the superior decree of His Excellency the Viceroy, Count de Gálvez, relative to the aid which has to be given from the Pious Fund to each of the religious of the College of San Fernando on their departure for one of the missions of this peninsula, and to the permission to enter or leave this peninsula which the above religious are obliged to obtain exclusively from His Excellency.

I shall keep in mind the above regulations, which are so fitting, so that they may be observed with all exactness, insofar as the matter lies in my power.

I am Your Lordship's obedient servant, and I pray that God Our Lord may keep you for many years in His holy grace.

San Luis [Obispo] Mission,
June 29, 1787.

57. To Don Pedro Fages

In accordance with your Lordship's esteemed official letter dated the twentieth of this month I shall instruct the missionary Fathers of San

Francisco and Santa Clara, if it should be possible and no notable inconvenience should result, to make available either from one or from both
of these missions six or eight Indian volunteers to assist in the building of
the warehouses and the construction of the defense works in the Royal
Presidio of San Francisco.

To facilitate this, I shall inform them of the grave urgency of these
works, the good treatment Your Lordship offers to the workmen, the
daily wages of one and a half reales, and the satisfying meals of which
meat forms a part.

I shall do likewise in regard to Your Lordship's instructions to me in
the postscript of your letter by giving you news of the crops of the
mission as soon as I receive the information.

I am at Your Lordship's service, and I beseech God Our Lord to keep
you for many years in His holy grace.

San Carlos Mission,
July 23, 1787.

58. To Don Pedro Fages

Your Lordship's esteemed letter of the twentieth of this month fills
me with joy. It brings to my mind the noble and glorious objectives
which, in the judgment of His Excellency the Viceroy, Count de
Gálvez,[1] should occupy Your Lordship's attention and that of your
troops in this province. And this province should surely enjoy a greater
measure of happiness if these points alone were exactly observed.

Occupying the last place among these points is that of forbidding to
the Indians the use and management of horses.[2] And Your Lordship
takes the view that the violation of this regulation is to be attributed
solely to me and to my missionaries.

It is something that is rare, but quite possible. And I would be glad
if it were actually so, in view of the ease with which it would be corrected, for no sooner would the admonition be given that the correction
would take place, instantly and without fail. We are, thank God, like
springs that are well adjusted, responsive to the least impulse that will
promote progress in this conquest.

No one is more concerned or more interested than the missionaries
that the Indian should continue in his native ignorance of horsemanship.
But Your Lordship is well aware of the cattle and horses which, with the
King's pleasure, every one of the missions possesses, and that horsemen
are needed to look after them. And these have to be Indians, for there
are no others.

If some missions go to excess in this matter, as Your Lordship states, I am convinced that it will neither be permitted nor approved by any Father, but will be reproved and punished wherever it is discovered.

What His Excellency is opposed to is, I presume, not just the excesses, nor, it would seem, those which Your Lordship surmises. The more, Sir, the military are withdrawn from aiding the missions and the missionaries, the less are the Indians prohibited from using and handling horses. There would be more prohibition [of Indians] if there were more aid [from the military]. I am not doing violence to my limited knowledge of Spanish by reading this meaning into the text.

This Mission of San Carlos possesses four saddles for the care and service of all its possessions located in the country; and the remaining missions are in the same condition, more or less.

As Your Lordship knows better than I, six mounted Indians are not in effect equal to one lone soldier; and there are usually more than six soldiers employed in caring for and otherwise managing the flocks and herds of the presidios.

Finally, Your Lordship may be assured beyond doubt that no missionary will contravene the esteemed instructions of His Excellency, Count de Gálvez; rather we shall do our utmost to carry them out promptly. And in this respect, would that our strength were in keeping with our incentives! We would then bring back to life that great Christian hero who was soldier and statesman. May he rest in peace.

I see that Your Lordship is committed to this noble enterprise, and it is for this reason that I have felt such deep satisfaction.

Your Lordship may have seen, on some rare occasion, that an Indian who accompanied the missionary on his journeys was carrying a sharp weapon. This was for the needs of the journey, in the same way as they are sometimes entrusted with axes, sickles, machetes, etc.; but never will it be seen or heard that we give them, or permit them, such arms apart from such services. How much of this there is which we do not cause, and which we cannot cure! Just as in the other case!

In the meantime, however, I take comfort from the fact that Your Lordship's assiduous and watchful vision extends to everything, and I, the least of your subjects, accept with the greatest humility your higher orders.

May God Our Lord keep Your Lordship for many years in His holy grace.

San Carlos Mission,
August 21, 1787.

---

[1] On the death of his father, Matías de Gálvez, in 1785, he succeeded to the position of viceroy. He was already captain general of Cuba and governor of Louisiana and

the Floridas. As viceroy, his jurisdiction was extended so as to include the Internal Provinces, and during his brief administration (he died during an epidemic in the fall of 1786) he took an active and practical interest in these frontier territories.

² By order of the King, Gálvez drew up a number of recommendations which he sent to the commandant general of the Internal Provinces, Don Jacobo Ugarte y Loyola. In all, there were two hundred and sixteen points. Twelve of these had reference to Sonora and California, and in the last of them Gálvez admonished Ugarte to require Governor Fages to "mantener en su innocencia á los Indios del Canal de Santa Bárbara, en quietud á los de las Misiones de San Diego, San Gabriel y San Francisco, y en el mas justo arreglo, subordinación y disciplina á unas Tropas que sola serven en el sistema presente para infundir respeto, dar buen exemplo á los Indios, castigar con prudencia los excesos que cometan, y prohiberles el uso y manejo del caballo." See Donald E. Worcester (ed.), *Instructions for Governing the Interior Provinces of New Spain, 1786, by Bernardo Gálvez* (Berkeley: Quivira Society, 1951), pp. 119-120.

59. To Don Pedro Fages

The Indian Bruno has taken refuge in the church of this Mission. As soon as I learned of this, I asked Corporal Briones whether he had a warrant against him, and he told me that he had.

Apart from the immunity of the holy place and the importance attached to it more than to any other place in the world, he comes to us suffering from blows received from the soldier Ríos, for he, being really provoked, took satisfaction or vengeance into his own hands.

Neither the military nor the Indians had been able to catch him in the twelve days during which he was wandering in the mountains, without attending Mass or the prayers.

He has now given himself up and is prepared to comply with both obligations, and since this is the object of our highest hopes in this country and the nature of the offense is not opposed to it, I hope and pray that after punishing him Your Lordship will permit him to go free.

I am, as always, Your Lordship's obedient servant; and I pray that God our Lord may keep you for many years in His holy grace.

San Carlos Mission,
September 6, 1787.

[Marginal note in the handwriting of Lasuén:]

At the present time they are carrying off Indians to the presidio on any pretext of guilt in order to have peons to work for nothing, perhaps in the orchard of His Lordship.

60. To the Missionaries

The Lord give you Peace. The Royal Governing Audiencia has sent by sea in a folder addressed "To His Lordship the Governor" sealed letters for each one of the missions.

I can infer that in these, as in mine, that high tribunal will regard as too high and excessive the price placed on otter pelts by agreement between the governor and Don Vicente Vasadre, and it demands that some reduction be made in it, keeping in mind and giving due consideration to the information which the tribunal is furnishing us.

Later a packet was sent by land addressed to me, containing open letters for each mission. In them orders are given to buy up pelts and to enforce the prohibitions affecting private persons. It contained, too, a plan drawn up by Don Vicente Vasadre and instructions from the President of the Audiencia ordering me to see to its exact fulfillment and to circulate it among the missions in my charge.

By this mail Your Reverences will each receive both sealed letters (the address was added here to those that came without it) and the plan itself which was sent to me, for it is impossible for me just now to make a copy.

It must be forwarded promptly from mission to mission. On arrival at San Diego, a copy is to be made, and the original sent on to Santa Barbara. There another copy must remain, and the original is to be sent to me, as it must be kept here.

In the meantime I shall inform the Fathers of Santa Clara and San Francisco of its substance until the last named can be supplied with a transcript.

A serious doubt and difficulty occurs to me, and I feel I cannot at this time give a definite decision for I do not have the time to give sufficient thought to the matter, and I barely have time to write about it.

Business matters press, and allow no respite, and require that reports be made in duplicate; and my pen, which is not idle for a minute, is all Your Reverences see and know of me.

I am in doubt and difficulty as to whether that illustrious superior authority which has written individual letters to all, will or will not be satisfied with a reply from me alone. I do not know whether its members will say that the prohibition of our college carries no weight with them, for, as we may suppose, they were not unaware of it, and yet they wrote individually to all.

In this predicament, for the present and in case the return of the boats does not allow me time to deliberate on it and to change my mind if necessary, it is my decision and my direction to Your Reverences that you are all to write, taking your cue from the answer I give, and offering to carry out what you are charged to do. But the letters must be sent unsealed, and addressed in exactly this manner: "To the Royal Governing Audiencia, Mexico." And there must be another sealed letter to the Father Guardian of San Fernando. This is the way I will do it myself.

The form of address to use is: "Your Highness." At the beginning and the middle of the letter, which must be a full sheet of paper, should be written: "Most Mighty Lord," and then, in the accustomed place, begin with: "My dear Sir" (although this may be omitted, according to the opinion of some), "I have received with the utmost respect, etc." After the words "May God keep Your Highness many years, etc.," there is again placed in the middle, or over the signature, "Most Mighty Lord" and below "Fray . . . kisses the hand of Your Highness," etc. I have been told, too, that the phrase "Kisses the hand of Your Highness" is not used, but that the signature is added after the words "Most Mighty Lord." I realize that they may have to tolerate infractions of recognized procedure on our part; but it is better to try to avoid them.

The great anxiety and perplexity I have to endure when I face this critical and delicate state of affairs is that I must make a reply to a request for a reduction put forward after the price had been agreed on. Those consulted are so numerous and of such diverse position: the governor, the Dominicans, etc.

The pelts acquired by private individuals this year are delivered to the ships without spot payment; more I do not know. The governor assures us that the price will be fixed and enforced according to the first evaluation; but this (make no mistake) ought to put us on our guard. This point is very important, and the danger of provocation very possible. Therefore, with the conditions as above, my decision from first to last was to leave the modification of the price to the judgment and disposition of His Highness, and to that I could see no alternative. But I shall first call his attention to these points: To what was the former low price due? Who caused the present higher price? Why is there such extensive stock-piling now? Who were the evaluators, and how well-informed were they about everything since they asked counsel of no one? And lastly, the fact that the Filipinos pay a considerably higher price for the pelts than the legally fixed one, as do the French gentlemen who were here—men, I might add, who are not likely to make mistakes when dealing with business matters.

If any well-founded reasons should occur to Your Reverences which might contribute to the maintenance of the prices that were assigned, I beg you to communicate them to me. And if the departure of the ships should prevent you from doing so, write it to the college, for there is no prohibition against sending a letter that goes no farther than that cloister.[1]

The pelts, therefore, are to be delivered to the presidios in accordance with the plan of Don Vicente, with the difference that this year the exact price is to be left undetermined, pending the decision of the Royal Audiencia. Delivery is to be made without balancing the debit and credit accounts, and simply by noting down the quality and sizes.

This letter has for its purpose the carrying out of strict repeated orders; and therefore I charge Your Reverences to advise me as to its receipt and that of the enclosed plan. And of the Fathers of San Diego I ask that they keep it safe until I ask for it, or give other instructions regarding it.

If it should be detained in some mission because the mail has been forwarded too soon, efforts should be made to take advantage of the earliest and safest opportunity so that it may follow its due course without serious delay.

With cordial affection I am at the service of Your Reverences, and I pray that God may keep you for many years in His holy grace.

San Carlos of Monterey Mission,
September 18, 1787.

P. S.

Our Reverend Father Guardian, under the date of May 8, strongly recommends to me our friend Don Francisco Hijosa[2] and instructs me to bring this to your notice so that you may meet his wishes in every way, and particularly what he asks for at this time, which is no more than three hundred arrobas of suet, without any admixture of lard, one hundred fanegas of the best wheat, and four or five of chick peas, all according to the standard of his approval and taste.

I have already written to San Antonio and San Luis, recommending that when the mules arrive to transport their provisions they may send what they can of wheat and chick peas, and, depending on what is sent, I shall then advise how to meet the remainder of the order.

Farewell.

1 Missionaries enjoyed free mailing privileges when communicating with the college.
2 He was commissary at San Blas, the port through which the supplies passed both to and from Mexico.

61. To the Royal Governing Audiencia

No sooner did I observe, Sir, in your superior order of the eighth of March that Your Grace had drawn attention to the excessively high price for otter pelts as given in the Price List and approved by the governor of this peninsula, and by the commissioner, Don Vicente Vasadre, than I made up my mind that, in so far as it pertained to me, I would leave any change or reduction to the judgment and disposition of Your Grace.

Later, when I read the notes which Your Grace was so kind as to send me, and when I had duly reflected on them, as I was instructed to do, I was confirmed all the more in my resolution.

Nevertheless, with your permission and in deference to your Grace, since I have lived in California ever since the expulsion of the former Jesuits, I would like to mention what I have observed in regard to this matter for it seems to me that it has a relation to the problem regarding which Your Grace has sent me instructions and recommendations.

It is true, Sir, that in the beginning it was customary to buy the otter pelts from the Indians for almost nothing. They were caught without much effort and were given away free. When I was in charge of the Mission of San Borja they were then the most plentiful of that variety of fish; so I sent a dozen or more otter pelts to His Excellency the Marqués de Sonora. His Excellency paid for them, on the plea that he did not wish to receive them as gifts. Neither before nor since, even up to last year, did I set any value on such pelts if someone wanted them to serve as a loin-cloth for an Indian. The price was small, Sir, and in keeping with it was the size of the catch. The Filipinos, people from San Blas, and people here and there began to show new interest in the natives here, and began to pay them a higher price than the one in the Price List. I discovered that the same was true of the Frenchmen who called here, all of them the type who know how to avoid mistakes when there is an advantage to be gained. The price went up, and the trend grew stronger as the interest in hunting and purchasing increased. Moreover, despite the fact that only those near the ports were able to benefit from this enterprise, otters were not caught in such large numbers, nor were so many pelts collected, as at present, now that the market for them is steady and profitable.

The trappers above mentioned decided on their own scale of prices without consulting anyone, so far as I know; and for this reason were presumed to know what they were doing. On the other hand, seeing that they themselves constituted a very opportune form of rivalry which obliged them to remain within the limits of what was just, I mentioned in my reply to Don Vicente Vasadre that the price agreed on seemed to me to be equitable, and that it was quite in accord with the basic objectives of the establishment; and this being the case, before it is decided what the ships should pay, in the light of this perhaps the King may be willing to pay them more.

It is very true, Sir, that I then pursued the matter further (as did the two who are mentioned, as I have no doubt), not so much in regard to the costs and other circumstances relative to our acquisition of otter pelts locally, as to the question whether in addition to the effective encouragement which it is proposed to give these new possessions there might not be added the permission, assistance, and convenience of selling direct to the Chinese, for from this source would flow many advantages and benefits which the missions were sacrificing by reason of their very fitting and wholehearted obedience to the disposition of the sovereign.

I have considered at greater length, Sir, the duty, the expense, and the burden that were being imposed on the missions in the person of their missionaries in regard to this matter, for they were being obliged to select the Indians who were to do the fishing, to support them from the common fund, to assign them according to their ability as far as possible, to supply them with rafts, canoes, and nets, and especially with provisions, and to pay them what is just and in accordance with their tastes. I have taken into account the fact that, although this is a free enterprise, private individuals or soldiers if they wished to obtain pelts would be obliged to have recourse to the very Indians who, for the most part, have been detailed to engage in fishing, thus robbing us of the labors of those we have employed, and cheating these in turn. Your Grace can easily infer this from the number of pelts which the missions forwarded so far this year, and from those forwarded by the *gente de razón* who continue to live in their own district.

Now that an absolute prohibition has been issued that applies to all classes of natives, and trading in pelts has been restricted to the missions alone—on the understanding that we are at liberty (if I may take the liberty of saying so) to sell the pelts, and in exchange for them receive, as at the present time, clothes that are useful for the Indians—it would seem that the time is opportune and the motives adequate for altering or modifying the original price. It will be the province of Your Grace to decide this, for no better person can be found, no one with a more discriminating and exalted judgment to decree such matters so as to bring it about that the Indians will not fail to apply themselves gladly to an enterprise which will confer an inestimable benefit on them, and from which at the same time the King may derive a like benefit, and the returns may justify the risks involved.

For this reason, the missions under my jurisdiction have been collecting pelts without assessing their value, keeping a record only of their quality and size, until such time as Your Grace makes a decision on the matter.

Further, with due deference to Your Grace's pleasure, I beg to state that up to the present we have had no accounting of the pelts which Don Vicente took last year so that we may pay for them in effects; that the practice has been introduced of increasing the freight charges to three pesos, something never known before; that here we do not have as many sea otters as along the coast of neighboring California; that one can find here pelts that are larger than the maximum specified in the schedule of prices; that in this latitude the waters of the coast, like everything else, are less temperate, or colder, than those further south—and consequently the work of the Indians is more difficult and dangerous; that the seals here are all the same color as a rule; that there are no beavers, or pine martens, and that martens are unknown; and that the furs of all the species found along these coasts will be collected if and as Your Grace so commands.

Finally, as the least among your subjects, and the most responsive to your superior orders I pray and beg God Our Lord to keep Your Grace for many years in His holy grace.

San Carlos of Monterey Mission,
September 24, 1787.

62. To Don Jacobo Ugarte y Loyola

It is impossible for me to complete in time for the next mail the report which Your Lordship requests in your official letter of April 22, which I had the honor to receive. It has reference to the mutual accusations of His Lordship Governor Don Pedro Fages and the Reverend Father Fray Francisco Palou.[1] These were included in the *expediente* which was forwarded to Your Lordship by the Royal Governing Audiencia of Mexico, and you were kind enough to forward a copy of it to me.

On my part I promise to see to it that your instructions are carried out in full, especially in regard to duties of mine which still remain undone; and I shall do so in the manner best calculated to assist Your Lordship in acquiring the information you desire, because of the respect which I owe to the higher service of God and King.

To achieve this and to satisfy, too, Your Lordship's devout wish to settle the dispute in the most just and competent manner in the interests of the peace and concord which should prevail, and of the support and stability of the missions, I shall send the information to Your Lordship, in accordance with your command, so that you may issue the instructions which you deem appropriate. And I shall make mention not only of the points at issue but also any others that seem appropriate for such an important objective.

Your Lordship is not mistaken in inferring that, in the meantime, my religious and I will do what we can to promote harmony and concord with His Lordship the Governor. Ever since the time when, in obedience to my college, I assumed the office of president, even more than during the years when I was a missionary, I have sought, Sir, both peace and concord with the leaders and the officials as the surest, as the only basis for all of the above. Everything contrary to this I have looked upon with indescribable abhorrence, and, thanks be to God, I have aimed at overcoming it at all cost.

Even in matters of well-grounded complaints, I decided recently, Sir, on examining the circumstances of these defections from the ideal to remain silent, to suffer, and to overlook, and, without seeking an occasion to speak of them, to take advantage of some opportunity that would spontaneously arise, such as the present.

This I shall do, Sir, with the frankness, uprightness, modesty, and circumspection which I owe; and I pledge myself, now and always, to serve Your Lordship as a gentleman for whom I profess the greatest respect, the most profound loyalty, and the most complete obedience.

May God Our Lord preserve Your Lordship for many years in His holy grace.

San Carlos of Monterey Mission,
September 25, 1787.

---

[1] Palou was then guardian of San Fernando College. As will appear in Letter 65 *infra*, the quarrel was not a personal one. Palou was defending the claims of the missionaries in California, who were his subjects, and the governor could say with much justice that in many instances he was merely enforcing a law for which he was not responsible, the *Reglamento* of Neve, his predecessor in office.

63. To Don Jacobo Ugarte y Loyola

I cannot bring myself to decline to oblige those who seek some favor by using me as an intermediary. This, and this alone, is the reason why one so insignificant as I am presumes to trouble Your Lordship in the midst of matters of greater moment.

Everyone ought to know how little weight my recommendation carries; but as long as there are some who find comfort in the fact that I try to do them a favor, they place me under an obligation to give them that comfort.

Ensign Don Ramon Laso de la Vega spoke to me on two or three occasions, and has now written me a letter in which he gives me to understand that his sole ambition is to get married. Whether this is due to an ardent inclination on his part or an obligation in conscience which is more compelling, or to both, I am convinced that it would be advisable to grant the permission.

The problem, however, is that he is not satisfied with this favor; he wishes, in addition, to continue to serve as an officer. He knows better

than I do that there is a difficulty involved in this; but we both know that
Your Lordship can overcome it.

In this affair, therefore, be pleased to see an appeal to Your Lordship's
compassion, and the sole motive that inspires it is a sentiment of charity.

I confess that in this petition I have completely forgotten who I am,
and I have kept in mind solely who Your Lordship is. This notwithstanding, if the favor is granted, it will be due exclusively to you, and
I shall add eternal gratitude to the homage and obedience which, in
justice, I owe Your Lordship.

May God Our Lord keep Your Lordship for many years in His
holy grace.

San Carlos of Monterey Mission,
September 26, 1787.

64. To the Royal Audiencia

In due submission to the superior order of Your Highness, dated
March 8, which I received together with the plan formulated by the
commissioner for otter skins, Don Vicente Vasadre, I wish to report
that I am in complete agreement with the strict observance of it, and I
have already taken steps to ensure that the same is put into execution in
the missions subject to my jurisdiction as President, for I have already
circulated the above-mentioned plan among all the Father Ministers as
Your Highness commands me.

Sir, as the least among your dependents and the most subservient to
your superior orders, I pray that God Our Lord may keep Your Highness many years in His holy grace.

San Carlos of Monterey Mission,
October 13, 1787.

65. To Don Jacobo Ugarte y Loyola

In due obedience to the superior order of April 22, issued by Your
Lordship, and in fulfillment of what I submitted to you in that regard
on September 25, and bearing in mind the copy which Your Lordship
sent me of the *expediente* drawn up by the Royal Governing Audiencia
of Mexico regarding the mutual complaints of Don Pedro Fages, governor of this province, and the religious missionaries of the Apostolic
College of San Fernando, I beg to state, Sir, that having lived in this

SAN BORJA MISSION, LOWER CALIFORNIA
as it appears today

peninsula at a time when no formal regulations yet governed it, and later when it was governed by the provisional code of Señor Echeveste, which was approved by His Excellency the Viceroy, Frey Don Antonio María Bucareli, Knight, and by the one framed by Commandant General Don Felipe de Neve, which was approved by His Majesty and governs it at the present time—I beg to state that it is my conviction that not only have we, the religious of San Fernando College, not opposed the observance of any of its articles so as to bring about grave, or even the slightest, harm to the royal service, but that if our lord the King had been here in person, His Majesty would have been well satisfied, for he would see that we were scrupulously engaged in the punctual and exact fulfilment of his sovereign laws and even of His Majesty's intentions, perhaps to a greater extent than might be expected from poor friars.

I shall deal with the grounds on which the said governor bases the regrettable charges he makes against us; and it will be seen, I think, that he has been mistaken because of his military activity and ardent zeal.

The first is, that in violation of Article 3, Number 15, of the *Reglamento*, Mass was not celebrated for more than three years in the Presidio of San Francisco, although it happens to be located close to the mission of the same name.

The governor made a casual reference to this in conversation the first time I met His Lordship shortly after I had been given the office of President. I told him immediately that I would exhort all the Fathers in the missions close to the presidios to give the latter the kind of assistance which, as His Lordship knew, I had given for ten years to the Presidio of San Diego. And what this was, those who reside at the presidio can relate.

Not long after, on March 24, of last year, Don José Antonio Rengel, the commandant general *ad interim*, filed a complaint with me that the Presidio of San Francisco had not had Mass for more than two years, according to a report made to him by Governor Don Pedro Fages. In reply, I told His Lordship truthfully that I had not known that Mass was not being said at that presidio, with the exception of the time when there was no church there, nor a becoming place that could be used as a substitute. I assured His Lordship that as long as such requirements were not lacking on the part of the presidios there would be no failure on the part of the missionaries to provide all due assistance, for this had been promised to the governor himself, Don Pedro Fages.

Consequently, Sir, the church was built, and the Fathers were notified. They blessed and dedicated it, and continue to say Mass there on all Sundays and holydays of obligation.

The missionaries of San Diego, of Santa Barbara, and of San Carlos follow the same procedure with regard to their respective presidios. Hence, neither with respect to Mass nor to all that pertains to their spiritual welfare, do those who reside at the presidios lack a chaplain who will give them the attention to which they have a claim.

So concerned have we been about this, Sir, that, as I explained to Señor Rengel, even the Fathers of San Buenaventura Mission, despite the great distance of eight or more leagues, attended the Presidio of Santa Barbara as often as they could until last year, when, in the immediate neighborhood of the presidio, a mission of the same name was founded.

How disinterested we were, let those to whom we ministered bear testimony. We have never claimed any recompense, and we have no recollection of receiving even the slightest.

It was not the lack of recompense but of gratitude that was a little exasperating, especially to the Fathers of San Francisco; but it never restrained them from giving spiritual assistance to those at the presidio. Officers and soldiers alike indulged in vain and inopportune boasting that the religious were chaplains to them and for that reason were therefore obliged to serve them as a matter of justice.

The second charge which the governor brings against us is that we refuse to recognize the rights of the government in matters pertaining to temporalities and the viceregal patronage.

It seems to me, Sir, that this accusation should be supported by reference to specific cases (I know of none), accompanied by the explanations given in regard to them by the missionaries. And if these are not regarded as juridical, Your Lordship could then make such regulations for the inquiry that is sought as would answer the questions *what*, and *how*, and *when*.

As regards the temporalities, Sir, they are acquired, increased, and conserved by the care and diligence, the vigilance and energy of the missionary, and by the labor of the Indian, with hardly any help whatever from the government. Their management, use, and distribution, and in addition the actual condition in which they are, should prove to their legitimate masters, and even to their very rivals, that the system of management is most expedient and just.

The entire burden of their administration which the King has entrusted to us overwhelms us with the worries and burdens of a task that has no equal; but we endure it in obedience to the royal will, and in the certain and unshaken belief that it is necessary.

This has been the opinion of men whose judgment is sound and unbiased, an outstanding example being His Excellency the Marqués de Sonora. His Excellency, with nothing to influence him but what he had seen, had to avail himself of the full force of his authority in order to induce us to take charge of the temporalities in Lower California, for the missions there had been delivered to us without this obligation. And in the discharge of that obligation, neither then nor later was it ever brought to our attention that there was a single statute which we might have violated.

I do not know what to say to Your Lordship regarding the vice-regal patronage beyond this, that in a country like this there are not opportunities for proving to the satisfaction of the governor that we recognize the high honor which is due to his worthy person. The King himself would recognize the absence of these opportunities not with displeasure but, rather, I think, with admiration and rejoicing, for he would see that we were doing the best we could. Your Lordship knows that we are dealing with pagans, and that we are training them to live as befits men. The King now regards them as sons; while we are fulfilling the obligation which His Majesty lays upon us of continuing to train them so that afterwards he may rule them as vassals.

Finally, may Your Lordship be pleased to formulate rules governing both matters, and you will see that we shall conform to them whole-heartedly.[1]

We are well aware, too, that Your Lordship has to guard against the danger of greed or private interest on the part of those who have to handle the temporalities of neophytes.

As to the third complaint, namely, that we do not want to bring the prices of seeds, goods, and produce of the missions into conformity with the regulated prices which are public, and approved by His Majesty, I would ask, Sir, that you make them public.

I am fully satisfied that nobody would accuse us of so great an irregularity. I have neither practiced it nor have I known of it.

I may cite for Your Lordship the instance of a missionary who lacked supplies for his Indians, and who, being requested by the governor to sell grain to the presidio which was in great need, with all respect suggested to His Lordship that in these circumstances the price should be raised. This made me indignant, and I wrote to him that he should help the presidio to the utmost. I reminded him that the question whether or not the price should be increased pertained to the governor, and that of proposing it concerned me. I confidently assured him that His Lordship would not refuse to do what was just. Heed was paid to public clamor and to reports from private individuals rather than to the sincerity and the actual procedure of the Fathers of that mission. Eventually, the governor, being fully and clearly acquainted with the scarcity existing in that and other missions, and being fully aware that these same missions might have had to pay twice the fixed price for the supplies which they offered as a courtesy to the troops, added two reales to the price of each fanega, but only in the case of corn, and even that was restricted to certain specified missions, and for a limited and very brief period.

Prior to this legal fixing of the prices the missionaries of the missions did not dare to increase by fifty per cent the price of the occasional fanega of grain which some persons in need removed almost forcibly, [but they did so later] for they were satisfied that the circumstances themselves demanded it.

The prices set for grain, in the price schedule referred to, are, in my view (subject always to superior judgment), at the lowest point to which they can decline in time of abundance. On the other hand, we have had years of scarcity; and in them, although the schedule makes provision for it, we did not raise the prices, and neither did we fail to provide for those at the presidio, and for the settlers who needed help.

Finally, Sir, it is my observation and belief that the market for grain, goods, and produce is more free, more useful, and more adapted to the needs of everyone as conducted in the missions rather than in the presidios. Do not take my word for it, Your Lordship, if the purchasers do not confirm it.

The fourth complaint of the governor implies that we do not send, at the prescribed time, exact inventories of the temporalities, with a report on the current harvest and the disposal of the previous one, in accordance with higher regulations.

The documents, Sir, which are sent annually to the governor on this subject are identical in every respect with those which are sent to me by the missionaries, and by me to my college. These were found adequate to satisfy the predecessor of both Don Pedro Fages in this government district and of Your Lordship in the commandancy. And finally, as the Reverend Father Guardian confirms for me in his latest letters, they met the requirements of the King in person, His Majesty Don Carlos III, whom God keep.

I have never heard that His Majesty has ever wished that we should give a detailed account of the disposal of the harvest; the report of what there is and what has been expended suffices. When I say that it suffices, Sir, I mean, of course, that in reckoning what was produced and what has been consumed the most just and reasonable wishes of the legitimate masters has been taken into account, according to the best legal procedure.

We are not administrators of haciendas. We have not the responsibility to make them a success, and we are not accountable if they fall short of expectations.

The meticulous and painstaking checking of receipts and expenditures are not necessary for our work, nor are they compatible with our principal daytime and nightime sacred duties. Be that as it may, it is for Your Lordship to determine, for we are willing to submit to everything that does not hinder us in the pursuit of objectives that are laudable— we who have already sacrificed ourselves to become exiles from the civilized world in order that we may win additional sons to the Holy Church of God, and vassals to the King.

The fifth of the governor's charges is that some of us embark for San Blas without permission, thus violating the ordinance which subjects us to this precise obligation.

When Don Felipe de Neve governed this province, one of our religious set sail with no other permission than that of his superior; and at that time, in the judgment and opinion of His Excellency the Viceroy, Don Martín de Mayorga, there was in the New World no order to which such action was in opposition. Later, our present Reverend Father Guardian, the then Father President, Fray Francisco Palou, embarked in the sight and presence of Governor Don Pedro Fages; hence, it would seem that His Lordship would be accountable for any violation committed in that case.

The following year I spoke to the same governor on the subject of the departure of the Reverend Father Fray Juan Riobó, and His Lordship told me there was no difficulty, provided we had a religious to substitute for him during his absence.

Finally, at this very time Father Fray Matías Noriega has proposed to withdraw from this Mission of San Carlos to his College of San Fernando; and as we were notified in advance by a decree of His Excellency the Viceroy, Count de Gálvez, that no missionaries should enter this peninsula or depart therefrom without his higher permission, this request has been forwarded to the governor.

Having answered the five charges or complaints of the governor, Don Pedro Fages, with the frankness which I promised, and having supported them with more evidence than was needed, with Your Lordship's permission, I shall set forth some ideas that occur to me with regard to the above decree of His Excellency Count de Gálvez.

It is the decree of His Excellency that the prohibition above-mentioned applies to the arrival and departure from this peninsula of the missionaries. He rules that his superior permission is a prerequisite and adds that "when there is a reason requiring the relief or change of religious, whether due to illness or other just cause, application must be made in due time by the respective superiors."

This we have already done, and it is to be attributed to our spirit of humble obedience. But, Sir, I must remind Your Lordship that there is no religious who makes up his mind to depart from his college for a destination like this who does not experience deep misgivings, and that there is nothing which can overcome them more effectively than the assurance that it would be possible to return, should climate or occupation prove unsuitable.

If this freedom is withdrawn, it will necessarily bring but little joy to those of us who are here, and cause the greatest repugnance to those who may have to succeed us. The three missionaries who have just arrived would not have come if the new regulation had not been concealed from them.

Besides this, Sir, what kind of sickness is it that can allow us to wait? And are there not just causes and motives that cannot wait? Is our status to be worse than that of the soldiers, for they can obtain a concession without need of recourse to a distant authority? Some of us have been twenty and more years in this service. Have we not deserved the privilege which our Papal Bulls and our King grant for a lesser period?

In my judgment, Sir, a ruling of this kind becomes tolerable only if it is directed solely to the religious ministers; that is to say, that without the express permission of a superior no one could be left as a solitary missionary in any mission.[2] But in that case, the concession would have to be made to our college, and the latter would have to insure without fail that we would have four or five supernumerary missionaries in these missions.

In this way, the superior decree of the viceroy and our own well-merited convenience could be secured at one and the same time.

The other points included in the *expediente* above-mentioned are cited by the Reverend Father Fray Francisco Palou, the present Guardian of our College of San Fernando. This means that my immediate superior in religion will speak in regard to them, and that I can keep silent. Your Lordship will have the satisfaction of obtaining information on this subject from a person of the highest repute. He deserves implicit confidence, for, in addition to his personal qualities, he was active for many long years in these and other missions, and was elected to the presidency of the missionaries of both Californias. All these are circumstances worthy of note and they serve to strengthen the truth of his arguments. The fact that in part I have relied on them with good results has caused me to speak at length in support and confirmation of them.

I shall only add that I would not wish to be involved in the fixing of prices; but in regard to them, I will not refuse to give such information as I may have, if it is demanded and I am consulted.

There is something which is totally repugnant to me personally, and something which I shall oppose to the utmost. It is the project of being alone in a mission. I am willing to submit to any kind of suffering, and I am willing to sacrifice my life in these parts, whenever my superiors so order me; but I am certain that there is no man who can convince me that I should submit to such banishment in this ministry. It seems, however, that this design has either been abandoned, or is no longer discussed; therefore, I am not discussing it further. But I will do so whenever it affects me.

Now, as always, I am searching for a way that will meet Your Lordship's approval as I endeavor to carry out the obligation imposed on me by your command. I may not, nor do I wish to, interfere in affairs of government, much less attribute blame to the government. But if the natural interconnection between its interests and ours renders both inseparable, and if my information should be more important than the rest, I have no other mind than to impart it to Your Lordship on request.

It is well known that a conquest of this nature cannot as a rule be achieved by us without the co-operation of the troops, nor by the troops without our co-operation. Well, Sir, whatever others may say to Your Lordship about us, my observation is that the military do not apply themselves to their proper duties in this joint enterprise. They busy themselves about too many things that distract them from the main objective, and that become a hindrance to the efficient protection of the territory. They have all grown so accustomed to peace that they neglect almost entirely the precautions necessary to preserve it. They have lost completely all prudent fear of hostile action—and such fear is very necessary in surroundings such as these. And should trouble ever begin, we would inevitably have to suffer the dreadful consequences of this lack of foresight.

Little is gained by giving just one soldier as an escort to a missionary when he goes on a long journey, or by assigning to the missions soldiers who are less efficient, weak in discipline, and poorly equipped. And what is worse, they leave them for long periods with one or two men short of the quota assigned. Many of the soldiers who have been assigned as a guard to the missions have introduced into them herds of cattle and other animals that cause much damage.

It is forbidden to sell to the missions any kind of animals for breeding, for they are not subject to tithes; and there is no desire to wait until the animals have grown up so that the tithes may then be collected.

And the same applies to mules, stallions, and horses that are still good for work. However, all of these can be purchased by the governor, the adjutant inspector, lower ranking officers and many others, without violating any law. It often happens that private individuals use one or other of these to pay debts which they have incurred at the missions and elsewhere or to obtain supplies they cannot find elsewhere. And the only advantage gained is the convenience of the public.

A charge was brought against me recently by the governor that in some missions an abuse is permitted, for more Indians are permitted to ride on horseback than are absolutely necessary to look after and round up the cattle. I satisfied His Lordship by pointing out the limited number of saddles and cowboys which each mission maintains for the purpose, and by adverting to the vigilance of the missionaries who are more concerned than anyone else that the Indians should not become adept in the use and management of horses. Immediately he told me again that His Lordship could not only limit their use and management but could forbid it altogether. So I felt it was very prudent to keep silent—as is my custom in such encounters—lest he bring to bear against us these and similar powers.

It is obvious to Your Lordship that without some mounted men, who have to be Indians in this place, the missions would lack an indispensable means for looking after, and making the most of, what is raised on the farm.

In cases like these the best we can do is to urge one argument or another, and we have already been told once that they will be disregarded. It is the power and authority of the one in command that always prevails.

It has happened very frequently that Indians are carried off to the presidios because they have killed some beast or animal, or simply because they ran away from the mission. There they are held technically as prisoners, but in reality as peons. The missionaries are not notified of this, even when they are captured through the efforts of the latter. It seems to me, Sir, that some provision is needed against such a mode of procedure because it is due to a greedy desire to obtain free labor, and because it is at variance with the control and care of the Indians which is our responsibility, because when there is reason for punishing them the Fathers usually can take care of the matter, and because of other inconveniences, too.

I think that some provision, too, is needed against the practice of the pueblos, especially that of San José, adjacent to Santa Clara Mission, in regard to the pagans, both men and women. They make use of them indiscriminately for all their house and field work. They are an immense hindrance to the conversion of the pagans, for they give them bad example, they scandalize them, and they actually persuade them not to become Christians, lest they would themselves suffer the loss of free labor. Here, Sir, are many abuses which justly demand a remedy.

It seems to me that the institution of alcaldes and regidores in the missions was untimely and unduly legalistic, for it makes such persons independent of the missionaries as regards punishment and dismissal from office when they deserve it, and it makes these officials lazy and haughty, connivers at wrongdoing and partners in it.

When I was in San Diego, we were informed of this decision; and a law was cited which ordains it. That law, however, made it subject to the proviso that an election for such an office must be held under the supervision of the parish priests. In conformity with these same terms of the law, I replied that there were no parish priests here and that the law made no reference to missions. Furthermore, there were no persons to be found in them who were capable of handling the economic affairs of their own families, and still less the political affairs of their pueblo.

The fact is this, that from that time on no such office was established in San Diego, either by the former governor or by the present incumbent; and only nominations were made of persons who have had the best reputation since their conversion from paganism. This method is in conformity with the constitution of the missions. So, too, is the method by which, in complete dependence on the missionaries, instructions are given to the neophytes in the management and discharge of their duties, in preparation for the time when they will become pueblos and be handed over to the secular clergy, as was successfully done in the case of the Sierra Gorda Missions.

The question of measures is one of major consideration in all kingdoms and provinces. Here where the heaped measure is applied to everything, we are exposed to much confusion and the prospect of serious losses in regard to grain which has to be measured by the use of the level measure.

To me it is clear beyond all doubt that, according to the practical judgment of Don Felipe de Neve, here in Monterey our measure exceeded by one half the level measure others use. For instance, a measure that contained a heaped fanega of corn was found to be a fanega and a half when filled with wheat. Many representations, both verbal and written, have been made to the governor in regard to this, and quite recently His Lordship told me that we would come to a mutual agreement regarding the best solution of this problem. I replied that I was entirely in favor of this. I hope he will consult me regarding a temporary solution pending a more definite one.

However, it seems to me, Sir, that so delicate a matter necessarily demands a decision emanating directly from Your Lordship which will enable us to determine, without further argument, the extent to which one measure exceeds another and the measurement which applies to each kind of grain.

Since last year I ordered from Mexico and from San Blas proper and standard European scales for measuring grain. They reached me with the latest ships, but they are not the type that will help to settle the matter exactly. It will be easy for Your Lordship to introduce them, if you judge it necessary.

I have heard it stated that the excessive breeding of cattle and horses at the presidios under care of the military pertains to the Royal Treasury; therefore I shall say nothing about it. It seems to me that all that remains for me is to bring to Your Lordship's attention the fact that if the province seeks its supplies from the mission livestock at royal expense, and on the other hand if it is maintained that the pueblos rather than the missions are to get preference in supplying the presidios with grain, the missions will have no means of acquiring what is necessary for survival, nor will they have even the means to clothe the Indians, as our lord the King desires.

The pueblos and presidios are not yet in a position to furnish completely the provisioning contemplated; and during the interval, which may not be very long, I must point out to Your Lordship that when the paymasters make purchases from the missions in order to supply the needs of the armed forces, as a rule they refuse to make payment in return in the form of goods that are useful for the Indians.

In this respect, in my judgment, they are offending against equity in buying and selling. They persuade the Indians to sell, but they give them no opportunity to buy, for there are no other shops or merchants here.

If they pay, as they usually do, with drafts or with Mexican currency, in addition to the delay involved in reimbursing the Indian, there is also the fact that the amount that is sent to the capital, and that he may wish to convert to his own benefit, suffers a considerable reduction; for in addition to the risks and other expenses, the freight from Mexico to San Blas costs him eleven reales per arroba regularly, and last year it rose to eighteen.

The moderate prices which have been fixed for the products of these new lands, it seems clear to me, were intended to bear an exact relationship to the reduced prices and the convenience with which those who sell here at Mexican prices would be able to acquire the items they need at the same price at the paymasters' stores.

It was the same person who was the author of the *Reglamento* and of the tariff, and it is evident that it was out of regard for the mutual benefit of buyers and sellers that he made that just arrangement. But this is not realized in cases in which the mission is not paid in goods.

Payment is made in this fashion as a matter of justice in the case of those from the pueblos who bring their produce to the presidios. How, then, can it be just to refuse to act in the same way towards the poor Indians?

Who can say that the Mexican merchants acted rightly if in the case of growers who sold them grain they absolutely refused to give cloth with which they could clothe themselves, and instead gave them money, thus making it imperative for them to expend it on purchases in Monterey? In that case the merchant would estimate the price in Mexico, and the poor worker would have to bear the expense of the losses and surcharges of having to bring them to a place so remote. This, precisely this, is what happens to our Indians.

These are the points which have occurred to me at this stage as being the most important, and matters of greater significance. Whatever Your Lordship decides in regard to them we shall accept with profound submission and ready obedience, in the same way as we have already accepted the decisions and resolutions of the Royal Governing Audiencia contained in the above-mentioned *expediente* which, insofar as it rests with me, I have already brought to the attention of all the missionaries.

In my judgment I have already carried out the superior mandate of Your Lordship. At least I have devoted to this end my understanding, my will, and my best efforts.

In this way lies my duty: always to obey Your Lordship with the certain and constant belief that only thus shall I fulfil my obligation.

May God Our Lord keep Your Lordship for many years in His holy grace.

San Carlos of Monterey Mission,
October 20, 1787.

[1] The Viceroy of Mexico, as vice-patron, shared in many of the privileges of the Royal Patronato. With the establishment of the Internal Provinces the commandant general of them enjoyed similar rights. It will be observed that Lasuén is not challenging the right of civil officials in Spain or its possessions to exercise such privileges. His attitude is: the precise privileges granted are perfectly legitimate; but they should not be extended arbitrarily, and they have little application in a mission country such as California.

[2] That is, because of the departure of the other missionary.

66. To Don Pedro Fages

I have made it a rule of life never to be wanting in respect and obedience to Your Lordship in all that is consistent with my status as a poor religious. This is merely as it should be, and I shall never fail to observe it.

I gladly accept the honor Your Lordship confers on me;[1] and I shall come tomorrow, with God's help, to say Mass at your presidio, and to sing it, if there is someone to assist.

Nothing pleases me more than to be of service to Your Lordship; and no task is ever more agreeable to me than that of proving beyond doubt that I am your most devoted and obedient servant.

May God Our Lord keep Your Lordship many years in His holy grace.

San Carlos Mission,
November 3, 1787.

¹ The governor had sent a cordial invitation to Lasuén to be his guest at the presidio for the celebration of the feast of St. Charles, the patron saint, whose feastday was the following day.

67. Memorandum

[In the handwriting of Lasuén but not signed by him]

1. The proclamation in regard to the monopoly and the prohibition in regard to sea otters has not been published, and no one wishes to believe what missionaries say concerning it.
2. The sea and land commandants are opposed to the observance of the plan of Don Vicente Vasadre which was approved and enjoined by the Royal Audiencia.
3. Goods of inferior quality and excessive prices by the California agent in payment for sea otters.
4. The denial of an escort for confessions and baptisms when, in such circumstances, the missionary has to spend the night away from the mission.
5. The frequent absence for long periods of one soldier, and even of two, from the escort assigned to the missions.
6. The holding of pagans and Christians as prisoners in the presidios, especially at Monterey, when work needs to be done, even when the crime merits a lighter sentence, or no term in prison.
7. The Indians of Santa Clara banished to Monterey, during the past three years, for the stories they concocted regarding Father Peña.
8. The encroachments of the pueblos on the Indians.

VI
The Year 1788

Although the extant letters for this year are few, the problems were not. They cover a wide range—the treatment of Indians, the price of otter pelts, and the reluctance of the governor to permit military escorts to accompany the missionaries when visiting the sick.

68. To Don Pedro Fages

HAVE RECEIVED THE DECISION OF HIS MAJesty in regard to the manner of procedure in divorce cases. I shall carry it out whenever a case arises, and in so far as it pertains to me.

With deepest respect I place myself at Your Lordship's service, and I pray that God Our Lord may keep your Lordship many years in His holy grace.

Santa Barbara Mission,
January 31, 1788.

69. To Don Jacobo Ugarte y Loyola

Enclosed with Your Lordship's esteemed official letter of November 21 of last year I received the copy of the royal order of the previous July 14, and a duplicate of the royal decrees which it cites, expressing the terms under which His Majesty has deemed it fit to divide the general ministry of the Indies into two distinct departments.

I have duly noted, and I shall carry out in accordance with the orders of Your Lordship, all these sovereign prescriptions insofar as they apply to me.

As always, I am at Your Lordship's service; and I pray that God Our Lord may keep you many years in His holy grace.

San Luis Obispo Mission,
May 11, 1788.

70. To Don Pedro Fages

I have this day received Your Lordship's esteemed official letter written at the nearby presidio on the tenth of the present month. In it you inform me that the commandant general has sentenced to perpetual banishment the Indian neophytes Carlos, of the Mission of San Diego, and María Regina, of San Gabriel. You further state that in virtue of it Your Lordship has decreed that the aforesaid Carlos, as well as one other named Agustín Merino, shall serve that sentence while attached to the Mission of Santa Clara, and the woman named Regina at that of San Antonio.

175

As you consider proper that Carlos should not be separated from his wife, you request and charge me to indicate the steps which I regard necessary so that she and her children may be transferred to the place where her husband is to serve his sentence.

It is not my wish, Sir, nor is it within my competence to oppose the authority and power of Your Lordship, once a decision has definitely been reached. And I cannot, on the other hand, deny myself the frankness and sincerity which are mine in the reply in which you are awaiting my opinion.

Your Lordship states that you feel that your decision will be in accordance with my zeal; but I frankly admit that this is not so. The missions are not intended as places for the maintenance of those who had to be banished from the missions. And surely they are not intended for the very desirable purpose of preventing people from lapsing into the same kind of criminal conduct which was the cause of their banishment.

They were obviously intended for the exact opposite of these, and no prudent missionary should be called on to undertake a burden so heavy, or to deal with subjects of such evil character.

It is in the presidio that the Indian Carlos has spent many years without either his wife or his children, for it is a suitable place for the punishment and restraint of those who are insubordinate. Through the clemency of the commandant general he was brought back to his own country and his mission and united with his wife and family. Instead of being grateful for the favor, he immediately became the ringleader in the very same kind of agitation, or a similar one, for which he had been expelled.

The wife and children of Carlos are not to blame, and so the missionaries do not think it right that heavy punishment should be inflicted on them.

It will be only as a result of exhortations that it will be possible to induce them to make the sacrifice of becoming strangers for the sake of their husband and father. If Your Lordship wishes, I will see to it that this is done, and anything else which Your Lordship may see fit to decide pursuant to it.

While it is true that I deem these objections worthy of the attention of Your Lordship, it is no less true that I make them with the same deference which I always show and will continue to show to your higher orders.

May God Our Lord keep Your Lordship for many years in His holy grace.

San Carlos Mission,
June 15, 1788.

MISSION SAN BORJA
An interior view

THE YEAR 1788 177

71. To Don Pedro Fages

The flattering official letter of Your Lordship dated today, which I have just received, and the graciousness you have shown by so kindly enclosing a copy of the decision of the commandant general in regard to the Indian woman, Toypurina, have given to the recommendations of my insignificant self more weight than they deserve. Would that my outward expressions of gratitude were in keeping with my inner sentiments.

In the past, Sir, I felt exactly as you do in regard to this Indian woman, and it so happens that I made reference to the case only yesterday.

She will be received gladly in any mission to which Your Lordship decides to send her and will receive all the help she needs on the way to her destination.

The higher orders of Your Lordship I shall hold in high regard. They are laws which I am under obligation to obey, and they afford in addition the pleasure and honor of doing what is pleasing to you.

May God Our Lord keep Your Lordship many years in His holy grace.

San Carlos Mission,
June 15, 1788.

72. To Don Manuel Antonio Flores

I beg to inform Your Excellency, in accordance with your superior order of March 1, that Don Vicente Vasadre y Vega, commissioner on behalf of the central government for the purchase of otter pelts, took sixty-four such pelts from the missions subject to me. Their price, as he reckons it in accordance with the price list, comes to four hundred and eleven pesos. This appears from a receipt he gave in accordance with which, at my request, he promises to apply this amount to the purchase of articles proper and suitable for our Indians, and to deliver them to our College of San Fernando so that they would be forwarded to these missions by way of San Blas. They did not arrive in the ships of last year, nor have we word up to the present that they may come in those we are expecting.

I have the same desire and the same obligation to obey Your Excellency in regard to your other command, but this is not so easy for me. I have already brought to the attention of the Royal Governing Audiencia, in connection with the considerations they submitted to His Highness, this additional one which had its beginnings here: the high value set on sea otters after they had formerly been regarded as almost worthless. This notable change owes its origin precisely to the fact that the Filipinos and those from San Blas actually paid a higher price for them than the one in Señor Vasadre's fixed price. From that it was inferred that that commodity brings a higher price in China, and the price it should command here was determined by comparison with it. In order to alter it, as Your Excellency orders me, I would need to have a competent knowledge about market conditions for such, and circumstances regarding such; and since I do not have this, it seems to me that the one and only thing I can decide on is, to accept what your Excellency regards as just and equitable.

Impelled by different reasons I suggested to the Royal Governing Audiencia that the price fixed in the above list might be reduced, and at the same time I pointed out to Your Excellency two reasons why it seems to me it could be lowered.

In this way I feel that I have carried out your superior order and left to your superior judgment the final decision on the point.

To this I had been looking forward without the least misgivings, and with deepest interest; and now I find myself with the same command repeated once more by Your Excellency, and with no more information than what I then imparted to the central government already mentioned. Furthermore, His Highness made no decision. And that is not all, for something new has arisen, a very substantial doubt in regard to the matter. I do not know, Most Excellent Sir, whether or not the fitting prohibition proposed by Don Vicente Vasadre, approved and ordered to be published by the Royal Audiencia, is to remain in force, for as long as it was observed the missions had the task of attending to all the activities essential to collecting the sea otters. Or it may be that free trade will be extended to this commodity, as decreed by Señor Don Fernando Joseph Mangino. In that case the Indian neophytes, the only people who hunt for this kind of creature, will waste their labor, and the missionaries who maintain and house them will be at a loss for the expenses incurred and for their efforts.

Therefore, Your Excellency, I do not dare decide; but I do take the liberty, and as is but fitting I take on myself the obligation, of gladly accepting whatever Your Excellency decides, and of promptly putting it into execution.

In regard to the last point which Your Excellency brings to my notice: that the price of the pelts due as of now should be paid by me immediately, in accordance with the fixed price of the aforesaid Vasadre, on the understanding that it will be in the form of clothing which the agent at these presidios holds by agreement for these missions, and which have already been received in each of them in accordance with the orders from the Royal Audiencia. In that case, all that remains for me to do is to forward the superior order of Your Excellency to the missionaries so that their respective missions may select from among the above-mentioned clothing an amount equal to the value of the pelts which had been forwarded.

I remain the least of Your Excellency's subjects, and the most submissive to your superior orders, and I pray that God Our Lord may keep Your Excellency many years in His holy grace.

San Carlos of Monterey Mission,
July 30, 1788.

73. To Fray Francisco Palou

It was Your Reverence who placed before the central government of Mexico City the just complaint that escorts were refused us for transactions necessary and becoming; and the same authority decided once and for all that for the attainment of the just and pious ends, which His Majesty approved in the new *Reglamento* for this peninsula, the governor should grant the religious missionaries the help they need for the more perfect carrying out of their pious objective, and should give them all the necessary armed escort in their indispensible trips to presidios and missions. It continues: As of this date, January 12, 1787, these instructions have been sent to Governor Don Pedro Fages.

The commandant general sent me a copy of these and other items; and in virtue of them and of the fact that obviously they are not observed, for the escorts were denied us just as before these provisions were issued, I informed Governor Don Pedro Fages of this, courteously and by word of mouth. He replied to me with a smile that he had secret instructions approved by His Majesty to do the opposite, and that nothing that I had proposed had come to him from the Mexican authorities.

Your Reverence will regard this answer as seriously as I do, and much more so; and the conclusion we shall reach is, that Don Pedro Fages will always do what he pleases with us,[1] and that no matter what concessions we get—I mean in regard to our apostolic ministry—they will carry no weight with His Lordship.

If I send him an official letter about something in particular, as I am now thinking of doing, it has reached the stage where, as he has already told me, he will reply that he has had recourse to higher authority; and then, between having recourse and not doing what is ordered, we are in the same position as if no orders had been issued to help us in the exact fulfillment of our sacred duties.

Just recently this very thing happened, and as this gives me an opportunity for doing so, I am bringing it to the attention of Your Reverence in order that, and with the firm hope that, you will act, as you always do, in the interests of our welfare.

I say the same in regard to the three Indians from Santa Clara, those who gave false evidence against Father Peña. They enjoy their freedom at this presidio, and the governor is being waited on by one of them in the capacity of page. Even on his journeys he waited on him hand and foot, a matter which could not but make us blush a great deal for shame.

The lieutenant at San Francisco has said at Santa Clara that he had instructions from the governor, verbally and in writing, that in case the troops sought out runaway Indians belonging to the missions, he was without fail to take them to the presidio to work. It is probable that the other lieutenants have the same instructions. But this is contrary to reason, as Your Reverence well knows, for then they become as wild as before, with the same lack of instruction as in the forest, and sometimes with an example worse than there.

Within the last few days the governor has been spreading the report through the military posts and the missions that we cannot keep Indians in prison beyond ten days. I do not know what is the source of these innovations. It is certain that they are very hurtful; and it is our hope that Your Reverence on learning about them will take steps to remedy them.

With the most profound respect I hold myself in readiness once more to carry out the higher orders of Your Reverence, and I pray that Our Lord God may keep you for many years in His holy grace.

San Carlos Mission,
August 9, 1788.

[1] Lasuén did not need to elaborate on the attitude of Fages towards the missionaries. More than sixteen years before, Palou himself had sent to the guardian of San Fernando College the following report: "[Governor Fages] considers himself as absolute, and that the missionaries count for less than the least of his soldiers, so that the missionaries cannot speak to him on the slightest matter concerning missions. He states that he is in charge of all; that the missionaries have nothing more to do than to obey, say Mass, administer the sacraments; that all the rest devolves upon him as commander . . . ." Palou to Verger, Loreto, October 2, 1771, cited by Geiger, *Life and Times of Junípero Serra,* I, 329.

74. To Don Pedro Fages

Since Your Lordship and I are aware of the charges and countercharges of the commandant and the missionaries of San Diego, I have begun to wish and actually believe that if we had a discussion among ourselves on the information we both have gleaned, our joint efforts would be all that would be needed to put an end to these dissensions and to bring about a more satisfactory settlement.

Actually, I had already written these religious all there was to be said in favor of so happy a result, and pointed out to them their duty in the matter. This I had done before being requested to do so by Your Lordship in your esteemed official letter of the sixth of the present month.

This letter placed me under a definite obligation to reply; and despite the fact that I did so on the eleventh of the same month, with all the deference of which I am capable and without introducing any incidents or digressions that were irrelevant, I am deeply grieved that, without intending it in the least, I caused Your Lordship the displeasure and annoyance which you bring to my attention in your other esteemed official letter of the day before yesterday.

Any prudent man will easily recognize this if he examines the three official letters in question.

I have always held the view that to submit to writing what can be said and settled by word of mouth, while it is not opposed to greater harmony and concord between those who frequently have dealings with one another, it by no means conduces to it. I am still more convinced of this when each of them delivers in person to the other the letters he has written.

This may not be the most apt way of doing things; but for me it has peace and concord for its objective. Hence, I would have refrained from replying to Your Lordship's official letter despite the reproach I might have incurred that by my silence I had concurred in all that had been written. However, because I feel that by my silence I might offend Your Lordship the more, and that if I seek to discuss the matter with you face to face it will not be pleasing to you—in a word, because I think Your Lordship wants me to reply to you in writing, I am going to do so.

If I am mistaken in this, Your Lordship should not read further. Tear up this letter. Call me; summon me; order me to come to your residence, and you will find me there promptly.

As regards the action taken by the Fathers at San Diego in regard to the corporal of the escort, it seems to me that it was not open opposition but a courteous request to him to suspend as far as possible the orders he had received from his commandant until such time as recourse could be had to the commandant. As regards what transpired later, I feel that allowance must be made for the natural feelings of the Fathers for they were neither listened to, nor was any notice taken of them. However, despite all this, in every case it is the duty of the inferior to carry out most faithfully what has been commanded him by a superior, and he should even be advised to do so.

This thought is well expressed in the paragraphs which are summarized in the passage under discussion, and in similar ones, which state: "As I write these words I am strengthening my determination not to open my mouth, nor to express in public even the least aversion I feel, in this or other instances, towards the transfer of Indians from the missions to the presidios."

As to those things which pertain to the missionary Fathers alone, matters such as the management, control, discipline, and education of the Indians, I maintain that we have a greater degree of competence than anyone else. I have made clear, too, by word and example, that as regards revolts, bloodshed, and crimes of a serious nature that cannot be prevented or corrected by the missionaries, or that call for a particular type of punishment, Your Lordship possesses all the competence one could desire, whereas we have none, beyond that of keeping Your Lordship informed.

That this is the real sense of my proposal is shown by the fact that I am speaking of apprehensions made at the instigation of the Fathers, and of punishments they had inflicted on their own initiative. In these circumstances, whatever action was taken in opposition to the Fathers and their will is prejudicial to us.

It is quite possible that the insolence of the Carmel Indians in consuming the King's cattle was curbed by the efforts of the military, and one can presume that the order came from Your Lordship and was carried out at your instance; but if this beneficial result has applied to those of the mission—something which I do not venture to assert—neither I nor those associated with me give our approval to any action of this nature which does not emanate from us.

In most instances, certainly, it is better if the search for runaway Indians be made by means of Indians; but there are some instances in which it is necessary for the troops to undertake it.

If the encounter which the latter had at the Channel had happened to our Indians, it is they who would have borne the brunt. In fact, a short time before, this is what almost happened to the new Christians of Santa Barbara who had been sent on a similar errand. As a general rule, the circumstances of the case must decide who should be sent to carry out this duty.

I have not given the natives, nor do I wish the missionaries to give them, any severer punishment than that of keeping them under instruction for long periods each day when they are being prepared to become Christians, and that of reprehending them when they are obstinate in their concubinages, or when they join with Christians in doing what is naturally wrong, or when guilty of sins of omission.

From other corporal punishments I excuse them as often as I can, and even from witnessing them; and I recommend the missionaries to do likewise.

In the whole of my official letter not a word will be found in reference to an order to refuse to supply an escort, or to one rescinding such an order. My sole reference was to an escort that, a short time ago, accompanied Father Mariner for half the journey, and then obliged him to return without fulfilling his sacred mission.

In order to show that this action was contrary to law, I quoted the one recently enacted by the central government. It has not been repealed, and it has not lost its force just because fifteen hundred others have been repealed, as Your Lordship knows.

If on this account Your Lordship is under obligation to supply the assistance prescribed, by the same token you are debarred from everything opposed to it.

On this subject I neither said nor wished to say anything in my official letter. As for the rest, I would like to sum up briefly once more, in keeping with what I have said above, that in order to please Your Lordship I shall always do a great deal, everything in fact, so as to obey you and carry out exactly and humbly your higher orders.

May God Our Lord keep Your Lordship many years in His holy grace.

San Carlos Mission,
August 18, 1788.

75. To Fray Francisco Palou

[This is identical with Letter 73 above. However, since part of the date is somewhat blurred, some have interpreted the month as *September 9*, and not as August. For that reason both dates are given here.]

76. To Don Pedro Fages

Felipe Gutiérrez, who was formerly a soldier of the Royal Presidio of Monterey, in the presence of Father Fray Antonio Paterna and of two witnesses, pledged himself to marry Francisca Ruelas, widow of Pablo Pinto, deceased, and bound himself to carry out this promise[1] on his recovery from the illness from which he suffered.

The poor widow has good grounds for suspecting, as she explained to me, that the person in question may leave the province, and may use this or some other device as a means of breaking his promise.

In these circumstances, it is Your Lordship, and not I, who has the power and authority to oblige this man to satisfy this grave obligation in justice.

With the utmost respect, therefore, I ask for the assistance of Your Lordship in this matter, and I have full confidence that I shall receive it because of your sense of justice and equity.

Always happy to obey the higher orders of Your Lordship, I pray that God Our Lord may keep you for many years in His holy grace.

Santa Clara Mission,
September 14, 1788.

[1] This was no merely private promise of marriage. It was a solemn and public espousal, or act of betrothal.

77. List of Missionaries

List of those of us, missionaries, who on this date are devoting ourselves to the administration of these Missions of New California, to the instruction of the neophytes, and the conversion of the pagans.

San Carlos	Fermín Francisco de Lasuén, President José Señán Pascual Arenaza
Our Father St. Francis	Pedro Benito Cambón Diego García Faustino Sola, supernumerary
Santa Clara	Tomás de la Peña Diego Noboa
San Antonio de Padua	Miguel Pieras Buenaventura Sitjar
San Luis Obispo	José Cavaller Miguel Giribet
Purísima Concepción	Vicente Fuster José Arroyta
Santa Barbara	Antonio Paterna Cristóbal Oramas

San Buenaventura   Francisco Dumets [*sic*]
                                    Vicente Santa María

San Gabriel   Antonio Cruzado
                                    Miguel Sánchez
                                    José Calzada, supernumerary

San Juan Capistrano   Pablo Mugartegui
                                    Juan Santiago

San Diego   Hilario Torrent
                                    Juan Mariner

                                    San Carlos Mission of Monterey,
                                    October 18, 1788.

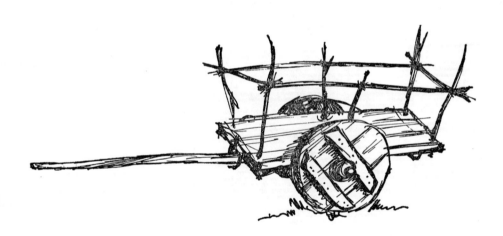

VII
The Year 1789

The few letters that have survived for this year would seem to indicate that it was one of the rare periods when the problems of the President were relatively few. During it provision was made for more detailed reports of mission activities throughout the succeeding years.

78. To Don Jacobo Ugarte y Loyola

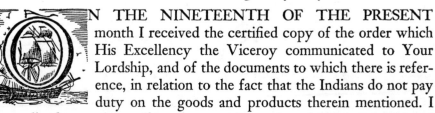N THE NINETEENTH OF THE PRESENT month I received the certified copy of the order which His Excellency the Viceroy communicated to Your Lordship, and of the documents to which there is reference, in relation to the fact that the Indians do not pay duty on the goods and products therein mentioned. I immediately put into effect the superior order of Your Lordship of September 12, 1788, the year just ended, by forwarding everything to the Reverend Missionary Fathers subject to my jurisdiction for their information and guidance.

I have the honor to be Your Lordship's devoted servant, and I shall not fail day by day to pray to God Our Lord for your success and happiness. May He keep you for many years in His holy grace.

Santa Clara Mission,
January 22, 1789.

79. To Fray Miguel Hidalgo

The Reverend Father Vicente Fuster, minister of the Mission of Purísima Concepción in this New California, appeals to me in a letter of the seventh of this month, begging that there be removed from that mission one of the servants named Rafael Rodríguez. Among the reasons which he gives for this, there are some which, in my opinion, may be a matter for the judgment of Your Paternity as Commissary of the Holy Office.[1]

For this reason, and in order that they may come to your notice with the least risk of major delay, I am sending you a faithful copy of them.

"Among those who are servants at this mission," writes the Father mentioned, "there is one named Rafael Rodríguez. On his own admission he has permitted the rumor to spread that he was one of those sought everywhere by the law, and that he had been brought a prisoner to San Blas when the frigate *Realejo* was brought to port. This individual has shown himself to be a blasphemous man, speaking evil of God and the saints; and this he has done on several occasions in the presence of his companions. He was worse than ever last Sunday, the fifth of the month, for he had been gambling with them all night, and one of them won some cigarette cases and a handkerchief. He tried to get a loan from one of them, but the latter did not feel he could trust him. Then he began to cast aspersions on the saints, shouting that he did not believe that the saints performed miracles, and invoking maledictions on any saint to whom he would pray. He spoke disparagingly of God, and finally he uttered other blasphemies offensive to the Divine Majesty and the saints.

"Two of his companions have reported to me that he uses love-charms for women, and for committing robbery, and for escaping from the law, and for making himself invisible. One of them told me that he heard him say that if he were to put an egg in the place where a woman was doing her grinding, and then bury it for nine days, then recover it, open it with the aid of many pins which should be placed in the egg as if they were thorns, and then throw these at the door of the woman's house they would turn into three worms. These worms would then fasten themselves to different parts of the woman's body, and the result would be that the woman would go in search of a man with whom to commit sin.

"In order to commit a robbery, (they say) one must first kill a cat by striking it, clubbing it well, and then burying it. After some months one must exhume it, use its bones to smoke with while standing before a mirror, and continue to smoke until the mirror becomes entirely dark or clouded. When that stage is reached, according to this man, the time is ripe to carry out the robbery openly, and without danger of detection.

"He spoke of knowing many other tricks, but the servants assure me that in their presence he never performed them, nor have they seen or heard that he did so.

"It must be about a month since he was caught one night in the ranchería. Sergeant José María Ortega placed him under arrest. After punishing him, he warned him, when setting him free, that if he did not mend his ways he would order him flogged. The other then went so far as to say that if anything like that happened to him, he would burn down the mission and the Blessed Sacrament.

"Finally as far as I have been able to gather, his blasphemies, curses, and oaths have all been uttered at times when he feels annoyed; but that is very frequent, for he has an impetuous and choleric disposition. He has not shown any caution, nor does he refrain from uttering any absurdity. His companions were scandalized, and for that reason they came and denounced him.

"I have just finished writing this when Ortega told me that one of the servants reported that this particular Rafael Rodríguez said that if he wanted to find out what was happening in Spain, or in his own house, he could find out by simply saying an incantation."

I certify that I have copied all the above from the Reverend Father Fray Vicente Fuster's letter, the original of which I immediately burned.

I place myself at the service of Your Reverend Paternity, and pray that God Our Lord may keep you for many years in His holy grace.

Santa Clara Mission,
April 17, 1789.

[1] Better known as the Inquisition. Regarding the scope of its functions in Mexico, see Geiger, *Palou's Life of Serra,* p. 361, note 37. It was empowered to deal with such matters as blasphemy, witchcraft, profanation of the Blessed Eucharist, etc. Hidalgo was superior of the Dominican missionaries in Lower California.

For a description of the Inquisition in its earlier stages, its scope and methods of procedure, see Richard E .Greenleaf, *Zumárraga and the Mexican Inquisition, 1536-1543* (Washington, D. C., 1961).

80. To Don Pedro Fages

In accordance with Your Lordship's esteemed official letter of the twenty-ninth of last month, I acknowledge receipt of the certified copy of the royal order of February 10th of last year, which approves the instructions issued by the central government of Mexico in regard to the allowances to be made from the Pious Fund of the Missions[1] for the journey by sea and land of missionaries who come to this peninsula. It further provides that the aforementioned central government shall determine the sending and the replacement of such religious and the execution of the royal orders which may be issued in the future in regard to such matters.

The orders which Your Lordship is so kind as to intimate to me shall serve to prove ever more clearly my profound obedience.

May God Our Lord keep Your Lordship for many years in His holy grace.

Santa Clara Mission,
May 13, 1789.

[1] A fund created by gifts and donations from private individuals for the evangelization of the Indians of the Californias, for the establishment and maintenance of missions among the Indians. It was initiated by the Jesuit Fathers in their mission in Lower California, and both Franciscan and Dominican missions later benefitted from it. For a further account of it, see Antonine Tibesar, *Writings of Junípero Serra* (Washington, D. C., 1956), II, 475-476, note 97. With the departure of the Jesuit missionaries the Fund was administered by the government, but it was not aided by public taxes.

81. To Don Jacobo Ugarte y Loyola

In compliance with Your Lordship's higher order of the fourteenth of last March, in which you enclosed the letter which the Most Excellent Viceroy Don Antonio Flores sent you on September 9, and the copy of the royal cedula of March 21, 1787, I shall draw up the Report required by His Majesty in regard to the missions under my charge, and I shall send it to you every two years, this being the interval designated by Your Lordship as a rule to be followed in order to bring about uniformity.

As you anticipate, I shall spare no effort in taking care of this and similar matters. I shall devote to them the attention which the royal will and the authoritative instructions of the Most Excellent Viceroy and Your Lordship demand. However, I am much preoccupied, constantly and ceaselessly, by duties assigned me by His Majesty, by His Excellency, and by Your Lordship, for I take care of all these missions, being at the same time in charge of the one in which I reside, and of the neighboring presidio, in what pertains to spiritual affairs. The result is that I have less time than I need in order to think over and compose all these documents, and then to draw them up in duplicate, as I am asked.

The fact is, Sir, that this year, as in the previous ones, I forwarded to Governor Don Pedro Fages the report on the spiritual and temporal status of every one of the missions at the end of the previous year. And so I took for granted that I had satisfied Your Lordship's higher order by merely referring to these reports, because they include all that Your Lordship requires of me for the time being, and because the governor himself told me that he had forwarded them to Your Lordship.

But now I suddenly find myself face to face with an official letter from the same governor in which, enclosing another copy of the same cedula, he informs me that I am to send him under separate cover the same report as I send Your Lordship.

Although I mention these grievances I am not making an issue of them, as I am doing my utmost to obey as best I can those who are in a position to command me. I shall therefore proceed forthwith to draw up the required Report in duplicate; but I shall be grateful to Your Lordship if you will kindly permit me to request that you advise how I should act in this regard in the future. May I also beg you, in this instance, kindly to overlook any defects that may be found in this document, and to be so good as to advise regarding the best way to prepare it in the future.

This request is inspired by my keen desire to carry out your higher orders to the entire satisfaction of Your Lordship—for this, after all, is the same thing as fulfilling my duty. And this, too, is the way I view that of praying to God Our Lord that He may keep Your Lordship for many years in His holy grace.

San Carlos of Monterey Mission,
July 7, 1789.

82. Memorandum

A report on the spiritual status of these missions of New California at the end of last year, 1788, which I am forwarding to Brigadier Don Jacobo Ugarte y Loyola, Commandant General of the Internal Provinces of New Spain, in accordance with his higher order of March 14 of the present year.

On the last day of December of the year '88 there were:

10,575 baptisms
2,284 marriages
3,576 deaths
6,750 living

Of these latter, all over five or six years of age receive instruction in Christian doctrine every day in church. One of the missionaries recites it with them, or some well-instructed Indian does it in his presence, once in the morning during Mass and before breakfast, and again in the evening before supper.

On many other days it is recited on two more occasions, with the boys and girls, in front of the missionary's door, at a time that is opportune in the morning and evening.

With these young people this instruction is quite effective; with those of middle age it is fairly satisfactory; but with the very old the bare essentials alone can be taught, and this with much difficulty.

The majority of the adults go to confession once a year; many go to communion; and there generally are some who receive these sacraments two or three times in the course of the year.

Almost invariably we find in all of them, as death approaches, a deeper and better attachment to the true religion that is ours than we could bring about or hope for while they were in good health. Thanks be to God. One would have to see a marvel like this in order to grasp it fully.

As a group, and as individuals, we never cease to instruct them in their Christian duties, taking advantage of every incident and occurence that of necessity arises at all hours when one is dealing with so many people and with such different characters.

When one hammers away at them like this, their hardness tends to soften, and they begin to realize that they are human beings and to appreciate the happy status they have attained after leaving the barbarism and brutality in which they grew up.

Those who fall sick when they are in the rancherías of the pagans, or in the places where they were born, to which they are accustomed to go with the permission which we find it necessary to give them from time to time, and even many of the pagans when they are sick, even though they may be twelve or more leagues from the mission—all of these send word to the Fathers asking for confession or for baptism, as the case may be, and, thanks be to God, it happens but rarely that they fail in their request.

Up to the sixth of July, 1784, five thousand three hundred and nine persons were confirmed. On that date the limit for the extraordinary concession of that faculty expired.[1] Later I was informed definitely that it had been renewed for twelve years, and that it had received the authorization [pasé] of the Council; but it has not arrived here. I know not why.

San Carlos of Monterey Mission,
July 8, 1789.

[1] Lasuén's predecessor in office, Fray Junípero Serra, for a number of years had been given the privilege of conferring this sacrament. For an earlier controversy regarding the right to administer Confirmation, see Tibesar, op. cit., III, 371-385, 460 (note 223); see also Geiger, Life and Times of Junípero Serra, II, 159-170.

83. To Don Pedro Fages

I am returning to Your Lordship the copy of the royal cedula which you sent me, along with your higher order of the sixth of the present month, requiring me to send Your Lordship a record of the baptisms in each of the missions under my charge for the entire preceding year, distinguishing between adults and children.

I have received an identical copy and similar orders from the commandant general, except that he does not distinguish between children and adults.

He asks for promptness and all possible dispatch, as Your Lordship does; but this requirement we could certainly not carry out if it were necessary to make the latter investigation. In the reports which I submitted to Your Lordship last year and in the other years, this breakdown is given; but perhaps it has not come to the attention of Your Lordship.

I have decided to quote these in order to carry out the above higher order of the commandant general as they fully cover all His Lordship asks; but as regards the esteemed order of Your Lordship, obviously I could not under any circumstances withhold from it my humble submission and obedience.

I therefore enclose for Your Lordship the document requested, drawn up in the form that, for the moment, seems to be adequate, keeping in mind the urgency with which it is sought. Nevertheless, should it appear otherwise to Your Lordship, I am always happy to carry out to the letter not only this, but any other task that you may be pleased to assign me.

May God Our Lord keep Your Lordship many years in His holy grace.

San Carlos of Monterey Mission,
July 9, 1789.

84. Memorandum

A report of the spiritual status of these missions of New California at the close of the year that is ended, 1788, which I am forwarding to Governor Don Pedro Fages, Lieutenant Colonel and Commandant Inspector of California, in accordance with his higher order of the sixth of last month.

On the last day of December of the year '88 there were:

> 10,575 baptisms
> 2,284 marriages
> 5,309 confirmations
> 3,576 deaths
> 6,750 living

The constant and unremitting instruction given them, and the spiritual progress thereby achieved, have been noted with approval by the governor, to whom I am sending the report.

All the neophytes have become favorably disposed towards Christian obligations in proportion to their capacity and to the length of time that has elapsed since their conversion. Already they have reached the stage where they appreciate highly the happy state to which they have passed from the unhappiness and misery of a life that was barbaric and brutal.

Finally, I feel certain that when the governor comes to making a report on the matter, he cannot but be just.

San Carlos of Monterey Mission,
July 9, 1789.

85. To Don Pedro Fages

At the first opportunity of getting in touch with San Antonio and Santa Clara Missions, I shall advise the Reverend Father Missionaries to get ready what Your Lordship requests and instructs me to provide, in your esteemed official letter of this date, so as to supply the packet boat *San Carlos* in full with all the items which Commandant Don Esteban José Martínez is requesting for the port of Nootka.[1]

With the same object in mind, this mission will contribute what it can. To assure the prompt and easy transport of the food supplies, it will help with its mule train, and the other two [missions] will help with theirs. And it will assign fifteen or twenty Indians to help in repairing the damage caused by the fire in the presidio.

I am always happy to carry out any dictates that Your Lordship sends. It is not only a duty I owe, but, in addition, a source of personal satisfaction.

May God Our Lord keep Your Lordship for many years in His holy grace.

San Carlos Mission,
August 14, 1789.

[1] Nootka is on the west coast of what is now Vancouver Island. Reports, especially those of La Pérouse, had reached the Spanish authorities that Russia seemed to be contemplating an extension of its possessions along the Pacific Coast, at least as far as Nootka. In 1788, and again in 1789. Esteban Martínez was sent north to investigate and to reassert the claims of Spain to the regions in the north. See Chapman, *op. cit.,* pp. 343-345.

86. To Don Pedro Fages

It is only by recommending his soul to God that we can find relief for the deep grief that we feel at the sad news, which Your Lordship conveys to me, of the death of His August Catholic Majesty, Don Carlos III.[1]

In this mission on next Monday we, the missionaries, will pray for him solemnly and in public, as day by day we do so privately and individually.

As regards the royal presidio, there is nothing more I can do than to celebrate Mass in it and to add such additional prayers for the repose of the soul of our deceased monarch as Your Lordship shall deign to recommend to me on the day or days which Your Lordship may select.

With this same purpose in mind, I shall convey the sad news to all the missionaries. I am always at your service to do as Your Lordship bids.

May God Our Lord keep Your Lordship for many years in His holy grace.

San Carlos Mission,
September 26, 1789.

¹ Carlos III died on December 14, 1788. When barely sixteen years of age he became Duke of Parma. Later he became King of the Two Sicilies; and for the last twenty-nine years of his life he was King of Spain.

87. To Fray Miguel Hidalgo

By courtesy of Father Preacher General,¹ Fray Cristóstomo Gómez, I am forwarding to Your Most Reverend Paternity the matters you committed to me.

The fact that the time was very near for the embarcation of the witnesses named therein, and the fact, too, that it is difficult or almost impossible to get the servants to undertake a long journey in order to appear in court, induced me to travel all the way from Monterey to San Diego. But the defendent and the four principal witnesses had already sailed from that port to San Blas, and the only one who remained in this country was the last, who is Antonio Dávila.

Would that my success were in keeping with my efforts! It is my constant hope, however, that Your Very Reverend Paternity will overlook my shortcomings and will command me as one whose duty and desire it is to obey you.

May God Our Lord keep Your Very Reverend Paternity for many years in His holy grace.

San Diego Mission,
December 1, 1789.

¹ A title of honor in the Dominican Order—the Order of Preachers. Gómez succeeded Hidalgo as president in Lower California. He died in office in the summer of 1800. The trial to which there is reference in this letter was to be conducted by the Inquisition of Mexico.

88. To the Missionaries

The Lord give you Peace. This day I received the copy of a letter sent by the Most Reverend Father Commissary General of the Indies¹ to our Reverend Father Guardian. In it he complains bitterly that he lacks the reports of the college and of its missions which are demanded by his decrees and by those of the Council [of the Indies].

Under holy obedience he orders them to be sent to him, and he threatens with severe punishments those who may be responsible for the delay.

In virtue of this, I enjoin on Your Reverences not to permit the least delay in drawing up in duplicate, according to the customary form, the report of the respective missions. Forward it to me promptly, so that I may have all of them before the end of January. They should be prepared in the same way as before, merely adding that which applies respectively to the notes of the attached form, which is a copy of the one sent by the Most Reverend Father to the college.

When it has been read, take a note of it to serve as a guide so that you will know what you are required to insert in the report. See that it is forwarded from mission to mission as far as San Francisco. And see to it that this letter accompanies it, and that it is well sealed. Finally, it is to be forwarded to me from San Francisco after the individual ministers have testified in the postscript that they have read it, and that they have either carried out, or will carry out, what is ordered.

Pueblos and Ministers: I shall record these in the Status Report.

Neophytes: This is identical with the figures for "Living"; but you are to exclude male and female children up to nine years of age, so that these may be given separately.

Pagans: They are numerous in the neighborhood, and their number cannot be ascertained.

Converted Nations: When the accepted name of the nation is known, the various languages which have been identified may be given.

Adjacent Nations: The same.

Geographical Position: I shall insert it.

Distance from College: Likewise.

Stipends: They are already known.

Assistance which the College Gives: The college itself will state this; or Your Reverences can state that it is responsible for obtaining our stipends and for obtaining and forwarding our supplies, and that as far as it can it responds to our appeals.

Marriages according to the Church: As in other years.

Our Reverend Father Guardian advises me that, as regards grievances for which a remedy is sought or desired, all are to avoid entering them in the report, unless some very unusual circumstance should arise, or some extraordinary necessity; and that will happen but rarely. Instead, it is better to advise me about them separately, so that I may take the steps that are needed.

Furthermore, I am forwarding to Your Reverences the decision of His Excellency the Viceroy, in virtue of which the Indians are to be taught the making of pottery, so that you may do the best you can while awaiting the arrival of the instructors who are to teach it.

The Reverend Father Guardian, whose letter of farewell you have already received, was much concerned regarding the problems about which Your Reverences wrote to him, and especially to me, from San Luis (May God Our Lord grant good Father Cavaller what is most fitting for him, and to good Father Giribet the comfort and strength that I wish him), San Antonio, San Carlos, and Santa Clara.

I, too, am concerned about the same problems, and I am most desirous to serve Your Reverences with true affection. In that spirit I pray that God Our Lord may keep Your Reverences for many years in His holy grace.

San Diego Mission,
December 4, 1789.

[1] The Commissary General was the intermediary at the highest level between the Franciscan missionaries and the Spanish administration. He was a Franciscan, resided at Madrid at royal expense, and had wide jurisdiction over all Franciscan missionaries. The office was established in 1572 and was abolished during the lifetime of Lasuén, as a subsequent letter indicates.

89. Summary Report on the Missions

Summary Report on the Status of the Missions entrusted to the Apostolic College of San Fernando.

Pueblos	Ministers	Neo-phytes	Boys and Girls up to 9 years***	Position	Church Mar-riages
San Diego	Hilario Torrent Juan Mariner	940	231	32 deg. 42 ms.	223
San Juan Capistrano	Vicente Fuster Juan Santiago	771	194	33 deg. 30 ms.	260
San Gabriel	Antonio Cruzado Miguel Sánchez	1,044	217	34 deg. 10 ms.	354
San Buena-ventura	Francisco Dumets Vicente Santa María	380	133	34 deg. 36 ms.	55
Santa Barbara	Fermín Lasuén Antonio Paterna	425	121	34 deg. 38 ms.	133
Purísima	José Arroita Crisóstomo Oramas	151	35	35 deg.	39
San Luis Obispo	Miguel Giribet José Calzada	582	152	35 deg. 38 ms.	203
San Antonio	Miguel Pieras Ventura Sitjar	1,064	326	36 deg. 30 ms.	335

Pueblos	Ministers	Neo-phytes	Boys and Girls up to 9 years***	Position	Church Mar-riages
San Carlos	Pascual Arenaza José Señán	732	198	36 deg. 48 ms.	393
Santa Clara	Tomás Peña Diego Noboa	787	439	37 deg.	188
Our father St. Francis	Pedro Cambón Diego Garcia Faustino Sola	429	130	37 deg. 56 ms.	182
TOTALS		7,305	2,176		2,465 [2,365]

***These are already included in the number of "neophytes."

Pagans: There are many in the environs of the missions as a whole, and of each particular one. It is not possible to ascertain the exact number.

Converted Nations: Among those discovered, there is no nation in the territory of the missions in which some have not been converted, and there is no one in which there are not still some to be converted.

The proper designation of each nation has not yet been ascertained; and the dialects which have been identified along the coast appear to be seventeen or eighteen.

Bordering Nations: The interior of the country has been explored to a slight extent, and it has been observed that the pagans there resemble those of the coast, and it appears that the same is true as regards diversity of dialects.

Distance from the College: Mexico [City] is commonly held to be 200 leagues from San Blas, by land; and from San Blas to San Diego the distance is 300 leagues by sea. From San Diego to San Francisco, going by the first route that was discovered, the distance was reckoned at 210 leagues. At the present time, in view of the alterations constantly made in it, it can be put down as 180 or 190 leagues.

Stipends: Our Lord the King (may God preserve him) sends two missionaries to each mission, and allots 400 pesos each year to each of them. Since there are twenty-two missions, the stipend for all amounts to 8,800 pesos each year.

Help given by the College: The college undertakes to collect our stipends, to furnish our supplies by means of them, to get them in readiness, and to see to it that they are transported to San Blas. As far as it can, it sees to it that our requests are given prompt attention.

VIII

End of the rule of Governor Fages

Two events of note took place during this period. One was significant in the religious field, for Lasuén was authorized to administer the sacrament of Confirmation, and the other affected the secular domain, for Don Pedro Fages, always the King's faithful servant but often the missionaries's jealous rival, ceased to be governor.

90. To Don Pedro Fages

 HAVE ON HAND AN ORIGINAL ROYAL CED-
ula dated March 21, 1787, in which His Majesty orders
that reports of the missions are to be forwarded to him
every two or three years. Then there is a dispatch from
the commandant general, dated March 14, '89, enclosing a copy of the royal cedula and ordering me to
complete and forward to him every two years the report prescribed by
His Majesty for the missions under my charge—the interval indicated by
His Lordship to be accepted as a general rule.

In accordance with this, I carried out the instructions of His Lordship at the end of the year '88, and consequently I do not need to
forward another until the end of '90.

In view of these weighty reasons, I had it in mind not to send Your
Lordship the reports (or they might be called inventories) annually, for
in accordance with the superior orders of His Majesty the King, and
of the commandant general, they are now only biennial reports, and it
is the commandant general who is the immediate channel for the forwarding of these documents to His Majesty.

However, as soon as I saw Your Lordship's worthy official letter,
dated the eighth of this month, in which you ask for the Annual Reports
or Inventories, I changed my mind and decided to send them to Your
Lordship this time, and in the meantime there will be no change in the
original plan.

One of the reports is missing, and for this reason I am not sending
them on this occasion.

I am at Your Lordship's service, and I pray that God Our Lord
may keep you for many years in His holy grace.

Santa Barbara Mission,
February 21, 1790.

91. To Don Jacobo Ugarte y Loyola

I learn from Your Lordship's superior edict of the fourteenth of last
November that on the seventeenth of the previous October His Excel-

lency the Count de Revilla Gigedo took over the functions of Viceroy,[1] Governor and Captain General of these Dominions, President of the Royal Audiencia of the Capital, and Superintendent Subdelegate of the Royal Treasury. In accordance with the instructions of Your Lordship, I have made this known to the religious who are immediately subject to me.

As in the past, I am always happy and eager to carry out the higher orders of Your Lordship, and to pray that God Our Lord may keep you for many years in His holy grace.

Santa Barbara Mission,
March 10, 1790.

[1] He was viceroy from 1789 to 1794. He transformed not only the capital city but much of the Mexican administration, too. He is not to be confused with the first Count of that name, who was his father. He, too, was Viceroy of Mexico, assuming office in 1746. The father died in 1766, the son in 1799.

92. To Don Jacobo Ugarte y Loyola

I have received the original patent from the Reverend Father Prefect, Fray Pedro Mariano de Iturbide, which Your Lordship was kind enough to enclose with your esteemed official letter of the second of March last. In that patent the faculty is granted me to administer the holy sacrament of Confirmation in these new mission fields.

However, the permission of the Most Illustrious Lord Bishop of Sonora has not yet reached me. This is the permission which Your Lordship was so kind as to request His Illustrious Lordship to send to me direct, so as to spare me the delay of having to make this request myself. I shall await it with confidence, for it cannot fail to arrive in view of the weighty influence of the person who asked for it.

With profound respect I place myself at your service and pray that God Our Savior may keep you for many years in His holy grace.

Santa Barbara Mission,
May 26, 1790.

93. To Don Fray José Joaquín Granados[1]

Together with Your Most Illustrious Lordship's esteemed letter of the eleventh of last April, I have received both your superior permission, granted on the third of the same month, to exercise the faculty of administering the holy sacrament of Confirmation in these new mission districts in accordance with what was granted by decree of the Sacred

Congregation *de Propaganda Fide,* given in Rome on the fourth of May, 1785, and also the delegation conferred on me for this purpose by the Reverend Father Prefect of the Apostolic Colleges, Fray Pedro Mariano de Iturbide, in accordance with his patent issued on the thirteenth of March, 1789.

I am deeply grateful to Your Most Illustrious Lordship for so signal a favor, and I promise to avail myself of it as often as possible for the benefit of this portion of your flock, and to help in satisfying Your Most Illustrious Lordship's pastoral zeal in these parts.

I beg Your Most Illustrious Lordship for your holy blessings. It is my desire and my delight to hold second place to no one in homage and submission, in deference and obedience to Your Most Illustrious person and to your higher orders. And I pray that God Our Lord may keep Your Most Illustrious Lordship for many years in his holy grace.

> *San Luis* [*Obispo*] *Mission,*
> July 15, 1790.

---

[1] José Joaquín Granados y Gálvez was the second bishop of Sonora. He was a native of Malaga, Spain, where he was born in the year 1743. He joined the Franciscan Order in the College of Santa Cruz at Querétaro. In March, 1788, he was appointed Bishop of Sonora, and in May of the following year received episcopal consecration, having acted as bishop-elect in the meantime. In February, 1794, he was officially transferred to the diocese of Durango, Mexico, but died the following August without having taken formal possession of the diocese. He was the author of a number of books in some of which he defended the right and aptitude of the Indians for higher education.

94. To Don Pedro Fages

This will acknowledge Your Lordship's worthy official letter of the thirteenth of the present month. In it you graciously inform me that it has been decided to grant the district of Santa Margarita to the retired corporal, Francisco Cayuelas, in accordance with the instructions of the authorities and the right vested in the wife of the above, herself a neophyte of San Luis Mission. No doubt this information is not sent in the hope that I may give my assent, because it has already been decided on. And in any case if my consent were necessary, I would not be able to give it.

If Your Lordship sends me this information so that I may know it, well and good. But if it is a request for my opinion, here it is: Your honor, as soon as Cayuelas married this neophyte, which happened very shortly after she was baptized, he took her away from that community and made her much more independent of the mission and of the direction of the missionaries than she should be. He separated her from her people and ceased to contribute in the slightest degree to the improving and cultivating of their land.

Her predecessors, too, have no claim whatever to any benefits or advantages of this kind; consequently, those who have undertaken such tasks and devoted their lives and constant labor to the common good will now be at a disadvantage by reason of this concession; and so will their descendants after them when, some day, the problem arises of dividing up these lands. It is at a cost of indescribable labor that these lands have been brought to the stage at which they are useful and productive so as to meet the needs of a civilized community; and by reason of what they produce they have become means towards a better living for all classes, awaiting the time when those who are civilized and those yet to be civilized can live comfortably as members of a settlement, gathered together as neophytes in the mission. Afterwards, in due time, each would receive his due proportion of land on which to live, and thus reach the stage when each by himself can manage his own affairs fittingly, like Indians in a pueblo.

Cayuelas gave no thought at all to this, and neither did the others who married Indian converts of this region. Instead, if it depended on them and they could make the choice, they would have taken them off, each to his own country, whether that country was in America or in Europe.

Apart from this, the Mission of San Luis is using the region of Santa Margarita for many purposes, and one of them is to breed swine which are kept in pasture there. In that particular place there is a ranchería of natives, and in San Luis there are many Christians who are natives of that place.

Furthermore, it should be kept in mind that there is a long distance and a bad highway between the mission and the place mentioned. This means that Cayuelas will be exposed to danger, and so will others of like position who claim that property, and so will the missionaries. All will be placed in serious jeopardy because of the accidents and mishaps to which as mortals we are all exposed.

With this I conclude what I have to say about the den and hideaway to be set up there for Christians and pagans alike, and all the evil consequences that will follow from it.

My only reason for bringing all this to the attention of Your Lordship is that I consider it very pertinent to my duty and to the rights of these poor Indians; and all, from the King down to Your Lordship, desire that I should safeguard these latter, as would a father, and that I should speak the truth clearly in their defense whenever occasion demands it.

I bring this matter to the attention of Your Lordship respectfully and humbly. I am not trying in any way to oppose your decision or that of any other superior. I do not consider that I am opposing your judgment or theirs; I like to think that I hold them in high regard. I am setting forth the facts which, naturally, you will be glad to have; and then without question I shall abide by your decision.

Furthermore, I shall acquaint our College of San Fernando with the matter by sending them a copy of this reply. As members of it we have the pleasant duty and task of teaching all the Indians to render whole-hearted submission, deference, and obedience to their legitimate superiors.

This is how I act towards Your Lordship in word and deed, and I promise that there will be no change in my attitude in the future. I pray that God Our Lord may keep Your Lordship many years in His holy grace.

San Antonio de Padua Mission,
July 26, 1790.

95. To Don Pedro Fages

I have received your esteemed official letter of the twentieth of the present month. It enclosed a certified copy of the higher order sent to Your Lordship under date of the seventeenth of last March by His Excellency Count de Revilla Gigedo, Viceroy of New Spain. In your letter you direct me to instruct the missionaries to attend to the taking of the census, for, in accordance with the esteemed order already cited, these lists are to be forwarded by the commandants of the presidios under the control of Your Lordship.

The circular has not yet reached me, the one to which there is reference in the letter and copy cited, and about which Your Lordship was wondering whether or not His Excellency had forwarded it direct to me. For this reason, and especially because of certain terms in the document which do not apply to me, terms such as *Pastor*, or *Curates, Salary, Pueblos*, I was of the opinion that the regulation in question did not apply to us, or to those in our charge, because we are known as Apostolic Missionaries *de Propaganda Fide*, and such we are; because our Indians are poor and destitute neophytes; and because the places where we bring them together so that they may learn that they are men are *missions*, and are known as such.

However, on the assumption that Your Lordship has received the instructions, and in accordance with them requests the co-operation of the missionaries in this project, with the first mail that leaves I, Sir, shall notify the religious under me to implement and make good what Your Lordship decrees.

This is my duty and I shall carry it out to the letter, for I am always happy to obey not only your weightiest precepts but your slightest hints.

May God our Lord keep Your Lordship for many years in His holy grace.

San Antonio de Padua Mission,
July 26, 1790.

96. To Don Pedro Fages

By order of His Excellency the Viceroy, our College of San Fernando is sending four religious to be members of the two foundations of which Your Lordship makes mention in your esteemed official letter of today. They have just arrived aboard the frigate anchored in this port.

By the same ship, too, there arrived the articles which are to be made ready for the two establishments, as the college requests. The only things now missing are the sacred vessels, the vestments, and the other church goods which go with them.

As soon as I receive them, and arrangements are made for the transport of everything to the place where it is needed, and the other preparations are completed which Your Lordship knows are indispensible, I am ready to begin the venture whenever Your Lordship decides.

I place myself in readiness once more to carry out the higher orders of Your Lordship, and I pray that God Our Lord may keep you for many years in His holy grace.

San Carlos Mission,
August 3, 1790.

97. To Count de Revilla Gigedo

Together with the higher orders of Your Excellency of the eighteenth of last May, I have received the revised tariff for sea otters which is to be in force from now on.

This makes me certain that when Your Excellency receives the one I drew up, in response to your superior orders, you will have no alternative but to accept what I said then: that for activities of that nature I am the most worthless of Your Excellency's subjects. But you must also believe what I now assert: that I am more enthusiastic about what Your Excellency has decided than what I proposed. And even though there is a vast difference between the two, I am content, for I was merely attempting to obey in the best way I knew.

In accordance with what Your Excellency expects and enjoins on me, I will therefore devote myself to seeing that all the regulations contained in the tariff are observed in regard to the collection, proper classification, and shipment of the pelts. This will make it easy to identify the different types and qualities and will obviate trouble in regard to balancing accounts and payment.

If Your Excellency would permit it, I would like to make three or four observations which, it seems to me, might be deserving of your attention. They pertain to the third regulation. But my complete submission to the decisions of Your Excellency prevents me from doing so and allows me only the freedom to say that I will obey it as punctiliously as the others and will see to its observance to the best of my ability.

My major superior, the Reverend Father Guardian of San Fernando, will, I have no doubt, lend his aid too, if Your Excellency so directs, and he will even do more than I can.

I have already charged the missionaries of San Francisco and Santa Clara to make every effort to have their Indians and their coastal areas effect the greatest possible catch of pelts, in accordance with Your Excellency's orders and the reasons given.

This, Your Excellency, I am confidant they will do; but the Fathers cannot help feeling, and with good reason, that in view of the fact that one mission is located near a presidio and the other near a pueblo, the troops and the settlers will defraud both alike, without distinction, and usurp from them their labor and their reward. The reason is that the soldiers and settlers will buy or seize most of the pelts, and the best of the lot, from Indians who had been assigned by the mission to the task [of collecting these pelts]; and then they will come to us so that the missions may buy what was already theirs.

And that is not all; it may happen that at the very time when the soldiers and the settlers are receiving seven pesos for every pelt, paid from the mission account, some Indian from whom they took them is presenting himself to the missionary, begging for food and clothing, and perhaps nets and rafts for trapping.

Something like this will happen everywhere; but neither this nor anything else will keep me from carrying out to the letter everything Your Excellency commands me.

With this good resolution I pray that God Our Lord may keep Your Excellency for many years in His holy grace.

Santa Clara Mission,
September 10, 1790.

98. To Don Pedro Fages

His Excellency Count de Revilla Gigedo, Viceroy of New Spain, did me the honor to send me by direct mail the same price list for sea otters which Your Lordship already sent me in your esteemed letter of the seventeenth of the present month, and which I received last evening. For twelve days or more I have been giving the matter all the personal attention possible in the circumstances, in accordance with Your Lordship's directions given in your superior order of the eighteenth of last May. As a consequence, I am very much on my guard so as not to omit even the slightest detail in what remains to be done, as occasion and opportunities permit, especially in regard to those items brought to my attention by His Excellency.

Your Lordship knows how exact and prompt I am in carrying out your orders. From this you can infer how much the more prompt and exact the foregoing will make me, coming as it does from no less an authority than the Viceroy himself, for he it was who did me the honor to assign me to this task and to send me directions in regard to it. And as I show deference and obedience to Your Lordship, as is but just, I owe the same in this instance, insofar as I can give expression to it. And be assured that without fail I shall continue to act in the future as I have done up to the present, with a view to pleasing and gratifying you.

May God Our Lord keep Your Lordship many years in His holy grace.

Mission of our father St. Francis,
September 25, 1790.

99. To Don Jacobo Ugarte y Loyola

Enclosed with the higher order of Your Lordship dated the second of last July I received a copy of the edict which, on the same date, Your Lordship ordered to be proclaimed within the confines of your higher jurisdiction, an edict regarding the formalities which the Indians and the rest of the people are to observe in order to change their location and to journey from place to place. In accordance with the instructions of Your Lordship I immediately made a copy of everything so as to circulate it at the first opportunity among the missions, in order to obtain the objectives cited at the end of the edict.

Having thus obeyed to the letter the above-mentioned higher order of Your Lordship, I have to confess frankly, but with all deference and due respect, that were it not for Your Lordship's order, I would never believe that the law quoted in the first article of the edict would apply to the Indians of the missions, but only to those of the pueblos.

It is only to the latter, it seems to me, that the liberty granted by the law is suitable. But regarding the above-mentioned liberty and what is explained, declared, and determined for its right use in the twelve articles of the proclamation, it is only with much difficulty that I can adapt them to mission Indians, especially our own. This is due to the form in which we found, maintain, and administer missions, always with an eye to the intentions of our Lord the King, to what the condition in which the Indians are, and to the circumstances of the country.

Our basic work consists in the care of the native population of these new possessions, in converting them to the bosom of the church, and in gathering into the missions the barbarous pagans scattered through the hills and beaches like animals, or living in a society far from civilized and scarcely human.

Now, in my poor judgment, the liberty we are speaking of is either directly opposed to this essential undertaking, or destroys it.

After the Indians have been converted and gathered together, they are instructed by the missionaries in living as rational beings, in being Christians, in the ways of politics and economics, and in mechanical skills. Out of twenty individuals, we estimate that there should be one who is so far ahead of the others that, benefiting from the instruction, he may serve the community profitably and may be of assistance to the missionary. If the one seeking, and consequently receiving, permission to transfer is from this group, his community obviously suffers a loss. And if the individual belongs to the remaining group, then the group to which he transfers is burdened; and neither here nor there can he aspire for a moment to more than the ration from the community kitchen, and to a piece of clothing that is not sufficient to cover him.

Hence, because of his natural inclination and because of his dialect, the migration of the Indian can never be very lasting. Although very prone to wandering, he is always drawn back to the place of his birth, or to the place where most of his people are.

We the missionaries pay very close attention to this in the transfers which take place when new missions are founded. We send to them Indians who were baptized in those already founded, but who are natives of the region or the neighborhood where the new mission is established. It has been found by experience that they like this; and in no other way can they be kept quiet and induced to continue their education.

It is not my understanding that our Indians can be transferred either to the presidios or to the pueblos, for in neither the one nor the other is there a resident priest. Instruction will not be given there; they will forget what they have learned; and living too much for the present world, they will completely forget the eternal.

Your Lordship, I protest that I hate and detest any form of independence; and it is my glory under God that I possess a docile spirit, dependent, submissive, and humble, and gladly subordinated to anyone who has jurisdiction over me.

This is the judgment, too, that I must form about my missionaries, and there is a good basis for it. For in this consideration, the experience I have acquired through many years as a missionary under the rule and method imposed by our College of San Fernando, and the zeal with which it is observed, have emboldened me—a person having no personal interest in the issue except that of the common good, and of the happy outcome of the work entrusted to us—these have emboldened me to say that the provision of His Excellency on whom rests the responsibility for the observance of the royal decree, and to carry out which Your Lordship has formulated the measures accompanying the above decree —this provision, I repeat, will be observed in these missions simply and solely and only insofar as it agrees with our Indians' way of thinking. It will never be observed as fully, as wholeheartedly, and as thoroughly as it would if left to the care of us, the missionaries, with no more interference on the part of judges, lieutenants, delegates, or justices of the peace, and no more dependence on them than that of affording us on request the help we need to restore transgressors to their proper place of residence.

This in no way militates against the faithful observance of Your Lordship's decree in all its parts, as I have stated. But if it should not be repugnant to Your Lordship, we might, without failing to obey, be able to suspend the carrying out of Article Three, pending such time as Your Lordship's decision, in the light of these considerations, sets forth for us definitely what we are to do.

I fully recognize, Sir, that the Indian will migrate, even if the missionary does not wish it, in view of the fact that in this case Your Lordship decrees that the certificate of the judge is sufficient in order to move. But if then or in the interval there is such a refusal on the part of the missionary, the above may serve to exculpate him if he is accused, or at least it should serve to suspend judgment, to see whether or not there are strong motives for refusing him [permission to move].

With profound humility I once more profess myself ready to carry out the higher orders of Your Lordship, and I pray that God Our Lord may keep you for many years in His holy grace.

San Antonio Mission,
November 19, 1790.

100. To the Missionaries

The Lord give you peace. If we had the sole right to decide whether or not to carry out what the commandant general explains, declares, and decides in the edict which I enclose, I would at the moment be inclined to the negative view. I would humbly point out to the Señor in question the inconveniences that I recognize, and would suspend publication until His Lordship might determine what he judged fitting. But as the interpretations and decisions of the edict in question have to be observed whether we like them or not, it will be better to "like" them, provided there is not something that hinders it or some grave inconvenience. Should that arise, you can say that a request and representation have been made by me to the commandant general regarding the point.

For this purpose, and to make it possible to deal with the question in the easiest and most successful way, I have thought it best to make known to Your Reverence my reply and representation. They are contained in the enclosed copy.

The order in my letter accompanying the edict is fulfilled if you will read or explain to the Indians the edict in question. Afterwards, you can elaborate at greater length so that all may understand the disposition of His Excellency the Marqués de Sonora and his resolute determination to see that it is observed—for this is the main point, the object, the basis, the beginning and the end of the entire affair.

This letter must not be shown to any layman, nor may its contents be divulged. I do not mean by this that I would fail to submit it to any judge or superior who might demand it of me; however, we'll cross that bridge when we reach it.

Although I am at the moment on my way to the missions in the south, because of the inclemency of the weather and other circumstances, I request the Reverend Fathers of the Mission of our father St. Francis that, when they have observed what is enjoined in these papers, they seal and address them, and forward them to the Mission of San Luis. From there they are to go in proper order from mission to mission for the same purpose until they reach San Diego. And when all has been complied with, they are to be placed in the archives there.

I place myself at the service of Your Reverences and pray that God Our Lord may keep you for many years in His holy service.

San Antonio de Padua,
November 19, 1790.

101. Memorandum regarding Confirmations

The faculty to administer the holy Sacrament of Confirmation, to whom and within what limits, is given at the beginning of this Book. It consists of the documents which are there assembled. It was extended for a further ten years by decree of the Sacred Congregation of the Propagation of the Faith, given in Rome on the fourth of May of the year 1785. The Reverend Father Prefect of the Missions, Fray Pedro Mariano Iturbide, confirmed it to me by Letter Patent issued on the thirteenth of March of the year 1787, so that I might make free use of it in these missions in the capacity of President thereof. It is expressed in substantially the same terms as the faculty given my predecessor, the venerable Father Fray Junípero Serra, the original of which, together with a copy thereof, collated and transcribed, can be found in this Book.

Moreover, the *expediente* of the above faculty, which was renewed and granted to me, was not available until the thirteenth of July of the present year of 1790. It reached me at the Mission of San Luis Obispo where I then happened to be, on my way to this Mission of San Carlos so that I might confer with the governor and reach an agreement with him in regard to procedures preliminary to, and necessary for, the founding of the two missions. These latter are to be located between this Mission of San Carlos and those of San Antonio and Santa Clara. They are to be known as the Soledad and Santa Cruz, and are to be established just as soon as the boat which we are expecting arrives.

Since it was necessary for me to arrive here as soon as possible so as to attend to these matters, I did the best I could in the meantime. So, on the fourteenth of the same month of July of the said year 1790, in the above-mentioned Mission of San Luis Obispo, I proceeded to administer the holy sacrament of Confirmation in complete conformity with the practical instructions of the Sacred Congregation of the Propagation of the Faith, granted in Rome. This [document] I carry with me for my direction, and this I have observed, and with God's help shall continue to observe most faithfully as often as I shall exercise the above-mentioned extraordinary faculty, with the intention, and with the earnest desire of attaining the sacred ends, no less pious than they are generous, for which the privilege was granted, namely, the greater glory of God, and the greater good of all the faithful of these missions, so that strengthened by the power of the seven-fold gifts of the Holy Spirit, they may *not only believe unto justice with their hearts, but with their mouths make confession unto salvation*,[1] *and show themselves followers of Christ even to the shedding of blood.*

In proof of the above I hereby certify and sign

Fr. Fermín Francisco de Lasuén

[1] Rom. 10: 10. (The quotation is given in Latin).

102. Considerations submitted to Reverend Father Guardian[1]

The missions will not always have the means of paying the military and private individuals for the pelts which they deliver to the missionaries.

It does not seem reasonable that the missions should guarantee the price of these articles to these people and then run the risk of accidents and losses in transport to the capital, as well as the expenses of storage, packing, and crating.

There are no trappers of sea otters other than Indians; and these are readily oppressed and imposed on by the *gente de razón*, while the mission supplies are for all alike, whether Christian or pagan, whether well or sick, whether they work or are unable to work.

Nevertheless, even when there is [no]* profit to the mission community, the latter will always pay the Indian for pelts, and pay in a form that suits him better and is more equitable than what the military and civilians pay. Through greed and self-interest each of these will leave much to be desired in their regard for the terms of their contract. They will cause the natives much vexation, and will prejudice and frustrate the efforts of the missionaries. Finally, with the granting of this privilege, one source of revenue for the missions is lost in a department dependent entirely on the industry of the Indians.

[1] This document is unsigned and undated, but it is in the handwriting of Lasuén.
* The "no" is missing in the text, but it was obviously intended. [Tr.]

103. To Don Jacobo Ugarte y Loyola

In compliance with the esteemed instructions of Your Lordship under date of the fourteenth of March, 1789, I am forwarding to you in person the accompanying report on the spiritual status of these missions at the end of December of the year just past.

When my actions meet the approval of Your Lordship I have satisfied my highest ambition, and that is, to carry out to your satisfaction the higher orders you issue.

May God Our Lord keep Your Lordship many years in His holy grace.

San Diego Mission,
February 28, 1791.

104. Memorandum

Report of the spiritual status of the missions of New California at the end of the year 1790. This is what I am forwarding to the Brigadier Commandant General of the Internal Provinces of New Spain, His Lordship Don Jacobo Ugarte y Loyola, in accordance with his higher order of March 14, 1789.

On the last day of December of the above-mentioned year of '90, according to the census there were:

12,877 baptisms
2,662 marriages
4,780 deaths
8,528 living

Of the latter, all who are five or six years of age and over receive instruction in Christian Doctrine every day in the church. One of the missionaries recites it with them, or some well-instructed Indian does it in his presence. There is one instruction in the morning during Mass and before breakfast, and another in the evening before supper.

On many days there is recitation of it on two other occasions in which the boys and girls take part. It takes place before the missionary's door, in the morning and evening at a time that is most opportune. The instruction is given alternately in their own language and in Castilian.

In the case of the young the results of the instruction are good; in the case of the middle-aged the progress is fair; but in the case of the very old nothing beyond the bare essentials is grasped, and then only after much effort.

They hear Mass every day, and they are now convinced that the person who fails to do so on Days of Obligation[1] deserves punishment.

The majority of the adults go to confession once a year; many receive Holy Communion; and there are usually some who receive these sacraments two or three times in the course of the year.

In the frequent problems and disputes, which are bound to arise at all hours when there are so many people who in this case are entirely dependent on the missionaries in temporal no less than in spiritual matters, we let no opportunity pass to instruct them in their Christian obligations. And we can already notice that these neophytes are showing a proper appreciation for what they profess and what it has done for them, and we notice as a consequence the progress corresponding both to their capacity and to the interval since their conversion. Thanks be to God.

Furthermore, many pagans who live a great distance from the mission, when they fall sick, send as a rule for the missionary in order to be baptized.

From the fourteenth day of last July up to the present, the number of those confirmed is four thousand three hundred and twenty-nine; and this, together with those in the Report for the year '88 brings the total of those confirmed in these mission districts to nine thousand six hundred and thirty-eight.

Mission of San Diego,
February 28, 1791.

---

[1] These were the ecclesiastical holydays, and in the Spanish possessions they were quite numerous at this time. In addition to the fifty-two Sundays, there were approximately thirty-four additional days on which attendance at Mass was prescribed. The Indians could see in this a certain measure of compensation, for manual work was forbidden on such days.

OLD pottery pitcher
+
Brass basin ...

IX

Governor Romeu's Brief Administration

A new era of peace and harmony characterized the brief administration of Governor Romeu. Two new missions are established, and the first group of distinguished foreign visitors become the guests of Lasuén.

105. To Don José Antonio de Romeu[1]

EFORE YOUR LORDSHIP TAKES POSSESSION OF YOUR NEW office as governor, in advance I gladly bind myself to carry out your orders, for afterwards the carrying out of them will be my duty.

Both now and later, and whenever the occasion presents itself, I desire to affirm my personal submission to Your Lordship's decrees, despite my own obvious worthlessness.

All the missionaries of New California offer the same assurance to Your Lordship, and with them I should like to let Your Lordship know how happy I am; and I offer my congratulations on your promotion to this new office.

At the same time I wish Your Lordship all success and happiness. May your good qualities win you even greater honors, a greater measure of the King's confidence, and above all, the attainment and the imperishable honor of eternal beatitude.

May this be God's gift to Your Lordship and your lady, whom I greet with deepest respect; and may He keep you in His holy grace for many years.

Mission of San Diego,
May 3, 1791.

[1] Romeu, a native of Valencia, Spain, served with Fages in the Sonora Indian wars. At the time of his appointment as governor he was acting as inspector of presidios, charged with the duty of bringing order into the presidio accounts which by that time were chaotic. He did not achieve very much, for he suffered greatly from ill health. He reached Monterey in October, 1791, and died on April 9, 1792. Cf. Bancroft, *op. cit.* I, 487-489.

106. To Don Pedro de Nava

The first definite news I have had of Your Lordship's promotion to the office of Commandant General was when I heard that Your Lordship had already assumed office.[1]

I would have preferred to have anticipated this by volunteering my obedience to your orders in advance; now I find myself under strict obligation to obey them. In these circumstances I find myself, poor Friar that I am, with nothing to offer but my prayers.

However, as Your Lordship knows, men differ greatly in their ways

of fulfilling their obligations, and those which I have so recently con-
tracted with Your Lordship I undertake to fulfill with the greatest
personal satisfaction and with the greatest exactitude. And so, while I
acknowledge Your Lordship as my most worthy superior, I am resolved
at the same time that Your Lordship will see in me the most humble and
obedient of all your subjects.

This, too, will be the experience of Your Lordship when you deal
with any of the missionaries of New California; and with them I tender
to Your Lordship our full measure of respect. I offer my congratulations
on your high position, and wish you all happiness in this life and in the
next.

May God Our Lord keep Your Lordship for many years in His
holy grace.

Mission of San Gabriel,
May 19, 1791.

---

[1] Pedro de Nava assumed the office of governor and commandant general on March
7, 1791. He transferred the administrative center from Arizpe to Villa de Chihuahua,
and held office until November 4, 1802.

107. To Don José Antonio de Romeu

I learn from Your Lordship's esteemed letter of the seventeenth of
last April that Your Lordship has been appointed Governor of this
Province. I wish to pay my respects and to place myself completely
at your service.

Furthermore, I have sent this information to the missionaries of the
presidency under my control. I have made known to them that they
are to acknowledge the appointment, and I have ordered them likewise
to make it known to all who are in their charge.

Accept my congratulations on your new office. I wish Your Lordship all happiness in it, and it gives me much pleasure to regard myself
as your most humble subject.

May God Our Lord keep Your Lordship for many years in His
holy grace.

Mission of San Gabriel,
May 20, 1791.

108. To Don José Antonio de Romeu

I have promptly carried out the higher order of Your Lordship of
the seventeenth of last April by recognizing Brigadier Don Pedro de

Nava as Commandant General of this and the other Interior Provinces and by notifying all the missionaries of the presidency in my charge that they are to acknowledge him as such.

May God Our Lord keep Your Lordship for many years in His holy grace.

Mission San Gabriel,
May 20, 1791.

109. To Don José Antonio de Romeu

In an envelope addressed to me I have received two official letters and a private letter from Your Lordship to the Reverend President[1] Fray Juan Crisóstomo Gómez. Since the contents of the three documents are of equal interest to the said Father and to myself, it appears to me that one address was mistaken for the other.

I have resolved, therefore, to reply to all of them on the assumption that by so doing I would cause less inconvenience than if I were to omit doing so.

Consequently, Sir, I am enclosing the official documents and this letter which is a reply to the one sent by Your Lordship which was so full of Christian sentiments.

I do not presume to place myself on an equality with the Reverend Father Crisóstomo in respect to Your Lordship's confidences, but I do not by any means wish to be found remiss in expressing in all earnestness my admiration for the religious zeal of Your Lordship.

Thanks be to God that He has inspired Your Lordship with such good intentions, for this is a pleasant foretaste of what is yet to be.

As soon as I found out that Your Lordship was to be our governor, I prayed to the Almighty for success in all your undertakings; and now with one voice all of us, missionaries, repeat that prayer; and since we all know the good dispositions of Your Lordship we shall offer it with greater assurance that it will be heard.

I extend a welcome to the province to Your Lordship, and to your wife and family. May the blessing of Heaven abound in you and yours, so that it may diffuse itself for the greater good of this entire vast territory under your charge.

I am eagerly awaiting the moment when I can present myself in person to Your Lordship to make profession of obedience, as I do now through the medium of this letter; and I warrant that my conduct will always be proof that I am your subject, never failing in it to show what a pleasure and honor I deem it to serve you.

May God Our Lord keep Your Lordship for many years in His holy grace.

San Gabriel,
May 20, 1791.

[1] President of the Dominican missionaries in Lower California.

110. To Count de Revilla Gigedo

No sooner did I receive Your Excellency's higher order of the twentieth of last January in regard to the founding of the two missions in the region of Soledad and Santa Cruz than I appointed the Fathers Fray Diego García[1] and Fray Mariano Rubi[2] as missionaries to the one, and Fathers Fray Alonso Isidro Salazar[3] and Fray Baldomero López[4] as missionaries to the other.

Consequently, for my part I shall take whatever steps are needed so that these missions may be founded with all possible speed. And there need not be any delay because the fittings for the church have not yet arrived, for they will gladly be supplied for the time being by the other missions, as Your Excellency anticipates.

May God Our Lord keep Your Excellency for many years in His holy grace.

San Carlos,
July 15, 1791.

[1] He became a member of the Franciscan Order in Andalusia, Spain, arrived in San Fernando College in 1787, and reached California shortly after. He served for brief periods at Dolores Mission (San Francisco), Santa Clara, Soledad, and others. He is not to be confused with a more famous missionary of a later date, Fray García Diego, who in 1840 became the first bishop of California.

[2] Lasuén had reason to regret the presence of this unworthy religious in California. He had been a member of the Province of Mallorca, and reached San Fernando College in 1788, and California in 1790. Three years later he was sent back to Mexico. His entire career in the New World, brief though it was, is crossed by many dark shadows. See Engelhardt, *op. cit.*, II, 497-505.

[3] He was one of the missionaries who arrived in California in 1791. He is the founder of Mission Santa Cruz, and he stayed at that mission until he retired in 1794. On his return to Mexico he wrote a report entitled "Condición Actual de California." See Bancroft, *op. cit.*, I, 597-580, 603-604.

[4] He, too, reached California in 1791 and was assigned to Santa Cruz. His career in California was undistinguished, and he returned to Mexico in 1796 for reasons of health. His health seems to have improved quickly, for in 1800 he became Vicar of San Fernando College. In 1812, and again in 1815 he was elected to the college council, and in 1818 and again in 1824 was appointed Guardian.

111. To the Missionaries

The Lord give you Peace. Our Reverend Father Guardian, in his letter of the third of last January, bids me make known to you the following regulations:

That the letters which are sent to the college must be addressed (a matter that has been brought to your attention on several occasions) to Don Andrés Mendívil, Accountant General and Director of the Mails for New Spain, or to the Administrator of Tax Exemption, because it is on this condition that exemption is granted. Some did not observe this, and the result was that last year the cost of mailing was eighteen pesos.

That the stockpiling of sea otter skins need not be discontinued, because in Mexico there will be no lack of private individuals who perchance will buy them at such a good price, or even at more than the amount fixed.

(It is not stated how or to whom they should be addressed. But it seems to me that they can be sent to our Brother Syndic, Señor Lazcano, but arranged in such a way that he alone may know what is being sent him. For this purpose, something else might be mixed up with them so that the official on board to whose kindness they are entrusted, and all others, may think they are something else, something that has little or no attraction for them, such as burial shrouds—but what to send and how to send it, Your Reverences may decide among yourselves. Señor Lazcano will be asked to forward the bundle or case to Mexico, each with the mark or brand peculiar to the mission[1] to which it belongs. And the Father Guardian, or Brother Sampelayo[2] must be advised in detail as to what is being sent to him.)

That he has been informed that the commissary at San Blas has complained that the tallow they send is more than he needs, and that this is the reason he takes it on himself to lower the price of it now, although he paid a good price for it in the past. He states that in order to avoid this he has written to Don Esteban Lazcano so that he may find out from the commandant the amount of tallow, more or less, that he will need; and then Your Reverences will be able to see whether it may not be best to agree about certain amounts so that the balance may be devoted to some useful purpose.

I would like to say in addition that I have an order from His Excellency the Viceroy that the missions of Santa Cruz and the Soledad are to be founded as soon as possible, even though the vestments and sacred vessels may not arrive for the present (and they did not).

All these have been left behind at San Blas, and His Excellency requests that in the meantime they be supplied from the other missions. By reason of this, and because it is a matter of concern to all of us to abide by this urgent injunction of the Viceroy, I beg Your Reverences to send me, at the first available opportunity, whatever you can reasonably spare in order to supply what is missing, especially chrismatories, some manuals, wafer-irons, etc. And when any particular mission feels it can give something, let it write in the margin what the item or items may be,[3] and this will serve as a guide to the others. Here we shall give two or three chasubles, two albs, one or two chalices, one bell, and anything else that we can.

I cannot recall where I saw three or four bells. They were not for the altar, for they were too big; nor for hanging, for they were too small; but a couple of them would be very welcome in this case.

I am sorry I have to bother you with a request like this; but, as you have observed, I have tried to save you from them as much as possible. But you will understand that in this case I have no alternative.

I am confident that in your wisdom and zeal Your Reverences will co-operate so that the pious wish of the Viceroy may be carried out for the glory of God, the good of souls, the honor of our Order, and as a proof of our humble obedience to the orders of our superiors, and of our competence and promptness in carrying them out.

I may add that what I have decided and what I am asking in this case are in accordance with the views, the opinion, and the will of our Father Guardian.

Whatever you may lend us, Reverend Fathers, I promise (with God's help) to return carefully and promptly as soon as the church fittings arrive for the missions in question.

I am at the service of Your Reverences, and I pray that God Our Lord may keep you many years in His holy grace.

San Carlos,
July 22, 1791.

P. S.

The statement above in regard to sea otters does not mean that you cannot look out for or take advantage of any opportunity of selling them to private individuals on sea or land, if that is found to be expedient.

[1] Each mission had its own characteristic brand.

[2] He was the procurator for the California missions and his name occurs frequently in connection with the requisitions for the missions. See, for instance, Arch. Gen. Nación. (Colegio de San Fernando), Cuentas, tom. 3, 2-16, 17-62.

[3] As requested, the missionaries indicated on the back of Lasuén's letter the items they could lend. Thus, San Gabriel offered a wafer box of tin, two corporals, an altar bell, two silk cinctures, six purificators, four finger towels, an altar stone, and an altar cloth.

112. To Don José Antonio de Romeu

In order to collect our stipends, as a favor from Your Lordship I need a certificate which, when added to the enclosed list, may suffice to make it clear in Mexico that we live here and take care of these missions, as set forth in the list.

Relying on the kindness of Your Lordship, I await this favor and obediently place myself at your service, and I pray that God Our Lord may keep Your Lordship many years in His holy grace.

San Carlos,
August 12, 1781.

113. List of Missionaries

List of the missionaries who at this time are engaged in the conversion of the pagans of New California, and in the instruction and maintenance of the converts.

San Carlos	Fermín Francisco de Lasuén Pascual Martínez de Arenaza José Señán
San Francisco	Pedro Benito Cambón Antonio Danti
Santa Clara	Tomás de la Peña Diego Noboa Martín Landaeta
Santa Cruz*	Alonso Ysidro Salazar Baldomero López
Soledad**	Diego García Mariano Rubí
San Antonio de Padua	Miguel Pieras Buenaventura Sitjar Bartolomé Gili
San Luis Obispo	Miguel Giribet Estevan Tapis
Purísima	Joseph Arroita Christóval Uramas
Santa Barbara	Antonio Paterna Joseph de Miguel
San Buenaventura	Francisco Dumetz Vicente de Santa María Antonio Cruzado
San Gabriel	Miguel Sánchez Joseph Calzada

San Juan Capistrano	Vicente Fuster
	Juan Norberto de Santiago
San Diego	Hilario Torrent
	Juan Mariner

**To be assigned to these missions.

San Carlos Mission,
August 10, 1791.

114. To Don José Antonio de Romeu

I offer a thousand thanks to God; and to Your Lordship, your wife, and your family I send my congratulations for having arrived in good health from the more dangerous and risky part of your trip, and for now being safe on dry land where your journey will be less hazardous —at this very moment you are possibly at San Diego.

I was greatly troubled at not receiving news of you for so long a time; but I was made equally happy by receiving it with the esteemed letter of Your Lordship, dated the sixteenth of last month. Thanks be to God; and I trust to His Most Holy Majesty that He will show the same favor by bringing Your Lordship and your family safe to the royal presidio, your future home, where we all ardently desire you to be, for the glory of God, for Your Lordship's relaxation, and for the good of this important conquest.

In virtue of a superior order of His Excellency the Viceroy, I on my part am taking whatever measures are feasible to bring about as soon as possible the founding of Santa Cruz and of the Soledad. And seeing that Your Lordship is so near, I cannot do less than express my joy that the beginning of your administration should coincide with the attainment of a goodly proportion of the principal reasons for your elevation to this high office, beginning as it does by adding natives to the Christian community, and gathering new sons to Holy Church, and new vassals to the Crown. In one word, you will inaugurate the putting into effect of the principal designs of His Majesty in regard to these, his vast possessions. Thanks be to God.

Pending Your Lordship's arrival, all I can do in this regard is to speed up preparations, God willing; and Your Lordship will be the person who will control and direct, inasmuch as you have been placed at the head of this great enterprise.

I am looking forward eagerly to the happy moment when I shall see Your Lordship, for it will be the signal for the more speedy execution of this project; and it will give me an opportunity to present myself personally, and to make clear that I am your most willing subject.

In keeping with this, I will give proof in the meantime by the most scrupulous observance of the slightest suggestions that Your Lordship may deign to address to me.

Extend my compliments to my lady, your wife. And may God grant Your Lordship and the family courage and inspiration to face what little remains [of the trip]; and may all of you be made joyful by reason of the large fund of merits[1] that you will inevitably acquire [when you undertake] enterprises that are so numerous and so vast.

Your Lordship, your Lady, and your family may look on this poor Friar as a chaplain who prays that God Our Lord may keep you for many years in His holy grace.

San Carlos,
August 12, 1791.

[1] In the opening lines of his letter to Lasuén, Romeu asserted that the only fund of merits to which he could lay claim was the earnest desire he had of doing his duty faithfully in California.

115. To Don José Arrillaga

I have good reason to believe that the new governor is still quite far off. Hence, if I have recourse to him for a certificate of our actual presence in these missions I may miss the assurance and convenience for the arrival in Mexico at an opportune time of this document, which the *Polera* affords, for it is soon to depart from this port for that of San Blas.

For this reason I have decided to send Your Lordship the enclosed list. It comprises the missionaries of this New California according to their various assignments. I am acting thus, for you hold the position of acting governor of this province, and up to now the actual governor has failed to arrive at the royal presidio which will be his residence.

May I ask you to be so kind as to make it valid for the payment of our stipends by affixing your signature to it.

May God Our Lord keep Your Lordship for many years in His holy grace.

Mission San Carlos,
August 21, 1791.

116. To Don Hermenegildo Sal

Today I received a letter from His Lordship Don José Antonio de

Romeu, enclosing a copy of an official letter from His Excellency the Viceroy. It was of the same tenor as the one which His Excellency sent me in regard to the two projected missions. He did me the honor of inviting me to participate in the event, and indicated that I need not await His Lordship's arrival in order to proceed with it.

This being the case, if it should meet with Your Grace's approval, just as soon as the road on which they are working is ready, you might take steps to forward the supplies without further delay. And in order to protect them, it has been suggested that the Indians there might put up a little building as soon as possible, one that is as good as the circumstances permit.

As soon as Your Grace has decided on the number and distribution of troops needed for the transport and protection of the supplies, plans will be made for the departure of the Fathers assigned to new establishment.

I appreciate very much the gracious and generous sentiments you have expressed in regard to the best and most efficacious ways of helping in this work. I thank you most cordially for them. To me they are a source of comfort and deep satisfaction, for they offer a well-founded hope for the happy outcome of our enterprise. All this I shall keep constantly in mind so that I may be duly grateful. And placing myself entirely at your service, and with cordial greetings to your wife, I pray that God Our Lord may preserve Your Grace through many years in His holy grace.

Santa Clara,
September 13, 1791.

117. To Don José Granados

On the thirteenth of the present month I happened to be at the Mission of Santa Clara on matters pertaining to the founding of the Mission of Santa Cruz, and already had it in mind to return here in order to deal with the founding of Soledad, when I received your esteemed order of April 30 last. In it, in accordance with the royal cedula of the sixth of March of last year, Your Illustrious Lordship instructs me that I am to take charge of the collection of the Ecclesiastical Subsidy granted to His Majesty on the value of specified incomes, that the rate is to be six per cent per annum for a space of four years, that it is based on the stipend and other forms of income which we, the missionaries of this peninsula, enjoy, that I am to obtain from each one a sworn statement of his income, and that I am to forward the amount to Your Illustrious Lordship as soon as possible.

So as to bring about the most prompt collection of this six per cent, you have named me Sub-collector for this area (which I understand to be the missions under my charge), and you instruct me to see to it that the missionaries each pay what is required of them at the Royal Treasury, or the paymaster's office, when they cash their stipends. Furthermore, I am to obtain from the ministers or the paymaster, in each case, a certificate or receipt which credits each amount, and these I am to forward to you so that you may add them to the other documents pertaining to this matter.

I humbly obey, as far as I can; but I wish to inform Your Illustrious Lordship that we, the missionaries of our New California, do not enjoy any income that could be called an ecclesiastical revenue. Our administration and ministration as regards the *gente de razón* is entirely gratuitous, just as it is for the Indians.

At present we number thirty; there are eleven missions, with twenty-two missionaries in charge of them.

These latter alone enjoy the stipend of 400 pesos per annum which the King our Lord (whom God preserve) pays to each as an alms. There are four supernumeraries who are paid nothing, but who are helped from the alms mentioned. And there are four others who are assigned to the two missions which are soon to be founded. For each member of this latter group two hundred pesos were obtained last year (when the foundations could not be established).

Our Brother Syndic in Mexico cashes these amounts when he pays for the articles which the procurator of these missions, a lay brother of our Apostolic College of San Fernando collects, in accordance with the want-lists which we send him for this purpose. In them we ask for necessities for ourselves, clothing and other necessaries for the Indians, and what we need for the church and for the fields.

In this way the alms that are given are expended; but we interfere neither in the collecting nor the spending of them, except to the extent of drawing up the want-list mentioned. And we receive the assistance in kind, paying the expenses of transport ourselves.

If you judge that the contribution of the six per cent is to be assessed in the case of our stipends, the matter will have to be referred to Mexico, so that our Brother Syndic may collect that much less from the Royal Treasury, and at the same time receive from these officials or paymasters the certificate for each, testifying that it is not the royal will to give each missionary more than 376 pesos yearly for the space of four years.

I have made this clear, so that it cannot be said that we, the apostolic

Franciscans, are making a contribution in money; for we have not received any, and never will, for all we receive is help when we need it, and then it is sent to us in kind—a method that appears to us to be more in keeping with our Franciscan profession. Your Lordship knows full well how cautious and circumspect we, the Friars Minor, need to be in regard to this.[1]

I always have to send to our College of San Fernando of Mexico a copy of the esteemed order of Your Illustrious Lordship and of my reply; and I am under obligation to carry out to the letter whatever you and my Father Guardian command me.

I would not wish to take an oath in regard to financial matters, Most Illustrious Lord, for in regard to these matters in particular, beyond a doubt, the precept not to lie is more than enough for me. However, yielding to the command of Your Lordship, and being unable to have at hand the sworn statements of the missionaries as promptly as you desire, for the present I am enclosing a testimonial in the name of all, and (God willing) I shall take care to send the others just as soon as I receive them from each one or each two of the missionary Fathers, in accordance with my request to them.

I wish to make clear that I acknowledge my bounden duty to obey Your Illustrious Lordship; that I am determined to do so at any cost; and that in the present instance I have found no other means than this of proving it. If I did not succeed, it was because I erred in judgment, for (as is but fitting) my sole desire is, to carry out to the letter what Your Lordship orders me.

May God Our Lord keep Your Illustrious Lordship for many years in His holy grace.

San Carlos Mission,
September 18, 1791.

[1] The recipient of this letter, the Bishop of Sonora, was himself a Franciscan. However, by reason of the office and the duties pertaining to it, he was no longer bound by the strict Franciscan obligation of poverty.

118. To Don José Granados

Now that the sworn certificates of the missionaries have reached me, I am forwarding them to Your Lordship without delay, in accordance with my promise and in compliance with your esteemed order of the thirtieth of last April.

In all that pertains to the respect and veneration, the submissiveness and obedience due to Your Illustrious Lordship, my whole attitude is, to respond promptly and wholeheartedly.

With these sentiments, which I shall show to be genuine on all occasions, I pray that God Our Lord may keep Your Illustrious Lordship many years in His holy grace.

San Carlos Mission,
December 23, 1791.

119. Certificate

I, the undersigned, certify on oath, which I make on the word of a priest and with hand on heart, that we, the missionaries of this New California, enjoy no income over and above what the ecclesiastical subsidy grants, merely the stipend alone; and this the King our lord (whom God preserve) gives us in the form of an alms, at the rate of four hundred pesos per annum for each of the twenty-two who are in charge of the eleven missions. The amount is sent to us by our College of San Fernando of Mexico, but it is first converted into things needful for our persons, or necessary for our missions or our Indians.

Last year, however, the amount of two hundred pesos was granted to each of the four religious assigned to two new foundations with which I am now preoccupied, and with which, God willing, I am determined to proceed.

I hereby affix my signature in this Mission of San Carlos of Monterey this eighteenth day of September, 1791.

120. To Don Alejandro Malaspina and Don José de Bustamante[1]

It was the generosity of Your Lordships rather than what (as you say) you experienced among us, as well as your noble heart and sentiments that inspired your esteemed and welcome letter, dated the day before yesterday, which I received today.

Your Lordships have regarded as a courtesy and a favor what we owe you in justice; and above all, it could only be a misapprehension springing from a noble and generous nature that could in some way cause such utterly undue expressions and proofs of gratitude.

It is not for this reason that I venture to feel satisfaction for having done what was no more than my duty; but, thanks be to God, I do indeed feel it because I did everything with more personal gratification than I can express, and with the true sentiments of a Spaniard. And the recognition of it by Your Lordships makes me delighted once more for having done so—leaving us to admire what masters you are at making others become your willing servants.

We have observed that Your Lordships, with your officers and crew, sacrifice yourselves to promote to the utmost the will of the sovereign and the glory of the nation. May God bless Your Lordships and grant you perseverance.

The demonstration given in this port by the two Spanish corvettes is proof that your expedition will be more glorious, more useful, and of more profit to the entire human society,[2] and of more renown to the monarchy than all others of this kind.

You yourselves, your officers and seamen when here, in the midst of Christians and pagans, have shown yourselves to be the types that can contribute without fail to that spiritual and temporal progress which Your Lordships desire and anticipate in this conquest.

Your Christian conduct, and your matchless regard for, and courtesy towards, those poor Friars Minor cannot but inspire in all who observed it a deep appreciation for what they preach and what they teach.

Gentlemen, it shall be my duty to guard with care Your Lordships' letter as something worthy to be kept in a glass frame to the right of the picture of the mission which the Count de la Pérouse left us.[3]

Finally, Your Lordships, I confess that I am incapable of matching the brilliant expressions in your letter, and less capable still of equalling the noble generosity of your gifts (and so that you may know that they were received I am recording them in the enclosed list). But I shall try to lessen my indebtedness by offering the gratitude of the religious, especially of the Franciscans. May God reward Your Lordships.

May God prosper and bless your undertaking. May God bring Your Lordships and your men back to your homes in happiness, health, and peace. And after they have obtained all the rewards and honors which our great Spanish King knows how to confer and can do so, may God grant that all who take part in this voyage may attain the honor and eternal reward of Glory.

For all this I pray, and with my colleagues I shall continue to pray to the Divine Majesty to keep Your Lordships for many years in His holy grace.

San Carlos Mission,
September 23, 1791.

A note attached to the letter of the naval officers enumerates the following items as the "gift":

> One piece of tinted baize
> A small chest with different items of hardware for common use

Two barrels of wine
Six bottles of olive oil
Twenty pounds of chocolate
One arroba of sugar
Two arrobas of vinegar
Six pounds of wax

[1] For an account of the visit of these commanders to California, and their activities there, see Cutter, *op. cit.*, especially pp. 25-40.

Malaspina was born in Palermo, Italy in 1754. He was a member of a family that could trace its noble lineage through at least eight centuries. He entered the Spanish naval service at an early age and took part in a number of engagements in one of which he was made prisoner by the English. Between the years 1789 and 1794 he was in charge of a round-the-world expedition which bears his name, and the ships that comprised it were the *Descubierta* and the *Atrevida*.

Bustamente, Malaspina's junior by five years, was Spanish by birth and descent. He began his naval career in 1770 and saw service in many distant assignments. He commanded the *Atrevida* during the expedition, and on his return to Spain, unlike Malaspina, he retained the favor of the court and subsequently held many official positions, both civil and political, until his death in Madrid in 1825.

[2] Instead, as Baron von Humboldt remarked, "this able navigator (Malaspina) is more famous for his misfortunes than for his discoveries." (Cited by Cutter, *op. cit.*, p. vii.)

[3] The picture to which there is reference was one painted by Gaspard de Vancy, a member of the expedition of La Pérouse and presented to Father Lasuén. The original has disappeared, but copies made from it are extant. A good reproduction of it may be seen in Cutter, *op. cit.*, pp. 42-43. For a description of it by one who was well acquainted with the original, see Angustias de la Guerra Ord, *Occurrences in Hispanic California* (tr. and ed. by Francis Price and William H. Ellison [Washington, D. C., 1956]), p. 27.

121. To Don José Antonio de Romeu

Towards the middle of last July I received from His Excellency the Viceroy the same official letter, word for word, which Your Lordship sends me in your letter of the eleventh of the present month.

I have already observed that the above-mentioned official letter was not forwarded, and I regret it very much because the carrying out of what was ordered in it was very much delayed. However, on seeing the higher order of His Excellency, I immediately named the missionaries. I sought and obtained from the commandant of this presidio the necessary help for a new exploration of the Soledad district, and a site was chosen that has many advantages over the two previously selected.

I had recourse to the missions for supplying the vestments and sacred vessels, and as soon as the commandant of the frigate *Aránzazu*[1] delivered what will serve as a "dowry" for the two foundations, I proceeded to Santa Clara in order to undertake in person the task of examining again the Santa Cruz site.

I crossed the sierra by a road that is very long and very rough. I found that this site was just as beautiful and just as suitable as had been reported to me. And furthermore, I came upon a channel of water close at hand, very plentiful, and very essential.

On the Feast of St. Augustine[2] I said Mass in the district, and the holy cross was raised in the very place where it is to be set up.

At that time many pagans, old and young, of both sexes, gave evidence that they would promptly enroll themselves under the sacred standard. Thanks be to God.

I returned to Santa Clara by a road that was rougher, but it was also shorter and more direct. I made arrangements for repairing it by means of the Indians of the mission I just mentioned; and an excellent job has been done, because for that job, as for all others, the commandant of the Presidio of San Francisco, Don Hermenegildo Sal, furnished all the help that was asked, with all speed and promptness.

I gave orders that a number of small houses resembling those of the Indians should be built in the locality, and I am inclined to think that by this time the two missionaries assigned to that foundation may be there.

Here in Monterey I happened to come upon the two corvettes of the Spanish Expedition, and at the urging of the commandants of them I felt obliged to remain here until their departure, on various matters pertaining to the royal service.

With the co-operation of Their Lordships I sought to transport the Santa Cruz supplies by sea, but it was not possible.

Some cargos were sent there the day before yesterday. One of the men who went along with them was from the schooner which came down from Nootka. (The schooner is under command of Don Juan Carrasco, pilot from the Department of San Blas, and it is at present at anchor in this port.) The objective is to see whether on the coast near Santa Cruz there is a shelter for this vessel; and if there is, to ship thence what is left here.

The answer is due tomorrow. We are interested in this method of solving the problem, for we are very short of beasts of burden.

This very day eleven Indians set out from here with a supply of implements to build a hut at Soledad so that we may accommodate the missionaries and the supplies.

I am busy with many preparations for that foundation. The missionaries of San Luis and San Antonio have been notified to make other preparations; and I shall be there, at latest, immediately after the Feast of St. Francis.[3]

I am giving Your Lordship this exhaustive account because I am convinced that this would be the best response to your esteemed official letter, inasmuch as I want to bring into focus, as well as I can, my ready obedience to the superior orders of His Excellency the Viceroy and of Your Lordship.

It is clear to me that only in this way can I fulfill my obligation; and I shall regard it as no less an obligation to pray that God Our Lord may keep Your Lordship for many years in His holy grace.

San Carlos Mission,
September 29, 1791.

[1] A small (205 ton) supply ship named after a famous shrine in the Basque country.
[2] August 28.
[3] October 4.

122. To Don José Antonio de Romeu

I am sending Your Lordship the enclosed certificates issued by the three naval surgeons, humbly requesting that in view of the grave and dangerous illness from which, according to the judgment of these three practitioners, the Reverend Father Fray Pedro Benito Cambón is suffering, Your Lordship may be so kind as to permit him to embark for San Blas in the packet boat *San Carlos* now at anchor in that port.

Despite the fact that I am advised by a decree from the office of the Viceroy of Mexico that such a permission is not to be granted to any missionary unless permission has already been obtained from the central government, I cannot help feeling completely convinced that the present case admits, and even calls for, a legitimate and prudent exception to the superior ordinance just cited. At least I do not see any reason for fearing that this viceregal authority will disapprove if, in the circumstances, this religious is given permission to return; but I would certainly fear even his anger if it were refused.

I have known the Reverend Father Cambón for years. I have seen him sick, and during the past two months I have observed a notable worsening in his condition so that the physician of the Spanish corvette gives as his prognosis that: "If he were to have to wait as long as is required for the permission of the central government to arrive, I have no hesitancy in giving as my opinion that this religious may die, in view of his present condition."

At different times he has moved because of his illness from San Francisco to Santa Clara, and has found relief. At other times he came to this Mission of San Carlos and felt somewhat better. At the present time, however, he does not find this to be the case anywhere. There is no medicine that brings him any relief; and in the midst of these anxieties, and so as not to be completely incapacitated, for many days in a row he has imposed on himself the secret penance of doing without water altogether.

For this reason, Sir, and because this missionary not only does not serve, but even lacks the ability to serve, in these missions, and because on the other hand we have available a suitable religious assigned to, and residing at, San Francisco to take his place, I hope that in your kindness Your Lordship will grant the favor I ask; and in that case I shall be eternally indebted and grateful.

May God Our Lord keep Your Lordship many years in His holy grace.

San Carlos Mission,
November 19, 1791.

123. To the Missionaries

The Lord give you Peace. According to the instructions which I believe the new governor brings, the Reports for the year just ending are required promptly by the first month of the new year. For this reason, and because the Most Reverend Commissary of the Indies, and also our College of San Fernando, wish the same, I hereby request you not to be tardy about it, and that you send the information to me in duplicate form at the beginning of the year by the first mail available.

The entire service which these documents can offer (as I understand it so far), and the whole purpose they are intended to fulfill, are adequately met if you use the enclosed form which is quite short, and which all will please follow for the sake of uniformity, as long as nothing else is prescribed.

I should be advised in a separate letter regarding anything else that might be considered worthy of notice, either with a view to bringing about a remedy, or for any other purpose; and, with God's help, I shall take care of what is fitting in the case.

May God Our Lord keep Your Reverences many years in His holy grace.

San Carlos Mission,
November 28, 1791.

Blessed be Jesus

Report on the State of this Mission of .... on December 31, ...

Baptisms: There were baptized during this year .... adults and .... children, and of these ... were *de razón,* making

	a total of . . . .; added to those of previous years equals a grand total of . . . . .
Marriages:	Marriages celebrated: . . . Indians; . . . . *de razón;* a total of . . . .; added to those of previous years making a grand total of . . . . . .
Deaths:	Indian adults deceased . . . ., Indian children . . . .; *de razón:* adults . . . ., children . . . .; total for all combined . . . .; added to those of previous years making a grand total of . . . . . .
Living:	The Indians who are actually on the rolls and attending the full program of religious and secular instruction are . . . . adults; the number less than nine years of age . . . . . .
Cattle:	Large and small combined . . . . , including draft-oxen, of which . . . . are broken to the yoke and . . . . unbroken.
Smaller Animals:	Sheep . . ., goats . . . ., swine . . . .
Horses:	The number of mares in herds with its corresponding stud burros . . . ., the number of donkeys. . . . . Altogether, both large and small, a total of . . . . head. The number of tame horses . . . ., the number broken in . . . .
Mules:	Number tame . . . ., number unbroken . . . .
Sowing:	There was sown for this year: wheat . . . ., barley . . . ., peas . . . ., corn, etc.
Harvests:	Amount harvested: of wheat . . . ., of barley . . . ., etc.
Building Construction:	What has been built: What has been acquired in the category of fittings for: the church, the house, the farm, etc.

Let a copy of the above be made for use in due time, and this copy is to be sent without delay from mission to mission as far as San Diego where it is to be kept.

San Carlos Mission,
November 28, 1791.

124. To Fray Pablo de Mugartegui

Salutations. I have been disabused at last regarding the violent friction between the missionaries at Soledad, for at Santa Clara on the fifth of this month I received a letter from Father García which I am enclosing. I set out on the seventh despite my illness and the bad weather, and notwithstanding all the risks and all the precautions that must be taken.

Nothing happened to me, nor did I get wet, thanks be to God; but after I arrived at the presidio the rains were so bad that for two days I was unable to go to Carmel.

Each of the Fathers at Soledad berated the other verbally in the presence of the governor. His Lordship himself knows that this was not the right thing to do, so he suggested to me that it might be very necessary to separate them.

I told him that I had little grounds for hoping that I would be able to make the journey here promptly. But when the letter of Father García reached me at Santa Clara I replied (and I brought the reply sealed), begging him for God's sake to return to his post as soon as possible, and to exercise a little patience until I could arrive there. I promised that I would stay with him until I had an opportunity of assigning another companion to him.

I told him, too, that seeing that Father García was still at Carmel, I would at once proceed with him to Soledad and would withdraw Father Rubí from there.

His Lordship afterwards pointed out how difficult and impossible it would be to place this religious elsewhere without a noisy scene, and without considerable inconvenience to the missionaries to whom he would be assigned. (To such an extent has he made himself known to all, this good Father.)

His Lordship expressed much sympathy with me, and suggested various reasons why it did not seem right to him that I should take the decision I did, knowing how disagreeable it was, and how incompatible with the discharge of my present urgent and grave responsibilities.

I recognized that he was right; and I protested to him repeatedly that I would never have discussed such matters with a layman and that I did so now at the cost of indescribable pain and sorrow because of the irregular action of the two religious who took their case to him. Then I told him: "There is now, Sir, no solution but this, and it is one that can give rise to inconveniences, and only the present urgency and necessity can justify it; and the [solution] is that Father Gili come to Soledad with Father Rubí, and Father García go to San Antonio with Father Ventura."

He immediately approved the suggestion, and I suspect that perhaps when Father Rubí found himself with the governor, he proposed the same thing and urged it; but both the governor and I believe that this association of Gili and Rubí can be ended with the arrival of the boat, for we have hopes that some religious will come in it.

Finally, Father García left here very pleased with his transfer, and took with him a letter to Father Gili. The latter replied to me that although he was happy at San Antonio he would proceed promptly to Soledad. Then, two or three days later, I had another letter from him in which he informed me that on the same morning when he was about to set out, Father Ventura awoke, having a high fever and suffering intensely from internal pains, that he had administered Viaticum to him, and that in his opinion it will soon be necessary to give him Extreme Unction.

I went immediately to the presidio and begged the governor to send the surgeon to San Antonio, and he went that same afternoon, the nineteenth of this month. Since then, the weather has kept us confined here because of the heavy rains and the furious winds which have us terrified; and to this date we have not heard a word further about the sick man.

Lieutenants Ortega and Goicoechoea had already been here at the presidio for some days when I arrived from Santa Clara. They have been busy checking their accounts, and the mail is being held back until they have completed them. I hope there will be some news of Father Ventura before it departs; and, with God's help, I shall let you know what it is.

The dissensions and disagreements of Rubí and García were of the most clamorous nature; so bad, in fact, that on one occasion García had to have recourse to the corporal of the guard and to take him home with him to restrain Rubí, for he feared that the latter might lay violent hands on him, or even do worse.

Father García has told me that the other carries side-arms, and that a horrible secret is attached to one of them, for he boasts that he had it with him in the college on the occasion of some disturbance unknown to me.

How painful and how sad it is for me to have to relate such things! But Your Reverence will understand that it is necessary for you to know these things down there so that a remedy can be found. At the same time you will be so kind as to give your blessing to the decision I have made in the transfer referred to, bearing in mind that responsibility for it is to be attributed not to me but to necessity.

Father García cannot adapt himself to what is new, as I explained elsewhere; but such as he is, he gives hope that he will be able to be of some service in these parts. As regards the other, there is no hope, judging by what one can see and by what all who know him report.

Recently I received Your Reverence's brief note of August 31, written in the infirmary, with the bitter extract drawn from the representation made to the viceroy concerning his decree for the expulsion of Father Peña. I was right in what I said about it in my first letter, written at Santa Clara.

The present governor has made no report; rather, he is surprised and astonished at the reports of his predecessor. I am much more surprised at the commandant general that he, without hearing a word from me, should have asked the viceroy for such a punishment for this religious.

In view of what Your Reverence has presented to the viceroy, I hope there will be a complete vindication at the time that is most opportune, that is, when the accuser of our brother has arrived at the capital. May God forgive him.

Ever since the beginning of this year the master carpenter, to whom His Excellency has reference in his letter, has been working at this mission.

A sweeping decision of the assessor has been sent to me by the commandant general, with an official letter and decree of his own, to the effect that the laws of the *patronato real* be carried out and enforced in the *doctrinas*[1] administered by the religious belonging to the presidency under my charge. Furthermore, according to the same ruling and decree, they have probably forwarded it to Your Reverence, and I wish to be advised regarding what I should do.

I have the reply already sealed in which I report to him that "the institutions administered by the religious included in the presidency under my charge are nothing but missions."

I have advised Father Peña of the favorable condition of his case, and I promised to send him on a more opportune occasion the letter and representation of Your Reverence.

I have letters ready for the other Fathers in which I send them your greetings and tell them about your accident. Perhaps no one will regret it more than I, just as no one will be more eager for your recovery, or more eager to carry out your slightest wish to the very letter.

May God Our Lord keep Your Reverence many years in His holy grace.

San Carlos Mission,
February 24, 1792.

The small tumor I suffered from at the end of the thigh burst, just one day after my return from Santa Clara. While not as big as before, it is always making me realize that it is in much worse condition than in the past, and is a source of almost constant worry to me.

---

[1] As here understood, a *doctrina* is a parish administered by religious and subject to the requirements of the Royal Patronato—privileges granted by Pope Julius II and other popes to the Spanish sovereigns, in virtue of which the Spanish king became in many administrative matters the vicar of the reigning pope. (The word must not be confused with a similar word commonly applied to the course of religious instruction imparted to pupils).

125. To Don Pedro de Nava

I have received Your Lordship's higher order of the eleventh of last October. Enclosed with it was a copy of the ruling of the Assessor of the

Commandancy General attesting that in the *doctrinas* which are administered by the religious belonging to the presidency under my charge, I should assist in the exact compliance and observance of what is expressed in the opinion therein issued. Furthermore, Your Lordship determines that in regard to parishes and *doctrinas* in the provinces subject to Your Lordship's control the laws of the *patronato real* are to be observed.

Sir, all the institutions which the religious of this presidency administer are missions; and my attitude in regard to them is to carry out to the letter everything that Your Lordship commands and disposes.

May God Our Lord keep Your Lordship for many years in His holy grace.

Mission of San Carlos of Monterey,
February 25, 1792.

126. To Fray Pablo de Mugartegui

The surgeon arrived last night and wrote to me from the presidio that Father Buenaventura was completely recovered. Thanks be to God. He reported that what the Father had suffered from was a severe cold, and that after he had begun to perspire he felt so much better that before he himself had arrived, the patient was already out of danger. Thanks be to God.

The Fathers Pieras and Tapis came up from San Luis when they heard of the sick man's condition. Both had written to me from San Antonio. Tapis had it in mind to return shortly to his mission, but I do not know yet how that will turn out, for the most furious storms of rain and wind continue.

Such floods as we have were never known at Carmel. The night before last the *pozolera*,[1] built of adobe with a tiled roof, collapsed. There was no further damage, thanks be to God.

Father Pieras, sometimes fearful and sometimes unconcerned, states that Father Ventura's illness has him puzzled; but no matter what be the outcome, he has begun the completion of the church for the Indians, but doubts if he will be able to finish it.

After he had been for more than six months in San Luis, and after he had returned to that very place from Purísima, whither his little wanderings had led him, he wrote to Santa Clara to tell me that he had got along well in San Luis and that he was very much better, but not entirely well. He mentioned that the Fathers at San Antonio had invited him often, but that he had acquired a horror and dislike for that mission; that having become disillusioned because of the many hazards and experiences he met there, it did not agree with him. He stated, moreover, that in any case he placed himself at my disposal in the most humble obedience.

In reply I told him that in view of the fact that he was not quite well and that he hoped to regain his health in San Luis where it suited him so well, he ought to continue there until he had completely recovered, and that he should inform me as soon as he had reached that stage. I added that if San Antonio proved to be too distasteful to him, I would do the best I could to get him settled in some other place of his choice, or in some place that seemed most suitable to his health.

The result is that now Father Diego García is a supernumerary at San Antonio, a position little in harmony with his disposition.

The Reverend Father Gili came with the surgeon as far as Soledad, and from there he writes to me that he is very happy with his companion, Rubí. Your Reverence cannot help smiling a little at this, for you can enjoy a good laugh, and keep a calm mind when things go wrong. Nor do I fail to rejoice a little and to give thanks to God because—and this is something which I do not deserve—Your Reverence has confidence in me and securely expects that I shall do whatever is most conducive to the honor and glory of God, and to the good name of our holy Institute.

Again I place myself at the service of Your Reverence, and I pray that God Our Lord may keep you for many years in His holy grace.

San Carlos Mission,
March 1, 1792.

P. S.

So far, neither the lieutenants nor the mail have left, and I have been able to conclude the short report on the missions which I sent Your Reverence. I must point out that the total number of those living for the preceding year was inaccurate, for it was given as 8,528, which was wrong; it should have been 7,718. As I calculated it, there would be fewer alive this year than last, and I knew this could not be the case. I was convinced that the figures for this year were right, and concluded that those for the preceding year were wrong; and so it turned out.

I am afraid that when adding totals [mistakes] will happen often, for I am in no sense an accountant; and for this reason I work all the more, and this at the risk of achieving all the less.

Within the past few days the Carmel River has swept away almost all this year's harvest, and is leaving us very little ground to be worked.

Four days ago, two soldiers and two servants set out on a fishing trip in the fishing-boat or small launch belonging to the presidio. No sooner had they left land than they encountered a violent storm of wind and rain which took them almost to the mouth of the Monterey River where the boat was wrecked. One of the servants escaped by a miracle, and the other three have not been seen dead or alive.

The Rancho del Rey,[2] as it is called, in the alluvial plains of the Monterey River is flooded. The rancheros, Cantúa and Diego Ruiz, suddenly found thmeselves in their little house up to their chests in water, and in that manner, and sometimes by swimming, they made their way the four leagues as far as the rising slope at Natividad where they made their escape. By this time they have made their way to the presidio, sound in health and feeling all right.

At the Soledad, too, they have had their moments of terror. We have no word from the other centers, but some mishaps are to be expected if they have had the same kind of weather we have had here.

In all humility I am,
Your Reverence's devoted servant.

March 7, [1792].

[1] Kitchen—the place where the *pozola* was prepared.
[2] Site of the present city of Salinas.

127. To Fray Pablo de Mugartegui

At last the mail, which has been so long delayed, will leave this afternoon to carry the news that Governor Don José Antonio de Romeu is no longer living. Yesterday, about ten in the morning, he died in my arms.

I assisted him since Tuesday of Holy Week, for on that day he made his confession; on Wednesday I gave him Holy Viaticum, and on Thursday Extreme Unction. He died fully resigned to the will of God, and with many signs that his death was a happy one.

His body was brought to the church of this mission. It is still here, awaiting the return of Father Arenaza from the presidio where he went to say Mass. Then, please God, it will be my lot to sing a Mass in the presence of the deceased, and to preside at the obsequies.

Lieutenants Ortega and Goicoechea and Ensign Sal have been here since last evening. When the ceremonies are ended, I believe they will not be slow to return each to his own house; nor can I, for the same reason, and because there is nothing new to add, be slow to bring this to an end.

With deepest humility I renew my obedience to Your Reverence, and I pray that God Our Lord may keep you many years in His holy grace.

San Carlos Mission,
April 10, 1792.

128. Memorandum regarding Confirmation

BOOK OF CONFIRMATIONS
Belonging to the Mission of Most Holy Mary
Our Lady of the Soledad

Founded at the expense of the Catholic King of the Spains, Don Carlos IV, the year, month, day, and place indicated in the other canonical books. This consists of one hundred and forty-six usable pages, numbered except for the first and last which are unnumbered.

Fray Fermín Francisco de Lasuén.

PREFACE

It is an article of faith that the ordinary minister of the sacrament of Confirmation is the bishop alone. Thus has it been defined by various general councils, and in the following words by the holy Council of Trent (Confirmation, sec. 7, canon 3): "If anyone shall say that the ordinary minister of holy Confirmation is not the bishop alone but any simple priest, let him be anathema."

Wherefore, when the Holy See in some cases grants to a simple priest the faculty of administering the said holy sacrament, he is warned that before making use of it he is obliged to make this known to all present.

This is my procedure wherever I confirm; and, furthermore, so that those who read this book may be aware of the above extraordinary faculty, the letters patent concerning its concession are faithfully transcribed in the following page. The above is attested and signed by me.

Fray Fermín Francisco de Lasuén.

Blessed be Jesus[1]

Fray Pedro Mariano de Iturbide of the Order of Minors of the Regular Observance of our holy Father St. Francis, Apostolic Missionary, former Guardian of this beloved (Friary) of Christ Crucified of Guatemala, Commissary Prefect of the Missions *de Propaganda Fide* in the West Indies, to Father Fray Fermín Francisco de Lasuén, Apostolic

Missionary of the College of San Fernando of Mexico, eternal health in the Lord.

Whereas our Supreme Pontiff Pius VI, Pope by Divine Providence, in order to promote the welfare of the neophytes of our missions graciously granted me the following faculty of which this is the purport:

At an audience granted by the Holy Father on April 24, 1785, Our Most Holy Father, by Divine Providence Pope Pius VI, at the request of the undersigned Secretary of the Sacred Congregation of *Propaganda Fide*, for a period of ten years graciously extended to Father Pedro Mariano Iturbide, Prefect of the Missions of the Order of St. Francis of the Observance of the Colleges of Holy Cross at Querétaro, of Guatemala, of Zacatecas, and of San Fernando of Mexico City, or diocese of North America, and to his successors within that period of ten years, the faculty formerly granted to his predecessor under date of July 8, 1774, the faculty, namely, of administering the holy sacrament of Confirmation by the use of chrism blessed by a Catholic bishop, even if the chrism is old, provided that the new cannot be obtained, and provided that in all cases the directions are followed which were issued by order of the same Sacred Congregation on March 21, 1774, for places belonging to these missions and not belonging to the bishop of any diocese—in which case the permission of the latter is to be obtained in writing. And there is granted the power of subdelegating this faculty in the form and manner described, to one member chosen by the above-mentioned Prefect from among the religious of each college by reason of his age and morals, or to one designated by the successors of the above. It shall be the duty of the one selected to visit often and exercise his ministrations in the territories subject to that particular college so that the faithful be not deprived of this spiritual support.

Given at Rome in the office of the aforesaid Sacred Congregation on the fourth day of May, 1785.

Stephen Borgia, Secretary.

Wherefore, in the light of the above faculty, by virtue of these presents signed by my hand, affixed with my seal, and confirmed by the signature of my secretary, I grant you this faculty, but only for the period of my good pleasure; and I impart it to the end that you may be pleased to use and exercise it as seems best to you in the Lord.

And if it should happen that by God's decree you should depart this life within that ten year period, it is to be understood that this same faculty is granted to Fray Pablo Mugartegui, Apostolic Preacher, and in his absence to Fray Pedro Benito Cambón, Apostolic Preacher and alumnus, too, of the aforesaid College of San Fernando.

Given at the said College of Christ Crucified of Guatemala, March 13, 1787.

> *Fray Pedro Mariano de Iturbide,*
> Commissary Prefect of the Missions.
> *Very Reverend Fray Mariano a Jesu Pérez de Guadalupe,*
> Secretary of the Missions.

I hereby certify that the above is a faithful copy of the original.
> *Fray Fermín Francisco de Lasuén.*

In addition to the original patent, I am keeping on file the permit to make free use of it which the Most Illustrious Don Fray José Joaquín Granados, Bishop of Sonora, sent me, signed and sealed, at the instance of Brigadier Commandant General Don Jacobo Ugarte y Loyola, as appears from his official letter of March 2, 1790. And this, too, I am keeping with the patent and permit above mentioned. At the same time I have in my possession and for my information the practical directions of the Sacred Congregation mentioned in the patent. These we have always observed, and with God's help we will observe them faithfully whenever we use this extraordinary faculty.

It is ever our desire that it may contribute to the greater honor and glory of the Divine Majesty, and to the strengthening in the faith of these new mission districts so that, by virtue of the Seven Gifts of the Holy Spirit, they may "not only believe in their heart whatever is necessary for justification, but in addition verbally confess what leads to salvation, and show themselves ready even to shed their blood for Christ."

Wherefore I so certify and sign.

On May 7, 1792, in the church of this Mission of Our Lady of the Soledad, the Reverend Father President of these Missions, Fray Fermín Francisco de Lasuén, having just sung the Mass and still clothed in priestly vestments, instructed all present that the bishop alone is the ordinary minister of the sacrament of Confirmation, and emphasized that the extraordinary faculty of the Holy See was granted in favor of these missions, and in virtue of it, although he was but a simple priest, he was empowered to administer it.

After instructing those present in all that pertains not only to an understanding of this sacrament but also to its fruitful reception, assisted by the two missionaries (mentioned), ministers of the above mission, and observing due form, he administered Confirmation to [here follow the names].

---

[1] The balance of this document is in Latin.

X

Administration of Don José de Arrillaga

The cordial relations between Church and State, so notable under Governor Romeu, continue under his successor, Don José de Arrillaga, who was interim governor. Skilled artisans arrive to train the Indians in crafts, and distinguished English visitors are entertained.

129. To Don José Joaquín de Arrillaga[1]

NDER DATE OF THE TWELFTH OF APRIL, I anticipated matters by acknowledging, in my own name and in that of my missionaries, your authority in this province for I had assumed, by reason of the death of His Lordship Don José Antonio de Romeu, that there and then it had devolved on your worthy self. In your esteemed letter of the seventh of last month you now formally notify me.

In virtue of it I am most happy once more to extend Your Grace our submission, and it is my ardent wish to give expression to it when an opportunity presents itself, and even to be outstanding in the punctual carrying out not only of your orders, but even of your suggestions. And we impose on ourselves the additional obligation of praying that God Our Lord may grant you a happy and prosperous administration, and may keep you for many years in His holy grace.

San Carlos Mission,
June 25, 1792.

[1] He had held the position of lieutenant-governor under Romeu. On the death of the latter he became acting governor. He permitted a month to pass before formally announcing it. He exercised the office until early in 1794 when the next regularly appointed governor assumed office.

130. To Don José Argüello[1]

Don Juan Francisco de la Quadra[2] sent me direct the same official document of which Your Grace sends me a copy in your letter of this date.

As a consequence, some time ago I was able to take the steps best calculated to accomplish the task assigned me; and in what remains to be done to complete it, God willing, I shall show the same zeal which, I believe, Your Grace will display in the part which devolves on you, and regarding which you have been notified.

May God Our Lord keep Your Grace for many years in His holy grace.

San Carlos Mission,
July 9, 1792.

[1] Argüello at the time was acting as commandant at Monterey.
[2] Quadra was the Spanish commissioner who had been given authority to negotiate

251

with the English regarding the conflicting claims of Spain and England on the Northwest coast. Quadra had notified the governor that it was very probable that certain English ships on their way to the Northwest might find it necessary to call at some California port to take on fresh food supplies. He asked that these facilities be extended to them. The letter, however, had been sent to Governor Romeu, who was now deceased; but Quadra had taken the precaution of writing direct to Lasuén.

131. To Fray Pablo de Mugartegui

I beg Your Reverence's holy blessing in order to inform you that on this date I am sending to the captain at Loreto, the acting governor, Don José Joaquín de Arrillaga, the names of us, the missionaries so that at the end of the document he may kindly certify that we are here so that our stipends may be cashed at the capital.

So that the document may reach you opportunely, I am asking him as a further favor, if he deems it fit, to forward it to the Reverend Father President,[1] Fray Juan Crisóstomo Gómez. And if it is sent to him, I am in turn asking him as a favor to forward it with this letter to Your Reverence.

Since my last letter the only news was that on the seventh of this month the frigate *Concepción*, under command of Don Francisco de Eliza, anchored in this port with our supplies. Father Sánchez was healthy, strong, and robust on arrival. For the time being I have assigned him to Santa Clara where the need is greatest, because on several occasions during the past month Father Peña felt himself exposed to insult. He is here at present and feels much improved after four bloodlettings.

Very respectfully I place myself once more at the service of Your Reverence, and I pray that God Our Lord may keep you for many years in His holy grace.

San Carlos Mission,
July 28, 1792.

[1] President of the Dominican missionaries of Lower California.

132. List of Missionaries

List of those of us, Missionaries Apostolic, who devote ourselves to the conversion of the pagans of New California and the instruction of the new converts.

San Carlo

Fermín Francisco de Lasuén
Pascual Martínez de Arenaza
José Señán

San Francisco

Antonio Danti
Martín Landaeta

Santa Clara	Tomás de la Peña
	Diego Noboa
	Francisco Sánchez
Santa Cruz	Alonso Isidro Salazar
	Baldomero López
Soledad	Mariano Rubí
	Bartolomé Gili
San Antonio	Miguel Pieras
	Buenaventura Sitjar
	Diego García
San Luis	Miguel Giribet
	Esteban Tapis
Purísima	José de Arroita
	Cristóbal Oramas
Santa Barbara	Antonio Paterna
	José de Miguel
San Buenaventura	Francisco Dumets [Dumetz]
	Vicente de Santa María
San Gabriel	Antonio Cruzado
	Miguel Sánchez
	José Calzada
San Juan Capistrano	Vicente Fuster
	Juan Norberto Santiago
San Diego	Hilario Torrent
	Juan Mariner

San Carlos Mission,
July 28, 1792.

133. To Don José Joaquín de Arrillaga

I am forwarding to Your Grace the enclosed draft which I have just received from the paymaster of Monterey. I respectfully request that you will be so kind as to authenticate it so that it may be cashed.

If Your Grace will do this favor, I hope you will also be so kind as to send it to the Very Reverend Father President Fray Juan Crisóstomo Gómez so that it will not be delayed. And I am asking him as a favor to send it from there to our College of San Fernando.

May God Our Lord keep Your Grace for many years in His holy grace.

San Carlos Mission,
August 2, 1792.

134. To Fray Lorenzo Revuelta

The Peace of God be with Your Reverence. I am sending you the duplicate of the list of supplies which I sent to our Reverend Father Guardian last March.

We have received the two *Santo-Cristos*. Seeing that according to the invoice they had come distinct from those packed, without a number referring to the case or package, I took it to mean that the reference was to items we had already received; and for that reason I told Your Reverence that only one of them had come.

The packages and cases have been opened, and the following items, although entered in the invoice, are missing: three loads of leather sacks, and a dozen large shears.

Furthermore, the following items not included in the invoice were added: three pozola ladles, and one piece of tanned cowhide.

It will be better if the cases come without locks, for then they will cost less and serve the purpose just as well, as appears from the poor condition in which they arrive even when supplied with them.

There is no special news. I am at the service of Your Reverence, and I pray that God Our Lord may keep you many years in His holy grace.

San Carlos Mission,
August 7, 1792.

135. To Father Guardian [Fray Tomás Pangua]

I have no doubt that the time has already come for the appointment of a new prelate; but who he is I do not know, not even his name.[1] Nevertheless, with deep humility and inward satisfaction I offer my obedience. I am filled with joy at your appointment, and sincerely wish you all success and happiness.

At the end of last July I advised Your Reverence's predecessor that on the twenty-fourth of the same month, seventeen days after the frigate *Concepción* put into port, Señor Zúñiga and Father Loriente arrived,[2] the latter without the commission's mandate, and both without any instructions whatever for its execution. They were awaiting them when, on the eleventh of last month, there anchored here the frigate *Santa Gertrudis* in command of Captain Don Alonso de Torres, and with a full crew of officers, sailors, and marines.

As soon as we established contact with them we noticed that many of them were surprised to see in these environs two individuals, each far away from his normal place of residence. For this reason they asked different questions; and while we avoided being untruthful we managed to conceal the truth from them. But since there are so many of them, and so many local residents, one has to presume that they will find out or suspect what the trouble is.

One thing is certain: we felt deeply embarrassed; and if there were anything in the affair to atone for, this unexpected coincidence more than made up for it. Finally, on the third of this month the *Concepción* sailed out from this port with the commissioners on board bound for Santa Barbara or San Diego, to await the instructions, and then to return. Your Reverence can imagine what will be our consternation and embarrassment in the case. God deliver us.

The compliments and respect that the skipper and officers of the *Gertrudis* have shown us, and the satisfaction they have all derived from the courtesy we have shown them, may be seen in the letter of the skipper, and in my reply, copies of which I enclose. Thanks be to God.

In this way we grow day by day in closer friendship and in mutual esteem.

This very day we heard that the day before yesterday there anchored in the port of San Francisco the sloop *Saturnina* on its way from San Blas, under command of Don Juan Carrasco, bound for Nootka or Fuca,[3] with a mail pouch for Señor Quadra. She sailed from San Blas around the month of June, went as far north as 38 degrees and 48 minutes, encountered bad weather, began to run short of water, and was fortunate to be able to arrive at the above port. It is reported that she will undergo repairs there, and resume her mission. There is not an officer who looks on the enterprise as insignificant, nor is there anyone who does not consider them lost for undertaking it. God prosper it.

With this in mind, we were happy to learn that Don Alonso de Torre[4] had been made a Captain of the Navy. A naval officer held me back from going this evening to offer my congratulations, saying that tomorrow we can both go together.

Both the *Concepción* and the *Gertrudis* were short of foodstuffs when they arrived, and Your Reverence can imagine how much it cost me in worry and effort to supply them with flour; but thanks be to God I am happy to have succeeded. I have arranged with the commandant that in the present circumstances it seems that the usual provincial tariff should not apply. This is because we find ourselves in the position of having to help the ships. This involved making great sacrifices at the missions so as to prevent greater hardships in the royal service.

He readily approved of this and asked me to send him an official letter on the matter, so that he could discuss it with the commissary at San Blas and submit it to the Viceroy.

I tremble to do this; but I shall profess very clearly that we ourselves are disinterested, and shall base my claim on the responsibility placed on us by the King our Sovereign to safeguard the temporal goods of our poor miserable Indians. And I shall give my word that what is agreed on by the superiors will be agreeable to us.

At the moment there is no particular news to send from these missions. The Reports on them I am forwarding in two separate packages.

I acknowledge that it is your will which controls my power to do or not to do; and so I desire and promise to carry out your will exactly as you are pleased to command me, in whatever manner or whatever place it may please you to specify.

I acknowledge that it is your will which controls my power to do or I renew my obedience to Your Reverence, and I pray that God Our Lord may keep you for many years in His holy grace.

San Carlos Mission,
September 12, 1792.

¹ More than three months earlier, on May 26, of that year a Chapter was held at San Fernando, and Lasuén's friend, Fray Tomás Pangua, was appointed guardian. Like Lasuén, Pangua too was a Basque. Thirty-three years before, on September 5, 1759, Lasuén, Pangua, and Prestamero another missionary destined for California, left Spain for the New World, making the trip in the same boat.

² These had been assigned to investigate the charges made against Fray Tomás de la Peña. Lasuén may have been acquainted with José de Zúñiga, for both had been stationed at San Diego. Towards the end of the preceding May Zúñiga had been appointed captain at Tucson. Father Loriente was a Dominican from Lower California.

³ Nootka is an island to the west of what is now Vancouver Island, and on the south the Straits of Juan de Fuca separate Vancouver Island from the State of Washington.

⁴ He was in charge of the *Santa Gertrudis*. For further information on ships that called at California during this period, see Marcial Gutiérrez Camarena *San Blas y las Californias* (Mexico: Editorial Jus, 1956).

136. To Father Guardian [Fray Tomás Pangua]

I ask Your Reverence's holy blessing, and beg to inform you that the two commissioners, Lieutenant Zúñiga and the Reverend Father Loriente, have written to me from San Gabriel, under date of the twentieth of last month, that they have received the order which they were awaiting, for carrying out their commission in accordance with the decree of His Excellency the Viceroy. This decree is: To ascertain with the greatest exactitude if the charges and accusations are well-founded which have been made to His Excellency against Father Fray Tomás de la Peña on his mistreatment of his Indians and on certain evil results which have followed therefrom.

[Marginal note:] Officially I know nothing of this, or of any other matter concerning the affair. What I do know I picked up incidentally, or from friendly correspondence.

No new instructions have been sent to them in regard to this new inquiry. They have nothing [to guide them] but the previous procedure in regard to this Father.

From this it can be inferred that this dreadful case, which was instigated and concluded by a former governor of this province, with a great deal of publicity and a great deal of embarrassment to us, is going to be started again, this time by the Viceroy of New Spain, and is going to be continued and concluded with even greater publicity and confusion to us. It has been entrusted to persons who dwell afar off, and who came here already during the shipping season in order to carry out their commission. They left for their distant homes without even opening the case, and before long they will be back once more, for all the province to see.

What concerns us most, of course, is that no other result can be expected from this procedure than what I explained to Your Reverence in my letter of the 30th of last July.

I need not, nor can I, explain how worried I am. I leave everything in God's hands and trust in His mercy. And in this confidence I make known to Your Reverence that I will do what I know to be my duty in the matter and whatever will contribute most towards its happy solution.

The schooners *Mexicana* and *Sutil* under command of Frigate Captains Don Dionisio Galiano and Don Cayetano Valdés,[1] after making a thorough exploration of the Straits of Fuca, anchored here on the twenty-third of last month.

I paid them a visit on the twenty-fourth, and on the twenty-fifth they attended Mass, and all who traveled in the cabin of both vessels, and of the frigate *Gertrudis*, dined in this mission. There were twenty-one of us at table. I am enclosing copies of the letter which I sent to the captains of these schooners regarding a gift they made me, and of their answer.

I claim no credit for myself for this and similar cases. I refer everything back to its source and inspiration, our holy college; and I am happy that this brings some additional honor to our apostolic institute, to the greater glory of God, and to the good of souls.

A brigantine, under the command of Commandant Quadra, and a sloop, which His Lordship purchased at Nootka, anchored in this port on the ninth of this month. On the tenth I called to offer my compliments, and on the eleventh Señor Quadra and many officers of all the vessels were here for dinner. They show us every respect and do many favors for us, and what is more to our liking, they are so agreeable and confiding in their contacts with us that they put us under an obligation to reciprocate. Thanks be to God.

The letter I enclose from the Reverend Father Oramas, and the one or two applications from the Reverend Father Calzada for a change of assignment, have obliged me to make changes in their appointments. I am sending the former as supernumerary to San Gabriel, and the latter as minister to Purísima. I trust Your Reverence will approve of this, or dispose as you think fit.

Just now the Reverend Father Fray José Señán informs me that he is going to write to Your Reverence asking for permission to return to the college. I have made it clear to him that I regret it very deeply, and I have asked him to give careful thought to the matter. He has informed me that he has given it much thought, that he has sought divine guidance, and that he is convinced that this would be the best for him. To this I did not need to reply; but I feel it my duty to tell Your Reverence that he is a good religious, a good worker, well-fitted to serve as a missionary here—in one word, he is a very good apostolic missionary.

Would that I were such! But what I think is not lacking in me is complete happiness, and an eager solicitude to pray that God Our Lord may keep you for many years in His holy grace.

San Carlos Mission,
October 20, 1792.

[1] The Journal of this voyage of discovery appeared in Spanish (Madrid, 1802) and English (London, 1930). Galiano and Valdés were lieutenants of the Malaspina expedition. See Cutter, *op. cit.,* pp. 2, 9 (note 5), *et. passim.*

137. To Don José Argüello

Your official letter, dated the twenty-fourth of this month, which I received yesterday, informs me that His Excellency the Viceroy has decreed that I am to assign to the missions under my charge, and according as I see fit, the skilled workers enumerated in the list which you enclose. They are those who up to now had come to Monterey under contract to teach their crafts to the natives of these parts. I was, of course, overjoyed both by reason of the advantage to us, and the confidence placed in me; and it shall be my highest ambition to make good use of the one, and to prove myself worthy of the other.

With these objectives in mind I am now proceeding to distribute the workers mentioned according to the plan which the list I am enclosing indicates. Inevitably there will be some barriers in the way because of the inclemency of the weather just now; the rains have appeared earlier than anticipated, and are causing damage. In the list you will see that we are waiting until the master mason and stone-cutter and the two journeymen complete the presidio church, as ordered by His Excellency the Viceroy in his superior order of the seventh of last April, a copy of which you sent me.

You will have observed, and of course informed the Honorable Interim Governor, that despite the fact that the craftsmen assigned here should have been master craftsmen capable of teaching their crafts perfectly, three of them are set down as merely journeymen. Furthermore, it was understood that all should bring with them the tools of their trade; but not even the carpenter, who from the beginning of this year worked at this mission, brought anything, and neither did the tanner, the blacksmith, or the master mason and stone-cutter, Manuel Ruiz.

I shall see to it, as you advise, that the tools already delivered, and those to be delivered, at the expense of the Royal Treasury are not put to other use than that prescribed, and that when an article is becoming useless, or shows signs of wearing out, the Fathers of the missions to which the master workmen are assigned should so certify.

At the present time the mission are not in need of tailors, for reasons that are not unknown to you, and for other considerations. These individuals can continue in whatever work they are engaged up to the present, or whatever seems best.

I am quite aware that the neighboring presidio does not have any broken-in animals paid for by the Royal Treasury, and you are aware, too, that at the missions there are not even unbroken animals paid for from the same source. Yet, when something pertaining to the Royal Service has to be done, the missions and their facilities are immediately alerted.

Just as soon as you decide that the craftsmen assigned to Santa Clara should get themselves ready, and have an escort available, I shall supply them with whatever is necessary for their journey.

Mission of San Carlos,
November 27, 1792.

Assignments of the Craftsmen made by the Undersigned:

The above-mentioned Royal Presidio

Master mason and stone-cutter . . .	Santiago Ruiz
Journeyman	Salvador Rivera
.. ..	Pedro Alcántara

San Carlos Mission

Master mason and stone-cutter . . .	Manuel Ruiz
Journeyman	Joaquín Riveras

Santa Clara Mission

Master carpenter who will also construct mills	Cajetano López
Master tanner, leather finisher, and shoemaker	Miguel Sangrador

Mission of Our Holy Father St. Francis

Master blacksmith and gunsmith . . .	Pedro González García

138. To the Honorable George Vancouver[1]

Your Lordship has been more than gracious towards both the humble Friars and the poor Indians.

What adds greater luster to the magnificent gift of Your Lordship is the fact that, apart from everything else and of itself, it is something truly worthy of the generosity of England and of the gratitude of Spain.

We shall make it known to all who are within the range of our limited correspondence. Radiating from here, the news should travel far. Then perhaps the delight of our Spanish people, as they express their pleasure on hearing it, will be the most fitting return on our part and the most agreeable to Your Lordship and your associates.

This, Sir, does not prevent us from reciprocating for the present with some poor token of our gratitude; and this will be presented to Your Lordship in the name of the missionaries and the Indians by the Reverend Father Fray Pascual de Arenaza. It is not, and it cannot be, an adequate recompense for the gracious kindness of Your Lordship. If that were the purpose, we know full well that it could not be accepted. It is merely a sample of the way we train the Indians in the duty of showing appreciation.

Will Your Lordship be so kind as to do us the honor of accepting it, both for the reason I have just mentioned, and for the additional one that in the case of a person in Your Lordship's position it is no less a mark of honor to receive insignificant gifts than to confer valuable ones.

For those which Your Lordship has made to us, accept our many thanks; and for those which you may do us the honor to accept, we give our word that, as is but just, we shall always retain a grateful memory of it.

In the name of all of us who have been so favored, I place myself at the service of Your Lordship. I wish you every happiness, and I remain from this time forward

Your most devoted and grateful servant,
and as such I kiss Your Lordship's hand.

San Carlos Mission,
December 15, 1792.

[1] In April, 1792, Vancouver "arrived off Cape Mendocino in the sloop *Discovery*, and continued the voyage to the Straits of Fuca. After making a number of surveys he sailed down the coast and entered San Francisco Bay on November 14th. During his stay of eleven days he visited the presidio, Mission Dolores, and Mission Santa Clara." (Engelhardt, *Missions and Missionaries*, II, 487). The *Discovery* cast anchor in Monterey Bay on November 27, and at Monterey and at Carmel Vancouver and his associates were lavishly entertained. On his return to England he wrote the story of his life in California in volumes iii and iv of his *Voyage of Discovery* (London, 1801). The pertinent passages may be found in Marguerite Eyer Wilbur, *Vancouver in California* (Los Angeles, 1954).

139. To Don José Joaquín de Arrillaga

In compliance with Your Grace's instructions of October 28, I beg to inform you that in all the missions of this New California, with the exception of one or two, open-air cemeteries[1] are to be found; but they are not located away from the places of habitation. They consist of a place enclosed by a palisade or an adobe wall, with a cross in the center. For the present there is no means of doing anything better.

On the assumption that one cemetery suffices for each mission, with later extensions as the needs of the settlement arise, the missions themselves, or each by itself, will set aside its own, at any distance that is required from the place of habitation.

The two pueblos for people *de razón*, as a rule, in each case carry their dead to the mission that is near them. The presidios sometimes do the same, and sometimes they bury their dead in their churches. It is in the church, as a rule, that those who are not Indians wish to be buried, and there is much trouble with the relatives of deceased persons before they agree to a burial in the cemetery.

In the Presidio of San Diego the cemetery is at the side of the church (it is different in others) and the commandant has imposed on the members of the presidio there the good custom that when they die they are to be buried there.

Your Grace will understand, as I do, that there are many reasons why it is convenient, and even necessary, that there should be a cemetery in every pueblo and presidio inasmuch as all of them are at a distance from the missions. The different commandants will advise Your Grace regarding the best way to lay them out.

My attitude is: Whatever Your Grace decides is what I want to do.

May God Our Lord keep Your Grace for many years in His holy grace.

San Carlos Mission,
December 20, 1792.

[1] On March 27, 1789 the King issued an order that all settlements should provide cemeteries at some distance from human habitations, as a precaution against epidemics. See *Provincial State Papers,* vol. 10, pp. 411-413, State Archives, Sacramento, California. (These papers are certified copies, not originals). In accordance with the royal decree, and as part of his very extensive program of social and hygienic reform, the viceroy had issued orders in regard to cemeteries, requiring that in future they be placed outside city limits. As this letter indicates, there was a prevalent custom of burying the dead beneath the floor of the church.

140. To Don José Joaquín de Arrillaga

I wish to acknowledge the copies that Your Grace sent me under date of October 27, last. [I am referring to] the orders and ordinances issued by His Excellency in regard to the skilled workers who are sent to these missions with the object of teaching their craft to the natives there.

I have already found out all I need to know on the matter from similar copies which Your Grace sent to the commandant of the Presidio at Monterey, for he had already informed me. He later forwarded me an official letter and gave me a list of the skilled workers attached to that presidio.

I take for granted that the commandant in question will forward you my reply, and the list of assignments. Notwithstanding this, in order to obey Your Grace as literally as I can, I shall repeat here certain points in my answer, and, as you expressed the wish, I shall add others which may prove useful to you in achieving the laudable purpose in mind.

The master stone-cutter and mason and the foreman who were assigned to this mission have come, the one arriving yesterday and the other the day before. The master blacksmith, who is going to San Francisco, and the master millwright who is going to Santa Clara, have not yet left the presidio.

Your Grace will notice that three of the artisans are in the category of officials, for they must all be masters capable of teaching their craft perfectly. It should be further noted that although the King is supplying the apparatus they need, some of them have none. In the case of the carpenter, who has been working at the mission since the beginning of this year, not a single implement has been paid for out of the royal treasury.

I have not given any assignment to the tailors principally because, judging by what I have seen and heard, they are not what we are looking for. Furthermore, there is no need of that craft at the missions, and there is not enough work to justify conducting courses in it. Neither at the present time nor for some years to come are there prospects that the sales will justify the expense involved; and with such expenditure it would be possible to find something just as important, and more easy to attain.

The little that the Indians would be able to pick up they would quickly forget through lack of practice in it. Consequently, we will not be making any progress for the future, for a time when, no doubt, this craft will be as useful as the others.

At the present time almost everyone is his own tailor, so scanty and so poor are the clothes they wear. This, more or less, is the case too at the presidios. In addition I do not regard it as best to send the Indians there, because there is no priest there, and because the soldiers of the presidio use them for work around the house. And not only do they not acquire the training that they are supposed to, but they lose the greater part of what they had acquired in religion.

Despie the fact that this is true, it may be necessary and opportune to look with favor on the royal privilege as a benefit to the country.

If you think it advisable, Your Grace may request two or more tailors who are men of good conduct, and suitable for teaching. To them could be assigned a number of missions and a group of boys, on the understanding that they are to travel and move from one mission to another, bringing their apprentices with them.

In this way, among all the missions which may be allocated to each master, instruction will continue with but little interruption; and the Indians will acquire sufficient knowledge so that, with care, judgment, and the industry of the missionaries, they will be able to exercise their craft, each in his own mission, and to ensure that they will continue instructing others in turn in their craft.

A few days ago, through my efforts, Antonio Domingo Henríquez arrived here from San Diego. He brought his wife, an Indian woman from San Diego. After getting married he succeeded in overcoming a vice for which he was well known—drinking.

In all the missions down south, as far as and including San Luis Obispo, he has made spinning-wheels, warping frames, combs, looms, and all the instruments of the craft with the exception of the cards. He has taught how to card, to spin, and to weave various quantities of wool, blankets, Franciscan coarse cloth (with which some Franciscans have already clothed themselves)—all of them finely woven. In San Gabriel and in San Luis he taught them to weave cotton shirting as well. He says that he will also give instructions in weaving full-width cloth, such as baize, and closely woven woollen material, and that it is very easy to give instruction in this process to those who have learned the narrow loom.

In view of this, should it appear desirable to Your Grace, this Henríquez could be hired in these missions in which this instruction is not given, and perhaps another equally gifted, or one with a knowledge of full-width textiles for the other missions, bringing two or three well furnished looms for the purpose, and some indigo for the baize. In this way the expenses of other weavers and workers would be saved.

It would be very helpful, however, if a master fuller would come for the final finishing of the coarse wool,[1] the baize, and the closely-woven goods, in case it should be decided to make some.

Having carried out in this manner the orders of Your Grace, I place myself once more in readiness to carry out any others you may give, and I pray that God Our Lord may keep Your Grace for many years in His holy grace.

San Carlos Mission,
December 21, 1792.

[1] Vancouver visited the two missions, San Francisco and Santa Clara, that year. He inspected cloth woven by the Indians of San Francisco and pronounced it "by no means despicable, and had it received the advantage of fulling, would have been very decent sort of clothing." Of the work of the Indians at Santa Clara he reported that "some of their woollen manufactures surpassed those we had before seen, and wanted only the operation of fulling, with which the fathers were unacquainted, to make them very decent blankets." See Webb, *op. cit.,* p. 209.

141. To Fray Tomás Pangua

I beg Your Reverence's holy blessing. I have already sent Your Reverence my congratulations on your appointment as prelate, although at the time I did not know your identity. I took it for granted that the most worthy subject would be chosen. Now I renew my congratulations, for I believed all along that Your Reverence would have to be the person. May God who has conferred this office add your name to the glorious list of holy guardians, and may He grant you all success and every blessing.

Would that I were Your Reverence's most worthy subject! This I am not; but may Your Reverence make and unmake me completely, just as you wish; and I trust in God, and with His help I promise to prove myself your devoted subject.

From July up to the present, eleven vessels have anchored in this port. Six of them have spent many days here, three Spanish and three English. They accept all kinds of attention from us; but that leaves us scarcely any time for other duties. At all hours of the day, and sometimes at night, we find ourselves surrounded by Englishmen. We give them all the attention and service possible, and they evidently appear grateful.[1] But there can be no doubt about this, that they have enjoyed it almost to extremes.

Their commandant, Señor Vancouver, has sent a magnificent gift, to be divided equally between the presidio, the mission, and Soledad. If I have time, I shall send you a note of the amount that fell to this mission of San Carlos,[2] and from that it will be easy to reckon the total.

It is now several days since Reverend Father Fray Mariano Rubí came here to recuperate, under the care of the presidio surgeon, from various ailments. A little while earlier Father Gili was here to take treatments, and from what I hear the physician say about them, both are seriously sick.

In view of Father Rubí's long sojourn here, when Father García had come here for a few days, he wished to return to San Antonio. I told him, instead, to stay with Father Gili at Soledad until Father Rubí could go there.

The commissioners for the affair at Santa Clara have not appeared, nor have they written to me for a long time. Some say that Señor Zúñiga will soon travel overland to embark at Loreto to take over his new assignment.

By this time there must be many serious problems submitted by me still awaiting a decision at the college. A decision in regard to them would bring inexpressible relief to me. I am looking forward to this favor from Your Reverence as soon as your grave occupations permit it.

For the moment no other matter of importance occurs to me, and I am afraid it may be because the seamen do not allow me time even to think. But neither they nor the whole world will ever be able to prevent me from carrying out with extreme care not only the orders, but even the suggestions, of Your Reverence.

May God Our Lord keep Your Reverence for many years in His holy grace.

San Carlos Mission,
December 23, 1792.

[1] The following are Vancouver's impressions and recollections of the reception he was given:

Our reception at the mission Carmel could not fail to convince us of the joy and satisfaction we communicated to the worthy and reverend fathers, who in return made

the most hospitable offers of every refreshment their homely abode afforded. On our
arrival at the entrance to the Mission the bells were rung, and the Rev. Fermin de
Lasuén, father president of the missionaries of the order of St. Francis in New Albion
[the name which Vancouver persistently applies to California to emphasize the visit
of Drake to its shores] together with the fathers of this mission came out to meet us,
and conduct us to the principal residence of the father president. This person was
about seventy-two years of age [he was actually but fifty-six], whose gentle manners,
united to a most venerable and placid countenance, indicated that tranquilized state
of mind that fitted him in an eminent degree for presiding over so benevolent an
institution. Wilbur, *op. cit.* pp. 63-64.
2 For the items received, see Letter No. 190 *infra.*

142. To Don Pablo Soler

In view of the length of time that the Reverend Father Fray Rubí
has been taking treatment and has been absent from his mission, I feel
obliged to ask Your Honor whether you consider that his illness will
render him incapable of carrying out the particular duties of his ministry,
or make them very difficult for him.

Your Honor knows that in order to replace him and to return him
to Mexico, the permission of the central government is needed; and in
order to avoid as far as possible the delay involved in making application
at such a distance, I find it necessary to make this representation so that
I may be able to give competent advice to the College of San Fernando
in a message to be sent by the boats which are about to leave this port
for San Blas.

I place myself at the service of Your Honor, and pray that God Our
Lord, etc., I kiss the hand of Your Honor.

Your devoted and faithful servant.

San Carlos Mission,
January 3, 1793.

143. To Fray Tomás Pangua

May I have Your Reverence's holy blessing, for I wish to inform you
that Doctor Don José Moziño, the naturalist in the expedition of Señor
Quadra, and a very devoted friend of our colleges, assures me that he
intends to make one or more visits to our College of San Fernando.

In that case, the least I can say is that he is deserving of every courtesy so that we may express our gratitude for the many very appreciated
favors which he extended to us at Monterey.

What he will report regarding these parts, and also regarding the
condition of the Reverend Father Rubí, will give Your Reverence as

clear a picture of what you wish to know as if you were yourself a witness.

With all respect and devotion I place myself entirely at the service of Your Reverence, and I pray that God Our Lord may keep you for many years in His holy grace.

San Carlos Mission,
January 6, 1793.

144. To Fray Tomás Pangua

Begging Your Reverence's holy blessing, I wish to inform you that in view of the protracted illness of Father Rubí I wrote in the following vein to the surgeon of the neighboring presidio:

[Here follows the full text of Letter No. 142 above, dated January 3, 1793, and addressed to Don Pablo Soler.]

I am sending Your Reverence the original report of the medical adviser, and I am adding for your information that Doctor Don José Moziño, naturalist of the expedition of Señor Quadra, is of the same opinion. Both agree that with care and medicine (which are lacking here, but not in Mexico or outside this province), this religious would be better in two months.

But he cannot leave here. He is not to embark—these are the words of this very harsh decree; and now there is no governor to give him a sympathetic ear.

May they yield in this, for God's sake, as soon as possible, for reasons present in this case, and for other very practical ones of the same order. What I mean is this: This ordinance should be revoked or modified. Up to the present there is no reasonable man who has heard it who does not disapprove of it.

Your Reverence will please pardon me. The ships do not permit time for more. Once again I place myself at the service of Your Reverence, and I pray that God Our Lord may keep you many years in His holy grace.

San Carlos,
January 6, 1793.

145. To Don José Argüello

The Reverend Father Fray Mariano Rubí, by reason of his infirmities, finds himself entirely unfitted for the duties of missionary in these parts.

And even if he were assigned as a supernumerary to one of the missions, he runs the risk, if he does not leave the land, of becoming worse and of being unfitted for any kind of work.

I believe this is the view of the surgeon, Don Pablo Soler, who is his attendant physician.

Keeping this in mind, and also the fact that at Mission Soledad, which was attended by this Father, I have already assigned another religious who is able to take care of the duties there, I beg Your Honor to permit the above-mentioned Father Rubí to embark in one of the ships which are about to sail from this port for San Blas.

May God Our Lord keep Your Honor for many years in His holy grace.

San Carlos Mission,
January 9, 1793.

Although the mere statement of Your Reverence as to the serious illness of Father Rubí is sufficient to satisfy me, however, since I have to give a report to the government, I hope Your Reverence will be so kind as to forward me a certificate from the physician so that, in virtue of it, I may approve of the embarkation, and rely on the document as my warrant for approving.

May God keep Your Reverence etc.

Monterey,
January 10, 1793.
José Argüello.

By courtesy of the same soldier who has delivered me the official letter of Your Honor asking me for a certificate from the physician regarding the seriousness of the illness which obliges me to take measures for the embarkation of the Reverend Father Fray Mariano Rubí, I am sending a request to the physician in question so that he may forward it to Your Honor.

May God Our Lord keep Your Honor many years in His holy grace.

San Carlos Mission,
January 10, 1793.

To Don Pablo Soler

I have just received an official letter from the commandant of this presidio, asking me for a certificate from Your Honor as to the seriousness of the sickness of Reverend Father Rubí for by reason of it I am asking that the Father in question may embark.

I most respectfully ask Your Honor if you will kindly put this in writing, have it sent to the official above mentioned, and be gracious enough in due time to advise me of the result (which I presume will be favorable), so that I may make the necessary arrangements with the naval personnel and reduce the requirements to a minimum so that we may reap the most benefit.

I am at the service of Your Honor, and I pray that God Our Lord may keep you many years in His holy grace.

(no date)

Copy of the Certificate:

Don Pablo Soler, surgeon approved by the Royal College of Surgeons of Barcelona, attached to the Royal Navy and residing at this Presidio of Monterey.

I hereby certify that Reverend Father Fray Mariano Rubí, missionary apostolic, has been suffering from an infirmity which has grown worse and for which a protracted treatment is necessary; and even if that were available here, in my opinion the aforesaid Father would be much exposed to the danger of further relapses (thereby becoming a greater burden) by reason of the indispensable ministerial duties of the Father in question—duties which aggravate the habitual infirmities from which he suffers. Wherefore, in good faith, I hereby testify to the above to promote objectives which I would favor.

Monterey,
January 10, 1793,
Pablo Soler.

In virtue of the above certificate the commandant at Monterey gave his permission so that the religious above mentioned may embark; and he took with him the original of the document so that he may present it to whom it may concern.

San Carlos Mission,
January 11, 1793,
Lasuén.

This mission provides the food for the missionaries who embark here. It supports those who come and go during the long intervals they spend here, and it takes care of the sick until they get better. I beg (if Your Reverence approves) that this be kept in mind when surcharges are made to the missions for expenses which are occasionally incurred in the coming and going of religious.

146. Memorandum

The above official letter is proof of the government's permission; and I, the undersigned, President of these Missions of New California, have requested it so that the aforesaid religious may embark. The latter, in turn, has repeatedly requested me to give him in addition my permission and blessing so that he may return to the Apostolic College of *Propaganda Fide* of San Fernando of Mexico.

Mission of San Carlos of Monterey,
January 11, 1793.

147. To Fray Tomás Pangua

I beg Your Reverence's holy blessing and, now that the ships happen to be delayed, I take the opportunity to inform you that we have all come to realize more and more how serious is the condition of Father Rubí and how utterly impossible it is for him to minister at any mission. For this reason, since he is sick and incapable of any service, I found it necessary to assign him to one of them as supernumerary.

The King grants nothing towards his support as long as he is in that capacity; and he would do nothing here except expose himself, so the physicians think, to the danger of getting worse, of dying, or of becoming entirely incapacitated, before another opportunity of embarking would arrive. Therefore, regarding myself as bound to do for this religious what I would wish my superior to do for me, I made it my business to request permission for him to sail; but I set out with more hope of doing my duty than of obtaining my objective.

It was God's will, however, that the permission of the commandant of the Presidio of Monterey should be forthcoming; and tomorrow, with God's help, our misionary will go aboard the frigate *Aránzazu*. The commander, Don Jacinto Caamaño, with the approval of his superior, Don Juan Francisco Quadra, has graciously offered to transport him with all possible care and comfort.

In all this I have been solicitous not only for the approval but also the complete satisfaction of Your Reverence, for my objective is that you may issue your instructions with the certainty that they will be carried out to the letter by me.

May God Our Lord keep Your Reverence for many years in His holy grace.

San Carlos Mission,
January 11, 1793.

P. S.

I beg Your Reverence (if it is possible) to forward, for the use of this mission, the work entitled *El Sacerdote Santificado.*

148. To Don José Joaquín Arrillaga

I beg to inform Your Honor that when I became aware, from the certificate of Don Pablo Soler, surgeon of the Presidio of Monterey, that the illness of the Reverend Father Fray Mariano Rubí, formerly minister of Soledad Mission, has made him entirely incapable of exercising his ministry in these parts, I gave him my permission to embark; and for the same purpose I sought and obtained the permission of Lieutenant Don José Argüello, commandant of the above presidio.

Thereupon the Father in question took ship for San Blas on his way to our College of San Fernando in Mexico, and in his place I appointed the Reverend Father Fray Diego García as minister of that mission.

May God Our Lord keep you many years in His holy grace.

Santa Clara Mission,
January 31, 1793.

149. To Fray Tomás Pangua

With Your Reverence's blessing I now report that as the Spanish and English ships have already sailed from Monterey, it has become possible for me to proceed to the missions in the north, but with great difficulty, however, because of the very bad roads.

When I had spent a few days at Santa Clara, I received a letter from Reverend Father Gili informing me that he had gone to Carmel, the mission of San Carlos, to recuperate, because his attacks had begun to recur, and because in his mission of Soledad he was already becoming apprehensive because of the climate.

This made me sad; and I felt more sorry still for the fact that his sickness is always of a nature that makes it necessary for him to leave the mission to which he is assigned, even when there is at no great distance a physician whom he could consult and from whom he could obtain medicine by merely writing.

I told him this in my reply; and because I have to see to it that no missionary is alone very long in any mission, I had to know as soon as possible whether or not he had it in mind to return to Soledad. If the state of his health makes him doubt about what he should do, I am instructing him to consult with his physician in regard to it, and to inform me immediately about his decision.

My view, which I should not fail to express, esteemed Father, is this: This religious is not fitted for that, or any other mission; neither his mind nor his spirit is inclined to this kind of work; they are not fitted for it, according to what I have seen and found out in the short time he has been in this work. It is possible that this is better understood at the college than here.

Keeping this in mind, and also the fact that he becomes ill far too frequently, Your Reverence might, if you think fit, obtain for him the permission of the Viceroy, and also grant him your own, so that he may retire.

This is what it will finally have to come to, anyway, for it is my belief that no sooner will a ship arrive than he will apply for it. Furthermore, when Father Rubí was taking treatments at Carmel, shortly after Father Gili had been there for the same purpose, the surgeon told me that both of them were really serious.

I would have already appointed Father Sánchez to Soledad, but I have to observe the precautions I mentioned before I proceed, for they are necessary, and many others, too, if we are to avoid, or at least lessen, the critical comments of our people. I will assign him as soon as I have a reply from the sick man and from the surgeon, to whom I also wrote; and I presume that one or the other, or perhaps both of them, may consider the climate of Soledad as bad for what is wrong with him. In that case I will think over what assignment to give to Father Gili.

Since the day before yesterday I have known the very sad news that since the end or the middle of last month Father Paterna has been very sick, and that since the beginning of this month he has become worse; and there was question of giving him the Last Sacraments.

Considering his advanced age, his death may be feared. May God's will be done; and if He takes him to Himself, in the short time I have had to give consideration to the case, it seems to me that I shall have to assign Father Gili to San Luis with Father Giribet, and Father Tapis to Santa Barbara with Father Fray José Miguel. I have not given expression to this thought beyond what I have written here, and I shall not, unless I am obliged to do so.

SAN GABRIEL MISSION

Lasuén's first assignment in California
as it appears today

This is clear proof that there is a pressing need that religious should come from the college to these missions as soon as it can be arranged; as soon as possible. There is further reason why the need is pressing. There is the very sickly and precarious condition of Father Peña; the advanced age of Father Cruzado; the recurrent attacks of his companion, Father Sánchez; the depression and hypochondria of Father Oramas which necessarily restrict him to the status and duties of a supernumerary; the exhaustion and weariness of Father Pieras; and whatever Your Reverences think is the matter with Father Lasuén.

It is known that Señor Arrillaga, Captain of Loreto and Interim Governor, is coming by road to conclude the adjustment of accounts begun by the late Señor Romeu. It is known, too, that the Reverend Father Loriente and Señor Zúñiga will come up in March or April to bring the Santa Clara affair to an end. May God be with us, and look on us with pity.

In these recent days there has been a rumor, based on the stories of the Indians of the other side of this port, that the English are planning a settlement, and that they have already made a settlement in the neighboring port of Bodega.[1]

There is no further news; and there will never be a change in my humble submission and ready obedience to the orders of Your Reverence, nor in my solicitude to pray that God Our Saviour may keep Your Reverence many years in His holy grace.

San Francisco Mission,
February 22, 1793.

[1] Bodega Bay is a rather open roadstead on the California coast north of San Francisco, near the junction of the present Marin and Sonoma counties. The English did not settle there; but twenty years later the Russians settled there and at Fort Ross, a little further to the north.

150. To Fray Tomás Pangua

I beg Your Reverence's holy blessing. Last evening I received a letter from the Reverend Father Fray José Miguel with the sad news, which I am imparting to Your Reverence, that on the thirteenth of this month, at three in the afternoon, the Reverend Father Fray Antonio Paterna,[1] Apostolic Preacher, died at Mission Santa Barbara, which he had founded in his old age, after having already founded San Gabriel Mission. He received the Last Sacraments devoutly, assisted by the above-mentioned Father Miguel, and Fathers Dumetz and Arroita.

Through all these years he acquitted himself as a good old man, and until the time of his death worked like a robust young man. In the judgment of all, he was outstanding for zeal in the performance of his apostolic duties.

In addition to this, I also received some further news. It reached me by word of mouth only, and so far I do not credit it. It is to the effect that Father Gili is already back at his Mission of Soledad, completely restored to health.

Since I have doubts about this, as I mentioned, and I am preoccupied with other cares, I am going to write to Father Sánchez to ask him, provided the weather and the roads permit, to make the journey from Santa Clara to Monterey and there to find out the condition and state of mind of Father Gili. And if he should need or desire a change of climate, or if he has not the strength to take care of Soledad, I am asking Father Sánchez himself to stay there. Father Gili would then go to San Luis, and Father Tapis to Santa Barbara.

But if he should find that Father Gili is content at Soledad and reconciled to it (I do not believe this can last long), he should in that case leave him there and say nothing further, but he himself should proceed to Santa Barbara as minister.

The most pressing need at the moment is the one I mentioned to Your Reverence in my letter of the twenty-second of the present month. I hope that Your Reverence will take care of it, that you will commend me to God, and that you will forward me your instructions so that I may submit to them, as is my duty.

May God Our Lord keep Your Reverence for many years in His holy grace.

Mission San Francisco,
February 24, 1793.

[1] He was a native of Seville, and was about seventy-two years of age at the time of his death. He had been in California since 1771.

151. To Fray Tomás Pangua

With a request for the blessing of Your Reverence, I wish to acknowledge the receipt of your letter of last July 17.

The displeasure of His Majesty (of which Your Reverence informs me) occasioned by the bad behavior of certain members of the missionary apostolic colleges, and the just annoyance and well-merited warnings of our Most Reverend Father Commissary General, together with all that they imply, have caused me sorrow and regret in keeping with the profound respect I profess for my King and my higher superior.

Inspired by this, I venture to assure Your Reverence that with the help of God, and as far as it rests with me as President of these Missions entrusted to our college, I will take means (as I did up to the present and, if possible, will take more efficacious ones) so that neither His Majesty nor the Most Reverend Father Superior, nor Your Reverence, shall have occasion for the least anxiety, but will find much to approve and to be pleased with.

With this in mind, I shall make a copy of your letter and send it as a circular to all the missionaries under me. Most of them, almost all of them (if I may presume your permission to say so) will be utterly astonished, thinking that all these distressing complaints and dreadful offenses should be laid at the door of our community when they can be attributed to but three or at the most four individual missionaries in these settlements. But in regard to all the others we have, by the mercy of God, maintained the same method of organization, the same devotion to duty, and the same observance of rules which, not so long ago, the King our Sovereign was pleased to approve (as he informs us), and to command that his thanks be extended to us in his name.

I shall therefore tell them, for I am taking it for granted, that Your Reverence will avail yourself of the opportunity to acquaint the Very Reverend Superior with so unusual and so noteworthy an event. It is also my ardent hope that you will facilitate the withdrawal of the religious of whom I spoke in another letter.

I shall continue, with the help of God, to watch over all entrusted to my care. I will keep you informed about what happens; and I expect with confidence that, aided by the apt and timely ordinances of Your Reverence which will be carried out to the best of my ability, both punctually and scrupulously, we your subjects will do all that is required of us to the complete and unqualified satisfaction of our superiors. This is what I desire, and also that God Our Lord may keep Your Reverence for many years in His holy grace.

San Francisco Mission,
February 27, 1793.

152. To Don Pedro de Nava

In accordance with the order of March 14, 1789, I am forwarding to Your Lordship the enclosed Report of the spiritual state of these missions at the end of December of last year.

It is always my pleasure, Sir, to keep in mind sentiments of most humble submission to the higher orders of Your Lordship, and to be solicitous to pray that God Our Lord may keep you many years in His holy grace.

Mission San Francisco,
March 6, 1793.

Report of the spiritual state of the missions of Upper California at the end of the year 1792, forwarded to Brigadier Pedro de Nava, Commandant General of the Internal Provinces of New Spain.

Baptisms 15,732
Marriages 3,276
Deaths 5,313
Number living 9,031

Of these (the number living), the report for those aged five or six years and over is the same as for the year 1790 which I forwarded to Señor Loyola on February 28, 1791.

During the period between February 28, 1791, and this date, 1,563 have been confirmed, bringing the total of all those confirmed in these mission districts to 11,201.

Mission San Francisco,
March 6, 1793.

153. To Fray Tomás Pangua

With the blessing of Your Reverence, I beg to remind you that in my letter of the twenty-fourth of last month I mentioned that I did not think that Father Gili was returning to his mission of Soledad. He was there, however, but it was only for a few hours, and merely to let Father García have a piece of his mind, and to get the same in return. There was nothing more than that; a great deal of loud talk—and it grew louder until the prompt return of Father Gili to San Carlos.

Arriving there, he found my letter, the one I wrote you about. The reply I am enclosing with the letter of the surgeon is the one he sent— and what a reply at a time when there is such a scarcity of missionaries!

The Father has at last declared openly what he is suffering from. It is simply an aversion for living in this country; and for this there is no remedy but to remove him from it; and, as Your Reverence knows very well, it is very important to take this step as soon as possible. In the meantime I shall see how, with God's help, I can deal with him by means of persuasion and kindness, for there is no other course to take.

Our ministry is performed before the public gaze; everyone knows us, and if you were to shout in San Francisco the echo would quickly be heard in San Diego.

Elsewhere when the failings of a religious become known, the latter simply loses ground; here one might say he loses everything. Keeping this firmly in mind I am making a systematic study so as to forestall at all costs any reason for a loss of that kind; and if I cannot do more, I will at least send timely recommendations to the college that should conduce to that end.

I have already written him that what he has told me about the attacks which he suffers, and what the surgeon has told me, are more grounds than I need for prescribing a change of climate for him; but that if he thinks it over carefully he will see that if he is to be excused from serving at Soledad Mission as well as from the others, something more is needed than my acquiescence. I pointed out that the present emergency does not allow him a liberty of that kind, nor does it allow me the right to acquiesce; that it is, instead, an indication that at the present time both are opposed to reason and to the manifold disposition of Divine Providence, and that we should submit to them, as we are in duty bound, and that we should reconcile with them, as best we can, the relief from the sufferings of which he complains, and which I desire no less than he.

I further pointed out that I had kept these objectives in mind, and in that letter made known my decision that in the meantime he should go to San Luis Mission, and that there he should be the companion of Father Giribet, helping him to the best of his ability. I further added that this was the way in which he could most honorably bring about his return to the college, and that I would direct my best efforts, and all the diligence he requested, in order to secure that objective.

In carrying out this promise there is no one who can be more helpful to me than Your Reverence. To carry it out is what I am attempting and so I ask you, for the love of God, to facilitate as quickly as you can the efforts of this religious to obtain the objective he so ardently desires. In the meantime, however, it is very important that he should undertake the office of which I spoke to him and which I assigned him, for on the one hand it is very necessary and urgent, and on the other I am entirely convinced that he can fill it.

Furthermore, as regards the last letter which I received from Your Reverence in which you enclosed a letter from the Most Reverend Father Commissary General in which he was very indignant with some of his subjects because of complaints against them which he had received from the King himself, I trust he will recognize that I make it my aim not only to fulfill my duty, but also to promote his welfare.

Father Sánchez accepts in a religious spirit his assignment to Soledad, but he dislikes very much having to associate with Father García. I am not surprised at this, because the odd escapades of this Andalusian, which have become public only too frequently, put everyone on his guard. I wrote to Father Pablo, the predecessor of Your Reverence, about the most conspicuous of them; I found myself compelled to do so. I have written to Father Sánchez asking him to bear with whatever inconvenience or unpleasantness there may be during the short interval until, please God, we see one another in his mission; and then, with God's help, I shall take what means are feasible to find a remedy.

I have written to Father Oramas that he should strive not to inconvenience him, taking into account his disabilities, and that he should keep them in mind when he is waiting on him; and I shall take cognizance of his needs, too, for the same Divine Providence who has so altered the conditions under which we live by reducing the missionaries to such straits can also so change his temperament and mind, can so remake him in body and soul that he can yet take charge of some mission. And I ask that he advise me so that I may be guided by it.

If this should come to pass, we have filled the vacancy at San Luis Mission; but if Father Gili leaves, I don't know how we can do it. And even if he goes there, I have little hope that he will remain or serve.

I see clearly that the Mission of Santa Barbara, with the added burden of the presidio, feels under no obligation to accommodate itself to Father Fray Cristóbal.

Several days have passed since I wrote the above, and the letter is not yet finished, for I was awaiting the reply from Father Gili, and it has not yet come. The day for the arrival of the monthly mail is approaching, and I have to seal this. With God's help I shall send you word about the outcome, but for the moment I have nothing further to say.

Accompanying this is a Report on the missions up to the end of last year, and a copy of the Report for the two years ended which I had already sent to the Commandant General, in accordance with what was stipulated in the year 1788.

I most humbly place myself at the service of Your Reverence, and pray that God Our Lord may keep you for many years in His holy grace.

San Francisco Mission,
March 30, 1793.

154. To Don José Joaquín de Arrillaga

I thank Your Grace for granting my request to permit the master weaver, Antonio Domingo Henríquez, to be included in the number of artisans, as you inform me in your esteemed letter of the twenty-eighth of last month.

Your Grace further informs me in the same letter that you have authorized Don José Argüello to stipulate a just salary to be paid to the above-mentioned Henríquez, after he has consulted me. In accordance with this, the officer in question has written me that it seems to him that he should be awarded the sum enjoyed by the master carpenter, José Antonio Ramírez, ten reales a day.

I am replying to him that I am in agreement with his opinion, but that if the interested party does not accept this wage on the ground that it is too small, I am of the opinion that it can be raised to twelve. He deserves all praise for the good name than he has earned in comparison with other craftsmen who receive a higher salary. The very useful instruction he gives in his art, the sole object of the liberal franchise given by the King, has not been equalled by any other, and has stood the test successfully in many missions.

To achieve this, it is obvious that he has had to bring into play an unusual amount of labor, application, and efficiency, and that he makes his efforts fruitful at the cost of much patience with the Indians, accommodating himself to them, and overlooking their faults.

His ingenuity, too, is outstanding, bringing big returns and great saving, for he has aligned, adjusted, and put in running order the spinning wheels and looms with all their parts needed in his art, with the exception of the cards.

This is the way I put it to the lieutenant, Don José Argüello, and thus I carry out, as best I can, the order of Your Grace. The official in question will report to you what I have done, and what the result was, and Your Honor will decide as you deem most fitting.

May God Our Lord keep Your Grace for many years in His holy grace.

Santa Clara Mission,
April 20, 1793.

155. To Don José Joaquín de Arrillaga

On the day following the receipt of the copy of the royal cedula which Your Grace sent me with your official letter of the first instant, we carried out here at Mission Santa Clara the royal will of our sovereign by celebrating a Mass of Thanksgiving for the happy delivery of his august spouse,[1] our Lady the Queen.

With this same object in mind I have already sent the notice, as Your Grace requests, to the other missions, San Francisco and Santa Cruz, taking advantage of a favorable opportunity which arose. When the same happens as regards the others, with God's help, I shall take the same action.

May God Our Lord keep Your Grace for many years in His holy grace.

Santa Clara,
April 22, 1793.

P. S.

The notification which is mentioned here, and which I promise to send to the remaining missions, I am sending by a mail which, I have just learned, is leaving for Monterey from this Mission of Santa Clara today, the twenty-fifth of the above-mentioned month and year.

[1] Better known, perhaps, as Maria Luisa of Parma, the frivolous wife of the easygoing, mediocre Carlos IV.

156. To Fray Tomás Pangua

Begging Your Reverence's blessing, I wish to inform you that I have just learned that Father Sánchez is at Soledad, Father Tapis at Santa Barbara, and Father Gili at San Luis. And in case something unforeseen should arise in regard to the latter, Father Oramas has stated in his reply that he is prepared to take care of the matter. Thanks be to God.

Señor Arrillaga is in San Diego. I have received a number of letters from him, all very cordial and confiding. Thanks be to God.

There is a report that Señor Zúñiga will arrive shortly at Monterey, and the Father President of the Dominicans writes me that the Viceroy has again ordered that the inquiry into the sad affair at this mission be instituted promptly, and that because Father Loriente is indisposed he has substituted Father Abada. The latter I do not know, not even by letter. May God in His infinite mercy see us safe through this dreadful misfortune.

God willing, I intend to spend this coming week at the neighboring mission of Santa Cruz, and I shall stay in that vicinity so that I can give what assistance I can, should it be necessary or helpful.

Father Gili asks me once more to bring about his return to the college, and to expedite it. I have already explained to Your Reverence that it is fitting and very desirable that he be granted his request.

I place myself once more at the service of Your Reverence to carry out your orders most humbly and gladly. And I pray that God Our Lord may keep you for many years in His holy grace.

Santa Clara,
April 26, 1793.

157. To Don José Joaquín de Arrillaga

In accordance with the instructions of Your Grace I have lost no time in enclosing herewith the Reports on the status of the thirteen missions under my control at the end of last year.

They include all that Your Grace requires from me, as well as anything I can contribute to the carrying out of the ordinance which the Most Excellent Viceroy informs me, under date of December 3 last, he has forwarded to Your Grace for the tabulation of a General Status of the presidios, missions, and pueblos, including the entire population both *de razón* and neophytes, the cattle, and the crops.

For this purpose, His Excellency asked me to co-operate with Your Grace by supplying any information you seek. This I have now done; and this is, and I trust always will be, my way of responding to the higher orders of His Excellency and of Your Grace.

May God Our Lord keep Your Grace for many years in His holy grace.

San Carlos Mission,
June 12, 1793.

158. To Don José Joaquín de Arrillaga

I beg to acknowledge your official letter of the first of this month, enclosing four copies of the royal cedula giving rules for the re-establishment of the office of Commandant General as distinct and independent, and leaving the unit made up of the Californias attached to the Viceroyalty of Mexico. I note, too, that it specifies the form of assent for the espousals and marriages of minors, and the respective licenses which must be furnished, and that there are regulations in regard to the military, to members of universities and conciliar seminaries,[1] houses and colleges for both sexes which are subject to the royal protection and royal patronage, and to the foundation of a College for American Nobles in the city of Granada.

Of all of this I shall make due and fitting use, subject to the instructions of Your Grace.

May God Our Lord keep Your Grace for many years in His holy grace.

San Carlos Mission,
June 12, 1793.

¹ Colleges for the training of candidates for the priesthood established and conducted in accordance with the decrees of the Council of Trent.

159. To Don José Joaquín de Arrillaga

I have received the Proclamation which Your Grace sent me with your letter of the thirty-first of last month, in which you instruct me to use all possible means to prevent fires which occur year by year and cause so much damage in this country.

Two days ago, after publishing it here, I sent it to Santa Clara Mission with a circular of my own for the other two missions in the north. I sent instructions that in each of the three a copy should be made, and be placed in the archives, so that it can be brought to the attention of the public each year, as Your Grace orders.

In due time I shall do the same for the other missions (God willing).

Every possible effort has been made in all of them, and every precaution taken, to remedy this very grave situation. This will be continued from now on, and by reason of Your Grace's timely foresight there is greater hope that the effect that is sought will be achieved.

The ministers of the missions through which Your Grace has passed must have felt deeply obligated to you, seeing that you were so gracious as personally to instruct the Indians in their obligation to abstain from this kind of misdemeanor, and for having warned them of the penalties if they fail to do so.

An exhortation of this kind, without doubt, will add much force to those we give, and perhaps will succeed in making them efficacious.

I take this opportunity to thank Your Grace for your resolve to extend the same favor to the remaining missions; and together with their ministers I place myself once more at your service.

May God Our Lord keep Your Grace for many years in His holy grace.

San Carlos Mission,
June 12, 1793.

160. To Fray Tomás Pangua

I ask Your Reverence's holy blessing, and beg to inform you that I spent the entire month of May at Santa Cruz awaiting the commissioners who are to inquire into the problem at Santa Clara. Under pressure of urgent business I left on the fifth of this month for San Carlos Mission, without hearing any word about them.

That very day when on the way I met the mail, and then I learned that they were already on their way, but traveling slowly. I received your three letters, too, dated November 26th, January 27th, and February 26th last. Also, I received the new patent as President, and from the new Prefect the faculty to confirm, and the extension of each of these [faculties] to Fathers Dumetz and Peña, in case something should happen to me.

I am grateful to Your Reverence for your kindness, and in all sincerity I repeat that I place myself in complete accord with your dispositions in my regard. I wish to assure you that it is a matter of indifference to me whether I continue to hold either office, or relinquish both.

I have sent the information to Father Peña, and I am awaiting an opportunity to do the same for Father Dumetz.

As for myself, I hold the opinion that the decennial of the faculty for Confirmation should be reckoned from the date on which it was granted in Rome, namely, May 4, 1785. As Your Reverence is aware, five years and eight days passed before it was possible to use this faculty. I began to exercise it on July 14, 1790, and some people tell me that it is from that date that the ten years granted are to be reckoned. On the other hand (until Your Reverence or the Reverend Father Prefect tells me otherwise) I hold and shall continue to hold that May 4, 1795 is the specified and final day on which this particular faculty expires. Not much time is now left, and I have no doubt that our Father Prefect and Commissary will keep this well in mind.

From His Excellency the Viceroy I have received an order requiring me to forward to the governor of this province any information he asks of me, information for the drawing up of a General Status which he has ordered him to do.

The latter has asked me for the Annual Reports, and I am sending them to him by this mail. Seeing that the whole burden of my reply to the Viceroy consist in telling him that I have carried out his higher orders, I am sending it to His Excellency direct.

I have already sent to the missions of the north the patent Your Reverence sent us, enclosing the patent of the Most Reverend and Illustrious Commissary General of the Indies, and I am now going to do the same for those of the south.

Father Pieras has been here for more than a month to recuperate, and the improvement so far has been very little. He is talking of going to San Antonio tomorrow. However, keeping in mind how he fared in that climate in the past, and the opinion of the doctor that a place like that would be bad for his condition, we have decided that should there be a recurrence of his bad attacks he may go to San Luis, where he made a good recovery two years ago. I have arranged with Father Gili that he can go to San Antonio while Father Pieras stays with Father Giribet until it is possible to make other arrangements.

This Father Pieras has resolutely pleaded to return to the college. Then someone (I know not who) played a trick on him by sending him the permission to do so by a letter patent which had all the appearance of a genuine one. He took it to be a genuine one, and agreed to take his departure this year, only to discover that it was all a joke. He kept up hopes, nevertheless, because of the real severity of the attacks, which could be confirmed by the testimony of the surgeon. Then he learned recently from the frigate anchored in San Francisco on the twenty-first of this month under command of Don Sal Fidalgo that Reverend Father Fray Magín Catalá remains as chaplain at Nootka; and so he has despaired of ever going back, and is making the sacrifice as has been said.

Governor Arrillaga cannot be long in coming. I am awaiting him to bring to his attention the pass from the Viceroy in favor of Father Oramas before sending it to His Reverence. The commissioners may come with him.

Don Fidalgo is constantly inviting me to San Francisco. This new development gives me a chance to visit Santa Clara, which is close to it, at a very opportune time, and I feel much inclined to return by that route.

I am very sorry that there has been a delay in regard to the mission to Spain[1] because of the death of Reverend Father Fray Angel. I am glad that they are asking for, and hope to get, a large number of missionaries through the efforts of Reverend Fathers Arévalo and Calzada. May God bring them safely and quickly.

It is known for certain that the commandants of these presidios have been given special powers to permit retired soldiers and others to establish themselves in ranches all around, even as far as a radius of four leagues. In regard to this innovation there was nothing I could say or do, because I came to know of it privately only long after it had been published. Nobody, however, is going to prevent me from speaking to Your Reverence about what is on my mind. I would like to point out that we, in the missions nearest the presidios, have the extra burden of caring for them, and it is a very heavy burden. It is entirely unreasonable to add the extra burden of the ranches, and there will be many of them. Furthermore, ranches like these will frequently degenerate into rancherías or clearings ["rochelas"], with [not only] Christians but gentiles and other additional labors.

It may be that some opportunity will present itself to Your Reverence in which perchance this information may be of value and may lead to a more favorable consideration of the case.

With the deepest respect I place myself once more at the service of Your Reverence, and I pray that God Our Lord may keep you for many years in His holy grace.

San Carlos Mission,
June 25, 1793.

[1] When San Fernando College needed new missionaries it was the custom to send one or more of their members to Spain to visit different Franciscan houses so as to obtain recruits. Seminarians as well as priests could volunteer. Junipero Serra, the first president, was a priest when he came to the New World. Lasuén, his successor in office, was a seminarian, but was already a deacon.

161. To Fray José Loriente and to Don José de Zúñiga

I have been notified by my superior, Reverend Father Guardian of the Apostolic College of San Fernando, that Your Reverence and Your Honor are members of the commission set up by decree of His Excellency the Viceroy to receive all the evidence which Reverend Father Fray Tomás de la Peña can present anew in reply to the accusations which various Indians of Santa Clara preferred against him before Don Pedro Fages, former governor of this province.

So, seeing that Your Reverence and Your Honor find it necessary, in order to carry out your commission, that I should notify the aforesaid Father on the point, as you request and charge me to do in your letter of the sixth of this month, I on this day sent him instructions that he is to satisfy you both in all that you require, within the terms of your commission.

I feel impelled, however, to let you know that I never suspected that this would come to pass, for I did not have a shadow of a doubt that all the authorities were entirely satisfied, and that the religious was completely exonerated. This, it seemed to me, would be the decision of everyone who has studied the official letter of Señor Fages, the original of which I enclose, sent in reply to a letter of mine, a copy of which I enclose.[1] I shall be grateful if you will attach both of these documents to your report of the inquiry, and send me an official receipt for the former.

If I had not been misled, as I naturally was, by the reply just cited of this gentleman, I would have pursued the matter more closely until Father Peña had given the most elaborate proof of innocence that is now demanded of him. In this way it could have been possible to avoid a repetition of the previous publicity which was so embarrassing, and which prejudiced our good name. And as I see it, we need such a good name if we are to attain the success which God and the King expect of us in these lands.

In all humility I take this opportunity to request Your Reverence and Your Honor to avoid anything that may give rise to publicity, without at the same time avoiding anything pertaining to the work of the commission.

May God Our Lord keep Your Reverence and Your Honor for many years in His holy grace.

San Carlos Mission,
July 7, 1793.

[1] The earlier letter to which he refers is Letter No. *55 supra.* The official letter of Governor Fages which he sent in reply is as follows:
M. R. P. Presidente
Muy Señor Mio:
Con el debido respeto he leido el de V. R. de 21 del mes pasado cuyo contenido corrobora el concepto que me forme de las diligencias practicadas contra los Indios calumniadores del R. P. Fr. Tomás de la Peña; y por las que yo forme satisfice de la conducta de dicho Religioso, y asi conoceria V. R. viendome desistir de que lo separase V. R. del Ministerio de la Mision, y como quiera que asi lo manifiesto en el informe con que acompañe los autos al Superior Gobierno no dudo venga de el su determinacion contra los maldicientes conforme la solicitud de V. R. pues para esa o cualquiera otra resulta se mantienen los reos con seguridad.
Repito a V. R. mis respetos, y deseos de complacerle, y de que Ntr. Sr. gue. su vida ms. as.

San Diego 18 de Abril de 1787
B.L.M. de V. R.
Su muy atto. agro. serdor.
Pedro Fages (rub.)

M.R.P. Fr. Fermín Franco. de Lasuén.
(A.G.N., Prov. Inter., tomo 1, fols. 85-87.)

162. To Fray Isidro Alonso Salazar and to Fray Baldomero López

The Lord give you Peace. Permit me, Reverend Fathers, to express my surprise, my great surprise, at receiving the appeal you made to me in writing under date of the twenty-first of the present month, requesting me to transfer you both from your present mission and to assign you to another.

I have never come upon, or seen, anything like this. I treat regularly with Your Reverences, and with the other missionaries, as with an equal, or as a brother to all. And this should have spared you the trouble of having recourse in this fashion.

In the past, whenever Your Reverences by word or in writing gave a hint of the request in question I answered in terms which, it seemed to me, convinced you that it was not in my power to grant such a request, or at least so mollified you that you were willing to continue.

So, with all the formality which the form of your request demands—it was delivered in person by one of Your Reverences—and in the presence of, and in the judgment of all who know the number and character of the missionaries engaged in these works of conversion, I declare that it is not in my power to grant the request you have made to me; that I would grant it with pleasure the first instant it should be possible for me; that with this mail I will forward your request and my reply to our College of San Fernando; and that only from there can come to Your Reverences the relief you seek. Bear in mind that if all your troubles and demands spring from the temporal affairs [of the missions], there is not even one mission in which I could place you without imposing on you at the same time the management of such affairs.

Such obligations are burdensome; but they do not discourage those who, with true zeal, have their hearts set on conversions. True, they are hindrances; but they are spiritual helps, too. If we look on them in any other way we have to regard them as a nuisance; and in that case it is little wonder that discouragement is the result.

The College of San Fernando itself, the other apostolic colleges, and all who engage in active missionary work, entrust such temporal affairs to the missionaries.

May God Our Lord keep Your Reverences many years in His holy grace.

Santa Clara Mission,
August 22, 1793.

163. To Fray Tomás Pangua

Begging Your Reverence's holy blessing, I wish to report that since I saw Reverend Father Espí in San Francisco I assigned him as supernumerary at Santa Clara to assist its two very sick missionaries there, for they have as an additional burden the care of the pueblo for the *gente de razón.*

A few days later I learned through the governor that a little restlessness had broken out among the Indians of San Antonio, and that Father Gili had withdrawn to Soledad. I foresaw immediately what could happen; and as Father Espí would have to come to Monterey on the frigate *Aránzazu* in which he was acting as chaplain, I awaited his arrival here in order to come to whatever decision the case called for.

Father Espí and Father Gili were now here. The latter is very weak and ill, and in the opinion of the surgeon, Don Pablo Soler, absolutely unfitted for the service of these missions for he is entirely averse to such service and to this entire country. This had reached such a stage that I heard him say, seriously and in public (the occasion was, when someone said that the infirmary at the college was a sorry affair), that he would rather be there suffering from a sickness so grave as to have to receive Viaticum than to be healthy and well in this country.

For this reason I assigned Father Espí to San Antonio. In an official letter, Señor Quadra instructs the above-mentioned Father to serve as chaplain in the frigate as far as Monterey. He goes on to say that if it is feasible another religious may be substituted with the same duties until the return of the vessel to San Blas. For this reason I have given permission in writing to Father Gili to embark and proceed with it as far as San Diego. I begged him, too, to take into his charge the spiritual needs of its people during the short voyage and the stop-over of the frigate in that port. He is already on board, and there is a report that she will sail tomorrow.

I told him by word of mouth that in view of his poor health, keeping in mind his reasons for being discouraged, and they are well-founded, and having regard to the fact that the medical officer made his report, not hesitatingly but readily, I gave permission for his return to the college; and I did so without any misgivings, but with a feeling that it was in accordance with justice, reason, and duty. I fear, however, that the skipper of the vessel may refuse to take him to San Blas unless he first sees the permit from the governor. We are expecting the arrival of the governor hourly; and when he comes I will explain to him how absolutely necessary is this trip to Mexico. And I will advise you of the result.

I am enclosing a letter from Father Pieras which I received recently at Santa Clara. Truly, if it were in my hands, he would embark on this occasion; and to fill the vacancy resulting in San Luis I would avail myself of Father Oramas. In view of the present emergency, I have good hopes that he will make the sacrifice by remaining here another year, or until Father Catalá[1] comes from Nootka.

The fact is that this Father is less handicapped than the other two

SAN DIEGO MISSION

Lasuén's home for five years
as seen a century later

for the work to be done here, and, while not ignoring any of the attendant circumstances, I find this course the most suitable.

I forgot to inform you in my previous letter that I received a very
gracious letter from Don José Manuel de Álava.[2] In it he placed at my
disposal all his good offices and his influence with His Excellency the
Viceroy for the successful dispatch of any business entrusted to me.
May God reward him.

In my reply I said nothing beyond acknowledging the letter, and
thanking him for his great courtesy. If Your Reverence should think it
right that I avail myself of that favor in some matter or other for the
good of these missions, I hope you will advise me what it might be, and
on what grounds it is sought. I have no desire to see my dependence on
your will and disposition grow less.

From the missionaries I hear many complaints, and very serious ones,
about their supplies, due to the mistakes or the carelessness of the Brother
Procurator. This has reached the stage that I have begun to fear someone
will create an outcry that will be heard outside the cloister. I try to
keep them calm by every means in my power, for I shudder at the
thought of such an impropriety or scandal. I find myself constrained,
however, to bring it to the notice of Your Reverence in the full assurance that in that way the matter will receive the proper attention that it
deserves.

With the most profound respect I place myself once more at the
service of Your Reverence, and I pray that God Our Lord may keep
Your Reverence for many years in His holy grace.

San Carlos Mission,
September 10, 1793.

P. S.

In two packages I am forwarding to Your Reverence the Reports
on the state of these missions at the end of last year.

[1] The memory of this saintly Catalan still survives in California. He received the
Franciscan habit in Barcelona in 1777. In October, 1786 he left Spain for the New
World. He was missionary at Santa Clara from the time of his arrival, the summer of
1794, until his death, November 22, 1830. He had "all the desirable qualities of a missionary save that of robust health," and because of impaired health he often sought
permission to retire, and in 1800, and again in 1804, he was given permission to return
to San Fernando College. See Bancroft, *op. cit.*, II, 600-601.

[2] On the death of Bodega y Quatro in 1793, Álava succeeded as commandant at San
Blas. Like other naval officers who visited California around this time, e.g. Galiano and
Valdés, he lost his life at the battle of Trafalgar (1803).

164. To Don José Joaquín de Arrillaga

It is my clear conviction that Reverend Father Fray Bartolomé Gili is absolutely incapable of serving in these missions, and consequently will be very burdensome to any to which he might be assigned. This opinion is shared, too, by the surgeon of the Royal Navy, Don Pablo Soler, who is in this presidio at present.

For this reason I have given him permission to embark on the frigate *Aránzazu* and to proceed to San Diego. My main purpose is that he may find, as he hopes, some distraction, but with the aim, too, that as far as possible he may be of spiritual assistance to those on board, for they lack a chaplain.

I have told him that, as far as I am concerned, I see no objection, but instead every reason and justice in his continuing to San Blas and even to Mexico, for at San Antonio Mission I have already replaced him with Reverend Father Fray José Espí. There is danger, however, that the skipper of the vessel may hesitate to agree to this in the absence of Your Grace's consent. Hence, I beg you kindly to take the view, as I do, that the necessity of the case serves as a substitute for the permission of His Excellency the Viceroy. Or you might take the view, and there are precedents for it, that in such cases the central government does not insist on this requisite.

May God Our Lord keep Your Grace in His holy grace for many years.

San Carlos Mission
September 17, 1793

At this Mission of Purísima the Monterey mail caught up with me. It arrived during the night, and left with haste for San Diego. I had been expecting that, without fail, there would be a reply to the official letter above, but I find there is none. But since at different times [the governor] spoke to me about giving consent in cases such as Father Gili's, I have now written to him that he may depart.

Purísima Concepción Mission,
October 21, 1793.

165. To Don Pablo Soler

I have already sent you word that the governor has finally asked that you issue the certificate in regard to Father Gili.

Recently a new problem has arisen for me. It is this: Father Pieras has just now written me from San Luis giving up all hope of finding any relief for his ills either there or in any of the missions. He is almost certain that he is soon to die, or at least that he will become a permanent invalid and obtain relief only when he reaches the other side, unless he is given permission to leave, now that there is an opportunity to take a boat.

With the knowledge that I possess on the subject, I feel that what the religious says is very true, and that his request is very just. This being so, I have sent his letter to my superior. I have informed him that if the decision were in my hands I would give him the permission to go. I would make use of Father Oramas to fill the vacancy thereby created at San Luis, for although this latter Father has permission to embark on this occasion, I have high hopes that because of the emergency he would make the sacrifice and stay until next year, or until Father Catalá would arrive in the ship from Nootka. By comparison, he would be less handicapped than Father Pieras for the work to be done here in the meantime.

Do me the favor, my dear sir, since you know the religious and his condition, to tell me in all confidence what is your professional opinion. Do this so that I may satisfy, with greater confidence, the obligation which devolves on me in the case.

Knowing the kindness of Your Honor, I feel confident that you will add this favor to the many others that I can recall. Be assured of the gratitude of your cordial friend,

Your faithful servant and chaplain who kisses your hand.

San Carlos Mission,
September 20, 1793.

166. To Fray Tomás Pangua

With a request for Your Reverence's holy blessing, I hereby send you the enclosed list which is duly certified.

After I had sent Your Reverence the letter that Father Pieras wrote me from San Luis I naturally felt apprehensive, so I wrote to the surgeon for his opinion. I am enclosing a copy of the letter and the original of the reply I received.

Reverend Father Fray Buenaventura has informed me now that five or six nights ago he made his confession as if he were to die, and once or twice they had to carry him bodily from the ranchería where he had collapsed. He further reports that to his knowledge, in San Luis they had to carry him in their arms from the altar to his bed, and that finally when Reverend Father Loriente was passing through San Luis he went with him to Santa Barbara with the firm determination of embarking for San Blas, a step he felt obliged to take as a matter of conscience. He has written something like this to the governor, and I am awaiting a reply from him. With God's help I shall do the best I can to reach this Father at Santa Barbara, and shall consider what is best to do in the circumstances. It is not my wish to take the attitude that the trip which he has in mind is just and necessary; but if it should be, I do not wish to oppose what is just and necessary.

He has come to the conclusion that if he remains here he will die shortly, but that if he leaves the country he will live—and in my opinion he is not in the mood at the present time to give up his right to hold on to life.

If I find myself in such straits I shall avail myself of Reverend Father Oramas, as I have already informed Your Reverence. And if this cannot be arranged, or does not work out, and if the three, Oramas, Pieras, and Gili of necessity have to leave, I shall appoint myself minister of Mission San Luis until someone else arrives.

So, with humble trust I am confessing to Your Reverence my very thoughts. Even when my plans are not carried out, it is my wish and hope that I may find out your opinion on them, so as to make it my guide when similar cases arise.

It is eight days since I arrived at this mission. I have attended to affairs here and, God willing, shall leave tomorrow for San Luis.

I thought that the reply of the governor to my letter regarding Father Gili would reach me here; but it has not yet arrived. As soon as it arrives, God willing, I shall give you a full report.

Happy, as always, to conform to Your Reverence's wishes, I pray that God Our Lord may keep you for many years in His holy grace.

San Antonio Mission,
October 6, 1793.

In this Mission of Purísima Concepción, Father Pieras got word that the ship had already left Santa Bárbara, and on the day I was about to leave San Luis I met him there to my surprise. He wanted to accompany me as far as San Diego so as to catch up with the ships, but he was not fit for such a journey, nor did I permit him to undertake it. He remains inconsolable and is living in hope that he will have all the permissions he needs for next year. The mail arrived tonight, is leaving without delay, and I have time for no more.

Purísima Concepción,
October 21, 1793.

167. To Don José Joaquín de Arrillaga

I have received Your Grace's official letter of the ninth of this month, enclosing a printed copy of the Proclamation and including the royal cedula of March 30 last, all of which His Excellency the Viceroy of New Spain ordered to be published so that the royal decree may be observed in which His Majesty resolved to declare war against France,[1] its possessions, and inhabitants.

This I shall duly make known to all who are under my jurisdiction, as Your Grace charges me; and as far as in me lies I shall see to it that all that is prescribed shall be duly carried out.

May God Our Lord keep Your Grace for many years in His holy grace.

Santa Barbara,
October 28, 1793.

[1] The sympathy of the Spanish monarchy, as would be expected, was with their beleaguered colleague, Louis XVI of France. In retaliation, the revolutionary government declared war on Spain in 1793. It ended in the peace of Basle in 1795, in which Spain ceded to France that portion of the island of Santo Domingo now known as Haiti.

168. To Don José Joaquín de Arrillaga

Together with Your Grace's official letter of the ninth of this month, I received the printed copy of the Proclamation, with the order for its publication issued by His Excellency the Viceroy of New Spain, so that the faithful and devoted vassals of His Majesty may be generous in their contributions for the support of the just war which has been declared against the French, and that they may fulfil with the greatest exactitude and punctuality the royal orders included in that Proclamation, and communicated by Their Excellencies Don Pedro de Acuña and Don Diego de Gardoqui.

I began immediately to help in this just war by means of the only contributions I can offer, and these are prayers to Heaven, begging that the Catholic arms may achieve glorious success, and that in the struggle they may obtain victory with honor, for on their side are justice and true zeal.

Those subject to me will do likewise. In accordance with the instructions of Your Grace, on this date I am imposing on them the same strict obligation, and the further one of pleading for contributions of a different kind from those whose good fortune it is to be able to furnish them.

May God Our Lord keep Your Grace for many years in His holy grace.

Santa Barbara,
October 28, 1793.

169. List of Missionaries

Assignments of Missionaries for the year 1793

San Carlos	[Fermín Francisco de] Lasuén**
	[Pascual] Arenaza
	[José] Señán
San Francisco	[Antonio] Danti
	[Martín] Landaeta
Santa Clara	[Tomás de la] Peña
	[Diego] Noboa
Santa Cruz	[Alonzo] Salazar
	[Baldomero] López
Soledad	[Diego] García
	[Miguel] Sánchez
San Antonio	[Miguel] Pieras
	[Buenaventura] Sitjar
San Luis Obispo	[Miguel] Giribet
	[Bartolomé] Gili
Purísima	[José de] Arroita
	[José] Calzada
Santa Barbara	[Esteban] Tapis
	[José de] Miguel
San Buenaventura	[Francisco] Dumezs [Dumetz]
	[Vicente de] Santa María
San Gabriel	[Antonio] Cruzado
	[Miguel] Sánchez
San Juan Capistrano	[Vicente] Fuster
	[Juan Norberto] Santiago
San Diego	[Hilario] Torrent
	[Juan] Mariner

** In this list, which is obviously a draft, Lasuén gave nothing beyond the family name of the missionaries.

170. To the Missionaries

The Lord give you Peace. Governor Don José Joaquín de Arrillaga has sent me two proclamations which are to be published by order of His Excellency the Viceroy of New Spain. One of them contains the royal cedula of March 13 last, ordering that the royal decree be carried out in which His Majesty has resolved to declare war on France, its possessions, and its people.

The other makes known the royal order set forth by Their Excellencies Don Pedro de Acuña and Don Diego de Gordoqui, directing the faithful and devoted vassals of His Majesty to come forward with their contributions to aid in this just war declared against France.

I am sending you this information, Reverend Fathers, and I charge you, whenever the occasion arises, to impress on your subjects the absolute justice of the decision of His Majesty in regard to France. And I charge both Your Reverences and all others to help the levying of this war with the contributions of which you are capable, that is to say, with fervent prayers, begging the God of Armies that the troops of Spain may win glorious victories, and that in the struggle they may win victory with honor, for on their side are justice and true zeal.

There are some who have the good fortune to be able to supply a different kind of help. Your Reverences are to exhort these to be generous with such contributions, thus co-operating in meeting the costs of the war in which are at stake the honor of God and of His Church, humanity, and the public order.

On reading this letter Your Reverences will certify that you have noted its contents and will be prompt to carry them out; and when all have so certified, the missionaries at San Diego will place it in the archives and notify me that they have done so.

May God Our Lord keep Your Reverences many years in His holy grace.

Santa Barbara,
October 28, 1793.

Marginal Note:

I sent a circular in the same tenor and on the same date to the missions in the north, from this Mission of Santa Barbara to San Francisco.

171. To Fray Tomás Pangua

I beg Your Reverence's holy blessing, and acknowledge receipt of your patent of the seventh of last June, with which you enclosed that of the Most Reverend Father Fray Juan de Moya, Commissary General of the Indies. I beg to inform you that I have forwarded it to the neighboring mission so that it may continue on to the last.

I did the same with the order of His Excellency the Viceroy, which you transcribed in your letter of the seventh of September, and which I received on the twelfth of the present month, in the same mail as the patent referred to above.

At the present time the cultivation of cereals to meet our basic needs does not allow us much time for the culture and care of hemp;[1] but, now that there is an Order from His Excellency and a recommendation from Your Reverence, I have no doubt that every possible effort will be made.

With God's help, my concern with the matter will be all that befits an order from so exalted a source. As regards items of ordinary consumption, they will be made available according to circumstances whenever the department at San Blas requests them.

The tallow was sent from time to time to the commissary at his request, and he received and paid for it, much to the advantage of the missions. Then he ceased to ask for it; I know not why. The skippers on the boats are cautious or reluctant to handle it, and the individual sailors at the present time try to get it at a lower price so as to resell it.

If it seems proper to His Excellency the Viceroy, His Excellency could arrange for the handling of this product, its shipment and delivery at San Blas, and even its price; and as there is an abundance of it in many missions, the department could supply its needs from it in great measure, to its own benefit and that of our Indians.

With this mail I received an order from His Excellency the Viceroy. He instructs me to send the Report of the Spiritual State of these missions direct to him, as formerly I was accustomed to send them every two years to the office of the commandant general, for the province has recently been separated from that dependency.

He informs me that he hopes I will continue to work for the successful propagation of our holy faith among these gentile nations. As my reply merely affirms that I will carry out the orders of His Excellency, I am sending it to him direct.

I had some inclination to drop the hint that I doubted whether His Excellency were aware that for years past I had not received a stipend (it has now become habitual), but I did not want to do so, and will not. Both the deceased governor and the present one gave much thought to this matter, and this is what makes me consider it—but only on condition that you regard it as worthy of attention. At all events, I am completely content and satisfied if I merely bring it to the attention of Your Reverence, leaving it entirely to your judgment whether or not to take any steps in regard to it.

With the most profound respect I place myself once more at the service of Your Reverence, and I pray that God Our Lord may keep you for many years in His holy grace.

San Diego,
December 16, 1793.

[1] Hemp was not raised extensively in California. In 1795 Governor Borica distributed hemp seed, but the annual reports from the missions have little to say about hemp. In Santa Barbara in 1808, the harvest of hemp amounted to 211 arrobas, or 5,475 pounds. Cf. Engelhardt, *Santa Barbara Mission* (San Francisco, 1923), p. 90.

172. To Fray Tomás Pangua

With Your Reverence's holy blessing, I wish to inform you that, thanks be to God, I have had the happiness to extend my campaign as far as San Diego, and on my return trip I have now been in San Juan Capistrano since the nineteenth of the present month. In three days, God willing, I have it in mind to go to San Gabriel and to stay there during the winter. I want to be of some help to those sickly missionaries on whom devolves the care of a pueblo of *gente de razón*, a place of considerable size, without any supernumerary to help them.

It was in just that place that I met Father Gili on his way up from San Diego as I was on my way down there. I felt no desire to leave him with the Fathers mentioned, nor did they suggest that he might stay, nor did he give the impression that he would welcome such an assignment. It is quite obvious that he is too ill and worn out to serve the missions.

I keenly regretted that he did not embark. Externally I tried to pose as indifferent as to whether he would implement his request to retire, or remain some years longer in these parts. I pretended not to be fully aware of the situation, and told him that inasmuch as his return to the college was assured by virtue of the certificate of the surgeon, he should be able to leave in the vessel from Nootka which might arrive in Monterey in May or June, and with this in mind he could stay in San Luis in the meantime. I am glad that you have informed the Viceroy about this person's condition.

I have not received the letter or letters for the month of May to which Your Reverence referred.

Thanks be to God and Your Reverence for the two hundred pesos which have been received for the return of the missionaries, and for the fact that negotiations have been under way and there are hopes that it will now be easier to arrange for the return of those who have completed the ten years, or have a just motive for leaving earlier. An arrangement such as this is a wonderful help.

I am delighted and very grateful that Your Reverence is sending us two or three religious this year and four or six in the coming one. But far greater is our joy that you have it in mind to afford us an opportunity of seeing you face to face, and to honor us and preside over us in person. What a moment to look forward to! May it never happen that we shall have to be content with the mere desire on your part.

I share in the joy which the nineteen new collaborators will bring Your Reverence. May God grant that they may be the type that are needed; and if they are not, may He make them such. With these, and with those yet to come, Your Reverence will be able to satisfy your zeal and attend to your affairs.

The three English ships of last year have been in San Francisco and Monterey once more,[1] and have anchored, too, at Santa Barbara and San Diego. They have not sought to spend the winter in any of these ports, because when they indicated what they had in mind, Señor Arrillaga imposed certain conditions which he considered necessary, but which they did not see their way to accept.[2]

Several have told me and written me that Commandant Wancouver [Vancouver] and the officers often asked about me. Finally I came upon them in San Diego without looking for them. I visited them, and they were very gracious to me. Señor Vancouver made me a gift of an organ. I saw it in his cabin the previous year, and noted how much he esteemed it. I would not have parted with it for anything, and the thought of such a present never entered my mind. By merely turning a small handle you get the most beautiful sound. It plays thirty-four brief melodies [tocadas], and none is far removed from what is sacred. It is an instrument of beauty and a truly precious piece. May God be his reward— for that was and can be the only price I can give in return.

He asked me to what church I would assign it, and I said to San Carlos of Monterey. He was much pleased; and now I find I have the unavoidable problem of transporting it there. The job will be a little risky, but not very difficult. It is now here in San Juan, and on Christmas Night and Christmas Day it was played to the indescribable delight and amazement of the Indians.

I arrived in San Diego for my routine duties on the fifth of this month, and at eight o'clock that morning the three ships set sail from that port.

Señor Vancouver left me the address for any letters I might wish to write to him, first at Nootka, where he says he will go next year, and after that at London. It is very kind of him to be concerned about any poor letters I might send him, for the matters I would write about will not afford him much pleasure, for they are not at all interesting. Nevertheless, I must take care to be grateful, although it can only be in a Franciscan way. (Marginal Note: I brought here the letter written in San Diego, and therefore the two can go under one cover.)

In the same [Franciscan] way it is my duty to obey Your Reverence, and I will do so, begging God Our Lord to keep you in His holy grace for many years.

San Juan Capistrano Mission,
December 27, 1793.

[1] These were the *Discovery*, the *Chatham*, and the *Daedalus*. The *Discovery* was the first non-Spanish ship to enter the port of San Francisco.

[2] In 1792, during the first of his visits, Vancouver was entertained lavishly and was permitted to travel freely. During this time Arrillaga was in Lower California. In 1793 when Vancouver next called Arrillaga had moved to Monterey and was concerned, as were other Spanish officials, lest the Englishman may not have sensed, as he did, the weakness of the Spanish defenses in California. Vancouver was quick to notice the change in attitude, and promptly withdrew. It is to the second visit that Lasuén here refers. There was one more visit the following year, but by that time Argüello was in charge at Monterey and Borica had replaced Arrillaga. On this occasion the courtesies of the first visit were repeated.

173. To Fray Tomás Pangua

I ask your blessing, and I wish to inform Your Reverence that as I was about to seal my last letter I heard vague rumors about restlessness among the Indians of Santa Cruz Mission.

At the present moment, through the mail which has arrived and will be quickly on its way, I have found out for certain that on the night of the fourteenth of last December the pagan Indians, and some Christian Indians, from the rancherías to the northwest of that mission made an assault on the guard, wounded the corporal in the hand, and another soldier in the shoulder, and set fire to the roof of the corral for the lambs, and the old guard house. The corporal fired a few shots, and with that they withdrew without serious injury to either side.

The two who were wounded are better already. Later, a reinforcement of troops arrived, and they have taken as prisoners to Monterey five Christians and I do not know how many pagans.

The motive they have given is this, that the soldiers had taken away to San Francisco various Christian Indians belonging to that place who had been fugitives from there for some time, and that they had taken a Christian Indian woman away from a pagan man, and it was he who was the principal instigator and leader of the disorder.

It appears that all is now quiet and peaceful, thanks be to God. And to keep it that way I ask if Your Reverence will plead for them in any way that may be fitting so that the matter may be regarded in a spirit of charity and compassion.

I would appreciate it a great deal if you would avail yourself of any favorable opportunities that arise to say a word in favor of Señor Don José Joaquín de Arrillaga, who is interim governor, so that he may become the actual governor of this province. He is a very gifted person and, in short, knows a great deal, or all that is to be known, about this country, and it is only what one would expect if great achievements and advantages would be the result.

The mail does not allow me time for a letter of greater length or better style; and in addition I have been bothered by a pustule in the chin for some days, and it causes me much pain.

Father Baldomero ends his letter to me with these words: "And for the sake of my health I ask Your Reverence to beg permission for me to return to the college, a favor for which I shall be extremely grateful." Your Reverence will do what you think best. I am not opposed to it, and I am fulfilling the request by forwarding it.

[On the margin:] All the reports have reached me, with the exception of the one from San Buenaventura; and this is an omission that occurs almost every year. Because of that, the Short Report is not included in this mail, but I shall see to it that it is not missing from the next.

[Text resumed] I am as always completely and gladly at your service; and I pray that God Our Lord may keep you for many years in His holy grace.

San Gabriel Mission,
February 3, 1794.

174. To Don Diego de Borica

Before Your Lordship assumes office as new governor[1] I gladly volunteer my service to carry out your orders, for at a later date compliance will be a matter of obligation.

Both now and then, and whenever occasion arises, I wish to give evidence of my very special obedience to the commands of Your Lordship, despite my very obvious inefficiency.

All the missionaries of our New California express these same sentiments towards Your Lordship; and I join with them in letting you know how happy we are, and we offer our congratulations on your promotion to this office. I wish you all success and happiness in it. May it be a stepping-stone to greater honors, leading to a greater share in the confidences of His Majesty; and above all, may it win you the privilege and imperishable honor of eternal beatitude.

May God Our Lord grant this to Your Lordship as well as to your spouse, whom I salute with deepest respect. And may He keep you many years in His holy grace.

Santa Barbara Mission,
March 31, 1784.

[1] He was governor of California from October 1794 to January 1800. Like Arrillaga, Lasuén, and many others who were prominent in early days in California, he was a Basque. Bancroft describes him as "one of the ablest and best rulers the country ever had, always striving for progress in different directions, avoiding controversy, and personally interesting himself in the welfare of all classes; a jovial bon-vivant, knight of Santiago, and man of wealth." Bancroft, *op. cit.*, II, 724.

175. To Fray Tomás Pangua

I beg your holy blessing. When I last wrote to you from San Gabriel at the end of February I had already heard that Fathers Pieras and Gili had gone from San Luis to Monterey; but I did not believe it. But I had no sooner reached the Presidio of Santa Barbara than its commandant handed me a letter from Father Pieras who informed me that they had heard that the vessel from Nootka would soon arrive, and they had made up their minds to come closer to, or to come as far as, Monterey so as to embark, and that for some days now they were at San Antonio awaiting that opportunity.

I wrote to them, greatly disapproving of their rash decision, and reproached them for the big scandal it would give rise to among the people, for they left only one missionary at San Luis while there were four of them at San Antonio.

I ordered that they should return immediately, or at least that one of them should, to be a companion to Father Giribet at San Luis. And in case they should fail to do this, I wrote to Father Espí, begging him to go to San Luis in the event that none of these Fathers had gone there within eight days of the receipt of my letter—for I had agreed to this.

When they got my letter, Father Gili was already in Monterey, and returned immediately to San Antonio. There, he informs me, he fell ill, and that Pieras was sick. Hence, Espí went to San Luis where he passed the holy season of Lent, thanks be to God, and there he still is until I come up, which, please God, will be some time next week. I do not understand, and I never will be able to understand, these two Fathers,

Pieras and Gili; and it is now your province, Father, to agree to the retirement they ask, or to take such steps as seem best to you.

On the Feast of St. Joseph we had the blessing and dedication of the very beautiful church of this mission,[1] and there was all the solemnity, splendor, peace and joy that one could desire. Thanks be to God.

The Reverend Father Fray Esteban Tapis has proved to be an excellent painter, and has embellished it with different designs, especially around the high altar, which he has frescoed. The result is something much more attractive than the paintings on canvas brought from a distance to San Luis, San Antonio, and Santa Clara. Thanks be to God.

In recent days, almost simultaneously, there was a disturbance among the Indians of Purísima and San Luis. It was due to a rumor started by two or three Christian boys who said that our soldiers were going to kill them all when they came together in church for Mass.

We hastened there quickly with some soldiers, so as to get them to return to their respective missions, for they had all taken to flight; and we succeeded with very little effort, and no one was the worse for it. There were no later developments.

The latest mail arrived at the presidio last night; and when we learned about it in the morning it was already ten or twelve leagues from here. The same thing can happen again; and that is the reason why this letter has to be on his way so hastily, and so unattractive in form.

As always, my services are at the free disposal of Your Reverence. May God Our Lord keep you many years in His holy grace.

Santa Barbara,
April 23, 1794.

P. S.

I am sending the enclosed exactly as they were sent to me from Santa Clara.

[1] When the mission was founded, a temporary church was constructed. As was the procedure in the other missions, the first church was simple and crude. Such churches were constructed of forked poles placed close together, supporting a series of cross beams, and roofed with tule and earth. In Santa Barbara a new church was built in 1789, a more permanent one. It was built of adobe and had a roof of tile. A new adobe church was begun in 1793 and completed the following year. This is the church to which Lasuén makes reference here. It was dedicated on the Feast of St. Joseph, March 19. It was so damaged by the earthquake of 1812 that it had to be taken down eventually. It was replaced by the present stone church, which is really the fourth mission church of Santa Barbara.

176. To Don Diego de Borica

I have circulated among the missions under my charge Your Lordship's welcome and gracious letter of the twentieth of last January which arrived in duplicate form on the twenty-second of the present month. I did this, for I wished that the missionaries might be filled with the same appreciation, gratitude, and joy which your noble and friendly sentiments inspired in me.

On behalf of all, I expressed in advance our good wishes on your appointment and our joyful acknowledgement of it, and I now repeat it. And we offer our ready submission to your worthy commands, even before we have incurred the joyous obligation of complying with them.

Seeing that at the beginning of March Your Lordship was already thinking of starting out for the coast of Sonora, it is possible that with your family you have already made the dangerous crossing by sea to Loreto. Would to God it were so, and that our opportunity to obey would come as quickly as possible. It is this that will reveal to Your Lordship the basic and principal traits in myself; and I venture to assure you that my religious, too, will be outstanding in obedience.

For the rest, Your Lordship will learn by experience that everything will depend more on your good pleasure than on ours.

To your spouse, my lady, my most profound respects. I trust she will accept such sentiments, for they spring from a sincere interest.

And now I wish Your Lordship all happiness and success; and I pray that God Our Lord may keep you for many years in His holy grace.

San Carlos Mission,
May 28, 1794.

177. To Fray Tomás Pangua

With Your Reverence's holy blessing, I beg to inform you that on the twenty-second of this month, after I had completed my last visitation of all the missions, I returned here to San Carlos. On the same day I received your latest letter, dated the twenty-seventh of last October. By the same mail I had a letter from Señor Álva, dated the eleventh of December, both of last year.

The notable delay between the one and the other is due to the fact that Your Reverence's letter was forwarded to the other Monterey, as has already happened on other occasions, and will always happen when the words *of California* are not added, or when this province is not written at the beginning of the address.

I am reminded in the letter quoted of various matters which Your Reverence mentions as having communicated to me in a letter of the end of last September, namely:

(1) The orders of His Excellency the Viceroy regarding the departure of Father Rubí;

(2) The 200 pesos which His Excellency assigned to those who returned from California after serving ten years there;

(3) The sowing of hemp which is to be carried out in these missions;

(4) The abrogating of the 200 pesos. Furthermore, to those who return after the completion of the ten years, the stipend is to be paid up to the time they reach the college;

(5) Orders from His Excellency the Viceroy regarding the behavior of Fathers Gili and Rubí, with a copy of an official letter from His Excellency dated the ninth of the same month of September, ordering me to institute proceedings to be conducted before the royal judges of this province in regard to faults and irregularities of which the Fathers in question may have been guilty.

I replied to nos. 2 and 3 in due time, but I have no recollection of having heard of the other three, nor can I find any letter in regard to them. Presumably it was lost.

I would not have known up to the present that Father Rubí had reached the college if he himself had not written it; and as he did not say anything to me either about His Excellency the Viceroy or about Reverend Father Guardian, I cannot help inferring that perhaps there was something remiss about the approval for his departure. But as far as I am concerned, I have nothing more to say beyond what I explained very fully at the time, borne out by the unanimous and unqualified opinion of the medical attendants, the formal certificate of one of them, and the permit from the commandant of this province.

I learned through the missionaries of Soledad and Santa Cruz that the 200 pesos had been cancelled. And in regard to this, there is not and there cannot be any other reply but one of regret. It may have been right to cancel it: it would have been better to pay it. The stipend which accrues to those who return at the end of ten years will be paid up to the time of their arrival at the college. I shall assume that this would be without prejudice to what will be enjoyed by those who happen to be already assigned to take their places.

I respect and accept with profound deference the higher orders of His Excellency the Viceroy in regard to the behavior of Fathers Gili and Rubí. And if, as is likely, the governor of the province has some instructions from His Excellency on the matter, and advises me of them, I will carry out punctilliously what he orders me. But I confess frankly that if I have to institute proceedings which have to be taken before the royal judges, I know of no faults or excesses which would demand it in the case of the Fathers mentioned.

On our part, the motive that definitely dictated the retirement of both has been illness; and there was a formal medical certificate to the effect that sickness rendered them incapable of ministering in these missions, and even made it absolutely necessary for them to have a change of location.

I reported that they were very pleased to depart from here. This was due to the complete and total repugnance of both of them for this kind of life and for this country. Neither the one nor the other felt embarrassment about repeating this publicly. And what greater harm can there be than this? There was no other remedy but to let them go, even if they were well. And if we did not, of what use here are minds filled with an unqualified abhorrence for everything that is to be done here? If they cannot get along with themselves, with whom can they get along?

Now, all of these altercations, those that were mutual between the two, and those that each in turn had with Father García during the time they were associated with him, all had their consequences for the public. But in truth it is not these things in themselves that caused so much commotion and surprise; it was rather the personality of the individuals and the office they held; and the further circumstances that, thanks be to God, up to that time, the public had never observed anything like that in the Fathers from San Fernando.

Nevertheless, neither this difficulty, nor the deep-seated aversion they both felt towards being in these parts would have been enough to inspire in me the least hope that they would retire. Difficulties that seemed too great were involved. What made it possible was the fact that they became completely incapacitated and unqualified, as was declared and certified by the attending physician.

The governor has written me that he has received the permission of His Excellency the Viceroy for Fathers Pieras, Noboa, and Gili to embark.

This makes me think that the letters which were left behind—and among them was the certificate regarding the indisposition of Father Gili—may have been sufficient to justify the need of this religious to withdraw to the college. (They were left behind because they failed to reach the boat at San Diego.)

Through the Fathers at Santa Cruz Mission I learned that five missionaries from the college will come in the boat we expect this year. And as it is customary for you to send me these notices the letter must have been lost, or forwarded to the other Monterey.

It will be my duty once more to make out the list of missionaries who served these missions in the year '92, with the proper verification, if the governor will be so kind as to give it to me.

In San Antonio I also met Fathers Gili and Pieras, and told them, and afterwards wrote to them, to go to San Luis and wait for the first opportunity to embark, for I had received notice that the permission had been granted them.

Here I found Father Peña so ill that one could not help feeling the greatest pity and compassion for him. He is dejected and very apprehensive, ceaselessly fretting, and talking to himself, and completely in the grip of a profound melancholia.

The day before yesterday he left for Santa Cruz on the advice of the surgeon. The latter did what he could for him, but without results. After a rest he will proceed to San Francisco, where he finds it less obnoxious than elsewhere.

Father Arenaza went with him to keep him company, and to go to Santa Clara to console and take care of Father Noboa, for the latter has written to say that he is very depressed, and very despondent because of his day-to-day infirmities.

I am sending along what is enclosed, and place it at the disposal of Your Reverence. And there, too, I place myself, always responsive to Your Reverence's commands. And I pray that God Our Lord may keep you for many years in His holy grace.

San Carlos Mission,
May 28, 1794.

178. To Don José Joaquín de Arrillaga

Your official letter of last month informs me that His Excellency the Viceroy of New Spain has given permission to retire from their missions to the following Reverend Fathers: Fray Antonio Paterna, Fray Cristóbal Oramas, Fray Diego de Noboa, Fray Miguel Pieras, and Fray Bartolomé Gili, all of whom are to be replaced this year by five others.

No doubt Your Lordship will bear in mind that the Reverend Father Paterna died in Santa Barbara Mission a little less than a year and a half ago,[1] and that the Reverend Father Oramas withdrew last year already, with the permission of His Excellency.

I shall give due notice to the other three at the proper time.

May God Our Lord keep Your Lordship for many years in His holy grace.

San Carlos Mission,
June 7, 1794.

[1] "On February 14, 1793, ecclesiastical burial was given in the church to the body of the Reverend Fray Antonio Paterna. He was a native of Seville, Spain. He arrived in these missions of New California after having labored in the missions of the Sierra Gorda in Mexico for twenty years, down to the month of May, 1770. He died yesterday,

February 13. He received all the sacraments with great devotion, and he was a true son of our father St. Francis. (Signed) Fray Francisco Dumetz." Mission Santa Barbara, *Libro de Difuntos*, No. 199.

179. To Don José Joaquín de Arrillaga

I have received Your Lordship's official letter of the thirty-first of last month. It enclosed a superior order from His Excellency the Viceroy declaring that the exchange value of the work accomplished by the skilled artisans pertains to the Royal Treasury after one half has been deducted. The half in question is to be divided into three parts, one part to go to the skilled artisan, and the other two to his apprentices whether they be few or many. It is further decreed that the collecting is to be the responsibility of the religious in charge of the mission in which they reside.

In accordance with Your Lordship's instructions I shall make known this official decree to the missionaries of Santa Clara, for there were skilled workmen there, and to those of San Francisco where there still are two others. I shall request them to put it into effect and to advise me regarding results, so that I may bring them to Your Lordship's attention.

As regards this mission of San Carlos, I observe that its skilled workers have not made any objects for sale. Their labor is of benefit to the mission. Most, or almost all of it, is devoted to the church which is being built, and the cornerstone of which was laid on the seventh of last July.

May God Our Lord keep Your Lordship for many years in His holy grace.

San Carlos Mission,
June 7, 1794.

180. To Fray Tomás Pangua

May I have Your Reverence's holy blessing, for I wish to inform you that yesterday I received your two letters of January 24, and February 28, last, with the further news that a mail was coming soon to Loreto with the mail sacks for the other group. In view of this, it seems to me opportune to send Your Reverence the enclosed, as evidence for the time being of the date of arrival of the last five religious.

Up to the present I have not been able to find out what in substance is the decision in regard to the just claim of Your Reverence, in connection with these religious, that some disbursement be made to cover traveling expenses on land and rations at sea.

In short, let the religious who are needed come, and let those who have a good motive for doing so be free to go, whether or not they are paid. And if they are paid, it is not the missionaries but the missions that gain. And if they are not paid, it is the missions and not they who are the losers. It might be well if they would form a correct idea in this matter of the difference between our method and that which the other missions observe.

I offer Your Reverence a thousand thanks for sending the Fathers mentioned, and for the welcome information you give regarding their good qualities. Thanks be to God.

I have planned a trip to San Francisco for the day after tomorrow (with God's help), and I have written to them to await me there, or in Santa Clara if they wish. I had it in mind to give them their assignments on the basis of their external appearances, and a brief conversation with them, but, thanks be to God, Your Reverence's words of advice arrived opportunely, and with the help of them I can hope to proceed in a more enlightened way.

Further, with God's help, I shall observe the disposition of the Fathers at Santa Cruz who go keenly after temporal things, and then declaim loudly against them; I shall attend to the departure of Father Noboa, the completely incapacitated condition of Father Peña who is still in Santa Cruz, but almost completely demented, and to one or other who is completely dissatisfied with his assignment. So, I trust in God that the assignments to be made will be for the best. With the help of God I shall send a report on everything as soon as possible.

I shall personally deliver to the Fathers at Santa Cruz Your Reverence's good letter, and I shall send the other to Father Gili by this mail.

I am somewhat comforted by what you tell me regarding the Santa Clara affair, and by the letter of my reverend and venerated Father Mugartegui (to whom, if I cannot write now, Your Reverence will please convey my kind regards and my affectionate greeting); but I will not have an easy mind until I know the decision, disposition, or declaration of the Viceroy, based on the latest inquiries carried out in a spirit of good faith, and right zeal for justice.

By means of the invoice which we received yesterday we learned of the allowance of 36 pesos referred to in the will of Señor Anteparaluceta.[1] May God grant him eternal rest. And then there are the books which Your Reverence sends us. A thousand thanks for everything.

I never expected anything else would happen but what happened in regard to the accounts of our poor Brother Revuelta. May God give him patience. I often find reason for suspecting that the restless follies of the age have made great advances towards the interior of the cloisters. May God give the remedy.

We already know that Señor Borica was appointed Governor. I sent him congratulations months ago; but before he could receive them he sent me his compliments, and very generous they were, from the *estancia* of Río Florida;[2] and I have replied to them in my own way. Would that he were a man like our good Arrillaga, for he is a grand person, with a deep affection for the clergy.

I am sending my good friend Reverend Father Fray Pablo an account of certain subjects who left the pueblos and found employment with rancheros, and with this information, and with what Your Reverence knows about these parts, there should be enough information to enable Your Reverence to give direction in any deliberation you choose to have.

Whatever it may be that you desire from this very humble subject, I shall consider and esteem as very fitting, and shall undertake most gladly. For this reason I do not suggest anything definitely, not even something which perhaps Your Reverence could anticipate, and I would naturally long for.

Nothing suits me better than to be completely subject to the orders and suggestions of Your Reverence, and I pray that God Our Lord may keep you for many years in His holy grace.

San Carlos Mission,
June 22, 1794.

---

[1] He was a canon in the Cathedral of Puebla, Mexico. In his will he left the sum of five hundred pesos for the missions of California. San Fernando College expended the money on the purchase of supplies for the missions. Santa Cruz Mission received the equivalent of sixty pesos, Soledad forty pesos, and the remaining missions the equivalent of thirty-six pesos each. See *Tomás Pangua to Lasuén,* Santa Barbara Missions Archives, Sec. 2, No. 217.
[2] This is the older name of Villa Coronado in the State of Chihuahua.

181. To Don José Joaquín de Arrillaga

[Summary of a Letter]

[Lasuén] acknowledges receipt of the official letter of the sixth inst. He declares that he has no authority to oblige anyone of his missionaries to go as chaplain aboard the *Aránzazu.* He refers to the instructions of Commandant Saavedra of Nootka that to that boat is to be given the chaplain of the missionaries' boat to replace the one who has to stay in these missions.

What the captain of the *Concepción* said places him under no obligation, namely, that "despite the fact that they are all indisposed, at least some one of the three religious whom the aforesaid Don Salvador

Merienda took on board his ship (the *Concepción*) will be able, perhaps, to agree, if he is asked, to return with it from Acapulco to San Blas."

San Francisco,
July 8, 1794.

182. To Don José Joaquín de Arrillaga

I am sending Your Lordship the enclosed list which pertains to the year 1792. I shall be grateful if you will certify to the actual presence here that year of the missionaries named in it. The reason is, that although it is certain that I already sent it to Your Lordship and that you signed it, it was misplaced by the royal officials. They are asking the Reverend Father Guardian of San Fernando of Mexico for a duplicate, and this Father is asking me for it.

May God Our Lord keep Your Lordship for many years in His holy grace.

San Carlos Mission,
August 1, 1794.

183. To Don José Joaquín de Arrillaga

I should like to bring to your notice that Reverend Father Fray Tomás de la Peña, Minister of the Mission of Santa Clara, has suffered from serious illnesses for more than a year. Despite this, he has done his utmost to serve that mission. He has had recourse to every expedient that was available. He sought a change of climate from time to time, staying now at San Francisco, now at Santa Clara, and at another time at San Carlos. Finally, he has fallen victim to a severe form of hypochondria which has rendered him absolutely unfitted for the service of these missions, and is a clear sign that he cannot regain his health in this land.

Don Pablo Soler, surgeon of the Royal Presidio, will corroborate this; but I did not ask him for a formal certificate, for he does not consent to issue any unless Your Lordship so orders him.

But above all, you yourself are a good witness in regard to the tragic and sad position in which this religious has found himself; and so, another religious has been appointed to take his place at Santa Clara.

So, with all due respect and deference, I am asking Your Lordship if you will be so kind as to grant him permission to embark for his college in Mexico aboard the frigate *Concepción* which is at anchor in this port and soon to set sail. It seems to me that we cannot await another opportunity without running the risk of a complete breakdown, or even the death of the patient. It will not easily happen, although it is true now, that while on the journey he will have the company and the attendance of other religious, and the advantage of disembarking at Acapulco.

I am quite certain that the fact that the petition to Your Lordship for the retirement of Reverend Father Peña comes from me is the best argument that can be found why, by reason of his condition, it is imperative that he should be retired. Furthermore, in this country there are neither ways nor means by which he could regain his health. And surely there is not a single other missionary with whom I would plead, as I would with him, to continue indefinitely in this mission work.

I trust that in your goodness Your Lordship will grant the favor I am asking; and I pray that God Our Lord may keep you for many years in His holy grace.

San Carlos Mission,
August 1, 1794.

XI
Inception of Borica's Rule

*A new governor, Don Diego de Borica, assumes of-
fice. He is a Basque, as is Lasuén, and a friendship,
often close but sometimes strained, grows up between them. Internal problems increase—missionaries
become incapacitated, fail to conform to the needs
of time and place, seek permission to return to Mexico.*

184. To Don Diego de Borica

I AM INFORMED THAT YOUR LORDSHIP AS-sumed the office of Civil and Military Governor of this Province on the fourteenth of last May, as your official letter of that date so testifies.

I acknowledge Your Lordship as Governor, and gladly make my obedience; and for the same purpose I am forwarding the corresponding notice to all the missionaries who are subject to me.

May God Our Lord keep Your Lordship for many years in His holy grace.

San Carlos Mission,
August 6, 1794.

185. To Don Diego de Borica

By virtue of the order of Your Lordship of last July 14, consequent upon that of His Excellency the Viceroy, Count de Revilla Gigedo, issued on the preceding April 7, I have been informed, and on this date I am making it known to the missionaries subject to me, that the King our Lord has granted permission to Don Román Márquez to lead an expedition which he has planned from the port of Cadiz to that of San Blas, and other ports on the coast of California. I am further advised that he enjoys full liberty to claim foodstuffs and manufactured articles pertaining to the nation to take on board for his outbound journey and also for his return. His Majesty orders, too, that in Spain and America this expedition is to be regarded with favor, and to be supplied with what it needs, without prejudice to the public treasury.

I am advising them to do this, too, in the interests of the missions under their charge, and to try to make collections of pelts and other products of the country such as would bring a return to the missions, trading them with that particular ship, or with other Spanish ships that come direct from Cádiz.

May God Our Lord keep Your Lordship for many years in His holy grace.

San Carlos Mission,
August 6, 1784.

315

186. To Fray Tomás Pangua

Begging Your Reverence's holy blessing, I wish to inform you that towards the end of last June, when I arrived at the Mission of Santa Clara, I sent Reverend Father Fray Gregorio Fernández from there to the Mission of San Luis where he is now with Father Giribet.

Providing for Santa Clara Mission entailed a great deal of thought, due to the unusual circumstance that the two religious who were attached to it left at the same time. Then I received a letter from Father Fray Francisco Sánchez who was extremely disconsolate and unreconciled at Soledad. He implored me in the most touching terms to change him to some other place. Recalling that he must know something about this same Santa Clara, having been there when he had the status of supernumerary, I assigned him there, much to his delight.

Father Espí sent me a similar request, asking for a transfer from San Antonio. I had with me a letter from Father García. He was aware of the request of Father Espí; and in the letter he was very insistent in asking for him as a companion, adding that he was sure it would suit Father Espí very well. I did so; and they are both at Soledad now. I have reason for thinking that Father Espí is still not satisfied, and it is going to be very difficult for me to satisfy him—a matter which worries me considerably.

I assigned Father Martiarena with Father Sitjar at San Antonio to take the place of Father Espí. It suits him quite well; and I think it will be the same no matter where I send him. Thanks be to God.

The Fathers at Santa Cruz have not breathed a word about their request for a transfer, despite the fact that I mentioned their old request incidentally; and I had it in mind to grant it. They have settled down there; but as it has come to my knowledge that they both continue earnestly to beg that they be recalled to the college, and knowing that Your Reverence has promised it to them for the following year, I have placed Father Fray Pedro Esteban with them in the capacity of supernumerary. In this way I am keeping in reserve for that eventuality someone who will have experience in the affairs of that mission.

One of these days I am expecting Father Fray Juan Martín here, for he has to pass this way as he goes to be supernumerary at San Gabriel. He has been detained at San Francisco during this time, for it was necessary for Father Danti to come to Monterey and then go to Santa Cruz, and return with Father Peña.

Father Margín Catalá is in Santa Clara as minister with Father Sánchez; and there, too, is Father Fray Manuel Fernández as supernumerary. Of the latter, I am told that nothing suits him; and I notice that none of the missionaries who have known him like him. But this is something which should be left to time; and he has been there too short a time yet to be known.

I have already advised Your Reverence regarding the serious and dangerous disabilities of Father Peña, and the enclosed copies will inform you about what we felt it necessary to do. On the eleventh of this month he embarked with Fathers Noboa and Gili on the frigate *Concepción;* and on the next day, the twelfth, it set sail from this port to Santa Barbara and San Diego, taking along the supplies for these presidios and missions.

Father Pieras is in Santa Barbara awaiting the boat. Because of what he endured on previous journeys he has given up the idea of going to San Diego by land, in order to embark there.

This frigate is due to go direct from San Diego to Acapulco; and this means that the Fathers will have the advantage and convenience of arriving by sea quite close to Mexico City. It may be that Father Gili will return by sea from Acapulco to San Blas to attend the spiritual needs of those on board, for there is no chaplain.

There is some doubt in the mind of the captain of the boat as to whether the Fathers have the privilege of meals during the voyage. I cannot say; but this I do know, that these three in particular have served these missions for many years and never even thought of giving or receiving an accounting of their stipend, for their only ambition was to develop these establishments of our Catholic King by the aid of their stipends, their sweat, and their labor. Those who doubt can investigate and examine, and they will find that their sole concern is to be back in their college, bringing with them nothing but their clothes such as they are, their breviary, perhaps a few books and papers which they brought with them, and over and above these, the various ailments and the shattered health they have incurred here. Thanks be to God.

I am certain that Your Reverence will not fail to do whatever is fitting in regard to this.

I have never claimed, as Your Reverence thought, that this mission should be reimbursed for what it did for others by assuming the heavy burden of the expenses of the missionaries who come and go. The only thing I ask is, that this mission be excused from contributing to the expenses of outsiders who come and go, especially when their comings and goings do not concern us.

I have many reasons for the latter view; but I have no reason for hesitating about conforming wholeheartedly to what Your Reverence enjoins. There is no personal interest or personal attachment to prejudice me in favor of this mission; but it does provide for my maintenance; it furnishes what I need for my frequent and lengthy journeys; and it pays for whatever I need from Mexico, even if I do not serve to a greater extent here than at the other missions.

The sloop *Valdés* has been in this port since the beginning of this month. It has returned from Manila and is under command of Frigate Lieutenant Don César Bertodona. According to reports, it will set sail at the beginning of next month and go direct to San Blas, which it is expected to reach much sooner than the *Concepción* will arrive at Acapulco. For this reason I will take advantage of it and send this letter, with the one enclosed which Father Baldomero sent to me open. I am sending, too, the certified list which Your Reverence asked for, to show that we were here in the year '92, seeing that the original one, which was sent to them in due time, was mislaid among the papers of the royal officials. By the same sloop I am sending, in addition, two packages containing the reports on the state of these missions at the end of last year.

In San Luis and in Purísima they have evidence of meetings and conspiracies on the part of the Indians, Christian and pagan, who it seems were plotting the murder of the Fathers and soldiers. They had them seized in time, and the leaders imprisoned; and with the precautions which have been taken, it appears that for the time being there is nothing more to be feared.

I do not hesitate to tell Your Reverence that any mediation which is possible in favor of the accused, so that every clemency may be shown to them, will always tend to promote the work of conquest and our peace of mind.

If all renumeration is abolished for the comings and goings of missionaries, it is only fair, too, to abolish the obligation of having to await the higher permission of the Viceroy so that religious may embark, whenever there is legitimate need or cause.

With the greatest respect, and in entire submission, I place myself once more at the service of Your Reverence, and I pray that God Our Lord may keep you for many years in His holy grace.

San Carlos Mission,
August 19, 1794.

P. S

It is now known that Señor Borica is in the province and is coming here. Señor Arrillaga is holding up the issuing of the certificate that testifies we are here; but, be that as it may, with God's help it will leave here at the latest by the frigate *Concepción*.

God willing, I expect to leave next week for the south, going as far as San Diego, so as to make the most of the short time that remains before the faculty for confirming expires, unless a renewal of it is sent sooner.

Well, at last, here is the certificate that we are actually staying in these posts to which we were actually assigned.

187. To Don José Joaquín de Arrillaga

It is necessary for me to obtain a verification of our actual residence in these missions. If I have recourse to the new governor at the distance at which I have reason to believe he is, I shall miss a good opportunity of sending that document safely and opportunely to Mexico by means of the sloop, for the vessel is ready to sail from this port to San Blas.

In view of the fact that you are the interim governor of this province, and that the governor is late in arriving at the royal presidio, his residence, I have decided to forward the enclosed list to Your Grace. It contains the names of the missionaries of Upper California and their respective assignments. I shall be grateful if you will validate it by indorsing it, so that it may be presented for the payment of our stipends.

May God Our Lord keep your Grace for many years in His holy grace.

San Carlos Mission,
August 24, 1794.

188. To Fray Tomás Pangua

May I have Your Reverence's holy blesing. I wish to report that in the course of my journey from Monterey to this place I received your esteemed letter of April 29 last. Enclosed with it was a letter from my dear confrere, Reverend Father Jubilarian Fray Miguel Urbina, and the newspaper clipping regarding the sad news from France.[1] Enclosed, too, were copies of decrees issued by His Excellency the Viceroy in virtue of representations Your Reverence made him with a view to bringing about better arrangements in regard to these missions and their ministers. May God Our Saviour reward Your Reverence for your holy zeal, and for the happy outcome of your pious and just requests.

With God's help, this very day I begin my return journey to Monterey, and I shall instruct all the remaining missionaries, including those here, that they are to specify in the Report the number of the living, and the distinctions according to sex.

I have already sent Your Reverence the certified list of our actual residence here for the year '92, in accordance with your instructions, in view of the fact that the original, which was sent at the proper time, was misplaced in the Secretariat.

The delay is a cause for much uneasiness, and is a basis for presuming that the eleven religious who, as Your Reverence informs me, embarked in Spain for the college on the sixth of November, may have been lost. May God Our Saviour protect them from Frenchmen and from shipwreck, and bring them safely to a place where they are badly needed.

In San Luis and Purísima missions rumors and evidences of revolt are again being noticed, and they owe their origin to nothing else but the same old fickleness of the Indian. The leaders were arrested very opportunely, and everything is quiet once more. Thanks be to God.

While I was on the way, a letter reached me containing an unsealed one from Father Danti. It was addressed to Your Reverence and the venerable council, and in it he repeated his request to retire. I merely sealed it, and placed it in an envelope, in care of the Administrator General of the Mails, and forwarded it immediately.

Likewise, when passing through Santa Barbara, Father Fray José de Miguel showed me the copy of a letter which he had sent to Your Reverence with the same request.

When someone comes to me with a suggestion like that, I persuade them not to go; but if they have already made up their minds, I accept their motives, assume they have been well advised, and leave it to God and to Your Reverence to reach the right solution.

I have been filled with joy by the decision of Your Reverence that supernumeraries are essential in these parts, and consequently I no longer fear that we may have to do without them.

At Soledad I came upon Father García, suffering from rheumatism and confined to bed. I left a note for Father Fray Juan Martín with instructions that if, on returning to the mission, he found the sick man still in the same condition he was to remain there with Father Espí. I entrusted this note to the latter, but he did not deliver it. Father García was still a patient when he returned, and now Father Juan Martín is back at his first post, San Gabriel. There, more than any other place, he will have opportunities for immersing himself thoroughly in Moral Theology; and Father Sánchez can be relied on to impart what knowledge he has in this regard.

I left it to the choice of Father Espí to continue at San Antonio or to change to Soledad. In the meantime Father Martiarena expressed no preference, being willing to accept whichever post the other did not want. Espí chose Soledad, and after a few days once more chose San Antonio. However, I have not been able to give way on account of the note, and also because Martiarena and Sitjar get along well together and are happy at San Antonio. This information may be of use to you when replying to whatever Father Espí may want to write to you.

Señor Borica and his family caught up with me at San Juan Capistrano. We greeted one another as fellow-countrymen, but, since we were traveling, we did not discuss much business, and we left any lengthy discussion of our affairs until my return to Monterey. He seems to have a pleasant disposition[2] and not to be prejudiced. May God Our Lord grant him all success and all peace.

We are assured that on most days of Lent there is the privilege of eating meat; but up to the present no document has reached us to authenticate it, and this would be necessary, for this is a serious matter.

I wish, too, to have some directions about the use of our faculties in the unusual case of one who comes, as did the last missionaries, without them.

The Señores Alva and Fidalgo have written to me from Nootka under date of the ninth of last month giving me word jointly of their commission in that port. Both of them, from the excess of their goodness, are extremely pleased that there is a definite hope that we shall see one another in Monterey some time this month or the next. I cannot tell how sorry I am, but I have misgivings that the distance at which I am, and my particular duties, will not permit me to enjoy so extraordinary a happiness. In that case, my sole consolation is the assurance that both of these gentlemen may themselves be convinced that if we have to miss that happiness, there must be some circumstance that made it utterly impossible.

I wish Your Reverence all happiness and perfect health. I continue unaltered in deepest submission even to your very suggestions, and pray that God Our Lord may keep you for many years in His holy grace.

San Diego,
October 27, 1794.

[1] King Louis XVI was put to death by guillotine the previous year.
[2] This seems to have been the opinion of all who have written about him. Bancroft, *op. cit.,* I, 531 speaks of him as "a fellow of infinite jest."

189. To Don Diego de Borica

By means of Your Lordship's official letter of the eleventh of this month, which I received yesterday, I am informed that on the twelfth of last July His Excellency the Marqués de Branciforte[1] assumed the office of Viceroy, Governor and Captain General of these dominions, President of the Royal Audiencia of its Metropolis, and Deputy Superintendent of the Royal Treasury. At the first opportunity that arises I shall see to it that the missionaries subject to me are so notified.

May God Our Lord keep Your Lordship for many years in His holy grace.

San Carlos Mission,
November 27, 1794.

[1] The new viceroy was of Italian descent, and was married to the sister of Godoy, the "Prince of Peace."

190. Memorandum

A list of the items that fell to the share of this Mission of San Carlos from the gift made by Don Jorge Wancober [George Vancouver] with the stipulation that it be divided equally between this mission, that of the Soledad, and the Presidio.

2 barrels of nails	11 pruning hooks
32 small axes	5 gardener's hoes
2 large saws	9 dozen rasps
5 handsaws	28 ditto of brass spoons
28 bundles of thread	1 set of copper kettles and another of tinplate
20 rolls of colored ribbon, woolen	
8 ditto, narrow	5 copper cups
⅓ piece of artificial galloon	5 ditto, tin
10 colored feather dusters	7 dozen small files
14 pieces of rope or cord for fishing	73 tin plates
33 axes	2 soldering irons
17 ditto, for carpenters	1 single grindstone, or whetstone, five spans in diameter, which had remained in this mission.
11 small iron shovels	
6 ditto, large	
2 sickles	

The mission presented him with six hundred large abalone shells, six sheep, and six otter skins, in addition to many sacks of different kinds of vegetables, and of potatoes,[1] besides frequent gifts that had some value.

[November, 1794?]

[1] Lasuén could well have regarded this gift as retribution. The first potatoes to be introduced into California, as far as is known, were a gift to San Carlos Mission from an earlier distinguished visitor, the Frenchman La Pérouse, during his visit to California in the latter part of the year 1786. In his memoirs La Perouse wrote: "Our gardener gave to the missionaries some potatoes from Chile, perfectly sound; I believe this is not one of the least of our gifts and that this root will succeed perfectly around Monterey." (Cited by Bancroft, *op. cit.,* I, 431)

191. To Don Diego de Borica

Manuel Esteban Ruiz is a master-mason and stonecutter. At a salary of eighteen reales a day he undertook to teach his crafts to the Indians of our New California, and in that capacity to continue here for a period of four years. He began to work at the Royal Presidio of Monterey on June 14, '91, and continued there by order of the governor, Don Pedro Fages, until December 20, '92. On that date he came to this mission of San Carlos in virtue of a higher order from His Excellency Count Revilla Gigedo, Viceroy of New Spain, who gave orders that the skilled workers should be distributed through the missions in order to teach the Indians. When the master-worker arrived here there was no supply of material awaiting him, and the period of the heavy rains had set in.

Eventually, the first stone of the church was laid on July 7, 1793,[1] and by this time about half the work is completed.

It would be very fitting if the person who began the work could complete it. But the time allowed in the contract is not adequate for that, and neither is it adequate for the proper instruction of the apprentices assigned to him.

He abides very well by the terms of his contract, and is a person of good character; and by reason of this, if there were other applicants who were skilled in the same arts and were of like character, they, too, would have been given a contract, and without a doubt the number of those who would have come would have equalled the number approved and authorized by the central government, to be paid for out of the Royal Treasury.

Seeing that in this master-craftsman, Manuel Esteban Ruiz, are combined all the qualities one could ask for in order to attain the pious objectives of the King—the welfare and progess of these, his new possessions—I humbly beg Your Lordship to issue a decree extending the contract of this craftsman an additional year or year and a half, or to take steps to see that it is so extended. This is the length of time he will need, he says, in order to have the church completed and the Indians sufficiently instructed.

May God Our Lord keep Your Lordship for many years in His holy grace.

San Carlos Mission,
December 10, 1794.

San Carlos Mission, January 3, 1795
This is a copy of the original, and to date I have not yet received a

reply. I have been merely told in conversation that my request had been forwarded to the Viceroy of Mexico.

Fr. Fermín Francisco de Lasuén.

[1] This is the stone church of Carmel Mission which is still standing. In the course of the years it has undergone some alterations, but it is still substantially the edifice that Ruiz built. The general plan reveals the work of a master craftsman, but in the execution of details one can readily detect the hand of neophytes who were still novices in the art.

As early as 1784 provision was already made for the construction of this building. When Fray Junipero Serra lay dying, in the month of August, 1784, he said to his friend Fray Francisco Palou, "I desire you to bury me in the church, quite close to Father Fray Juan Crespi for the present; and when the stone church is built, they can put me wherever they want." (Geiger, *Palou's Life of Serra*, p. 247). The grave of Serra is in the sanctuary of the stone church, and so is the grave of Lasuén. There is no evidence that the bodies were reinterred. Instead, the sanctuary of the old church became the sanctuary of the new stone church.

192. To the Missionaries

The Lord give you Peace. I wish to inform Your Reverences that on the nineteenth of last July His Excellency the Marqués de Branciforte assumed the office of Viceroy, Governor and Captain General of these Dominions, President of the Royal Audiencia of his Metropolis, and Superintendent Sub-delegate of the Royal Treasury.

Our Father Guardian in his letter of the twenty-sixth of the same month of July greets Your Reverences, and charges me to bring to your notice that should the new chief of the province require or order you to effect some change in the management, methods, or procedure which have been observed in these missions, or question or consult you, especially in writing, in any matter that could refer to it, let your reply be, that this does not lie within your competence and should be directed to me. It is earnestly recommended that one should proceed with much circumspection and care in this matter.

The eleven Fathers who on the fifth of last January were taken prisoners by the French were kept manacled in jail in the city of Pointe-a-Petre[1] until the twelfth of April, when the English took the city by force of arms. They released them immediately, and by the third of May had them brought to Puerto Rico. Three days after their arrival Reverend Father Fray Gregorio Samaniego, a priest of the Province of Burgos, died there. Of the remaining ten, five are students and one a lay-brother. According to a letter from Reverend Father Oramas, dated the eighth of August and written at the same time that the mail from Spain reached Mexico, three more of this number had already died, one of them the president. Another was in his last agony, and grave fears were entertained for the others, for they were suffering from the *black vomit*.[2]

Three or four days after arriving there a certain Father Fray Lóndriz from Burgos died of the same disease at Veracruz. He had come from Cádiz with the collector of the seventeen who arrived at the college in September, and of the eleven who were made prisoners. This latter is Fray Jaime, and he should be at the college by this time.

Others who died were Brother Murguía, and Father Preacher Fray Antonio Brillas, and one of the newly arrived, a student deacon, Fray Luis Ramírez. Four others of them have already begun to break down and are constantly in the infirmary because the climate does not suit them. Fathers Sancho and Bocanegra find themselves very lacking in strength.

The Reverend Father Arévalo has already received the official authorization in regard to his commission to collect twenty-two more religious. The men of the Council[3] did him the honor of reading in plenary session the Reports and the Spiritual and Temporal Status of these missions. They were all highly pleased with the great and outstanding progress which, in comparison with other larger missions, has been revealed.

They thank us in the name of the King through the medium of the Reverend Father Guardian, and he in turn adds his own and that of the college.

On the thirtieth of last March our Most Reverend Father Moya was consecrated bishop. The sponsor was our Lord the King, and he appointed him Archdeacon Prebendary of Valencia and Inquisitor General. The position of Commissary General of the Indies fell to the Most Reverend Fray Pablo de Moya, nephew of the former.

In appreciation of the many and special favors shown to our College of San Fernando by His Excellency the Count of Revilla Gigedo, the Reverend Father Guardian sent him a Letter of Affiliation, and he appreciated it so much that he sent the following letter, and His Reverence has sent me this copy of it:

"I am grateful for the affectionate expressions which Your Reverence in your own name and in that of the Apostolic College offers me in your letter of the twenty-fifth of this month, together with your Letter of Affiliation. For this reason I repeat to Your Reverence that wherever I am, it will afford me particular satisfaction to contribute to the welfare of your community which exercises and discharges the high and commendable obligations of its sacred institution in a manner so becoming and so deserving of praise.

"It is my earnest hope that in your prayers you will commend me to God; and I pray that He may keep, etc."

A few hours before leaving Mexico His Excellency sent the following to our Father Guardian:

"Since the new Viceroy is about to take over the command of these dominions, I shall no longer have occasion to transact official business with Your Reverence. Nevertheless, I shall not fail to retain an eager disposition to promote whatever will redound to the satisfaction of Your Reverence, of your community, and of every member of it, no matter what or where my assignment may be.[4]

"May God keep, etc."

In each of the missions, when this circular letter is received, the fact that it has been read is to be attested; and the Reverend Fathers at San Diego will take care to return it to me.

If because of the speedy departure of the mails which carry it, it should remain behind somewhere instead of proceeding with them, it is recommended that it be dispatched promptly with Indians so that its arrival everywhere should not be retarded.

I wish Your Reverences all happiness and, placing myself at your disposal, beg your prayers. And I pray that God Our Lord may keep you for many years in His holy grace.

San Carlos Mission,
January 2, 1795.

[1] The principal port of the island of Guadeloupe, part of the French West Indies.
[2] A symptom of the yellow fever.
[3] This was the Council of the Indies, a very powerful body, for the administration of imperial affairs in Spain was vested in it. See C. H. Haring *The Spanish Empire in America* (New York, 1947), pp. 102-118.
[4] When Revilla Gigedo ceased to be Viceroy—his term had not expired—he went to Spain, but the influence he could exert at court was much less that either he or the missionaries had anticipated, for he found it necessary to defend himself against critics and detractors. In the course of a few years, however, he was restored to favor.

193. To Fray Joseph Manuel de Martiarena

The Lord give you Peace. After Mass today, when I wanted to write this letter they told me that the Indians who were to take it had already left. I am happy about the service being had from the horses and mule.

I am very sorry to learn about the breakdown of my dear Padre Fray Buenaventura. I send him greetings. And I wish to assure you that I am ready to do what I can, even by personal effort, to promote his recovery.

In my estimation it would be better if notification of the election of justices is not sent to the governor until such time as His Lordship asks for it. And in case he asks for it, simply write: January 6 of the year ... in this Mission of ... X X were elected alcaldes, and X X *regidores*.

I am very busy; I am leaving immediately for the presidio. I wish Your Reverence and my friend Father Ventura all happiness. I am at the service of both of you; and I pray that God Our Lord may preserve you both in His holy grace through many years.

San Carlos Mission,
January 13, 1795.

194. To Fray Tomás Pangua

On the twenty-eighth of last month I received your letter of the twenty-sixth of last July. I am happy, in the first place, that His Excellency Count de Revilla Gigedo appreciated the Letter of Affiliation which you so justly and fittingly sent him. His expressions of gratitude, of which you sent me a copy, give us good ground for hoping for his powerful protection at Court. Thanks be to God.

I have sent this information among the missions in the form of a circular letter. And I also sent the further news you gave me in the letter mentioned. That is to say, that Brother Murguía died at the college (this we knew already), and Fathers Brillas and Ramírez; that Father Samaniego died in Puerto Rico; and according to a letter of Father Oramas, of the eighth of last August, in the same place three others of those released by the English, one of whom was the president. And finally, in Veracruz, Father Lóndriz.

I am always circumspect and careful, and now more than ever, in regard to the civil government. I will do just what you tell me in every case when there is a question of introducing innovations; and I have instructed the missionaries, in the name of Your Reverence, how they are to reply in such circumstances.

I have informed them of the thanks extended to us by the members of the Council in the name of the King for the happy and progressive condition of these missions. And I have let them know, too, the expressions of thanks you added in your own name and in that of the college. Thanks be to God.

Father Pedro Esteban has been here for more than a month and a half. He came in a launch which some English brought to Santa Cruz for a cargo of beans and vegetables. He had met with a slight accident and was suffering from a minor injury. He was given treatment, and is thinking of returning to his post as soon as the weather allows; but that has turned to rain. I delivered to him the letter you enclosed, and I gave him the message you told me to give.

At the end of November Señor Wancober [Vancouver] sailed from this port with the frigate and brigantine under his command. He insisted very strongly that I should write to him in London where he hopes to be within eight months, and where he will be eager to hear about the Franciscans who are engaged in this work of conversion, for they hold the first place in his esteem and affection. May God reward him. He made presents of whatever he could to this mission, and to those of Santa Cruz, Santa Clara, and San Francisco, for they took pains to show him courtesy.

The Englishman commissioned for the evacuation of Nootka did not arrive there when Brigadier Álava was expecting him. For that reason he had to come down to Monterey where he will remain until April. He will then return to Nootka to carry out his commission on the part of Spain.

I thought I might be able to repay some fragment of the endless amount I owe to such an illustrious house, if I could pay my respects to Don José Manuel de Álava, even if only in a poor Franciscan way. But I fear he is leaving me still more his debtor, for he surpasses himself in the honors and favors he confers on me. May God reward him for it.

Today, the twenty-sixth of the current month, I received two letters from you. One was dated the thirteenth of August, and the other the thirtieth of last September, containing directions regarding the processing of tallow. I do not believe that in this country it will be practicable, because here we do not slaughter sheep. Nor is it possible to slaughter animals in the months of November and December[1] after we have had two or three frosts, for as a rule by that time they all are thin. In addition, it would take many years to get our plant and our workers adapted to the many details involved.

All the tallow, or almost all, that is sold and can be sent to San Blas is from cattle. Despite this, I will send the information to the missions in a circular letter, and will do all I can to see that there are stockpiles of tallow of the best condition possible.

As soon as it arrives, I will distribute the hemp seed to the twelve missions, for Father Arenaza has sown it for three or four years in this mission in small quantities. He was able to raise enough to keep on hand a sufficient supply of seed, and to distribute it even this very year to the other missions and the pueblos.[2]

The small quantity sown here did well, but I understand it never reached the stage when it could be made into rope. I already told Your Reverence that up to the present they are engaged in activities (to express it that way) of primary necessity; and work on such crops allows little or no time for attention to other produce. I repeat, nevertheless, the same offer I made on another occasion, namely, to devote all my efforts to attain this end, in so far as it lies in my power, so as to satisfy my obligation of complying with the superior order of His Excellency the Viceroy and of Your Reverence.

Tomorrow Father Fray Pedro will leave for Santa Cruz and I am already thinking of giving him another assignment, because his temperament does not harmonize with that of the Fathers of that mission. It is only too true that he is very melancholy.

The Fathers at Santa Clara tell me that Father Fray Manuel Fernández is getting along very well. Thanks be to God.

I am glad, and I appreciate it very much, that this year you are determined to send two or three religious, those that you know to be the type needed. May God bring them safe.

At the moment there is nothing new of any importance. And there never will be anything new in my obedience and submission to the orders and instructions of Your Reverence, nor in my cordial wish that God Our Lord may keep you for many years in His holy grace.

San Carlos Mission,
January 26, 1795.

[1] Writing almost fifty years later, Sir James Douglas noted that the slaughtering season began "about the middle of June and lasts about three months." Other writers seem to agree. Cf. Edith Buckland Webb, *op. cit.*, p. 176.

[2] In at least one mission museum, that of San Juan Bautista, hemp carders, dating back to mission days, can still be seen. Furthermore, writers have assumed that hemp was introduced into California by Governor Borica in this year of 1795, but this letter makes it clear that Father Arenaza had been cultivating it "for three or four years" previously.

195. To the Missionaries

The Lord give you Peace. The King our Lord, in a royal official letter of the twenty-third of July, 1793, commands that schools of the Spanish language are to be established in all pueblos of this government so that the Indians may learn to read, write, and speak it, and that they be forbidden to speak their native tongue.

The governor has sent me an authentic copy of this royal order, and he knows what can be done in these active reductions to attain the objective desired so that (as is but right and just), what the King has ordered may be brought about, as far as possible. He places an obligation on me, and I hereby pass it on to Your Reverences, namely, that you take pains to teach the Spanish language to the different converts, and that you forbid them, as far as possible, to use their native language, availing yourselves for this purpose of whatever means your well-known zeal suggests.

Before forwarding this, let someone in each mission sign it, certifying that it has been read; and it is to be returned to me from San Diego so that it may be available if called for at any time.

May God Our Lord keep Your Reverences for many years in His holy grace.

San Carlos Mission,
February 23, 1795.

Herewith I enclose the Instruction which I received yesterday after the missionaries from the north had taken note of it. And in the meantime, pending the return thence to me of the patent of our Most Reverend Father [Commissary] of the Indies, which I intend to forward, I wish to inform Your Reverences that the person who sent the information on behalf of the Council was the Reverend Father Pablo de Moya. He informs us that to complete the ten years, as required by the law and by our General Constitutions, the period is to be reckoned from the first day of embarkation at any port in Spain.

And in like manner, in order to carry out successfully and to the satisfaction of God and of our Catholic Monarch the just desires of the latter, he hopes that we will help with our sacrifices and prayers. And he exhorts us at the same time to remember Our Most Holy Father, Pope Pius VI, our Catholic sovereigns, the Most Serene Prince, and all royal persons. All of this I now impose as an obligation on Your Reverences until I am able to send you the actual patent.

Furthermore, despite the fact that the method indicated to us as a means of processing the tallow is not practicable here (and I have replied in this vein to our Father Guardian), please make every endeavor to collect as much as possible of this item, and let it be the best quality according to our best judgment.

March 1, of the above year.

196. To the Missionaries

The Lord give you Peace. I am sending Your Reverences the enclosed sample so that, in obedience to the higher orders of His Excellency the Viceroy and of our Reverend Father Guardian, you may be guided by it in the Report which Your Reverences will be required to send me every two years, in accordance with the aforementioned higher orders. (At the same time you are not to omit the customary annual one.)

What this adds to your work is the number of *gente de razón* of your respective missions, with their increase or decrease in the two years, as well as the baptisms, marriages, and deaths among them. You will give also the rise or fall in the population which, for the two year period, will appear in the total of Indians and of *gente de razón* in comparison with the preceding years.

The placing of these particulars in their proper columns will be my responsibility. Your Reverences will give them to me in unbroken lines. Do the same in regard to the notes to be inserted in the Form.

Let a copy of this be made at each mission so that it may serve as a guide when it is needed. And let the original printed copy be passed along as quickly as possible, until it reaches San Diego.

In accordance with this Form, Your Reverences are each to make out your Reports immediately in regard to the last two years, namely, '93 and '94, because it is so ordered. And you will send them to me as early as possible.

As you forward this, you will testify that you have read it, and that you have received the printed Form; and let the oldest add his signature to it. The printed Form is to be placed in the archives at San Diego, and the Fathers there will return this letter to me in the conditions specified in order to meet requirements.

May God Our Lord keep Your Reverences for many years in His holy grace.

Mission San Carlos,
March 4, 1795.

P. S.

It is not necessary for this Report to come in duplicate form like the other; one copy suffices. It is only the general one which concerns me and has to be sent in triplicate. Pray for me.

It has not been possible for me to mail this letter on time, so today, the sixth of this month, I have had some time to spend with the governor, and we agreed that, as regards the information requested concerning Spaniards and other people, I will deal with this by stating ahead of the notes that in these missions there are no Spanish settlers, with the exceptions of the families of those who serve as military escort, and in some cases a major-domo. Your Reverences are thus excused from including such persons in your Report.

In the customary annual report, however, you will be careful to enter these baptisms, marriages, and deaths, differentiating them in each case from the Indians. There will be nothing new for you to do in regard to each biennial report, because if you draw up the annual one in accordance with the differences mentioned, and with the other details as requested, it will be possible for me (as I am now doing) to draw up a new one in full every two years in accordance with regulations.

It is certainly fitting, and is something I request, that Your Reverences would always and without fail advise me every two years on all matters that you judge important for the advancement of each one of your missions, provided such information would be in accord with the *Notes* in the Form.

Mission [name not given, but evidently San Carlos]
the sixth of the above.

197. Fray Tomás Pangua

I am grateful that Your Reverence took the trouble to deliver in person my letter to His Most Illustrious Lordship, Señor Martínez.[1] He has already replied with all becoming gravity, but without a promise of anything, not even under show of courtesy. Perhaps your recommendation slipped his memory, for he addressed the letter to *The President of the Missions of San Carlos of Monterey in Sonora*.

All of this is of little importance in view of the concessions which His Illustrious Lordship granted at the request of Your Reverence, as you informed me in your letter of the twenty-fifth of last October. I have already notified all the missions in regard to them.

Furthermore, I have circulated among all of them the patent which you sent me, together with that of our Most Reverend Fray Pablo de Moya, Commissary General of the Indies.

I acknowledge, too, receipt of the higher order of His Excellency the Marqués de Branciforte, Viceroy of New Spain, relative to the biennial reports on the spiritual status of these missions, in accordance with the requirements in the Form drawn up and printed by order of His Excellency, and forwarded to me by Your Reverence.

If I am correct in assuming that His Excellency made additional printed forms available, it would be well if we had eight or ten of those that contain directions, so that we could send them to all the missions. And we should have, in addition, a good number of the ruled Forms with the blanks to be filled in, so that the President may have a good supply on hand; for since he has to forward three clean copies every two years it is possible that at least three others may become spoiled because of the distractions or problems he has in mind when preparing them.

I have already expended much effort on this Report, as I did on three or four biennial reports in the past, and would have sent it on its way if the mail had been one day later.

I was quite worried because the new order arrived on the very day on which, according to directions, I was to have it completed. I received it the second last day of last month.

I referred my problem to the Governor (a good man, a good fellow-countryman, a person of great vision and remarkably active), and His Lordship was good enough to volunteer to draw them up in triplicate for me, provided I would send him, even in a rough draft, the data and the information to go with it. I have put them together without waiting for the reports of the missionaries for this year. I have sent them to him, and with his help and support—and may God reward him for it—I shall be able to send you these documents by this mail, that is to say by the frigate *Princesa* which is due to sail shortly for San Blas.

This, too, is an opportune time to send Your Reverence, in two packages, the Annual Reports of the Missions, and the usual general summary of the condition of all of them. This was a most trying task for me, especially at the present time when the others are being sent. By referring to them it will be possible to correct and clarify it. I hope Your Reverence will pardon and overlook the corrections and erasures.

It has come to my attention that by means of a series of questions the Governor has tried to find out from the commandants of these presidios how much spiritual assistance we, the neighboring missionaries, give them. The answers, with a few exceptions, have been very favorable. As a consequence, at the present time the governor in a report is petitioning the viceroy for full-time chaplains for the different presidios, with the exception of Santa Barbara, at a salary of 400 pesos, and with the specific condition that they be from San Fernando College; for should they be from some other group or other institute there would be bound to be a considerable amount of misunderstanding and friction (and this is but too true).

I leave to Your Reverence and the venerable council the solution of the difficulties this issue raises. I would point out, however, that even to the governor himself the salary or stipend he mentions seems small, if it is to provide a suitable and decent living for the religious, unless the neighboring missions come to his assistance. And there is no reason why communities as poor as these are should assume the burden of subsidizing a few royal chaplains. A surgeon who lives and works exclusively in this presidio enjoys a salary of about 1,000 pesos; and a phlebotomist (a no-body, as everybody knows) who has been assigned to him so that he can have an easier life still, he gets more than 400. I do not like to be making comparisons; but I would like to point out that a chaplain needs a sacristan and a cook—and these are not to be had for nothing.

I am suggesting an idea, and let its value be what it may. Three missionaries could be assigned as supernumeraries at the same salary. These could easily be sent to reside in the three presidios, but on the definite understanding that should a mission be short a missionary, one of the three could be transferred to it immediately if no other missionary is to be had. In this case his stipend of 400 pesos would accrue to the mission whose Fathers now take care of the presidio whence he came.

With this temporary remuneration of the missions in the vicinity of the presidios, and with the open-mindedness of the missionaries, the latter would have less repugnance to residing at the presidios and submitting to their administration. Missionaries in the neighborhood would be less reluctant to afford help to those to whose lot it fell; and the presidio would always be assured of the help needed, for during the time they were awaiting the replacement the aforementioned would be under obligation to give more assistance.

I have never made it my business to plead for chaplaincies in presidios, still less for the establishment of new foundations, having regard to the fewness of members in the college; and so, what I am saying here in regard to the former, and in the attached triplicate in regard to the latter, is simply my attempt to carry out the unavoidable duty which the esteemed orders of His Excellency and Your Reverence impose on me, and the new request of this government to which reference is made above.

In the middle of last month the brigantine *Activo* cast anchor in this port after a voyage of forty days from San Blas. It brought the English commissioner for the evacuation of Nootka; and after Señor Álava embarked on her they set sail from this port for that latitude on the first of the present month.

I wish Your Reverence all happiness, and I place myself once more at your service, with the same humble compliance as always. And I pray that God Our Lord may keep you for many years in His holy grace.

San Carlos Mission,
March 12, 1795.

P. S.

The remark in the triplicate report that I am ignoring the distinction between Spaniards and people of other casts was suggested by the governor. I gladly accepted it, for in that way the matter is made clear, seeing that His Lordship in his over-all view gives account of these people, and because in excusing us from giving it, as he says, he makes the Report less laborious for us.

[1] Damien Martínez de Galinzonga, third bishop of Sonora, was a native of the Province of Murcia, Spain, where he was born in June, 1738. He was a member of the Franciscan Order. In February, 1794 he was named Bishop of Sonora, and took possession of his diocese in December of that year. Shortly afterwards he was transferred to another diocese, and died in Spain in 1802.

198. To Fray Tomás Pangua

I ask Your Reverence's holy blessing, and with all due respect I beg to inform you that it is confidence in God and nothing else that keeps me from saying that I am not capable of further effort. The fatigue I endure from writing is becoming so great that when all my other activities are combined with it, and it with them, the result is that I am constantly so confused in mind that my life becomes exceedingly wearisome. When I have the good fortune to take up the work in the spirit of penance, all becomes easy; but it is always a penance, and it is always in the power of Your Reverence to remove it or to continue it.

A great deal of what I have to suffer can be traced to the disgust and repugnance that are felt and revealed continuously by Fathers Salazar and Baldomero by reason of the fact that they are still assigned here. Your Reverence has already let me know how Father Salazar has importuned you even at this distance. You can imagine what my position is, being much nearer to him and with much less authority.

I know quite well that Your Reverence will leave nothing undone to comfort both, nor will I fail to use all possible means to bring about their contentment and peace of mind.

The tribute I paid in my other letter to our new governor is to be understood as applying to what we have seen up to the present. I am not coming forward as a surety for the future. Two or three times in the course of conversation, and in a passing remark, he has given me to understand that before I assign any missionary to a place, or change him from it, I should first obtain a permit or approval from him.

I am not in the humor to ask him for it, for it has never been customary; and it seems to me that everything pertaining to the royal *patronato* (and this is what he bases it on) has already been dealt with in the capital where you are when the missionaries set out from the college, leaving nothing to be done here beyond the simple plotting out as is done here, of the places where they are to exercise their ministry, this being the purpose for which they were called from afar, and sent on their way equipped with all they need.

Despite all this, if the case reaches the point when an official letter is issued, or the problem seems to be developing into a legal issue, I will give way in the best manner I know, calmly proposing what I have set out here, for I will then point out that I will have recourse to my college, with the firm and inflexible resolution of doing or avoiding precisely what it orders me to do or to avoid.

Therefore, I beg Your Reverence kindly to inform or direct me as to what I am to do in the matter.

This year continues to be an extremely dry one everywhere, and we are afraid that supplies will be extraordinarily scarce. But there are hopes at the moment that the condition may improve, for we can see rain-clouds forming.

In the missions to the north there have been many baptisms in recent months, and next Monday, God willing, I shall go there to confirm so that I may be finished before the sixth of May arrives when I shall no longer be able to do so.

I wish Your Reverence all happiness, and am always at your service. And I pray that God Our Lord may keep you for many years in His holy grace.

San Carlos Mission,
March 20, 1795.

199. To the Missionaries

The Lord give you Peace. Up to the present the higher authorities have been content with the Annual Reports which have been made up in compliance with the rules which I sent Your Reverences for this purpose under date of November 28, 1791. They now wish that the sections on Baptism and on the Living are to be given in the manner explained in the accompanying paper.

In these circumstances I strongly urge Your Reverences to observe the regulation mentioned, neither adding anything nor taking anything away, for the sake of uniformity (and as a precaution, so that we shall not give the government any loophole for imposing extra work on us).

In order to fill out this particular Report, which must be made at the end of every two years, there is to be added to the usual annual one a separate sheet, in simple form, with the information given as in the sample I enclose. (Keep in mind, in regard to the annual one, that it is to be made out in duplicate, each copy in a separate sheet, so that I can send one to the college and the other to the governor of the province.)

Your Reverences are to make copies of it for your own guidance, and certify that you have done so. See that it is forwarded with this to the Mission of our father St. Francis, whence it is to be forwarded to me so that I may have proof of it.

May God keep Your Reverences many years in His holy grace.

San Carlos Mission,
May 22, 1795.

Formula for the Reports. May 22, 1795

Blessed be Jesus

The statistics for *Baptisms* and for *Living*, as demanded by the authorities in the annual reports, should be given in the following form (being careful to observe for all other particulars the formula given for them at the end of the letter):

BAPTISMS: In this year the number of those who were baptized was: (so many) adults; (so many) children; (so many) were children of the above-mentioned newly baptized; (so many) were children of pagans. (So many) were *de razón;* (so many) were children under mission influence. In all, both children and adults, the total is (so many). This, added to the total for previous years, is a grand total of (so many).

LIVING: The number of Indians on the rolls and taking the full course of Christian and secular instruction equals (so many) adults and (so many) under nine years of age. The total number of men is (so many), and the total of women (so many), making a grand total of (so many).

FOR EACH TWO YEAR PERIOD

Report of the state of this Mission of (name) from the first day of the year 1795 until the last day of 1796.

INDIANS

Total for 1796: men (so many); women (so many); in all (so many).
Living in 1794: men (so many); women (so many); in all (so many).
This indicates an increase / decrease of (so many) men, an increase / decrease of (so many) women, and a total increase / decrease of (so many) souls.
In this two-year period the number of marriages of Indians was (so many), of baptisms was (so many), and of deaths (so many).
During the same period among the others there were (so many) marriages, (so many) baptisms, and (so many) deaths.

NOTES. Under this title (and the space may be left blank if there is nothing to add), one can state anything noteworthy that has occurred if it would serve to explain what is in the printed formulary, or if it would be important for the missions that the authorities should know it.

Mission of   (name)   , December 31, 1796
Fr. —————————————— Fr. ——————————————

San Carlos Mission,
May 22, 1795.

200. To Don Diego de Borica

I am reliably informed that Your Lordship has given orders that a military guard is not to be given to a missionary if the latter is to spend the night in the country, even if the purpose is to instruct or baptize a pagan or to hear the confession of a Christian. I have no doubt Your Lordship has reasons to justify your decision; and my purpose is simply to present mine, with the intention of humbly begging that this assistance be not denied us so that we may carry out our ministry when emergencies of major importance arise. And an emergency there certainly is when there is question of the baptism of a pagan or the confession of a Christian when their condition is serious.

Word reaches us that there are sick people living at a distance, and they are asking for a Father. A call like that can come at any hour. The Father is duly notified of a case. There is no chance or possibility that the sick can come of themselves, or be carried; and there is a well-founded hope that he would be able to help them. In that case he is strictly obliged to go, even at risk of his life, for he knows that he is under obligation to subordinate his own life to the spiritual good of his neighbor.[1] In fact, how to reconcile this precept with the safety of the missionary in face of such risks may well have been one of the principal reasons why the King our master maintains military forces in these parts.

Given this protection, the missionary attends to his duties with a greater sense of security. Without it, he risks his life. Naturally he has reason to fear, not so much for his own life as for the vengeance that will be meted out to the Indians as a consequence, should they succeed in bringing about his death, or should they attack him because they find him unarmed. In that case, the duties of the troops would be greater and more wearisome, the work of conversion would be retarded, and peace would be at an end.

Grave difficulties like these are avoided if a small escort is given to the missionary; and should some misfortune then befall, there is the satisfaction and comfort that it happened in the line of duty after every step that was reasonably possible had been taken in order to avoid it.

Your Lordship must not conclude that when we say the missionary is away over night we mean that he retires to rest in the place to which he goes, or even on the road. We simply mean that he utilizes the night to complete the task he was not able to complete during the day. Or it may be a case of waiting for daylight, for only with the aid of that would it be possible to negotiate some dangerous pass where, in the darkness, there is risk of falling over a precipice. Or it may be a case of taking some rest so as to be able to continue the task. For undertakings like these, the missionary never takes with him more clothes than what he is wearing and, unless impeded by some of the obstacles mentioned, he will go and return with no more delay than the business on hand definitely demands.

How many difficulties there are! And so many things can happen. Let us suppose, or consider, what has happened frequently. A Christian woman, or a pagan, in child-birth, the care she needs, and the infant. A Christian or a pagan who is unconscious. The missionary sets out to visit a sick man who is reported to be living near at hand, and after traveling for leagues they admit that it would involve a long journey; that he had already been to confession, or been baptized, but that he is dying. In the meantime it has become known that in the same place there is an additional one or more who are sick, and in the same necessity.

I myself have set out to do something that seemed to require but a half a day, and not even in a day and a half, and taking in the night, too, has it been possible to conclude the task. I have gone on a journey with the intention of returning the next day, in order to baptize a pagan woman who had sent for me. I began that night to instruct her in the Christian doctrine, and before I could finish I had to hasten to another who was dying. I instructed and baptized her; then returned to the first and did the same for her.

I retired a distance of two or three musket shots to the ranchería to rest for what little remained of the night, and there I learned that the ranchería was suffering from the plague. This I saw for myself the following morning. The sick wanted my help, and those who were well pressed for it, too. In the end I had to stay for nine nights and days with these pagans, a dozen leagues from the mission, and I baptized and buried many.

I know I would not have abandoned this work to which I was in duty bound even if the escort had departed. It was composed of two men; and I wonder if the Indians would have been as peaceful as they were, were it not for their respect for the escort, such as it was.

Furthermore, Sir, it is worthy of consideration that the rugged sierras, the valleys, and the beaches where the Indians live abound in bears, and other wild animals. And I am inclined to say that above all others I fear the very animal on which I ride, for I am quite unskilled in managing it—a failing in which we, the Franciscans, all share alike in these parts.

What heart, then, (and least of all that of Your Lordship), will bear to see a poor Friar on a dark night, engaged on the one hand in a truly religious enterprise which brings honor to our Catholic Nation, in behalf of the largest and most attractive among these barbarous nations, and on the other, surrounded by so much danger, so many things that cause anguish and anxiety, all of which can be remedied with two or three soldiers?

Even these latter are safer in duties of this nature than in others in which they frequently engage day and night in the country, and which cannot be more necessary or more important. Yes, my Lord, a calamity is less likely to befall them in the company of the former, for in the present circumstances, nothing can contribute more to what they have to endure than some mischief or harm which they may commit—and it is not easy for them to commit such excesses in the presence of the Father.

Through the mercy of God, never once has any misfortune occurred in journeys of that nature in the course of all these years.

This is how I see it, and this is what I feel obliged to bring to the attention of Your Lordship, begging that you may be so kind as to grant us the favor of ordering that we be afforded fitting protection for the accomplishment of objectives that are so serious and so indispensible.

Whatever be the outcome, the orders of Your Lordship for me are always matters deserving the greatest veneration and respect.

May God Our Lord keep Your Lordship for many years in His holy grace.

San Carlos Mission,
June 15, 1795.

[1] Lasuén has stated very briefly and clearly a basic universal law applying to all priests charged with the care of souls.

201. To Reverend Father Guardian [Fray Antonio Nogueyra][1]

With a request for Your Reverence's holy blessing, and with the deepest respect and humility I offer my congratulations on your appointment to so exalted an office. It affords me great pleasure to acknowledge you as my major superior, and I shall be highly pleased if you look upon me as your most devoted servant. Let Your Reverence command me and dispose of me, and you can do so with the definite assurance that you will not find in me any other will but your own. I wish you all success and happiness.

I am forwarding Your Reverence the enclosed copy. After I had found out by word of mouth what the mental attitude of the governor was, I put before him in the same way the evil results and inconveniences; but I could not dissuade him from his opinion. His Lordship went so far as to post this ordinance of his in the barracks or guardrooms of the missions. I showed him the rough draft of the official letter with a view to finding out if he approved of it, before sending it to him.

He agreed to it, and I sent it. He received it on the date it was written. Nevertheless, fifteen days have passed since then and he has not sent any reply.

On two other occasions on which we discussed the matter, His Lordship told me that with this mail he is sending the Viceroy the actual document I sent him, and that he will do whatever the Viceroy determines, without altering in the meantime what he himself has ordered.

Your Reverence will know very well what has to be done to assure a favorable consideration for that request. Even those who refuse to grant it have no argument to bring against it, no reply to make to it.

It is my opinion that by this mail the governor is informing the Viceroy of a chance misfortune that occurred in San Francisco. Shortly after many Indians from the other side of the Bay had been baptized in that mission, several of them ran away to their own country. The Fathers sent ten or twelve reliable Christians to bring them back, warning them strongly on no account to go beyond a certain ranchería. They did not find them there; and forgetting or ignoring the advice of the Fathers, they went into the interior and unexpectedly found themselves among a multitude of warlike Indians. The latter, ignoring the fact that the Christians were unarmed, and paying no attention to their cries as they begged them to desist, or their plea that they had not the least hostile intent, slaughtered them all with the exception of two. It was only with much effort that these latter were able to escape, and it was they who brought me the news.

There was no risk involved in the enterprise, if only it had been carried out according to the instructions of the Fathers. And this information may be of service to you should some recrimination be made in regard to it.

Yesterday I received word that for some days Father Manuel Fernández has been very ill in Santa Clara, suffering from a persistent fever.   He has been sent some medicines which the surgeon of the presidio prescribed.

I am happy to be so dependent on Your Reverence that with the least effort you can do with me what you please, even if you have reason to think it is the most repugnant to me. In this mind, and with the greatest submission I place myself at the service of Your Reverence, and I pray that God Our Lord may keep you for many years in His holy grace.

San Carlos Mission,
June 30, 1795.

---

[1] The new guardian, whose name Lasuén did not know, was Fray Antonio de Nogueyra, or Nogueyra as he is more commonly known. He was elected in the chapter held on May 23, 1795. Previously he had been a member of the college council for a three-year period, beginning with July 1, 1786. His administration as guardian was brief: he died in office on October 30, 1796.

202. To Fray Diego García

The Lord give you Peace. Even if it were true that I made the promise to which you refer in your letter of the twelfth of the present month, it does not seem right that you should reproach me in such terms for not carrying it out.   Much less are you justified in not doing what you are ordered, as neither this nor anything else is a reason for omitting it.

Assuming, then, that in the opinion of Your Reverence that foundation was a mistake, and that there are others who, in obedience to higher orders, judged it a success, there is no reason why Your Reverence should suffer and cause others to suffer the annoyances, troubles, and inconveniences that have their source in your opinion. And there is no reason why we ourselves should not have an opportunity to take suitable measures to the end that this location may display to the best advantage the same aptitudes it has already shown of being able to maintain the establishment that is there.

Wherefore, in virtue of this, I order Your Reverence to proceed as quickly as possible to the Mission of San Antonio in the capacity of supernumerary, and to remain there until, on the arrival of the ships, some other course is decided on.

May God Our Lord keep Your Reverence many years in His holy grace.

San Carlos,
July 18, 1795.

203. To Reverend Father Guardian
[Fray Antonio Nogueyra]

May I have Your Reverence's holy blessing, for I wish to inform you that despite the fact that at every step, and for a long time, I had clear proof that Father Fray Diego García was not a fit administrator for the new Mission of Soledad, I retained him there for a time through necessity. Moreover, I had hopes, and it was my sincere desire, that by forbearance and tolerance, by gentle persuasion and warnings, I would be able to avoid the harsh measure of withdrawing him from that post.

In a year like this, which is unusually dry, he failed to take advantage, or did not wish to take advantage, of a large expanse of ditch through which, from November almost to the end of May, it would be possible to channel enough water for a good harvest of wheat and barley that would not fail. I passed it over almost in silence with merely a slight indication of my feeling of regret.

Having lost an opportunity like that, which was very important and involved but little effort, on my last visit to the mission I instructed him to devote himself as much as possible to the opening of that ditch; and I promised to use my influence with the governor to get him the aid of a soldier who was very willing to direct that work, and very skilled in carrying it out.

This I did; His Lordship let me have him, and I sent word to the Father. His reply was, that despite the little profit he anticipated from such an enterprise, or the total absence of any profit, on the following day he would promptly send some peons with the soldier to begin it.

After some days I learned that not only did he not do so, but that he put obstacles in the way. I reproached him twice with all gentleness, and when I least expected it I found myself with the letter (of which I am enclosing a copy), and with the necessity of making a decision. And what that decision was you can see from the tone of my reply.

Father Martiarena was here at the time. After sending me two applications for permission to leave San Antonio—for he found that climate bad for him, causing him since he went there a profound depression and bad headaches—he now came to consult the surgeon of the presidio here.

This practitioner decided that he must definitely have a change of climate. I immediately appointed him minister of Soledad, and he set out for it on the twentieth of this month, taking with him the letter to Father García that I mentioned. He has written me from there that this Father will start within a few days for San Antonio.

This is the principal, almost the only news of the day. To the regret of all who have come to know him, Father Fray Pedro Esteban[1] has declared that he is no longer fitted for the work here. Father Calzada writes me that he is suffering a great deal from an old ailment, hemorrhoids, and that he is applying to Your Reverence to be retired.

Father Danti is very querulous[2] with me for he has not received any reply from the college regarding the request he has sent twice, and he expresses himself to me in such bitter terms that if it were in my hands I would certainly send him away by the first boat. (He is running the risk, in his opinion, of going blind if he does not get treatments immediately.)

I have learned that Father Fray Manuel Fernández, who was on the point of being given Extreme Unction, is now out of danger and sufficiently recovered.

I am more at your service than at my own in any way you may wish to use me or utilize me, worthless though I am.

I pray that God Our Lord may keep Your Reverence for many years in His holy grace.

San Carlos Mission,
July 30, 1795.

[1] Fray Pedro de San José Esteban was a native of Castile. He joined the College of San Fernando in 1793, arrived in California in 1794, was a missionary mainly at San Diego and San Gabriel, and returned to Mexico in October, 1802.
[2] Bancroft speaks of Danti's "fiery temperament", and Governor Borica refers to it as "genio de polvora." Cf. Bancroft, *op. cit.,* I, 713.

204. To Don Diego de Borica

From time to time the thought has occured to me that in this year of scarcity perhaps grain is listed in the low category of fixed prices because we the missionaries, under whose care are the temporalities of these missions, have entered no complaints, despite the fact that in this past year of '94 the harvest showed a falling off of five thousand three hundred fanegas as compared with the preceding year of '93.

Your Lordship can be quite certain that we always have to be slow or hesitant about having such recourse for, in addition to avoiding any intrusion on our part into matters that are subject to your exclusive control, we shall never consider excessive any effort we can make, if it can increase more and more in public estimation our well-established reputation for being disinterested. I would not even have made this request to Your Lordship if the circumstances of the time did not demand it in view of the unusual and notable scarcity, and if there was any doubt in my mind that it was absolutely necessary to make sure that a just price is paid for the products.

Having thus satisfied whatever obligation I may be under in this regard, I shall consider that Your Lordship has carried out your duties in full, no matter whether you increase the price of grain or leave it as it is.

In this respect the indifference we feel has gone so far that it could not go any further. It is in a class with the deep dislike we have of making even the least suggestion in regard to this matter. We raised no objection to the second fixed price which now holds, and which lowers the level of the first, despite the fact that in it the price is fixed at the lowest level to which it could drop in time of plenty. When the first price list was in effect, which made provision for higher prices in years of scarcity, there were such years, and we agreed that there should be no increase, but that the missions, for that reason, should not cease to come to the aid of the presidios and their residents whenever they were in need.

We accept in silence the fact that the missions not only sell their fruit and produce at the reduced price mentioned, and also the fact that the price is subject to regulation every year, and every season during the year. We tolerate the fact that for the most part it will be the price that best suits the purchaser rather than the missions. As a rule, they have to supply the grain when the pueblos are in no position to do so. This will often arise when the missions themselves are in need of it, and always when it is necessary to wait a long time for the harvest. In a word, the only thing we are looking for is some way by which the need may be met, or some way by which we may meet it.

It is evident that the administrators of the missions are concerned not with the legitimate rights of property alone, but also with the more important problem of providing for the needy, even at the cost of suffering loss thereby. This kind of burden was imposed very definitely when, after the enactment of the *Reglamento* of Señor Neve, in which the pay of the troops was announced, the price list associated with the name of the same individual was published, fixing the price of the goods and effects which [the troops] consume. By keeping the price of these low it was sought to make the pay of the latter sufficient, and the inescapable interdependence between supplies and salaries became evident.

Obviously the trader would pay no attention to this, but it is not likely that the government ignores it. It is obvious that the missionaries cannot fail to give thought to it.

These latter discussed the matter with the person who formulated the *Reglamento* and the price list; but they did so by word of mouth and informally, as is their custom. And they departed highly pleased to hear him say that he would certainly convert the price for goods supplied into clothing for the Indians, equipment for the farm, and other necessaries for common use, and that they would find all of it at the presidio stores at prime Mexican costs.

Since this was the only way in which, in our case, equity could be maintained in buying and selling with benefit to both parties, and since we had the word of the governor for it, the man authorized to make laws for this province, we considered it so certain and secure that we needed a great deal of experience, and many instances, before we realized that all of this was just words and nothing more. The fact is, that the produce taken from the missions for the presidios is paid for in money, or in drafts on Mexico. The result is, not only is there delay in obtaining help for the Indians, but as soon as the money sent to the capital is converted to use, it is subject to a considerable rebate, for, in addition to the risks and other expenses, the cost of transport from Mexico to San Blas amounts to at least eleven reales per arroba. In this way the missions enjoy the advantage of shopping in Mexico, but this advantage is lost in the surcharges and costs which of necessity have to be incurred in transferring goods from there to New California.

We complained from the beginning about the losses involved for the missions, and looked forward eagerly to what had been offered to us with a view to making the trade an equitable one. But they induced us to be silent by every manner of subterfuge and pretext, and by courteously urging us to defer our hopes to a later date. Thus was introduced this practice, or whatever you want to call it, and no one has had the courage to oppose it formally.

What I marvel at is not so much this matter, as myself, for here I am, drawing up this formal statement much against my will. But the present scarcity is far beyond the ordinary. It is such that, if in former times of scarcity some good or bad excuse could be given for keeping silence, the present time does not admit any.

The effort of Your Lordship to do justice to everything is deserving of all praise; but perhaps in the short period of your administration there has not been an opportunity for examining such matters. I am making these suggestions, then, with profound respect, accepting in advance whatever the well-known justice and integrity of Your Lordship may decree.

May God Our Lord keep Your Lordship many years in His holy grace.

San Carlos Mission,
August 16, 1795.

205. To Reverend Father Guardian
[Fray Antonio Nogueyra]

Begging Your Reverence's holy blessing, I wish to inform you that on the twenty-fourth of last month the frigate *Aránzazu* cast anchor in this port. On board were Fathers Jayme and Ciprés; and on the following day, the twenty-fifth, they came to the mission and they were in good health.

I have not yet decided on their assignment; but I am inclined to leave Father Jayme here and to send Father Ciprés to San Antonio. In this latter place, in addition to Father Sitjar, there are also Fathers García and Esteban as supernumeraries, and I shall have to consider very carefully where I shall have to put them in the same capacity.

I must state that Father García, by reason of his peculiar disposition and his ailments, and the other because of his irresoluteness and his scruples are likely to be little or no use in this ministry. I realize that there is not anyone among the missionary Fathers who will be too happy to welcome them, and I find myself with a thousand perplexities and anxieties in my effort to find an assignment for them. I shall consider the matter very carefully and let Your Reverence know my decision.

I cannot help being filled with anxiety because of the very urgent request of Father Danti to retire to the college. I have sent a formal request to the governor, and I am enclosing a copy of it. He has not replied to me; but I am convinced that he is so inflexible in adhering to the rigor of the terms of the decree that forbids it, that he requires nothing less than an express declaration from the Viceroy—and all that in order to promote justice, and to make provision for a legitimate exception to which every law is susceptible.

That stern decree is the cause of much suffering for me. In view of the fact—and I have the information from the predecessor of Your Reverence—that there is news that efforts are being made to revoke it or moderate it, Your Reverence could not do us a greater favor than to use your best efforts to bring this about.

I have received a copy of the official letter of the *fiscal* for Civil Affairs and for the Royal Treasury, in which justice is done to the Reverend Father Fray Tomás de la Peña, declaring him innocent, and his conduct both good and religious. Thanks be to God. May He be blessed forever. This has lifted from my shoulders a horrible burden that has weighted me down in a manner no words can describe almost from the first moment when, in obedience to the college, I became president of these missions.

Only one month and six days are lacking in order to complete ten years. Your Reverence will follow your own counsels in regard to me. In that respect, my sole ambition is to do what Your Reverence orders me, even if it be to withdraw from here, or to become a supernumerary in any particular mission.

Yes, Reverend Father, I hope with the merciful assistance of God Our Lord that the commands and suggestions of Your Reverence will always find me without any special preference of my own, but determined to do what Your Reverence decides.

Father Calzada is very insistent that I should interest myself in obtaining his recall to the college. The reasons seem to me to be sufficient for granting what he asks, for his old ailment has now become aggravated.

Father Danti is returning to his former assignment, San Francisco, with the definite assurance and the sole consolation that without any doubt he will be leaving the following year. For this purpose I most earnestly beg you to send him his authorization, and that of the Viceroy if it should be necessary.

My faculty to confirm came to an end on the fourth of last May. Both before that date and after it I notified the holy college about it, and I am informing Your Reverence so that you may be gracious enough to obtain an extension of it through the Reverend Father Prefect. The reasons for asking for it are the same as before.

I wish Your Reverence all happiness, and I pray that God Our Lord may keep you for many years in His holy grace.

San Carlos Mission,
September 1, 1795.

206. To Fray Tomás Pangua

At last, and in a worthy manner, you have brought to an end your term of office. Congratulations. And me you have left laboring under my burden, and without a thought perhaps on your part of coming here to relieve me of it. But whether you come or stay, I must always remain your subject just to show how much I appreciate what you did when in office.

Your Reverence has given me by way of dessert a draught of the best wine, for you sent me the decree of the fiscal for Civil Affairs and the Royal Treasury in which justice is done to the becoming zeal and religious conduct of good Father Peña. Thanks be to God. It has been the means of relieving me of the bitter worries and cruel embarrassments which I was made to suffer for almost ten years, that *cause célèbre* was so like a plague. May God forgive those who brought it about.

I have assigned Father Jayme[1] to this mission of San Carlos, and Father Ciprés[2] to San Antonio. As supernumeraries at Santa Clara I wanted to place either Father García or Father Esteban according to what might be the choice of the Fathers there; but they closed that door on me with a bang, and did not want to admit either the one or the other.

I have had to assign them, the first to San Francisco, and the second to San Diego. I have told both of them that they are to take over, respectively, from the Fathers of these missions the ministrations which the presidios nearby require.

I am still afraid of meeting a refusal from some other source, and it is something which makes me feel very uneasy. The frankness of Father Gili was disarming. His problem is how to get away from the ten-year requirement.

I believe I am not mistaken in hoping that the influence Your Reverence always exercised up to the present for the good of this country, when there was a question of requests such as these, cannot but bring about these results, which are so necessary and desirous.

I have already mentioned that, in what pertains to my will, it is you who are in control. Let Your Reverence but put it to the test and it will be seen that my obedience is most prompt and wholehearted.

And so I pray that God Our Lord may keep you for many years in His holy grace.

San Carlos Mission,
September 22, 1795.

[1] Fray Antonio Mariano Jayme spent but one year at San Carlos; then he was transferred to Soledad where he spent twenty-five. His last years were spent in semi-retirement in Santa Barbara, for his health was impaired. He died in Santa Barbara in December 19, 1829, and is buried in the mission vaults. He was a native of the island of Mallorca.

[2] Fray Marcelino Ciprés was a native of Aragon, Spain, and became a member of San Fernando College in 1793. In 1795 he reached California and was stationed at San Antonio Mission from then until 1804, and at San Luis Obispo from then until his death in 1810. He is buried in the sanctuary of San Miguel Mission where he died during the course of a visit there. Bancroft speaks of him as a "zealous missionary, (who) learned the native language of San Antonio, and devoted himself most assiduously to the work of caring for the sick and attending to the spiritual welfare of the neophytes. He was ever ready to start when summoned, regardless of the hour, the distance, or the difficulties of the way." Bancroft, *op. cit.,* II, 148-149.

207. To Reverend Father Guardian
[Fray Antonio Nogueyra]

I wrote to Your Reverence, intending the letter to go by the overland mail for this month, for that is carried by a very speedy route so as to catch at Loreto the boat for San Blas. I described in it the steps I had taken for the embarkation of Father Danti, at his urgent request.

However, the mail was sent forward at an unexpected hour, and for that reason the letters were returned to me from the presidio, and were unable to catch up with it. It was necessary to send them by boat, and Your Reverence will receive them according to schedule at the same time as this.

At long last I assigned Father Antonio Jayme to this mission of San Carlos, and Father Fray Marcelino Ciprés to San Antonio. I wrote to the Fathers of Santa Clara that Fathers Diego García and Pedro de Esteban would continue as supernumeraries, and that, taking it for granted that one of the two would have to remain there, they were to advise me promptly as to which of them would suit them best.

In place of a reply, Father Sánchez came here without further delay with the message that they were absolutely determined that they did not want either of the two, making it clear that in that case both he and his companion would prefer to be assigned elsewhere.

This kind of strong opposition I have endured often, and I have yielded before it, not so much because of its force as for the sake of harmony and so as not to give scandal to the public.

This was told him in due course, and also the fact that an occasion could arise when, despite my best efforts, I might have to override such objections, fully assured and satisfied that all in authority would have to recognize that I had not been the cause of them.

I pointed out that it was natural to place a supernumerary in a mission which, like theirs, was adjoining the chapel of a pueblo, and that if the other missionaries declined in the same way I might have to send the supernumeraries to the barracks.

Finally, in the same spirit of appeasement, and keeping in mind that it may not be necessary to wait very long for the appointment of chaplains, as asked for by the governor, I assigned Father García to San Francisco and Father Esteban to San Diego (as the enclosed certified list indicates). I told them that each, in the particular mission to which he was assigned as supernumerary, should help these Fathers as much as possible in taking care of the presidio assigned to them.

I cannot help fearing still some other refusal, which will be very distressing to me.

Father Baldomero has written to me, deeply resenting the fact that the college has not replied to the applications he has made for returning to it, and asking me to bring it once more to their attention, and to give it my support in the hope that it may be granted to him. I do this very gladly, for I am convinced that a religious who is fully determined on retiring, while he may be very useful elsewhere, gives no promise of being of any use here.

In connection with this and other petitioners, I have heard complaints not so much on the grounds that the petition was not granted, as on the grounds that there was no reply to it.

As is obvious, I am unable to assign blame to anyone for not replying; but I would appreciate it a great deal if this favor is not denied them when it is not possible to grant them the other, and if the reason would be indicated, so that they might still keep alive their hopes for a more opportune occasion.

There is no further news that deserves mention. I wish you all happiness and success; and with the greatest respect and humility I place myself at your disposal and in obedience to you. And I pray that God Our Lord may keep you for many years in His holy grace.

San Carlos Mission,
September 28, 1795.

208. To Reverend Father Guardian
[Fray Antonio Nogueyra]

Under date of the sixteenth of September of last year the Most Excellent Don Eugenio de Llaguno forwarded to me the following royal order: "Most Excellent Sir:

I have given a report to the King on the subject of the letter of Your Excellency, No. 661, dated September 30 of last year, in regard to the procedure with reference to the documents enclosed, signed by the central government. These documents concerned the travelling expenses and remuneration of the missionaries who come and go to Old California. Keeping in mind all that has gone before, and the decisions given in regard thereto, His Majesty has decided that just as the expenses of the missionaries are paid on their out-going journey as far as their destination, the same procedure should be followed for the return journey, when they retire to their convents or colleges on the completion of the ten-year period, or because they are sickly, or because they have become incapacitated by reason of exhaustion from mission work, the royal order of April 20 of the year just ended is to be regarded as null and void in regard to these matters.

"It is decreed that as a general rule, and without distinction between one mission and another, missionaries will continue to be paid the same stipend they received at the missions by way of helping towards the expenses of the journey (care being taken that the amount is proportionate to the distance), until they arrive back in Mexico, provided, however, that they have obtained the proper permissions to leave their assignments, and that they can certify that they make the journey to the capital by a direct route, and without voluntary delays. This sum is to be paid them irrespective of whether their stipends are paid from the fund from vacant offices,[1] or from the Pious Fund of the Californias; and it is to be paid in lieu of the remuneration which it was the custom to give to those who returned from the Province and to certain others.

"Finally, as regards the return of the missionaries of California: due to the great distance, and to the dearth of shipping facilities, it will suffice if they have the permission of the Governor of California and of their respective superiors. These in turn are required to inform Your Excellency, and those who succeed to the office, that they have issued them, and to state the reasons and motives for doing so.

"In virtue of the royal order I am conveying this information to Your Excellency so that you may put it into execution in so far as it pertains to you, and that you may make this royal decision known to the superiors of the Orders of St. Dominic and St. Francis under whose care the California missions are being conducted. And you are to make it known, too, to all others to whom it pertains.

"I am sending this to Your Reverence for your information.

May God keep Your Reverence for many years.

Mexico, June 8, 1795.

Branciforte

Rev. Fr. President of the Missions of San Fernando of New California."

My reply is limited to saying that I have received the information regarding the royal order which he sent, that in all that pertains to me personally I promise the most exact compliance, and that I will observe it in the same way as I always carry out my obligation of being punctilious in doing whatever His Excellency orders me.

San Carlos Mission,
October 16, 1795.

[1] When a diocese was without a bishop, either through the death of the latter or his removal for any causes, certain diocesan incomes during that period became part of this fund, and could be used for purposes such as the one here mentioned. (In regard to the Pious Fund of the Californias, see Letter 80, note 1, *supra.*)

209. To Don Diego de Borica

I have received Your Lordship's official letter of the sixteenth of this month together with a certified copy of another, dated the sixteenth of last June, which His Excellency the Viceroy, the Marqués de Branciforte, sent to Your Lordship. By way of reply I would like to fulfil to the utmost the desires of Your Lordship and His Excellency, for these in

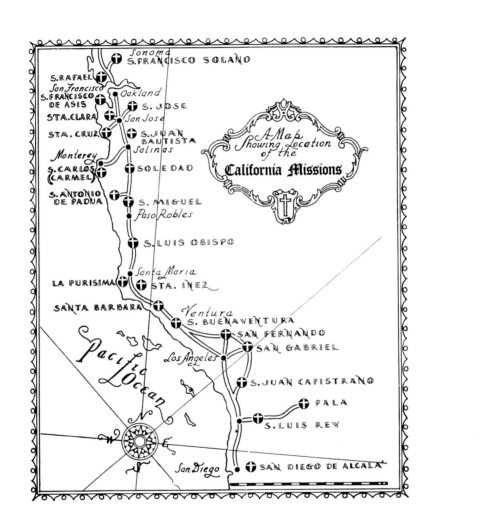

themselves cannot exceed my own desires to contribute to the progress of the war against the French, and to ending it for the glory of the Catholic religion, of the Spanish nation, and of our King.

Your Lordship expects from my zeal—would that my talents were in keeping with it—(and no other appeal was necessary for the purpose), and from the missionaries subject to me, that we on our part and in the name of the neophytes whose temporalities we administer, should give proof of the love which the holy Order of St. Francis has always manifested for the King and the fatherland.

If in our day Franciscans, to their credit, give proof of such sentiments of loyalty, surely we who are their confreres cannot do less. We are engaged in educating the Indians who were recently converted, and in civilizing and converting, in preaching to and in teaching, the pagan Indians. And this is a pious work in the highest degree, the most acceptable and commendable by all standards, and the primary and principal concern of the King our Lord. This is what His Majesty expressly stated in one of the laws which he included in the royal cedula of February 15, 1791.

We, the Franciscans who are engaged in this work, number thirty. Twenty-six receive a stipend, and the other four, of whom I am one, do not.

I am in charge of this mission of San Carlos, and while residing here I assist at the neighboring presidio just as do the other missionaries. And I am at the service of the other missionaries and of all the missions. I am very happy to do this; and I mention it not with a view to advertising what I do, but because the occasion seems to call for it. I want to make it clear that there is nothing more I can offer in this respect, unless it be to abandon this post, or, with the same willingness and disinterestedness, merely to exchange it for another in which the King my Lord may wish me to serve him, if permitted by my superior on whom, by His Majesty's wish, I depend. In my opinion the Fathers who work with me are of the same mind. True, they enjoy a stipend; but after they have deducted from it the pittance a Franciscan needs in order to live, they devote the balance to the maintenance and progress of these settlements.

To promote this holy and important objective we set aside all the Mass stipends which, as a rule, are given us from time to time, and alms offered us on occasion by natives or by sailors for any function of the church, as their devotion spontaneously prompts them, and anything else, no matter how great, that comes to us.

We the missionaries from the neighboring missions serve the four presidios without salary, or free-will offering, or remuneration of any kind. We exercise all the functions of a chaplain; and even if the amount paid to each was no more than five hundred pesos, it would amount to two thousand each year, and to a considerable sum over a long period. In regard to one of the presidios mentioned, the central government of Mexico decided that some remuneration should be paid out of the Royal Treasury to the religious of the adjoining mission. That was years ago. It has not been put into effect, and I have not claimed it. I have maintained silence, and I would not have spoken now unless I heard that the present crisis confronts me with the question: What are you doing for the royal service?

To these unselfish duties we add the truly arduous one of managing and caring for, as a whole, the temporalities of those in our charge. Individually, they own nothing whatever; and as organizations they have less means and more needs than any hospital. We are satisfied with the growth of Christianity and the improvement of human society, of the quality of their food and shelter, even if in the quantity of these things they do not enjoy an advantage or notable improvement in comparison with the pagans. They are very poorly fed and clothed; but they work in the fields and churches, dwelling houses, granaries, and offices, thus promoting the work of conquest and bringing about its major development as far as their condition allows.

All our income is absorbed in these operations, and in supplying implements and other things needed. This is always the case, even in years of plenty, as we would call them. In such times, if we devote some effort to adorning and embellishing the churches to some extent, it is not for the purpose of using up a surplus—the vast numbers here would take care of that—but it means that when there is an opportunity like that it brings to our minds the need of attending to such matters.

This year, as it happens, is one of great scarcity, for it has been a year of unusual drought.

At the present time if steps were taken to withdraw part of the resources, funds, products of industry, or other means of support, and to deflect them to some other objective, it would assuredly bring but little benefit to the latter, and result in much hardship in our work, which is so highly esteemed by the King. Furthermore, it is evident that our total lack of concern about personal gain is proof that in this point we are completely unselfish.

The Fathers are vowed to poverty by profession, and the converts are poor by nature, and both are engaged in a service very pleasing to our Catholic Sovereign. Hence, I feel that His Majesty does not require from us any other worldly contribution beyond the one we are making. (And it is this conviction which enables me to draw my breath, for the present request has placed me in a painful position, pressed on the one side by my zeal as a Spanish subject, and on the other by my lot as a poor Franciscan.) Furthermore, that my conclusion is correct can be inferred, if I am not mistaken, from the official letter which His Excellency sent Your Lordship.

The spiritual contribution began as soon as we learned about the war, and has continued ever since. As soon as I received copies of the Proclamation of it, and learned through Señor Arrillaga, then interim governor of this province, of the subsidies requested in order to meet the expenses of conducting it, I sent him the reply that there and then I had begun to assist in this just war against the French by affording the only help of which I am capable, namely, prayers to heaven. These I offer; and I celebrate many Masses for the same intention.

I also wrote to all the missionaries, charging them to be careful to impress on all who are subject to them, whenever an occasion arises, how just is the decision of our monarch against France, and urging that their Reverences and their Indians should give their support to so just a war with such contributions as they are capable of making, that is, with fervent and continued prayers. I exhorted them to pray to the God of Armies that Spanish arms might win a glorious victory, and that in this campaign they may achieve a degree of triumph and honor in keeping with the justice of their cause, and their zeal for God.

As regards those who are in the fortunate position of being able to afford help of a different order, I recommended that they should exhort them, too, to contribute generously from what they had, helping in this way to meet the costs of the war—for with it are linked up the honor of God and of His Church, humanity, and the public order.

I shall send them the same message once more. I shall not fail to send them as a circular letter the official letter of Your Lordship, with the above-mentioned copy enclosed. And I shall exhort them, while the major emergency lasts, to celebrate two Masses each month in each mission—sung Masses if possible. One of these Masses should be of the Immaculate Conception, and the other of the glorious Apostle St. James. They can add other Masses in accordance with the devotion of each, and the opportunities available.

May God Our Lord keep Your Lordship for many years in His holy grace.

San Carlos Mission,
October 18, 1795.

Note: Here there are no private possessions. Everything is for the good of the community, thus serving to support and extend the conquest, and these constitute a genuine royal service in fact.

210. To Fray Antonio Nogueyra

I have received your deeply appreciated letter of the twenty-sixth of last May, and now know that the office of superior of the holy college most justly has fallen to your worthy self. I accept your holy blessing with reverence and, with the deepest respect, convey to you once more the good wishes I expressed in my former letters. I renew my profound submission and my glad subordination to your will, not as a mere courtesy or formality that is expected from me, but as a sincere expression of my religious acknowledgment [of the relationship], and of my unqualified dependence; and I promise, with the help of God, to give proof of it constantly.

By the first mail, I shall convey to the missionary Fathers here Your Reverence's paternal greetings. I shall include in my letter the very phrases from yours, for they best express your cordial affection, and your regrets that you could not on that occasion convey them to each individually, by reason of the unavoidable and tedious duties which are the lot of a new Guardian of San Fernando College of Mexico.

Likewise, I shall notify them at the same time of the request, of the favor that Your Reverence asks in regard to offering Masses for your intention, seeing that the community was so heavily obligated in that regard that, at the time of writing, more than seven thousand remained to be offered. I shall let you know what their response is.

I have already begun to offer them and, with God's help, will continue to offer all I can until I reach one or two hundred, or until Your Reverence tells me that it is already enough. And I shall be careful to let you know the number offered.

My companions, Fray Pascual and Fray Antonio,[1] report that they, too, will offer all they can.

I am forwarding you the enclosed copies. In regard to these matters, as well as to all others, I do not wish to go beyond the role of secretary, giving as my reply neither more nor less than what Your Reverence dictates. But in this instance, as the need of replying in time does not give me an opportunity to wait for it, it does give me an opportunity, after Your Reverence has considered my replies, to retract with my signature what I have written, as I shall immediately do the moment you so direct, and as and how you direct.

In regard to the royal order which His Excellency the Viceroy sent me, a copy of which is included among the enclosed, the following questions occur to me:

1. whether *having completed ten years* is to be interpreted as "since arriving at the missions" or as "since arriving from Europe";

2. whether by reason of this motive alone—and it is sufficient grounds for asking it—I can grant this permission to a missionary, even to a supernumerary, without waiting for someone to replace him; and

3. whether, in the absence of someone to replace him, I can grant this permission to a missionary Father for this first reason, or for some other one of those mentioned, or for all combined, when, as a consequence of giving it, or through lack of a supernumerary, a missionary is left all alone in the mission from which the other wishes to depart.

Your decision, which I await, will be to me a law to be observed faithfully and to the letter.

Your Reverence may rest well assured that you have in me the least important of subjects; but do not doubt that in carrying out the orders given me I am to be regarded, God willing, as on a par with those whose obedience is the most exemplary.

Such are my innermost feelings. For Your Reverence I wish the fullest measure of happiness. And I pray that God Our Lord may keep you for many years in His holy grace.

San Carlos Mission,
October 19, 1795.

[1] Fray Pascual Martínez and Fray Antonio Jayme.

211. To the Missionaries at Santa Cruz, Santa Clara, and San Francisco

May the Lord give you Peace. Our Reverend Father Guardian, Fray Antonio Nogueyra, under date of the twenty-sixth of last May, informs me:

"It is not possible for me at the present time to write to each of my missionary Fathers exiled in these remote places, and so well occupied in the cultivation of that vineyard of the Lord, by reason of the unavoidable, weighty duties of a new guardian in Mexico, one who depends on so many, and needs the help of all.

"This I hope to do at a more opportune time; and so I beg Your Reverences to take the trouble (such as I am now doing) to bring this to the attention of the others so that for the time being they may excuse me.

"Forced by necessity, but relying on the tender affection of my brethren for their college, I am taking the liberty of asking a favor from them; and I shall not forget to thank them for it, and to repay them in some manner.

"By reason of the death of so many religious both at home, in the college, in Puerto Rico, and Veracruz, as well as those of other colleges with which there is a fraternity of suffrages,[1] the community finds itself heavily obligated for Masses, so that those that remain to be said at this date exceed seven thousand.

"Consequently, I call upon and beg Your Reverences to say for my intention as many Masses as each one conveniently can, and I ask you to inform me at your convenience regarding the number you are pleased to say."

I have replied to him that in this mail I am carrying out all his instructions in regard to Your Reverences; that I have already begun to offer Masses for his intention, and that, with God's help, I will continue to offer all I can, taking care to inform him each month regarding those already offered; and that I will advise him about Your Reverence's response in regard to this matter.

His Excellency the Viceroy, the Margués de Branciforte, in an official letter of the eighth of last June, informs me of the Royal Order which, on the sixteenth of the previous September, the Most Excellent Don Eugenio de Llaguno forwarded to His Excellency, namely:

"Just as the travelling expenses of the missionaries are taken care of when they are on their way to their destination, the same will be observed for their return to the college after the ten years have been completed, or because of illness, or because they have become incapacitated by the labors of the missions.

"Further, as a general rule, in place of the allowance which it was customary to give to those who returned from this Peninsula, they are to continue to receive the same stipend they received at the mission in order to help them to meet travelling expenses until they return to Mexico, provided they have the proper permits to leave their assignments, and provided they can prove that they made the journey direct to the capital, and without unreasonable delays.

"And finally, for the return of the missionaries of the Californias it suffices that they have the permits of the governor of Monterey and of their respective prelate. It shall be the duty of the latter to inform His Excellency that they have issued them, and they shall state the reasons and motives they had for so doing."

I replied to him that in all that pertained to me in this matter I promise the most exact obedience in such wise as to satisfy my obligation of always doing with the greatest exactitude whatever His Excellency orders me.

Our Brother Revuelta complains that he has had to face many embarrassments in connection with the mail or the Mexican courier. The reason is that certain letters from here were sent to private individuals outside the college, under cover of the Administrator General, Don

Andrés de Mendívil. Those who act in that fashion expose all of us to the risk of being deprived of the franking privilege we enjoy, and which is so important to us. And to forestall any misfortune such as that, on the occasion when I announced the concession of the privilege, I gave timely warning that no religious, either down there or even up here, should include in the mail of the province any letter addressed to any person who was obliged to pay postal rates. I now repeat the same injunction.

I think it very fitting to forward the enclosed copies to Your Reverences. They will enable you to know what is expected of us and of our Indians. And they will enable you to know my reply on the point.

Before the governor read my reply, perhaps he guessed it from comments I dropped in my conversation, for he said: "Your Reverence is probably not aware of the true state of certain missions. One has two thousand pesos, another more, another less." "Very well," I told him. "But Your Lordship knows that where there are approximately two thousand pesos there are also approximately two thousand persons, and all of them so very poor that these figures would not suffice to take care of them. If by means of these pesos the missionaries could help, or had an opportunity to help, the needy Christians who are faced with poverty, a poverty that is not just threatening, but is actually present—perhaps at the very time that Your Lordship is telling me this, they would not be able to let each of them have even half a peso. We have to exercise economy, then, in everything we handle; and although we cannot with this money remedy everything, it may be that by means of it relief is given when it is needed most."

Finally, will Your Reverences think it over; and if you have any observations to make, please do not fail to advise me. I am sending identical copies down south, and also to the college.

As this is forwarded, Your Reverences will place your acknowledgment, thus: Santa Cruz, (date) November, received, Fr. (name). And when the attached copies have been placed in the archives of the Mission of our father St. Francis, the Reverend Ministers there will return this with the above-mentioned acknowledgments.

May God Our Lord keep Your Reverences for many years in His holy grace.

San Carlos Mission,
October 22, 1795.

---

[1] When notification has been received of the death of a member of the Order, certain prayers are offered in his behalf. These are meant by the "suffrages." From time to time this privilege is extended to those who are not members of the Order, and among these were the Dominican missionaries in Lower California.

212. To the Margués de Branciforte

Fray Fermín Francisco de Lasuén, missionary, and President of the Missions of New California, most respectfully presents his compliments to Your Excellency, and begs a favor so necessary that it seems to merit the attention of Your Excellency.

This Mission of San Carlos of Monterey was able to proceed to build a beautiful church, the need of which has long been felt, solely because it was granted the privilege of having a master-mason and stonecutter. This expert arrived there towards the end of the year '92, but there was no supply of material on hand for him, and the season for heavy rain had already set in. For this reason it was not possible to lay the first stone until July 7, '93. From that date on, the work proceeded without intermission. Many oxen and wagons have been employed in it. Much iron has gone into it, and much labor, too.

The church is not so well advanced, however, that it would be possible to complete it by June, '96, when the extension granted to the expert comes to an end; but it could be completed by that date in '97. From this it is obvious that he could have completed it if he had worked here for the four years of his contract.

The mission in the first instance would not have begun a work of these dimensions if it did not have the privilege of having this expert, and now it can not bear the cost of completing it [without him], for the harvest this year has been very scanty.

It follows from this that our work is in vain unless Your Excellency is so kind as to grant a further extension of one year to this person's sojourn, or (what will not add much more to it) until such time as the church is completed.

And so, Sir, the one who asks is the one who is in need; and the one he asks is one who not only knows how to grant it but actually can —and that person is Your Excellency.

May God Our Lord keep Your Excellency for many years in His holy grace.

Mission San Carlos of Monterey,
November 18, 1795.

213. To Fray Antonio Nogueyra

Give me your blessing, Your Reverence. I wish to thank you, and also the venerable council, for the expression of confidence when you re-elected me, worthless though I am, as President of these Missions.

I welcome the opportunity to continue in office in a spirit of penance, devoting all my energies, such as they are, to carrying out my duties, despite the great obstacles and the many sacrifices involved. This is my ambition, and this is what I am determined to do.

I place my confidence in holy Obedience. This it is which imposes it on me and induces me to continue as before. It has the power to lighten the most difficult tasks, even when they devolve on a person of such little account as I am.

I had already sent Your Reverence a copy of the royal resolution in regard to meeting the needs of missionaries as they come and go, and the requirements for their return, when I received the enclosure in your esteemed letter of the eighth of last July. I am awaiting the solution of the "doubts" which I referred to you in regard to the matter, so as to be guided by it in all such cases.

At the present time those who are most insistent on retiring are Fathers Danti and Baldomero.

I recommend as earnestly as I possibly can the enclosed petition. It is unsealed, and it is intended for the Viceroy. I beg you to intervene, and to use all the fervor and influence in your power to obtain a favorable answer to my request. When you see it, I think you will regard the matter as very just. If not, ignore it.

I suspect that our governors did not regard it as proper that I should be entrusted with the locating of the artisans engaged at the expense of the Royal Treasury to work for four years in these missions and to instruct the Indians in the crafts they knew. Be that as it may, this was the decision of the central government at the beginning of the year '90, and I was not informed until the end of '92, after the expert who began, and is working on, our church had been working more than a year and a half at the neighboring presidio.

On July 7, '93, he laid the first stone, and the present state of the work makes it clear that it would have been finished if he had worked at it for the four years for which he was engaged.

True it is that about this time last year I was told that by devoting to it all this year and half of next, it could be finished; and perhaps for that reason an extension of stay was granted the expert until mid-June of '96. But I now see that I was mistaken, for in addition to the fact that up to then there had not been even three years of work, there were, in addition, occasional mishaps which have delayed us a great deal. For instance, thirteen or fourteen yoke of oxen died, and the crops have been very poor, especially for this year.

Furthermore, the expert admits that the work itself has been re-quiring more labor than he had expected, and he had not wished to forego it because of his own good name, because it gave an opportunity for more thorough training for his apprentices, and because they had finally discovered a first-rate quarry for the purpose.

Despite all of this, there is nothing superfluous or showy, but just a little added elegance.

Now more than ever would I wish that it were possible for me to be looked on with favor by the Viceroy; and I give my word that His Excellency, despite all his power, could not give me a reward, could not afford me greater pleasure or satisfaction, than by extending the leave of our artisan, which is the petition I am making.

The goodness of His Excellency will be all that is needed to secure this favor and benefit for the Mission, and for us the missionaries, of San Carlos. How much stronger will our case be if Your Reverence takes it upon himself to be our advocate, and that is what we are hoping for.

In the letter of Your Reverence I have noticed that you refer to earlier ones; but I have received only one earlier letter. The letters which are addressed to this Monterey are in the habit of going to the other. They are delayed a great deal, and sometimes they get lost. For this reason it is much safer to write "California" alone, without Monterey; or, if you do write "Monterey," let California be added after it.

I wish Your Reverence all happiness, and I pray that God Our Lord may keep you for many years in His holy grace.

San Carlos,
November 25, 1795.

214. To Fray Antonio Nogueyra

May I have Your Reverence's holy blessing, for I wish to inform you that Reverend Father Fray Antonio Jayme, after I had left it to his choice either to stay here or to go to San Francisco or San Antonio, decided on this place, and was very happy here for a few days. Then he went to San Antonio to visit his countryman and acquaintance, Fray Buenaventura.

After fifteen days he returned, and after approximately the same length of time he began to complain of a series of ailments all of which had their source in a profound melancholia, the cause of which he did not know. He was convinced, however, that he would get better if he returned to San Antonio for a few days.

It has been about fourteen days since he left, and I know that he has improved, and that he has made up his mind to come back soon. But he is always apprehensive that the melancholia will return, and he has obtained my permission in advance to go back again, in case circumstances require it. He has asked me, too, to assign him there as supernumerary when the occasion arises.

I am giving Your Reverence this information in advance, so that if it should come to pass you may know the reason.

I am not transferring Father Ciprés from there, because he is not only a robust young man, the kind that is needed to help good Father Sitjar in his old age and infirmaties, but he is also a person quite gifted in learning the dialect; and we should see to it that such a favorable opportunity is not missed at that mission.

The governor has decided on the survey and exploration of five sites for five missions in the intervening territory between San Diego and San Juan Capistrano, between San Gabriel and San Buenaventura, between San Luis and San Antonio, between this mission and Santa Clara, and between Santa Clara and San Francisco. And His Lordship has asked me to assign in each case some religious to take part in the project.

The result was, that Father Mariner went to the first site, Father Santa María to the second, Father Sitjar to the third, and Father Danti to the fourth and fifth. It is only a few days since Father Danti left, as the weather has been very wet. So far he has not sent me news of the expedition, but it can be taken for granted that they discovered sites.

The honorable governor asked me to ask him for these foundations so that in this way he might make a stronger representation to the Viceroy, but I refused him, saying that it was none of my business. I told him that down there Your Reverence will consult with His Excellency should questions arise by reason of the report of His Lordship.

Last month there was a fight among the pagans in the neighborhood of San Buenaventura. Two lost their lives in it, and two others were injured. Eight Christians became involved, and these have been taken prisoners to the Presidio of Santa Barbara.

Almost immediately after that, a Christian Indian was found dead and decapitated near the garden of the same Mission of San Buenaventura. It has now become known that the attackers were his own wife, two other Christians, and the woman's brother who is a pagan. They are all prisoners in the presidio just mentioned. You can well imagine how grief-stricken the Fathers are.

It is their wish that those who are guilty should have the benefit of all the clemency the case allows, for although it is a shocking one, it is the work of those who little realize its gravity. Should you have an opportunity down there to make a plea for clemency in behalf of this woman and the other poor creatures, we hope you will do so.

By this time Your Reverence will have been supplied with evidence, both direct and circumstantial, from Fathers Salazar and Señán who were eyewitnesses, in regard to the copious spring that has gushed forth at San Diego. With it the truth of what the venerable Father Junípero often said begins to appear. I myself have heard him say it more than once. His statement was, that he regarded it as certain that San Diego Mission was bound to become the best of all. "And if you ask me why," added the venerable Father, "my answer is that I do not know."

Today Father Jayme arrived back, and he is very insistent in regard to what I mentioned, and which I have to grant him whenever occasion arises.

Father Fuster has written that he will offer fifty Masses. Fathers Arenaza and Jayme each will offer the same number. Several of the others advise me that they are saying them, and others that they will do so and give me notice of the number. There are others who will give you notice direct. Up to the present I have offered fifteen, and with God's help will continue to do so, as I have already informed Your Reverence.

In this matter, and to any extent you wish, I will comply with your will, most humbly and wholeheartedly. And at the same time I will pray that God Our Lord may keep you many years in His holy grace.

San Carlos,
November 28, 1795.

Father Espí advises me that he has said twenty [Masses], and Father Martiarena eight; and they will continue to do so, as I understand.

XII

The Year 1796

Misunderstandings regarding the status of the artisan teachers accumulate, while internal problems, which in the circumstances admit of no easy solution, absorb much of his time. However, superiors show their confidence in Lasuén by appointing him, first, an official of the Holy Office (or Inquisition), and, later, a local representative of the Bishop of Sonora.

215. To Fray Antonio Nogueyra

WITH THE BLESSING OF YOUR REVERENCE I beg to inform you that on the very day on which my last letter was dated, the twenty-eighth of November, Father Fray Antonio Jayme arrived at this mission on his way back from San Antonio. He immediately expressed a very strong desire to be transferred once and for all to that post. The reason he gives is the fear he experiences lest, if he is not granted this request, he will possibly lose his reason or his life.

Now I do not need such strong motives before granting (if it is within the bounds of possibility) the request of a religious. So, I told him that he could go when he pleased, and that he could do as he wished and as he felt inclined.

He has already forwarded his belongings to San Antonio. I have already written there that he is going there in order to be of some help to Father Fray Buenaventura. Fray Marcelino has to come here temporarily, but he will not for that reason cease to be minister at San Antonio, for he is to return to it as soon as there is someone who can be given an assignment here, unless circumstances should arise which may force me to change my mind.

I am convinced, however, that Father Fray Buenaventura cannot be left with only Father Jayme, and that it will be necessary to give him someone else to help him.

There is no further news, except that the rains are becoming very scanty, and frosts are recurring and doing considerable harm.

With the most profound respect I place myself once more at the service of Your Reverence's orders and suggestions, and I pray that God Our Lord may keep you for many years in His holy grace.

San Carlos,
January 2, 1796.

[In the margin]:
During the past month I have been able to offer only ten Masses [for your intention]. Added to the others that I have reported, this brings the number to twenty-five. I shall continue in accordance with the offer I made.

216. To Fray Antonio Nogueyra

May I have Your Reverence's holy blessing. This month's mail has been detained until tomorrow. Being of the opinion that it would leave on the third according to schedule, I wrote to you, it seems to me, on the second. To that letter, which you will receive in due time with this, I have merely to add that the Fathers at Santa Barbara inform me that during last month they were able to offer only ten Masses [for your intention], but that they will continue to do so. Father Fray Juan Norberto de Santiago tells me that he will offer fifty.

The drought continues, and the extraordinary and unusual frosts still keep on. There is reason to be uneasy. Numerous and grave calamities already threaten us. May God protect us.

I am completely at the service of Your Reverence, and desire to give proof of it often by the most punctual obedience to whatever you order me.

May God Our Lord keep Your Reverence for many years in His holy grace.

San Carlos,
January 10, 1796.

217. Notes on projected Foundations

1. Between San Diego and San Juan the place called Pala is very good. It has all the distinctive features a foundation requires. It is fourteen leagues from San Diego, eighteen from Capistrano, and six leagues east of the Camino Real. [Added note: I have seen it, and it is absolutely unsuitable.] [1]

2. Between San Gabriel and San Buenaventura. [2] The reports that are made of this district are not satisfactory for the purpose of deciding once for all where the foundation between these two places should be located. The one regarded as most suitable is far from firewood, too far from San Buenaventura, and too close to San Gabriel. It is only eight or nine leagues from the latter, and as many as sixteen or seventeen from the former. It is a little more than two leagues from the Camino Real. It will be necessary to discuss this matter with the explorers in regard to the other places to which they refer; for although these may not have all the advantages of the place mentioned, they may have advantages from the point of view of distance, and as a consequence may be better for the conversion of the Indians who inhabit them.

3. Between San Luis and San Antonio. [3] The place of the waterholes is good from every point of view. It is situated on the Camino Real

Nº 70   6 Aug.   Viva Jesus   92

Señor Governador

Muy Señor mio: quedo entendido, haber tomado V.S. posesion
del Govierno Politico y Militar de esa Provincia el dia
11 de Maio ulto. segun me lo hace constar en su Oficio de
la misma fha.

Reconosco, y me subordino à V.S. gustosamte. como à
mi Govor, y a ese mismo fin paso el correspondte. aviso
a todos los Religiosos mis Subditos.

Dios Nro Sor Gue à V.S. en su Sta Gracia ms as. fier-
ron de S. Carlos, y Agosto 6 de 1794. 11.

BLm. à V.S.
Su mas Att. Servr y menor Capp.n

Dr Fermin Fran.co de Lasuen

Sor Tente. Coronl. Comandte Inspr.
Dn. Diego de Borica

LETTER OF LASUEN
with characteristic *rubric*, or flourish added
to the signature

itself, and is practically midway between the two missions mentioned, with little to spare one way or the other.

4. Between San Carlos and Santa Clara. Here there are two places close to the Camino Real that offer good advantages for a foundation. They are three or four leagues apart. The one to the north is near the place known as San Bernardino, and the stone for building the foundations is very far away. It will be eleven or twelve leagues from Santa Clara, and fourteen or fifteen from San Carlos. The one to the south is near San Benito,[4] about eleven or twelve leagues from San Carlos, and fourteen or fifteen from Santa Clara. It is important in the selection of a site to consider and reflect carefully on this: which of the two offers the best prospects for the conversion of the largest number of Indians?

5. About seven or eight leagues to the north from Santa Clara there is a very suitable site for a mission, despite the fact that it is somewhat short of firewood and lumber. One has to leave behind the road to San Francisco since the *Estero*, an arm of the sea which extends from that port, comes between that mission and the place surveyed. The discoverers have named it St. Francis Solano.[5]

All the places mentioned have a considerable number of pagans, and all the usual facilities—though not to the same extent—for the purpose of civilizing these people and bringing them into communities.

This is what can be gathered from the Reports, it seems to me.

Fray Fermín Francisco de Lasuén,
January 12, 1796.

[1] The Note was obviously added at a later date. What is now San Luis Rey was chosen as the site for the new mission, but Pala was not forgotten. Some twenty years later it became an *asistencia*, a mission station under San Luis Rey.

[2] Under date of September 3, 1795, Fray Vicente de Santa María sent Lasuén an account of his exploration for a suitable site for a mission in that region. See Zephyrin Engelhardt, *San Fernando Rey,* the *Mission of the Valley* (Chicago, 1927), pp. 3-9.

[3] For Fray Buenaventura Sitjar's account of the search for a suitable site, see Zephyrin Engelhardt, *Mission San Miguel Arcangel* (Santa Barbara, California, 1929), pp. 3-6. (The "place of the waterholes" did become the site of San Miguel Mission).

[4] This was the site ultimately chosen for Mission San Juan Bautista.

[5] Father Danti and his companions named the chosen site St. Francis Solano. The Viceroy, however, had the right to bestow a name on a new mission. Branciforte named the new site San Carlos Borromeo; but when informed that there was another mission of the same name already (Carmel Mission), he named it San José, the name by which it is still known.

218. To Don Diego de Borica

Last evening I received Your Lordship's official letter of the twenty-first of the current month, together with the certified copy of the contract made with the artisans Don Joaquín Botello, Manuel Muñoz,

Mariano Tapia, and Mariano José Mendoza, these being masters in the art of the tailor, ribbon-maker, potter, and weaver of broad-loom cloth. In addition, Your Lordship bids me to give due effect to this, in so far as it pertains to me.

In this regard the central government of Mexico has given me the task of distributing them among the missions in my charge according to their professions and as it seems best to me, after I have been informed of the arrival of the artisans and their implements.

Having regard to this superior order, I remarked to Your Lordship when we discussed this point that the master potter could teach his craft in the Mission of our father St. Francis, and the weaver of broad-loom cloth in San Diego. As regards the art of ribbon-making, since it cannot be practised in any of the missions because of the lack of materials and because it has neither use nor utility, there is no possibility that it can be taught to the neophytes in them.

As regards the master tailor, while I recognize the great importance of his craft, I realize that for the present and for many years to come he will not be able to find enough work in any mission, or in all of them together, to enable him to teach the Indians effectively, which is the object of the King our Lord in making this provision. For this reason, it seemed to me, Your Lordship could dispose of these two artisans as you please.

I repeat the same now; and I extend it to include the others as well as myself, for I pledge myself, in the whole range of my duties, to obey punctually all who, like Your Lordship, can give me orders.

Will Your Lordship tell me if I am right in judging that it is not the rule that the master tailor is to receive one-eighth part of the value of the clothes he will make, but rather of the work he contributes. The same problem arises in regard to the potter and the weaver—assuming in their case, as in the former, that the material they require for their work has to be supplied free.

Let Your Lordship make the decision in these matters and I shall carry it out.

May God Our Lord keep Your Lordship for many years in His holy grace.

Mission San Carlos,
January 26, 1796.

219. To Don Diego de Borica

In reply to the communication which I have this day received from Your Lordship I beg to inform you that I will abide by what I have promised; and so, I will observe the dispositions of Your Lordship in regard to the eighth part of the value of their work which by contract is granted to the artisans.

With regard to the question of the Indian youths which Your Lordship proposes, I can send them, if you so wish, to the presidio there, so that they may learn the art from Don Joaquín Botello, the master tailor, when he comes. I will not fail to do my part so that some from this mission may acquire such useful knowledge. I am assuming that in view of the prudent measures which you have in mind to take in this matter, the result will not be the undoing of our effort, for this has been the unfortunate outcome up to the present when we sent neophytes to the presidio for the purpose of instruction.

May God Our Lord keep Your Lordship for many years in His holy grace.

Mission San Carlos,
January 29, 1796.

220. To Fray Antonio Nogueyra

I beg Your Reverence's holy blessing, and I wish to acknowledge the receipt of your two esteemed letters, one dated the seventh and the other the eleventh of last November. They arrived together in the mail which reached me the day before yesterday. I wish to thank you a thousand times for the honor you were pleased to obtain for me of Commissary of the Holy Office. I have already received notification of the title and the instructions pertaining. I wish to thank you, too, for the concession you gained for us, at the cost of so many laborious efforts, to the effect that we shall not be denied an escort on occasions when, in case of more urgent necessity, we are obliged to spend the night in the country.

With the last mail the Governor received the first resolution which was taken on that point. When I met His Lordship, he gave it to me to read, as if flattering himself that his way of thinking had been approved.

I showed myself somewhat surprised, and I remarked that my request, considering the form in which I presented it, did not merit a negative answer in such terms. He agreed on this point, and attributed it to the fact that the lay Brother to whom it was referred as our agent in the case might have added to my request some irregular claim (as he put it) that the troops should be at our disposal in such cases.

His Lordship was of the opinion that something of that nature was necessary in order to explain why the answer to my request was made in those terms.

Finally, I concluded, saying with all possible calmness: I shall give a great deal of thought to the matter; and if I think it is right, I shall repeat the request.

Your Reverence has saved me that work, and has afforded me the pleasing satisfaction of being able to say to His Lordship: Now you see that the final decision was the one they sent me, the one that was seen to be the only possible one after they had given full thought to the matter. Thanks be to God.

I have already put before you my doubts regarding the permission which, in the name of the governor and myself, has to be given to the missionaries when they ask leave to retire. I am awaiting the decision in order to put it into effect. In the meantime, as it is very necessary to maintain the present number of missionaries, it will be very difficult for me to give permission to anyone, unless I have first someone to replace him—provided a necessity does not arise which cannot be met in any other way. And even if I permit it, the governor is certain to advert to this very thing, and in particular (as I have heard him point out) he is certain to advert to the expenses to the Royal Treasury of the allowances given to those who come and go. This animosity against the friars consumes them; but, in their conception, there is always enough in the Royal Treasury to add thousands of pesos to their own salary. But, perhaps if we ourselves were lay people, we would look at things in the same way.

It seems to me (always with deferences to the opinion of Your Reverence) that two additional supernumeraries should come, and others to replace those who have seriously asked to be retired by showing clearly that they are dissatisfied and despondent (reasons which are sufficient, but which are not likely to be regarded as such by the governor if others do not come to replace them), like Fathers Danti, Baldomero, and perhaps others. In this way, if it were possible, we would number thirty-two missionaries here. This would create a difficulty only for me, but it would be an advantage to the community. It would make it easier for some to retire, and would make it less onerous to put off replacing them until the arrival of another boat.

I do not know when our good Fray Antonio Jayme will make up his mind. He vacillates about everything, and comes to no decision. After his baggage had been sent to San Antonio several days previously, with the intention that he would go there once for all, he suggested to me that he was thinking of staying here, and of having his baggage returned. I agreed to this, as I did to everything he has asked. Later he told me that if it were not too inconvenient he would like to go to San Antonio on a matter of great importance, and that he would return promptly. "Very well," I told him, "Your Reverence may go when you please." The following day he went to the presidio to ask for an escort for his journey. He returned in the evening, expressing a thousand fears lest in that mission he would again become morose, become ill, and end up by becoming incapacitated. I told him to do what suited him best, but that he should reach a decision as soon as possible. Finally, he left for San Antonio. There, as I learned, he changed his mind every day. First, he wanted to come; then to remain. Finally, he set out from there with the intention of coming back here and of remaining here.

On the way, he fell from his horse, as he wrote me, and arrived at the Soledad in such pain and so fatigued that as a result he had a hemorrhage from the mouth. For that reason he had to stay there. For days already I had been conducting affairs at this mission with no one but Father Fray Pascual, and Lent had already begun. I had already given warning that either he, or Father Marcelino, or someone from the Soledad would have to come here without delay. I urged Father Espí earnestly and strongly to come, and as a result for the past eight or ten days this Father has been here assisting us in our duties.

I have later heard, and Fray Antonio himself has written me from the Soledad, that he is somewhat better.

Yesterday, when Father Espí returned from the presidio to which he had gone to say Mass, he reported that the governor had said to him in a tone of disgust: "His Reverence has once again consigned Father Jayme to San Antonio."

It may be that this is not so, because from the information we have the opposite can be inferred. What is certain is, that this religious up to the present has given evidence of poorer health and more tenseness than was the case here. But in mentioning this—and it seems only right that I should—I am not saying that I have given up all hope that he will ever get better, or be able to be used or be of service.

Up to the present I have offered forty Masses [for your intention], in addition to the four I say each month for your intention; and, with God's help, I shall continue to do as I have promised. Father Fray Buenaventura notified me more than a month ago that he had said thirty, and Father Marcelino twent-four, not counting the four monthly ones which he will continue to say. Fray Hilaro has said thirteen, Fray Pedro twelve, Fray Martín Landaeta seven; and they report that they will continue to offer all they can. I have advised them to keep a constant record of all of them so as to obviate any mistake or confusion which could arise at the end because some of these individual notifications of theirs had been lost or forgotten.

Time and time again I have instructed the Fathers that when they write to the college they send the letters "Care Of" the Administrator General of the Mails, Don Ramón Mendívil. It is less than two months since I again warned them about it. In accordance with your instruction I shall repeat the instruction, and refer them to the order of Your Reverence.

The rains continue to be very sparse, and day by day the frosts grow more severe. May God be blessed. I am enclosing a general summary of the state of these missions at the end of last year. The decrease which is shown in the complete returns as compared with the previous year approached six thousand fanegas, and in turn that year of '94 had five thousand three hundred and more fanegas less than the year '93. Despite this, the price of the produce is the same the whole time.

And so I place myself at your service, and with sentiments of affection pray that God Our Lord may keep you for many years in His holy grace.

San Carlos,
February 29, 1796.

P. S.

It now occurs to me that the royal decree on the power of the governor and the President to grant permission for the return of the missionaries is given, it would appear, in terms which limit the faculty of both of us to cases where those who have to leave have completed the ten years, or are sickly, or have rendered themselves unserviceable for the work of the missions.

When these requirements are not present, the governor, presumably, will have to refuse, and I shall not know what to do, nor how to satisfy the Most Excellent Viceroy for, according to the same royal decree, notice must be given to him of the causes and motives which one might have had for permitting the return. Will Your Reverence be so kind as to remove these doubts for me; and in the interval, with the help of God, I will endeavor to do the best I can in the emergencies which arise.

As ever your devoted servant,
[Rubric of Lasuén, but no signature]

221. Certificate

At Mission San Carlos of Monterey on this, the second day of March of the year one thousand seven hundred and ninety-six, I, Fray Fermín Francisco de Lasuén, of the Regular Observance of Our Holy Father St. Francis, Apostolic Preacher of the College of the *Propaganda*

Fide of San Fernando in Mexico, hereby certify that having received
the title of Commissary of the Holy Office which the honorable In-
quisitors of Mexico deigned to confer on me, I took the oath of fidelity
and secrecy as prescribed.

The witness was Reverend Father Fray Pascual de Arenaza, and,
there being no official notary, Reverend Father Fray José de la Cruz
Espí served as such.

In testimony of the truth of the above, the following affix their
signatures with me at the aforesaid Mission on the day, month, and year
mentioned.

Fray Fermín Francisco de Lasuén
Fray Pascual Martínez de Arenaza

In the absence of a Notary, executed before me,
Fray José de la Cruz.

222. To the Missionaries

The Lord give you Peace. By order of the honorable governor, in
consequence of orders given him by His Excellency the Viceroy, the
Marqués de Branciforte, I am sending Your Reverences the agreeable
news that peace has been concluded with the French nation.

In another official letter in which His Lordship encloses one sent
him by His Excellency, he requests and enjoins that in each mission and
presidio one Solemn Mass be celebrated to express humble thanks to the
Almighty, the Lord King of Armies, for the benefits He confers on us,
and those which we anticipate from this lasting and honorable peace.

I immediately replied that on the following day there would be celebrated here and in the neighboring presidio that just and religious
demonstration of gratitude of which he spoke, and that Your Reverences
in turn would do the same (just as soon as you were able) at the first
opportunity after being notified by means of this circular.

My request for permission to spend the night in the country with
the escort in unavoidable cases was entrusted by the college to Brother
Revuelta. In the first instance it was rejected and denied in very pointed
language. Notice that this was received by the governor in the last mail
but one. In that mail I had no mail from overseas, so he gave it to me
to read at our first meeting.

It surprised me very much and I mentioned that my letter did not
merit such an unfriendly official answer. He admitted it, and attributed
it to the Father Procurator. Be that as it may, as soon as our Father
Guardian took the matter in hand it was successful. And now there

has arrived the notice that what was asked for has been granted, as is but just. There is the further note, too, that the matter had not previously been given the attention it deserved. Thanks be to God.

The same Reverend Father again orders me to instruct Your Reverences when sending a letter to the college to send it care of Don Andrés de Mendívil y Amirola, Administrator General of the Mails, for otherwise postage has to be paid. Even should there be no such advantage, one must always follow the admonition of the superior.

Let this be forwarded, and due acknowledgement of its receipt be made at all the missions, and let it then be returned to me from San Diego.

May God Our Lord keep Your Reverences in His holy grace for many years.

San Carlos,
March 5, 1796.

223. To Don Diego de Borica

In obedience to the higher order of His Excellency the Viceroy, the Marqués de Branciforte, dated the twenty-seventh of last October, and the subsequent instruction which Your Lordship gives me in your official letter of the ninth of the present month, which I received the day before yesterday, I shall send fitting instructions at the first opportunity so that the missionaries to whose missions any master workman who happens to be married is sent are to assign to the latter a Christian Indian man and woman to wait on him. He in turn has the obligation of educating, maintaining, and looking after them.

May God Our Lord keep Your Lordship for many years in His holy grace.

Mission San Carlos,
March 29, 1796.

224. To Fray Antonio Nogueyra

May I have Your Reverence's holy blessing, for I wish to let you know that I am sending the Annual Reports of these missions in two packages. I am availing myself of the opportunity offered for this purpose by the sloop *Valdés,* under command of Señor Cañizares,[1] which anchored in this port on the twenty-second of last month, and will sail for San Blas in three days.

The only news which transpired since my last letter, and it is very good news, is that this month we have had very good rain, and the weather still continues rainy. This has taken care of many of our present ills, and fears of greater misfortunes in the future have been lessened. Thanks be to God.

Father Fray Antonio Jayme is still staying at Soledad. As I have known all along, although it cannot be told him, Father Espí will return there, for he gets sick very readily. He is afraid to come here, and he has no desire to be at San Antonio. His only wish is to be with Father Marcelino.

If from all this the only result for the moment is a little more inconvenience for me, I leave to time the best solution of the affair.

With the most profound respect and submission I place myself once more at the service of Your Reverence, and I pray that God Our Lord may keep you for many years in His holy grace.

Mission San Carlos,
April 12, 1796.

[1] He had been plying the California waters since the arrival of the first expeditions. He was evidently the first white man to pass through the Golden Gate, the entrance to San Francisco Bay.

225. Memorandum

In the matter of the juridical proceedings concerning the lands claimed by Manuel Pérez Nieto in the neighborhood of the Mission of San Gabriel, the original of which were forwarded to me by order of His Lordship the Governor, Don Diego de Borica, in accordance with his decree of May 5, 1796, I added the following as a supplement to it:

Fray Fermín Francisco de Lasuén, Apostolic Preacher of the College of the Propogation of the Faith of San Fernando of Mexico, President of these Missions of New California TESTIFIES:

That, whereas the missionaries have no power to grant, deny, or hinder anyone from taking possession of lands, the fact that their opinion is sought regarding these matters must be due to the fact that, being charged with the conversion of the Indians, and as a consequence with inducing them not to wander among the mountains and beaches, and with bringing them together into a civilized and Christian community, it is their duty to procure for them a suitable and profitable way of making a living in it.

It is the wish of our Lord the King, therefore, that all the land which is necessary for this purpose should belong to the Indians, and against that sovereign will there is no right in favor of anyone.

It is more than twenty years since the missionaries of San Gabriel took over the administration of it. I have seen them when they were happy to produce one or two fanegas of wheat, half or less than half that amount of corn, and the same as regards other cereals. Last year they had to sow one hundred and seventy-nine fanegas of the first, twelve of the second, and the same amount of the others. Despite that, it did not suffice to support the Indians, and they had to send half of them away to the mountains, and to place the rest on half rations.

So, when these missionaries want to occupy the lands that are in dispute, it cannot be thought that they are doing so for the sole purpose of dispossessing Nieto, or because they have seen that he gets profit from it. They do it because they need these lands.

To try to get the mission to use other lands which are more difficult to reach or to work, and to give up those that are easier and more convenient, so that a particular individual may benefit from them, is to place it in jeopardy in regard to the above right. This allocating or possession (call it what you will) which has been accorded to Nieto cannot be shown to be, at least in writing, the exact place he occupies. Rather, it is another place which is at a good distance, and is [beside] the flume along the road to Monterey, or the place known as Los Coyotes.

San Gabriel Mission has more than twelve hundred Christians, and there are still many pagans in its environs. With the pueblo of Santa María de Los Angeles on one side and the Sierra on the other, it is easy to see that it needs the flume to which there is reference and the adjoining lands, and it needs them not only for the present in which we now see what the situation is, but much more for the days ahead. It is clear that from now on we have to make provision for the Indians to make a living for themselves and not to be depending entirely on the common ration, on a blanket, a shirt, and a loin-cloth. Rather, they should look to the produce of the arable land which is to be given to them as their own, with building lots, improvements, and livestock.

In these respects the mission has already suffered considerable damage and loss because of the inconveniences which the above-mentioned Nieto and others who have settled nearby have occasioned it. What will happen, then? I believe that the King will not have to give his assent to it.

Despite all I have set forth, and I have no doubt the governor will give it all the attention it merits, I am far from placing myself in opposition; rather, I ardently desire, and so do all the other missionaries, that all may have a chance to make a living. In my opinion it would be possible for Nieto to continue where he is (for the present, and without in any way prejudicing legitimate claims),[1] if the governor were to make provision, if that be agreeable to him, for some way whereby the mission as well as Nieto, each for his own tillage, can have the benefit of the water supply which has its source in the same irrigation ditch, without prejudice to either.

Mission San Carlos of Monterey,
May 6, 1796.

I certify the above is a faithful copy.

San Carlos,
May 9, 1796.
(signed)

---

[1] He did continue to operate the rancho, and died in 1804. In time the Nieto Tract, as it was called, became quite extensive. It included all the lands between the Santa Ana and San Gabriel Rivers, from the sea to the hills. The greater part of what is now Long Beach was included in it, and so were Huntington Beach, Garden Grove, and many other settlements.

226. To Don Diego de Borica

I beg to acknowledge Your Lordship's official letter of this date. In it you notify me of the order of His Excellency the Viceroy, the Marqués de Branciforte, dated the eleventh of last January, to the effect that the fruits of the labor of artisans recently arrived in this province are to accrue to the Royal Treasury. Your Lordship tells me that if it would be agreeable to the missions to accept them on these terms, arrangements could be made to send the weaver and potter to them.

It seems to me, Sir, that this arrangement will not be agreeable to them, for they will have to supply the workers with material, and will have to see that their workshops and implements are in good condition, as has been the case up to the present.

Sir, it is only if they are granted the same privilege which they have enjoyed from the King our Lord that these two crafts can be of any use or advantage to these missions.

When the missions have supplied themselves with what they need from the articles made by the potter, it is all right to refund to the Royal Treasury the price of the articles sold, provided it is the artisan who is in charge of the transaction. But as regards the weaver on the broad loom, there are but few missions in which it will be possible to offer such items for sale. And since all the missions by this time have instructions in narrow loom weaving—and as a rule all the wool is devoted to it—they could acquire the other kind of weaving without additional expense. Obviously they cannot acquire it as quickly as with an artisan; but they can do so, little by little.

May God Our Lord keep Your Lordship many years in His holy grace.

San Carlos Mission,
May 11, 1796.

227. To Fray Manuel Fernández[1]

By reason of the fact that Your Reverence mentioned to Ensign Carrillo (I presume in the course of a simple conversation) that once during an expedition that you made in search of Christian Indians and pagans, when a Christian resisted being captured you knocked him down with your horse on some muddy ground, and that another Indian who had hidden himself among the grass or reeds of the marsh then fired an arrow at Your Reverence which passed through your mantle and habit, the governor gave instructions to institute certain inquiries to enable him to obtain full particulars in the case.

Yesterday after Mass at the presidio I had the great humiliation of being reproached in regard to these matters by His Lordship.

They say nothing about the shooting of the arrow, but present evidence that Your Reverence devoted three days and two nights to that expedition; that accompanied by a soldier, by the major-domo of the mission, and some Indians, you boldly and boisterously entered different rancherías, and that you took away the arms of the pagans and gave them to the Christians. I do not believe it.

I say I do not believe it, for I credit Your Reverence with enough intelligence to know that such enterprises require, as a *sine qua non,* a very careful preparation, prudent action, and a justifiable necessity.

All of these necessary circumstances are lacking, according to the investigation which has been carried out with all due formality; and in the absence of them I do not wish to believe that Your Reverence has done this, and I do not wish that you ever should. Moreover, as I had no previous notification of this occurrence, and now find myself faced with a formal charge regarding the consequences, it becomes necessary that you acquaint me with what happened, and I impose on Your Reverence the obligation of doing so, in order that I may face the charge, either asserting in all truth that such excesses never happened, or giving a firm promise that they will be avoided in the future.

I place myself at the service of Your Reverence, and I pray that God Our Lord may keep you for many years in His holy grace.

San Carlos,
May 23, 1796.

I certify that the above is a faithful copy.

San Carlos,
May 27, 1796.
(signed)

---

[1] He was a native of Galicia, where he was born in 1767. He became a member of the College of San Fernando in 1793, and was sent to California the following year. Bancroft (*op. cit.*, I, 498) describes him as "impetuous, violent, cruel, and a bad manager of neophytes . . . or at least over-zealous in converting pagans." He returned to Mexico in October, 1798.

228. To Fray Antonio Nogueyra

With your holy blessing, I am sending you the enclosed copies for they will acquaint you with the most notable news of the day. It is the best I can do, for I spend all my time writing, and to write about all that happens is more than I have time for.

It is bound to cause you some concern to see us under a government which institutes juridical enquiries because of a simple conversation of no great importance which could easily be explained away. I admit I share this concern myself, although so far I cannot find any basis for suspecting any sinister motive.

Today the governor has gone to Santa Cruz. I would have accompanied him, but I felt that was not what he wanted.

I read to him the letter I am writing to Fray Manuel, and one of his retinue is taking it. Some similar examples of inconsiderate haste have been observed in that religious, and I do not know where we will end. I will keep you informed, with God's help, about the outcome.

We have spoken several times about the affair at San Gabriel, and I never thought it would reach such a formal state. On the most sacred day of the Ascension of the Lord, after the sacred ceremonies in the presidio, and immediately after I had had chocolate, I was conducted by the governor to his office.

They are now giving to Nieto (he said) the lands which he occupies, for I know quite well that the mission does not need them, and it is forbidden under grave penalties to *eject* any person from the place where he has settled, and which he has improved by his labors.

I expressed my opinion sincerely and calmly; and on account of that and of another point to which I took exception firmly, and with religious becomingness, he became quite upset. He shouted as I had never heard him before, while I raised my voice just a little only once, but, thanks be to God, it led to no breach in the good peace and harmony.

He produced the pertinent papers, added his authorization so that they might be transferred to me, and handed them to me. He assured me that he had a repugnance for that kind of thing, and that he had never written anything whatever against us. May God grant that he never may. Finally we sat down to the same table and enjoyed our meal. Two days later I returned the papers with the comments indicated in the copy.

The first time I happened to meet His Lordship after this encounter he said nothing, and was very agreeable. On the next occasion he gave me to understand that Nieto was remaining in that place in the capacity of one tolerated, or permitted to remain, but without any right of possession; rather, without prejudice or detriment to the legitimate title. I am now reporting it in this manner to the Fathers at San Gabriel, and placing them under obligation to exercise much care in regard to it.

I am telling them that in my judgment I would not have added the last paragraph, and that I did so only in response to the earnestness with which they persuaded me to do so in the letter which they sent me in the same mail which brought the official documents. Notwithstanding all this, as soon as I began to garnish it with a parenthesis like "for the present", "and without", and so on, I found it a pleasure to do so.

Father Arroita[1] has asked me in a very formal manner for permission to retire to the college on the first boat that calls at any of these ports, for he has already completed the ten years, and finds himself worn out with the fatigues of a new foundation, fatigues which he endured at Purísima Mission.

In my reply I have acknowledged that his request is very just; but I have encouraged him to continue and begged him to wait at least until the supply ship arrives, for we hope that some missionaries will come in it. I do not know what he will decide, nor what I shall have to do; but I trust in God that what is best will be done.

Some days ago the governor told me, in a very confused way, that Your Reverence had written him, I know not what, in regard to the faculty to confirm. "Well, then," I said, "the letter that it was customary to write to me in regard to the matter must have been lost." Nothing more was said; and I am giving you this information for I think you will be pleased to know it.

The governor has given orders to the commandant at Santa Barbara to take census of all the natives at that entire channel, from San Buenaventura to Purísima. When the information is available he will consult the Viceroy regarding some ways and means of converting them without removing them from their homes.

I understand that one suggestion is, to place an additional missionary at Purísima, and another at Santa Barbara. This he told me in conversation, and I told him that it would be more apropos to put the matter before the college, and that it would be decided there. Certain it is that the proposal has some aspects that make such a procedure necessary, or very convenient; and there are other aspects that render it impossible, or very difficult. May God Our Lord grant there may be devoted to this matter that degree of deliberation which will best promote the honor and glory of His Holy Name, and the true good of so many gentiles.

With the most profound humility I place myself once more at the service of Your Reverence, and I pray that God Our Lord may keep you for many years in His holy grace.

San Carlos,
May 27, 1796.

P. S.

The packet boat *San Carlos* will sail from here to San Diego tomorrow, under command of Señor Saavedra.[2] This *caballero* was made a Knight of the Order of St. James[3] on Pentecost day in this presidio. The only time I witnessed that most religious ceremony I took the part in it that properly belongs to a priest in that same Order. But what suits me best is the same position in the Franciscan Order.

[1] Fray Francisco Arroita was a member of the Franciscan Province of Cantabria who joined San Fernando College in 1784. He was one of the missionaries who reached California in the summer of 1786. He was assigned for a time to San Luis Obispo, and in 1788 became one of the founders of Purísima Mission. There he labored until June, 1796 when he retired to Mexico. He died in San Fernando College in 1821.

[2] He was a Spanish officer in charge of transport and exploring vessels on the coast between the years 1790 and 1797.

[3] This was a military and hospitaler Order founded in Spain in the twelfth century. Beginning as a religious order, it was active in expelling the Moors from Spain. Later it acquired much wealth and power, ceased to be purely religious in aim, and became subject to the jurisdiction of the Spanish monarchs. It became an Order of Merit, but retained some of the titles and distinctions that belonged to it when it was a duly constituted religious order.

229. To Fray Antonio Nogueyra

With a request for Your Reverence's holy blessing, I wish to let you know that I went to the Mission of Santa Cruz in regard to business concerning Father Fray Manuel Fernández,[1] a matter about which I have already informed you.

The result is that he remains there, and I have assigned Father Espí as his companion, for the Reverend Father Baldomero has renewed his application to retire, and did so in a way that I cannot refuse. For this reason Reverend Father Jayme will remain at Soledad with Father Martiarena.

Neither have I been able to restrain Fathers Calzada and Arroita, despite all my pleadings, prayers, and requests—and I made them as forceable as I could—that they would stay, even one of them. Instead, they have placed me in a position in which I cannot do otherwise than give them permission to retire to the college. To take their places at the Mission of Purísima, I have assigned Fathers Fray Gregorio Fernández and Fray Juan Martín.

When I was thinking of returning from Santa Cruz to Monterey I learned of the arrival of the frigate *Aránzazu* at this port, and it was most opportune, for it gave me an opportunity to become acquainted with the new missionaries, and to give them their assignments as quickly as possible.

Father Fray José María Fernández remains here in place of Father Danti who has to leave at this time; and this very day Father Viader left for Santa Clara as supernumerary, Father Payeras for San Carlos, Father Peyrí for San Luis, and Father Cortés for San Gabriel.

The only one among these who has the faculties[2] from Reverend Father Prefect is Father Payeras, and only last night the others asked me whether or not they could hear confessions without them. I did not know what to tell them; but perhaps I shall send them word that they may, for I can recall that the present Father Prefect himself, when he withdrew to the missions in Texas, said (it seems to me) that he was granting faculties to the religious who, during their stay in these parts, would be assigned by the prelate of that college to missions among pagans.

This is a very confusing problem, and I ask Your Reverence, for the love of God, to free me from the confusion as soon as possible. Clarify the point for me; and as far as you are concerned, do what you can to see that those who come will have these faculties. This will obviate the countless inconveniences that arise when this is not observed.

Father Fray Francisco Sánchez sent me a formal and earnest request for permission to leave on this ship, and I owe him a great favor, for he has heeded my request to remain until next year. I have assured him that I will then give him the permission; and I beg Your Reverence to keep this in mind, if it is your pleasure, so that you may send someone to take his place.

This very day, and within one hour, the mail will definitely leave. This is the only day I have been able to write since I came here, and I have devoted the entire time to it, with all the fatigue a task like that involves. The result is, that Your Reverence will have to overlook both the form and the substance of this letter.

With the most profound respect I place myself once more at the service of Your Reverence, and I pray that God Our Lord may keep you for many years in His holy grace.

Mission of San Francisco,
June 30, 1796.

---

[1] Little is known about Fray José María Fernández. He reached California in the summer of 1796. He was stationed at San Francisco, and is described as a kind-hearted man. However, as a result of receiving accidentally a blow on the head his mind became so affected that he was rendered incapable of missionary work. He was sent back to Mexico the following year.

[2] At the rite of ordination the candidate for Holy Orders receives the power to administer certain sacraments. To exercise these powers, outside of certain cases of necessity, he needs the permission of the major superior in whom the power of jurisdiction is vested. This is what is meant by granting faculties. In this instance, the Father Prefect, or a still higher superior could have given it either directly, or through a representative so delegated.

230. To Don Diego de Borica

I beg to notify Your Lordship that I have given permission to four missionaries to return to the college after they had made a formal request to me for it.

To Father Fray Antonio Danti, who suffers from pains in the legs and severe inflamation of the eyes, which cause him to fear complete loss of sight.

To Father Fray Baldomero López, who suffers from a constant attack of hypochondria, for it daily increases his unfitness for the ministry.

To Father Fray Antonio Calzada, who is suffering from hemorrhoids. During all this year his condition was so serious as to make it almost impossible for him to serve in the missions. Recently he has been suffering from severe headaches.

To Father Fray José Arroita, too, for he has completed the ten years in the Mission Purísima which he founded, for he is worn out and exhausted by the labors of that service.

The other three have also completed the ten years as members of the college, including the time they spent here, which, in the case of Father Danti is six years, of Father López five years, and of Father Calzada, nine.

All will be replaced by the religious who, as Your Lordship knows, have arrived on the frigate *Aránzazu*; and in order to return in the same vessel, the four mentioned, through me, with all due respect and devotion beg Your Lordship to grant your permission and license, trusting to obtain this favor because of Your Lordship's kindness, and promising to be ever grateful.

May God Our Lord keep Your Lordship for many years in His holy grace.

Mission San Carlos,
July 20, 1796.

231. To Fray Antonio Nogueyra

May I have Your Reverence's holy blessing, for I wish to let you know that, under date of the thirtieth of last month, I wrote to you from the Mission of our holy father St. Francis to the effect that the great efforts I had made in the hope that Fathers Baldomero, Arroita, and Calzada, despite everything, would continue in these missions have been brought to nought, and I have been forced to permit them to retire, and to permit Father Danti also.

For this reason, and because I feared an importune and perhaps a noisy scene on the part of Señor Borica, I have said nothing to Father Fray Diego García. He continues as supernumerary at San Francisco, with the sole obligation of relieving the ministers there of the burden of serving the presidio.

This is the way, it seemed to me, Your Reverence would have acted in the present circumstances. I hope that in the future more opportune ones will arise so that I can observe in regard to them the instructions of Your Reverence which I keep well in mind.

The Father García of whom we are speaking informs me that he has celebrated forty-three Masses for your intention. The total I have celebrated is seventy-two; and in taking care of the increased number entrusted to this mission, as I told Your Reverence, I will continue (with God's help) to celebrate Mass for this intention in keeping with what I had offered to do.

I also informed Your Reverence of the formal request which Father Fray Francisco Sánchez made to me for his retirement, and that, in response to my pressing entreaties, he will remain for this year on the assurance I have given him that he may go next year.

I had the same experience with Father Arenaza. In view of the fact that there has not been in this mission for the whole of this year any permanent missionary who could have become familiar with its management because of the comings and goings of Father Jayme, he is making the sacrifice and will continue until the other ship arrives. Both are determined to leave on it without fail, and I have assured them of it, being satisfied that Your Reverence will approve and that you will send others in their place.

This leaves Father Fray José María Fernández in San Francisco, Father Viader at Santa Clara, Father Payeras at San Carlos, Father Peyrí at San Luis, and Father Cortés at San Gabriel. Father Espí went to Santa Cruz in place of Father Baldomero, leaving Father Jayme with Father Martiarena at Soledad, and Father Fray Gregorio Fernández stationed at Purísima with Father Fray Juan Martín.

In a confidential letter I informed the governor that I had distributed these missionaries in this manner and had given them these assignments, and although he gave me a rather vague answer there has been no new development up to the present.

His Excellency the Viceroy has answered my letter and granted an extension to the master mason up to the end of June, of '97. May God reward him and fill him with blessings. The governor had already closed the account of this workman as of the beginning of this month, and terminated his salary. On the ninth of the month he received notice, as did I, that His Excellency had granted the extension.

This procedure on the part of the governor is highly displeasing to the artisan, for in the ordinary course of events there is an interval of some months between the end of June and the time where there is an opportunity to embark for home. When he left home he was receiving a salary, and he thinks that according to the contract he should be paid a salary up to the time he leaves the province, or until he is returned to his country, provided that for this purpose he avails himself of the first opportunity that arises after the contract has come to an end. And so, I am referring the matter to Your Reverence in case an opportunity should arise to do something in favor of the claim.

Brother Revuelta has sent us nothing but the packages. He did not include the invoices which would indicate the cost of the goods, and the credits and debits respectively of the missions. It is an innovation which brings serious inconveniences to the missionaries, and can have evil consequences. In regard to this matter, as to everything else, Your Reverence will decide what you deem most fitting.

Father Espí accepted the assignment to Santa Cruz with great joy. He knew the condition of Father Fray Manuel Fernández, and I pointed it out to him so as to prepare him for the sacrifice he would have to make. He did not pose any objection. And before three days had elapsed since his arrival there he wrote me a letter, like those he is accustomed to write, objecting to that assignment most vehemently, and asking that I give him another one promptly. This is the case everywhere. He is a big problem for me.

He adapts himself very poorly in any mission. It may be that he may like a chaplaincy or pro-chaplaincy in a presidio. He has no taste for the work for which missionaries should come here. He gives signs of wishing to leave, and I tell him that at this time I will not permit it anyhow, in order not to contribute to the criticism which is bound to arise in the present circumstances. I have added that, next year or any other year he could make an application, asking Your Reverence for the permission—and I would not regret it in any way if he were to receive it.

The pilot Don José Tovar[1] has been in this port for some days with the sloop in which he went a little beyond Nootka, exploring the coast to see if he could find there any foreign settlement. He found a Boston frigate,[2] and in it he heard the news (so they relate) that there are sailing, or have already set out from London, I know not how many ships, with orders to attack any Spanish ships they may sight in these waters. May God protect us.

They have always been saying that this sloop would not leave until the frigate *Aránzazu* has arrived from San Francisco. She still has not come; and now I have received a letter from Tovar with the news that this very day he is sailing for San Blas. For this reason, this letter is being dispatched with all speed.

I have learned that Father Fray Hilario Torrent (for months past) has been suffering from acute depression which causes him to spend almost all the time weeping. He went to San Capistrano, and it seems he is beginning to recover.

With most profound respect I place myself once more at your service and pray that God Our Lord may keep you for many years in His holy grace.

San Carlos Mission,
July 21, 1796.

[1] Captain Tovar was in charge of the *Sutil.*
[2] This, no doubt, was the *Otter,* under command of Captain Dorr.

232. To Don Diego de Borica

As Your Lordship mentions in your official letter of the twenty-second of this month, it is evident that the new regulation which requires that seven-eights of the products of the work of the artisans be credited to the Royal Treasury makes it impossible to assign them to the missions, so that they may teach their craft to the Indians. But it is no less obvious that if the artisans are placed at the presidios, as Your Lordship has planned, it will be impossible, or at least very difficult, as experience shows, to give the Indians the instruction contemplated. They are neophytes; and to be at the presidio, away from the missionaries and independent of them, is very much in conflict with such a status.

The problem arose in this manner. As soon as it was decided to send skilled workmen, at the expense of the Royal Treasury, to teach their crafts to these natives, the central government ordered that the President of these Missions should distribute them through the missions as he saw best. This provision has not been revoked, for it was regarded as the only or the best way to teach manual arts to our neophytes. Realizing that this has now been rendered impracticable by reason of the new regulation, I find myself embarrassed, as I already said, in trying to adapt myself to the other course which Your Lordship proposes to me, that of sending the Indians to the presidio where it has been decided that the skilled tailor, potter, and ribbon-maker shall remain.

But since it is never my wish to place obstacles in the way of obedience, I will do what I can to send four youths, youths to whom it may be least obnoxious, two to be potters and two to be tailors. And I shall encourage the missionaries of San Francisco, Santa Clara, Santa Cruz, Soledad, and San Antonio to do the same.

It seems to me that the other missions are too far away for this purpose; and up to the present the profession of ribbon-maker is of no importance in any of them.

May Our Lord keep Your Lordship for many years in His holy grace.

Mission San Carlos,
July 23, 1796.

233. To the Missionaries

The Lord give you Peace. Your Reverences will see in the enclosed the new decision, and it can be presumed to have had its origin in the reports of the governor. But whatever its origin, it renders it impossible to assign or distribute the skilled workmen among the missions; as a consequence, it renders almost impossible the instruction of our neophytes. Yet this was the sole objective of the King, and it could be attained only by the concession made by His Majesty which has now been withdrawn.

As regards the new expedient which the honorable governor has hit upon: that we should send Indians to the presidio to be taught, Your

Reverences will observe that I promise to do only what can be done. If you do this, and it is not enough to attain the objective, advise me accordingly. And so that you may know what I desire, it is this: that four boys be sent from each mission, not in the hope that they could possibly derive any benefit while at the presidio, but with the purpose of disillusioning the government in a practical way so that it may be made clear that the economic project of the Royal Treasury nullifies the objective of the King.

I am sending the original as it is not possible for me to make a copy, and I request that it be returned to me, with this, as soon as possible from San Francisco. I will then send this and the other document to the two missions in the south.

I place myself at the service of Your Reverences, and pray that God Our Lord may keep you for many years in His holy grace.

San Carlos,
July 28, 1796.

234. To Don Diego de Borica

I have received Your Lordship's letter of this date and the accompanying official letter (which I am returning) of the artisans, the tailor, potter, and ribbon-maker, Don Joaquín Botello, Mariano Tapia, and Manuel Muñoz, who have been assigned to the presidio to teach their crafts. Your Lordship is of the opinion that these people are within their rights when they ask that an Indian man and woman be assigned to each of them to be their servants, in accordance with the superior order of His Excellency the Viceroy, the Marqués de Branciforte, dated October 27 of last year. Your Lordship reminds me that you enclosed it in your official letter to me of March 9 of this year, which I received on the twenty-seventh of that month. On the twenty-ninth of the same month I replied to Your Lordship that at the first opportunity I would forward the above instructions (and I did forward them) to the missionaries to whose missions some particular artisan who was married would be assigned, and that they were to assign an Indian man and woman to him to act as servants. At the time I wrote I judged that this was as it should be, for I had the impression that this was what His Excellency the Viceroy ordered. And when Your Lordship made no further comment to me I was convinced that I had come to the right conclusion.

I now perceive that although the above-mentioned artisans are assigned not to any particular mission but to the presidio, Your Lordship thinks it just that the missions without further delay should furnish them with servants. It is easy for me to obey this, but very difficult for me to put it into effect. I submit my will, Sir, but I shall carry it out only if I can overcome the difficulties I meet on the way. What these difficulties are I have made known to Your Lordship in an official letter, but not with the intention that they should clash with the proposal to send neophytes to the presidio to serve as apprentices. It is quite likely that His Excellency the Viceroy does not favor such a course, for it is well known that when the artisans were engaged to teach their crafts to these natives it was agreed that they were to be sent to the different missions. Should this become impossible because of the new arrangement mentioned, I have told Your Lordship that in case the instruction of the Indians is rendered impossible thereby I was of the opinion that in such a case the ordinance imposed no obligation to supply Indian men, and certainly not Indian women, to act as servants. But I repeat, Sir, that I shall obey; and if I am slow in carrying out what is required, it is because it is necessary first to bring it down to the level of the possible.

As regards my obedience, submission, reverence for authority, acknowledgement of it and respect for it—to this I never admit an exception, even when, as in the present instance, the very orders themselves would seem to invite it. By God's mercy, of this I have given proof during the thirty-three years of my ministry, some twelve of them in the office of President, in contact with all types of superiors from the lowly corporal of the guard to the Captain General and the Viceroy. And now the three mechanics mentioned would impair all this, cast aspersions on it, would weaken and complicate it when, under an incredibly grave misapprehension, they make the statement: We have come to Carmel, and the answer they have given us again and again, in short, is, that unless the Viceroy orders it, they have no intention of helping. They are wrong. They are absolutely wrong. They are under a false impression.

I am the President of these Missions and, during such time as I reside here, the principal minister of this Mission of San Carlos, popularly known as Carmel. I would prefer that my tongue would cleave to my palate, and my hand to the paper and the table, rather than that I would speak or write anything so unbecoming.

It is well known that here there is a certain religious, a minister, moreover, of this mission, one who has a light-hearted disposition, quick with a rejoinder, but guileless, too. Once when in characteristic fashion he was giving all his attention to some problem, he was taken unawares and reproached by one of the artisans in regard to the Indian man and woman. His reply was: Away with you, Sir. The Viceroy does not know what goes on here. And he added later: As to all these matters, they pertain to the Father President. Speak to him. He will tell you. This is exactly what happened; not the story as they tell it. I forgive them with all my heart. I pray and beg that they be not punished for it in any way. On the other hand, I plead with them and beseech them to retract what they said, and to remove from their statement what is so calumnious and uncalled-for.

The fact that this has reached me through your hands is evidence that, at the very least, Your Lordship has suspended judgment until I am given a hearing. There is danger, however, that the ordinary people who no doubt heard about the matter may accept it as true. This would be nothing less than to give scandal of the most harmful kind. Steps should be taken to bring it to an end.

May God Our Lord [keep Your Lordship many years in His holy grace.]

San Carlos Mission,
August 6, 1796.

235. To the Marqués de Branciforte

In accordance with the royal order of the sixteenth of September of the year '94, I beg to inform Your Excellency that, after they had sent me a formal request for it, I gave permission to four missionaries of this New California to retire to the College of San Fernando.

To Father Fray Antonio Danti because he was ill with pains of the legs and serious inflammation of the eyes, which caused him to fear total loss of sight.

To Father Fray Baldomero López because he had become a victim of chronic hypochondria which day by day decreases his fitness for the ministry.

To Father Fray José Antonio Calzada for he is suffering from hemorrhoids which in the course of the year became so bad as to make it almost impossible for him to serve the missions; and in addition he is suffering from severe headaches, a new and recent development.

To Father Fray José Arroita, for he has completed his ten years at Purísima Mission which he founded, and because he is worn out and exhausted by the labors involved.

May God Our Lord keep Your Excellency for many years in His holy grace.

Mission San Carlos,
August 15, 1796.

236. To Fray Antonio Nogueyra

Give me Your Reverence's holy blessing, and with it I shall have grounds for hoping that I shall not be overcome by a succession of exasperating problems by which I am overwhelmed by the government.

Fathers Danti and López were here on the occasion of the last unfortunate affair. They are carrying copies of the official letters in regard to it, and can give information about the other circumstances surrounding it. Despite this, I shall explain to Your Reverence step by step all that is needed for a full understanding of it.

When the central government of Mexico, at the expense of the Royal Treasury, decided to provide skilled workers to teach their crafts to the Indians of these missions, it ordered that I should allocate them in the missions according as I saw fitting. This I have carried out, without abusing the confidence placed in me, and without disturbing thereby in any way the good relations with the governor of the province. I gave him a report on everything, passing over in silence the occasions when on his own authority he interfered in the matter.

By means of an official letter he informed me that in the course of this year the Viceroy was sending a tailor, a ribbon-maker, a weaver on the broad loom, and a potter. He added that he sent me this information so that I might put into effect the part that concerned me.

I replied to him that the part which the central government of Mexico ordered that I should have in this matter was this: on being notified of the arrival of the workers and their implements, I was to allocate them among the missions under my charge, according to their professions and as I judged suitable. I mentioned that this was my understanding when on previous occasions I told him, when we were discussing this matter verbally, that the potter could begin to teach his trade at the Mission of San Francisco, and the weaver in that of San Juan Capistrano, that the art of making ribbons, since it could not be practiced at any of the missions because of lack of material, of use or utility, could not be taught to the neophytes. In regard to the master tailor, I remarked that while I recognized the great importance of his trade, it was clear to me that neither now nor in many years to come would he be able to find work in any individual mission, nor in all of them put together, which would enable him to impart to the Indians the full instruction which is the object of our Lord the King in making this provision. For this reason I suggested that His Lordship could dispose of these two skilled workers as he chose.

His Lordship agreed to this, placed the two workers at the presidio, and asked that apprentices be sent to them. I placed many obstacles in the way of this, for it is contrary to the status of neophytes to live at a presidio, away from the missionaries and independent of them. Furthermore, it is our experience that such a procedure is futile. I pointed out that by declining to accept these workmen at the missions it followed that I declined to accept their services for the Indians, but despite this, I would do whatever was possible so that a certain number of youths might attend from missions near enough to permit it.

Later he sent me an order from His Excellency the Viceroy to the effect that an Indian man and an Indian woman should be assigned to wait on the workers recently engaged. I replied that I would send that regulation to the missionaries at the missions to which any particular worker was assigned so that they could comply with it. The governor raised no objection to this.

Recently His Lordship informed me of another order of the central government to the effect that the products of the labors of these workmen should revert to the Royal Treasury; and when I pointed out that it was impossible for the missions to accept workers on these terms, the governor was very much in agreement with me.

When they had taken up residence at the presidio they sent a request to the governor for the Indian man and woman who were to wait on them, with other remarks that Your Reverence can read in the copy that the Fathers are taking along. They are also taking along a copy of my reply and my request that the workers should withdraw their demand, and that they should erase from their request a clause that is very definitely ill-founded.

The reply of the governor was, that he was ready to order that satisfaction should be given and the clause in question erased, after he had heard the parties in my presence or that of another religious whom I might name. It was now the first vespers of the Feast of St. Laurence, and therefore it was my duty on that day to say Mass at the presidio. For this reason I was a witness to the proceedings which lasted all morning and a great part of the afternoon. As a result, it transpired that the tailor alone was the author of the formal request. He stood by what he had stated in it, merely changing the statement that he had recourse, not to Carmel, but only to Father Arenaza who happened to be at the presidio. The ribbon-maker and the potter stated that they had not read the petition, but had signed it under pressure from the tailor and without reading its contents. They stated that they had not been given an unfriendly reception, but had been given all the gracious attention that could be offered.

The two witnesses testified, and it was true in substance that Father

Fray Pascual had said to the tailor: "Even if the Viceroy did order it, the Viceroy does not know what goes on here."

Of the two witnesses, one said that he did not notice, and the other that he did notice that the Father replied that in any case the Father President was over there: see him, and he will decide what is to be done. The same person added that it was his impression and judgment that the comment was an aside, and not seriously meant.

When the proceedings were concluded, the presiding judge, who was the lieutenant at the presidio, handed the record to the governor, and he issued the order that it should be passed on to me so that, seeing that I had been present as witness, I could declare whether everything had been done to my satisfaction, or whether there should be a more extended inquiry.

When the governor was handing it to me I said to him (recalling a comment we are accustomed to make among ourselves when there is a question as to whether the English will come to cause us trouble): "I assure you that if they attack us their bullets will not have to be as powerful, in order to drive me away from this land, as the impact of seeing such matters reduced to a judicial formality."

I received them. I took them with me and added the comment: "In obedience to the governor I witnessed these inquiries with deep humiliation. In obedience to his decree, which precedes this, I affirm that for my part I would be satisfied with much less; and consequently there is no need of a more extended inquiry."

There the matter rested. How I wish I could now express in words what my feelings were! That a genial or humorous sharpness of wit could possibly give rise to so much commotion, become so hateful, consume so much time, and disturb the peace!

It is my opinion that no suit should be permitted, or at least no permission to proceed should be given it, if, in the first instance, it contained a complaint or an accusation based on what is false, or calumnious, or on evidence that has no bearing on the complaint. If this course had been followed the matter would have been finished and settled the moment these workmen were brought face to face with me or with the other religious.

I am very sorry to have caused Your Reverence this humiliation, but my purpose is to spare you a greater one, should these stories reach the Viceroy, which is what I fear. Further, if this should happen, so that you may know what are my sentiments in the matter, I am copying the following communication which I have drawn up in draft with the purpose of forwarding and putting it into execution when I can:

His Honor the Governor

My dear Sir:

It is not my understanding that His Excellency the Viceroy, the Marqués de Branciforte, would wish or that he has given an order that in the case of the skilled workmen definitely assigned to the presidio the missions should be obliged to supply Indian men and women to serve them. The problem arises because the missions have declined some of the artisans who recently arrived in this province for reasons which I have explained to Your Lordship, and also because the missions were unable to admit any, in view of the new regulations which Your Lordship sent me. Rather, His Excellency issued this order on the understanding that the artisans would be sent to the different missions, as the earlier order stipulated.

However, repressing my own opinion out of deference to Your Lordship's, I am sending three youths as soon as possible, one for each of the craftsmen.

The potter and the ribbon-maker, it seems, are not asking to get Indian women; and it is going to be difficult to please the master tailor, because there is no girl who wants to go. If we use force, it will not be long before she becomes a fugitive to the forest. If we try to induce her to like it, the result will not last. And no matter by what device she may be kept in his house, she is going to be not so much a help as a burden; and in addition one must consider the consequences of having her associate with the Indian man, her co-worker.

May God Our Lord keep Your Lordship for many years in His holy grace.

It will be a severe penalty for this mission of San Carlos and for any other, to have to supply servants by force and without pay, to the people of the presidio, for if they do anything for the missions, the missions have to pay for it like anybody else. But we will endure it, until, perchance, the Viceroy when better informed decides otherwise.

The official letter for His Excellency is attached, in addition to the notification I have to give him of the reasons for which I have permitted the four missionaries to withdraw from here to the college down there. With the information it contains (for it goes open), and with what I have already told Your Reverence, I believe that he, too, will declare himself satisfied that it was not possible for me to do anything else.

With this I bring to an end all the trouble I am causing you; but I am not bringing to an end the profound respect with which I place myself at the service of your orders and suggestions. I pray that God Our Lord may keep you for many years in His holy grace.

San Carlos,
August 21, 1796.

P. S.

I am also enclosing the certificate of our residence here.

237. List of Missionaries[1]

San Carlos	Fermín Francisco de Lasuén Pascual Martínez de Arenaza Mariano Payeras
San Francisco	Martín de Landaeta José María Fernández Diego García
Santa Clara	Francisco Miguel Sánchez Magín Catalá José Viader
Santa Cruz	José de la Cruz Espí Manuel Fernández
Soledad	José Manuel Martiarena Antonio Jayme
San Antonio	Buenaventura Sitjar Marcelino Ciprés
San Luis Obispo	Miguel Giribet Antonio Peyrí
Purísima	Gregorio Fernández Juan Martín
Santa Barbara	Esteban Tapis José de Miguel
San Buenaventura	Francisco Dumets [Dumetz] Vicente de Santa María
San Gabriel	Antonio Cruzado Miguel Sánchez Juan Cortés
San Juan Capistrano	Vicente Fuster Juan Norberto de Santiago
San Diego	Juan Mariner Hilario Torrent Pedro de Esteban

August 23, 1796.

---

[1] As in every case, Lasuén first submitted the list to the governor to obtain his approval. In this case he added an unusually lengthy array of titles to the name of the governor: Professed Knight of the Order of Santiago, Army Colonel of Cavalry, Political and Military Governor of the Peninsula of California, Commandant Inspector of the Garrison Troops.

238. To Fray Antonio Nogueyra

May I have Your Reverence's blessing. I wish to acknowledge your letter of the thirteenth of last April, and this is in reply to it. I have informed Your Reverence that it was not possible for me to detain Fathers Arroita, Calzada, and Baldomero, and that I was able to defer the departure of Father Sánchez until next year.

Those who apply to leave because they have completed the ten years say that these years must be reckoned from the day of their departure from Europe, according to the declaration of His Excellency Count de Revilla Gigedo. They believe that in urging their claim they have the Viceroy of New Spain on their side, and on the other hand, if their claim is denied, they threaten that they will have recourse to him.

It would be possible to encounter some unpleasant controversy with this government if someone presented proof of having completed the ten years and I did not accede to it. It would be better, therefore, to have some authoritative and definitive rule regarding this point, so that we could follow it consistently and without contradiction.

On another point which Don Fages tried to put in the *Reglamento* (may God forgive him for it) to the effect that there ought to be but one religious in each mission, I wrote to the late Reverend Father, Fray Francisco Pangua, who was then Guardian of the College, that in a situation like that I would not wish to be a missionary. And I shall repeat it all the days of my life. This would be equivalent to condemning a religious to an intolerable life, without help when he would be sick, and without the sacraments when dying. In this we are looking on it from the spiritual point of view. But how do you think the King will look on it? And, a weightier consideration, what will be the attitude of His Majesty seeing that he wishes us to keep the temporal affairs of the missions in our control?

In obedience to Your Reverence, I have searched these archives, and I have seen a copy of what your venerable council wrote to the central government on this point, seeking permission for Most Illustrious Señor Verger to proceed to Spain to collect missionaries. I came upon a letter from the above-mentioned Reverend Father Pangua in which he writes to the venerable Father Junípero that he regarded it as a lesser evil to let a mission be without a religious than that a religious should be alone in a mission. And he replied to me in the same vein when I wrote to him what I have said, and he gave me permission, in such an eventuality, to take my departure as best I could.

Likewise, I have found a quarter sheet of loose paper in the handwriting of the late Father Palou with the notes, unsigned, of the substance of his reply to a certain letter of Don Fages. This being the case, there is nothing to worry about. Enclosed is an exact copy of it, even to the last detail.

I wish Your Reverence success in this matter more than in any other; for if we fail, what Your Reverence says will happen: not a single religious will want to come, and those of us who are in the missions will not wish to be alone.

I wish to thank you sincerely for all the care you devoted to the insignia[1] you sent me through Father Payeras.

I am continuing to offer what Masses I can for your intention. The total up to the present is sixty-six. Father Fray Esteban Tapis informs me that he has already offered fifty-nine, and will say an additional forty-one, bringing the total to a hundred.

In the name of Your Reverence I was instructed by Reverend Father Peña to propose for the office of President of these Missions some of the religious here whom I consider suitable. I do not wish to have any act or part in this matter; but so as to carry out what I am ordered, I beg to state that the following seem to me to have the qualifications: Father Fuster, Father Torrent (at the moment I do not know how this will suit him, for it is more than a month since I heard that he was suffering from a severe attack of melancholia), and Father Tapis.[2]

Without any wish to interefere in what does not concern me, but with the greatest obedience, respect, and devotion to the will of Your Reverence, I suggest that perhaps it would be very opportune to appoint a priest as Procurator of these missions in matters that require recourse to a superior outside the cloister, and who will direct the lay Brother Procurator in certain other matters.

I understand that the Dominicans have such a person, and we, the missionaries of San Fernando, would not wish to be inferior in this respect, if Your Reverence should so desire. At the present time there are some experienced individuals down there; and what a pleasure it would be if Your Reverence would favor Father Peña.[3]

I have sent congratulations to the Most Illustrious Señor Rouset,[4] and entrusted the letter to Don Borica who flatters himself that he obtained the mitre for him because he obtained for him a commission which he carried out brilliantly, and as a result he is a great friend of his. Certainly I have seen letters from the Most Illustrious Señor which make clear that there is a close friendship and understanding between them.

For this reason I suspect that inevitably there will be certain innovations which can be disturbing to us, for I notice that the governor, when speaking with others rather than with me, frequently raises doubts on our faculties in the military jurisdiction as regards the soldiers, and in the ordinary jurisdiction for the pueblos and the *gente de razón*. I would appreciate it very much if Your Reverence would kindly give me some direction in the matter.

I am completely at the will of Your Reverence. I wish you all happiness, and I pray that God Our Lord may keep you for many years in His holy grace.

Mission San Carlos,
September 3, 1796.

I took the opportunity to send His Excellency the Viceroy direct an acknowledgement of and a reply to an order His Excellency sent, to the effect that the ships from San Blas can supply the mission with what they need, provided in return they suffer no loss in the quality of the refund or the equivalence in value to the Royal Treasury.

¹ Sp. *venera*. At that time the most popular place of pilgrimage in Spain was the shrine of St. James of Compostella, in Galicia. Those who completed the pilgrimage were entitled to wear the insignia or heraldic symbol of St. James, which is a shell shaped like a scallop.

² Father Tapis received the appointment. He succeeded Lasuén, and held the office of President from 1803 to December, 1812.

³ The recommendation was evidently followed, for Peña kept a record of the articles sent to the missions, as the account-books of San Fernando testify. See Geiger, *Palou,* pp. 411-412.

⁴ He was a native of Havana, Cuba, and became the fourth bishop of Sonora. He joined the Franciscan Order at the College of Zacatecas, Mexico, in May, 1775, and served as missionary to the Indians of Tarahumara. In October, 1795 he was appointed bishop of Sonora. He did not reach his cathedral city of Arispe until the following September. He retired in 1810, and died in 1814.

239. To Don José Argüello

When I took my leave of the Lord Governor to pay a visit to this Mission of our father St. Francis I was aware that His Lordship had been informed that there had been certain disagreements between the missionary Fathers there. One such disagreement of itself was of such a nature that on the part of neither of the Fathers was there anything blameworthy, except the fact that it had taken place in public.

It is but right that Your Honor should know about it; but it is not becoming that I should describe these disputes in detail (as you ask me to do), or even do it in a general way when religious in anger have an occasional altercation. And least of all is it necessary that they should issue a signed statement so that the information I give may be regarded as a true and faithful record.

These are what the Lord Governor wishes: that the work of the Indians be made light; that there be more moderation in punishing them; and that they be given their rations cooked. All this has been put into effect quietly. The Fathers are in agreement about it, to meet my satisfaction. The Lord Governor, too, will be satisfied; and thus I satisfy your letter of this date.

May God Our Savior, etc.

Mission of our father St. Francis,
September 22, 1796.

240. To Don Diego de Borica

What can my fellow countryman and my lord expect from a poor Friar who never says in full what is in his mind and never takes a definite stand? And what can he expect when this same person is hemmed in by restrictions which no one understands better than Your Lordship? Every man is subject to restrictions; and those peculiar to this country as a rule make it possible for a person to do his duty only if he makes prudent use of kindness and tolerance, for [such restrictions] so block the way or make it so rough that he carries out his obligations without enthusiasm, or simply because he is under obligation to do so.

When affairs reach a crisis, or when firmness is called for, Your Lordship will not deny that I know how to use it. I recognize, nevertheless, that I shall fail often enough; and may God forgive me for it.

In the present case, Your Lordship has seen that an old man of sixty has journeyed nearly sixty leagues to remedy an evil. If this painful effort should prove to have been in vain, one must not suppose that he will fail to discipline severely one who failed to conform gracefully.

I know to whom I am speaking. Passion took over, Sir; it was given complete sway. When it met with an obstacle, it sought to overcome it by methods and means which it well knows how to devise. I wish I could travel like a bird to consult with Your Lordship in regard to the case. I would come to speak my mind, with all the confidence with which your kindness inspires me. My purpose would be to acquire ideas that would be useful for the future, and not in the least to awaken unpleasant memories of the past.

I am not trying to make saints out of the Fathers who have been in charge of this mission. They may have gone to extremes in disciplining. I have neither witnessed them, nor heard about them, nor received any reports about them. What is said about the work cannot be denied. It is evidenced by the big projects accomplished in a short time, for much of it was forced labor. I reprimanded them, and placed them under obligation to be more forebearing. What is it Your Lordship wants me to do?

The situation is this: It is as difficult to get them to work slowly here as it is, after much effort, to get them to do enough work elsewhere. Everything has been corrected and is in good order. Father Landaeta has agreed to more than I could wish, and to more than I would agree to. But it is necessary; and he agrees to conform and to allow time for a better agreement, for that will come in due time.

Between him and Father Fernández there has been only one incident in which there was a disagreement, and if this had not taken place in public it would not have reflected on either the one or the other.

Beginning with the twenty-second of the current month, pozole is being served to the Indians. For this purpose they have bought two cauldrons from the paymaster's office, and efforts are being made to obtain others from Mexico.

Of those who ran away and crossed the bay, these have come back: three men, a woman with a nursing baby that has been baptized, and a girl of sixteen or seventeen who is receiving instructions with a view to baptism. They report that they did not run away, and the others are not staying away, because of fear of punishment or aversion for the work; rather, they fled through fear of a contagious and fatal disease that broke out here. They are not accustomed to come of themselves, and no one went to bring them back. Your Honor, they were placed in the mission on the spur of the moment, and it is now necessary to give some thought to the best way to remedy that error. I have given instructions that they should try to win them over, and be much more kind in dealing with them, and that they should give them permission to go to their rancherías when they ask for it. And they should send them even without being asked whenever they see that they are declining in health or becoming homesick. I have hopes that it will not be long before all of them return.

Your Lordship says very truly that for two fellow countrymen to dispute, to the scandal of the province, would be a shame; and now I wish to say that precisely when that begins my administration comes to an end.

For years I have carried the burden in peace, and my only reward was the satisfaction I derived from serving the Order and the State. Scandal does harm; it injures both the one and the other. Far be it from me to decline what is just up to the point where it would be necessary to appeal to the technicalities of law. I welcome what is just, no matter in what form it appears. The threat of Your Lordship would have hurt me much more if it had not been obvious that it contained a good objective, but at the same time a serious and determined will not to put it into effect.

No, my lord and my countryman, there will be no lawsuits, for, in the first place, I do not wish that anyone should hate them more than I do; and it takes two to make a quarrel. In the second place, a bad settlement is better than a good lawsuit. And if the latter is always bad, no matter how good it may be, then, I will always choose the lesser of two evils. In the third place, as soon as Your Lordship initiates any proceedings, you are in the right; and when there is a question of right, I never oppose. In the fourth case, what chance has a poor Father Lasuén against a señor like Don Borica?

Your kindly disposition will understand why my heart, more sorely oppressed on this occasion than on any other in my life, should unburden itself in this fashion to one such as Your Lordship who can and will contribute to my comfort.

A thousand thanks, a thousand regards, greetings, and respects from Your most obedient countryman, your most devoted servant and chaplain who kisses the hand of Your Lordship.

Mission San Francisco,
September 26, 1796.

241. To the Missionaries

The Lord gives you Peace. I have learned that the honorable governor by means of an official letter has placed on you the obligation of holding the annual election for alcaldes and *regidores*. Let this be duly done, for His Lordship orders it; let it be done in a manner befitting missions where there is no obligation in law to do so.

In these (missions) we continue to prepare neophytes to observe the law, but they are not subject to these laws until such time as these cease to be missions and are declared to be pueblos or *doctrinas* by the King our Lord.

When that time is reached we must leave them, but in the meantime, no; the election in question can be held only by way of preparation and instruction for the future, but by no means can it be held in virtue of the law cited, for this does not apply to missions. This you will be able to explain to the governor when reporting to him that you have obeyed the order.

Furthermore, you would not in the least be violating, rather you would be acting in accordance with, the ordinances of our holy college if, in similar directives which introduce something new, the matter were referred to me.

May God Our Lord keep Your Reverences for many years in His holy grace.

San Carlos,
November 2, 1796.

242. To Fray Antonio Nogueyra

I beg Your Reverence's holy blessing, and wish to say that at the moment I can hardly do more than acknowledge receipt of your esteemed letter of the thirteenth of last July, for it reached me just as the government mail was about to be dispatched.

In my own name and in that of all the others, I wish to express thanks for the blankets and handkerchiefs which Your Reverence is getting ready in order to express appreciation to the missions, in return for the Masses offered in them for your intention.

I am very sorry that the faculty to confirm is being delayed so much; but if our Father Prefect calls when he is over there I believe he will be able to facilitate matters if he presents a permit from the Viceroy.

At the beginning of last month I returned from San Francisco, a place to which I was obliged to go because of the gravest and most trying problem I ever faced in all my life. The Reverend Fathers Fray Diego García and Fray José María Fernández had plotted with fanatical zeal to expel Fray Landaeta from that mission. The Indians joined in the conspiracy, and the officers of the presidio, Alberni and Argüello, joined it or tended that way. For this purpose they collected accounts of different unbecoming incidents that took place at different times in the past, giving them the appearance of cruel, enormous, and monstrous crimes, and these they attributed to Fathers Danti and Landaeta.

I worked hard to put an end to all this by means of letters. In this I was not successful, so I went there myself. I had to put up with a great deal, but, thanks be to God, everything ended in a peaceful solution, and to the complete satisfaction of the governor. Thanks be to God.

I think it very important that for the present a strict and rigorous silence be observed both there and here in regard to this matter until an occasion arises to withdraw Father Diego from the country, without making any reference to this affair. May God forgive him and grant him every happiness.

In a letter which he wrote in August and which I received in October, Father Fray José de Miguel asked me for permission to retire. If there is any way of sending a substitute for him I would appreciate it very highly, so that this religious may enjoy the consolation which he so desires, and which, so he tells me, he has often sought.

There is nothing I can add to the profound respect and submission with which I strive to accomplish in everything the will of Your Reverence. And I pray that God Our Lord may keep you for many years in His holy grace.

San Carlos,
November 2, 1796.

[In the margin]: I have offered ninety-two Masses, and I am continuing to do so. Father Torrent had offered sixty up to the fourteenth of last September.

243. To Don Diego de Borica

The Reverend Fathers of this Mission of San Carlos have forwarded me an official letter from Your Lordship, dated the twenty-second of last September. In it they were reminded that in the archives of the government there are references to various directives sent during the year 1792 to the Reverend Father Ministers of certain missions in regard to the election of alcaldes and *regidores,* and that Your Lordship has observed that thereafter [what was prescribed] was generally omitted.

Wherefore, seeing that nothing becomes the service of the King better than to put his laws into force, you charge them kindly to see to it in the future that they furnish in due time a report in regard to it, so that due credit may be given.

In this connection Your Lordship cites Law number fifteen, title number three, of the fourth book of the *Recopilación* of these kingdoms.[1]

The Fathers of this mission replied, referring the matter to me as the principal minister of this mission and the President of the others.

I have told them, and I have written to all the other missionaries, that they are to hold such an annual election all right, because Your Lordship orders it, but only in a manner that can be observed in missions, for there is no law that makes it obligatory for them. I pointed out to them that in the missions our duty is to continue to prepare the neophytes to observe the laws, but in order that they be formally bound by them, they would have to await the time when these places would cease to be missions, and the king would declare them to be pueblos or *doctrinas.* I added that when that stage is reached it will be our duty to leave them; but until then, no; an election of this kind should be held by way of preparation and instruction merely, as a preparation for the future, but by no means in the name of the law cited, for this does not apply to missions.

In obedience to the sovereign ordinances as I know them, and adhering to them strictly and scrupulously, this is the instruction, I repeat it, this is the instruction I have given my religious, and this is the answer I give, with all due respect, to Your Lordship.

May God Our Lord keep Your Lordship for many years in His holy grace.

San Carlos Mission,
November 12, 1796.

[1] Lasuén either did not notice, or is too courteous to point out, that Governor Borica gave the wrong reference for the regulation he cited from the *Recopilación de Leyes de las Indias.* Borica invoked Law 15, title 3, Book 6, *not* Book 4. The law is as follows: We ordain that in each village and reduction there be an alcalde, an Indian of the same reduction; and if there are more than eighty families, two alcaldes and two regidores, also Indians. Although the village be very large, there should never be more than two alcaldes and four regidores; and if there are under eighty (families) but more than thirty-nine, never more than one alcalde and one regidor. Each year a new administration must be elected in the presence of the parish priests (en presencia de los Curas) as is done in Spanish as well as Indian villages.

244. To Fray Antonio Nogueyra

I beg Your Reverence's holy blessing, and am happy to inform you that I have carried out what I proposed to you. I think I did what was most in conformity with your will when I did not send Father García away from here. At the time that I ought to have done so the governor and the officials of San Francisco were much devoted to him. So, in view of the peculiar dispositions of the Father and of the governor, we would have exposed ourselves to strong opposition; and this, with the fault-finding of the former, and the tendency of the latter to make legal issues out of matters, would bring our good intentions to naught, and we would find ourselves burdened with added worries.

The matter now appears in a less unfavorable light. The reason is, that the irresponsible and utterly imprudent action which the Andalusian, with the cooperation of Father Fernández, decided upon (I mentioned the incident in my previous letter to Your Reverence) of presenting themselves before me in public and in the presence of the honorable Alberni and Argüello, demanding that Father Landaeta should leave San Francisco, loudly attributing to him inhuman atrocities when they were nothing but unfortunate accidents, mixing up incidents that had no foundation other than his diseased mind with complaints that he was piqued by his departure from the Soledad, and his failure to receive the treatment and attention of the Fathers of that mission which were due to him. By doing so, I repeat, he has lost in great measure the esteem of his devotees who formerly gave him almost the same credence as Father Fernández when they heard him relate these tall tales.

As a consequence, when there is a question of transferring him, the latter will not raise any particular outcry, nor will the governor either, for he already knows about it. But it will always be very desirable, in order to avoid scenes, to have recourse to some motive or pretext as far removed as possible from what has happened. I shall be on the alert to take advantage of anything that may arise, and down where you are, perhaps some opportune reason may arise for recalling him.

Enclosed is the correspondence I sent to the governor, and in it is transcribed the letter of His Most Illustrious Lordship. I delivered it to him myself, and it made him very ill at ease, even before he read it. I have gone into the matter very deeply, for, seeing they are but missions, how can I concede any more than that the election be held in them in the manner in which circumstances allow?

If they wish to remove them from the category to which they belong and make them *doctrinas* or parishes, our Lord the King can do it whenever he wishes, but we know that he does not desire this yet, and that when that time comes, he will want us to leave them.

It has been my opinion that the only way to fulfill my obligation is the way I have mentioned; and I want very much to fulfill it. I am as eager to obey the orders of the King as I am to respect his prerogatives and privileges. I hold each in equal regard, for so the King would have it; and there is absolutely nothing more in my persistence than obedience to the royal will.

After he had read my official letter he continued to make every effort to make me desist from my purpose; and being unable to succeeed he told me that he would make copies of the documents concerning the affair, and that he would send them, together with my letter, to His Excellency the Viceroy for a decision. To save Your Reverence greater trouble, I am sending Father Peña various particulars on the point and possibly these may have some value so that you may understand and handle the matter.

In any event, in regard to that matter as well as to anything else, I will do what Your Reverence orders me, for my will is very much yours.

May God Our Lord keep Your Reverence many years in His holy grace.

San Carlos Mission,
November 26, 1796.

P. S.

I am sending Your Reverence copies of a confidential letter from His Lordship the Governor, and of a letter from Señor Argüello, as well as my reply. All have reference to the affair at the Mission of our father St. Francis.

245. To Fray Antonio Nogueyra (?)[1]

As these gentlemen were annoyed and wearied by the requests of the two Fathers that Father Landaeta would have to leave that mission, they thought that the outcome would be a lengthy lawsuit and controversy.

What is astonishing is, that although Father Landaeta did not contradict anything they said, and they made no charge whatever against him, they should make such an intense, strong, irresponsible, and irregular demand. It is more than I can understand. And when Father Diego saw that I was settling the matter without having recourse to "the big stick", he thereupon made the monstrous charge which I passed on to Your Reverence in my letter.

At last, everything is settled. All are at peace. There is quiet and calm. Thanks be to God.

The truth is, that from time to time I am assailed by fears that new disturbances may arise, or old ones be revived.

May Your Reverence bear all this annoyance in patience, and send such orders as you please to

Your humble and most worthless servant
Who kisses your hand.

San Carlos,
November 28, 1796.

[1] This letter is possibly a postscript to the letter of November 26, above. It was obviously addressed to Father Nogueyra, but lacks his name and the customary opening greetings of a letter by Lasuén.

246. To Don Fray Francisco Rouset

With all due respect and gratitude, I received the paternal, esteemed, and gracious letter of Your Illustrious Lordship dated the thirtieth of last September. It condescends to honor and favor the least of those dependent on you, and the most insignificant of your subjects; and to the same degree it redounds to the honor of Your Illustrious Lordship.

I am going to make it known to my religious for their consolation, which is bound to be great. And I am making it known, too, so that from all directions there may spring forth an outburst of gratitude great enough to equal the generous and distinguished favor which you have deigned to confer upon us. I shall make it known to our College of San Fernando with the same object in mind. Furthermore, I want to obtain from my Father Guardian his blessing, and his permission to exercise the new faculties which Your Illustrious Lordship has conferred on me.

And if in the meantime there should arise some problem pertaining to them, I shall, without fail, attend to the matter in the manner that I consider most in accord with the will of Your Illustrious Lordship.

In view of the fact that Your Lordship is giving me Military Faculties in case I should find myself chaplain to any presidio, I shall explain with all due frankness all that is to be told about this matter in the course of this conquest from the beginning up to the present.

There has never been the formal assignment, appointment, title, office, or salary of a chaplain. We the missionaries entered with the armed forces, and we have been ministering to them and to the Indians without distinction. The missionaries of the missions nearest to the presidios take care of the garrisons there, and those of the other missions take care of their escorts. This has been done at the request and on the instructions of the Lords Viceroy, and with the full knowledge of their Lordships the Bishops.

In the second *Reglamento* which was drawn up, and which has force at the present day, it was laid down that there should be but one missionary at each mission, but that there shall be two in those nearest to a presidio, one of them to act as chaplain at the presidio.

We notice that this is not observed, for in each mission two missionaries have always been maintained, and they receive the corresponding stipends. Consequently, the situation remains the same as before, with sometimes the one, sometimes the other, or each missionary in succession, taking care of the presidios from the missions nearest them.

In view of this, when there is one to spare, I assign them some religious in the capacity of supernumerary. In this way he helps to bear the additional burden, despite the fact that for this service there has never been paid an additional stipend or gratuity in the case of those who were not receiving them.

My regular residence is in this Mission of San Carlos, beside the royal presidio of the same name. I serve its occupants as far as they need me, taking my turn with the other two missionaries, supplying them with Mass and spiritual assistance on all days of obligation.

I am accustomed to alternate similarly with the Fathers in the other missions which, by reason of their nearness to a presidio, take care of its needs. Sometimes during my residence in them I take this on myself exclusively to relieve the Fathers, my fellow-workers, of that work for the time.

Knowing these matters, Your Illustrious Lordship will decide in accordance with your higher will, and we, the missionaries of New California, in profound submissiveness will be the most scrupulous in carrying out your decisions.

I am well aware how worthless I am in carrying out what may be entrusted to me by Your Illustrious Lordship; but this should not hinder Your Illustrious Lordship from being assured that in loyalty, respect, and obedience to you there is no one who will surpass me, because I make no reservation, not even of life itself, whenever it may be for me a question of satisfying these obligations.

I wish Your Illustrious Lordship all happiness, and I pray that God Our Lord may keep you for many years in His holy grace.

San Carlos Mission,
December 16, 1796.

247. To the Missionaries

The Lord give you Peace. The Most Illustrious Lord Bishop,[1] Don Fray Francisco Rouset, expresses his gratitude for the greetings I extended him in my own name and in that of Your Reverences on his promotion to the sacred mitre of Sonora. He places his high office at our disposal for anything that may conduce to our benefit and that of our missions.

In proof of his willingness to be of service to us, and of his appreciation for all of us his brethren, so His Illustrious Lordship states, he grants me all the faculties he can delegate in regard to the administration of sacraments to Indians and Spaniards in all these missions subject to me, with the power of subdelegating the same in his name to such missionaries as, in my judgment, may need them and will make fitting use of them. All of this is without prejudice to those we might hold by commission of the Prefect of the Missions, and others which we may legitimately obtain in the capacity of missionaries. In this regard, too, he makes me his Vicar Forane[2] for the Spaniards who may reside at these missions; and he has granted me Military Faculties.

None of the predecessors of His Illustrious Lordship has claimed recognition in these parts either in these terms or in any other. Yet we must not doubt that he knows perfectly well what his rights are, and what ours are.

I have replied with becoming gratitude and respect; and I have sent a copy of everything to our college so that they may be informed about the matter and instruct us in regard to this delicate innovation.

In the meantime, in order to guard against any misgiving, fear, or doubt about it which may arise, in the name of the above-mentioned Bishop, for now and until further notice, I subdelegate to each and all of Your Reverences all the faculties that can be subdelegated according to the tenor of the concession mentioned by His Illustrious Lordship. You will also be able to use the Military Faculties until such time as His Lordship decides to the contrary, and at this writing I have made it my business to inform him regarding our relationship with the occupation forces from the beginning up to now.

May God Our Lord keep Your Reverences for many years in His holy grace.[3]

San Carlos Mission,
December 18, 1796.

[1] These two words, although legible, have been erased.

[2] One empowered by the bishop to exercise a limited measure of jurisdiction over an administrative division of the diocese; a diocesan dean.

[3] On the same date Lasuén sent a circular letter to the missionaries of Santa Cruz, Santa Clara, and San Francisco. It is identical with the above, but it carries the following postscript: Either Your Reverences may notify me that you have received this, or you may so certify as you forward it, and then return it to me from San Francisco. See S.B.M.A., sec. 2, No. 278.

248. To Fray Antonio Nogueyra

Give me your holy blessing, Your Reverence. I am sending you the enclosed copies. In them you will see the steps by which the Lord Bishop of Sonora insinuates himself here, and those I felt in a position to discuss by way of reply to His Excellency. Thanks be to God that the first blow of the crozier was so gentle and gracious; perhaps pastors of old would have used more force.

The moment Your Reverence grasps the problem, I know you will keep it in mind, and so will the venerable council, and that you will study it and come to a decision in regard to it. With all possible haste, will you then send me clear and detailed instructions as to how to conduct myself.

Your Reverence knows the answer, and I am full of confidence [that you will send it], so that I may be in a position to refer to it without fail in regard to everything which His Most Illustrious Lordship may claim.

I am lacking in other ways and means; and I am lacking ideas for the proper conduct of this business and for the correct order of relationship and dependence which this new development brings with it.

My first and principal loyalty is to our college, and I shall never abandon that, no matter to what extent I profess allegiance, give assurance, or pay homage or tribute to those who are in a position to issue orders to me.

The present ideas of the Lord Bishop may have been suggested by the governor, and I have no doubt that they and others had to have his approval.

On this supposition, it seems to me that in order to contend with such authority, skill is of more value than force; and since His Illustrious Lordship shows himself so favorable and moderate, Your Reverence and the venerable council will be able to adjust matters in the most peaceful and conciliatory atmosphere.

Pueblos and ranches of the *gente de razón* have been established, separated entirely from the missions. Those that are to be established (so I hear) will have no connection whatever with them. In short, the presidios and escorts garrison and help them, but they will now be subject to military jurisdiction. The missions must be careful not to take a single step out of their present role. In those circumstances, at least, I no longer serve them because I cannot; and if my will were mine and not yours, I would say it is because I do not wish to.

So it will be a worthy object of the manifest zeal and tested judgment of the venerable council to teach us, in the present circumstances, where the limits lie between episcopal jurisdiction and ours; to explain to us the difference between the present and the former interpretation of the clause repeated in our faculties, especially in #25a: "Where there are no bishops, or ordinaries, or vicars thereof"; and, consequently, to take opportune measures to see that no missionary comes here who cannot exercise the administration which is granted to him, or tell us how a person who is here may qualify for that purpose.

How am I to know what Your Reverences will say about my circular letter to the missions? What I wish is, that you will be so kind as to read it with patience, and I will be satisfied that you will feel as I do that to change in the least my status as mere missionary leaves me good for nothing else.

I am telling the missionaries that they will be able to use the military faculties, for, keeping in mind the expressions used by the bishop, I am of the opinion that for the present and as long as His Illustrious Lordship does not ordain otherwise, they can so act, and in this way confusion or discord among them can be avoided.

All have in their missions some part of the presidios by reason of the soldiers of the escort assigned them, and these they have regarded as their parishioners in the same way as the missionaries nearest the presidios regard the presidial soldiers.

For many reasons it is fitting to follow this rule, as the religious who were up here can explain.

The gravity of the matter, and the need of dealing with it authoritatively so as to exclude as far as possible every possible form of doubt and difficulty, these add the greatest importance to my humble petition that Your Reverence reply without fail, and as soon as possible, giving full instructions so that I may act in accordance with them in all the points discussed.

With the most profound respect, I place myself once more at the service of Your Reverence, and I pray that God Our Lord may keep you for many years in His holy grace.

San Carlos Mission,
December 28, 1796.

I do not know how it came about that the governor said to me the other day, in the course of a conversation: "That hospice, which has been discussed so often, and the founding of which would seem to pertain to the Pious Fund, since it is for the promotion of this conquest, will, without a doubt, be a great asset to these missions and their missionaries.

"Your Reverence could send me an official letter regarding this problem, and I would give it my approval, send it to the Viceroy, and urge it strongly, so that it would be acted on."

Before I could reply to him (because he knows me well by this time) he added: "Obviously you do not wish to be involved in this without the opinion and permission of the college. If so, you can inform the Father Guardian and we shall see what happens." "Yes, I shall do that," I said; and so, I am keeping my word.